YOGA AND PARAPSYCHOLOGY
Empirical Research and Theoretical Essays

YOGA AND PARAPSYCHOLOGY

Empirical Research and Theoretical Essays

Edited by
K. RAMAKRISHNA RAO

Foreword by
KARAN SINGH

MOTILAL BANARSIDASS PUBLISHERS
PRIVATE LIMITED • DELHI

First Edition : Delhi, ***2010***

ISBN : 978-81-208-3473-6

MOTILAL BANARSIDASS
41 U.A. Bungalow Road, Jawahar Nagar, Delhi 110 007
8 Mahalaxmi Chamber, 22 Bhulabhai Desai Road, Mumbai 400 026
203 Royapettah High Road, Mylapore, Chennai 600 004
236, 9th Main III Block, Jayanagar, Bangalore 560 011
Sanas Plaza, 1302 Baji Rao Road, Pune 411 002
8 Camac Street, Kolkata 700 017
Ashok Rajpath, Patna 800 004
Chowk, Varanasi 221 001

PRINTED IN INDIA
BY JAINENDRA PRAKASH JAIN AT SHRI JAINENDRA PRESS,
A-45, NARAINA, PHASE-I, NEW DELHI 110 028
AND PUBLISHED BY NARENDRA PRAKASH JAIN FOR
MOTILAL BANARSIDASS PUBLISHERS PRIVATE LIMITED,
BUNGALOW ROAD, DELHI 110 007

To

GERTRUDE MAURIN

Friend and Benefactor

Contents

Foreword

KARAN SINGH

There is a curious misconception prevalent in the West that parapsychology is not in the realm of science but of religion. This is perhaps because the western definition of the 'mind' is limited only to what may be called 'normal consciousness', the sub-conscious and the unconscious dimensions. In the East, however, particularly in India we have known for many centuries that the mind has remarkable dimensions far beyond and above what may be called normal experience. The classic work on Yoga, Patañjali's *Yoga-Sūtra*s clearly describes the paranormal faculties that can be developed as a result of following the discipline of yoga. These include telepathy, telekinesis, hearing at great distance and other such faculties which may appear supernatural but are, in fact, a result of rigorous training of the mind so that it transcends its normal barriers.

The study of parapsychology, therefore, is as much a subject of rigorous scientific exploration as is classical psychology. There is also a very close link between Yoga and parapsychology. Yoga comes from the same root as the word 'yoke', and implies joining the *Ātman* with the *Brahman*, God immanent with God transcendent or, to put it in more familiar terms, the human and the divine. Indeed it is the enhanced abilities of the mind which are often exhibited by saints and seers, Sufis and mystics of all the great traditional religions that in some way represent the foundation of religious beliefs and practices.

There has been of late an enhanced interest in the West in the study of what are known as paranormal phenomena. This interest did not translate itself into productive research and fruitful understanding of the phenomena convincing to the scientific community in general, because they are considered anomalous or supernatural. What is required is to understand and accept as a natural fact that the human mind has tremendous vistas for growth and expansion, a virtually unlimited potential to exponentially increase its range and depth. Indeed, if we consider the mental faculties of primitive peoples and compare them with those of an Einstein, one can see in a dramatic fashion how the human brain can expand its capacities. There is, as Sri Aurobindo pointed out, no logical reason to presume that our present mental capacities have exhausted evolutionary process. Parapsychology provides us with valuable guidelines for pursuing what is surely the most exciting adventure in science today, the study of consciousness itself.

We live in a world which, despite its tremendous scientific and technological achievements, has still not been able to tackle the most exciting and enigmatic of all phenomena on this planet – the human mind. It is there, as the famous opening lines of UNESCO point out, that wars began, and not only wars between nations but civil strife, violence, crime and growing stress and tension in the minds of men. It is, therefore, necessary for us to start turning the searchlight inwards to see what it is that moves our thoughts and actions, and whether we can transcend our normal consciousness and move into a more holistic and integrated view of life.

Prof. K. Ramakrishna Rao who heads the Indian Council of Philosophical Research has performed an extremely useful service by editing this volume entitled ***Yoga and Parapsychology*** in which, apart from some of his own erudite articles, he has brought together a whole spectrum of papers by scholars from around the world including the United States, the United Kingdom, Sri Lanka, Germany and the Netherlands. It represents a major contribution towards a better understanding both of Yoga and parapsychology and of their symbiotic relationship, and I warmly commend this volume to students and teachers of psychology around the world.

July1, 2008

Preface

K. Ramakrishna Rao

Yoga and parapsychology are two areas to which I devoted a significant amount of my professional life. Parapsychology considered as the discipline to study psi (psychic abilities) is essentially the science of *siddhi*s (extraordinary human abilities). Yoga is considered to be an effective psycho-spiritual pursuit that results in the manifestation of a variety of supernormal phenomena. In fact, Patañjali's *Yoga-Sūtra*s is the foundational text of psychic science. One of its four parts, *Vibhūti Pāda*, is filled with the description and discussion of a variety of paranormal phenomena. There is thus an intrinsic commonality between yoga and parapsychology, which remains essentially unexplored in any systematic way. A serious and scientific study of the two and the resultant synergy of their confluence could result in resolving many of the riddles that puzzle parapsychology today and be a harbinger of a vibrant science opening up new frontiers. Further, it could be seen as a productive East-West meet in a profound sense.

Since industrial revolution in the West, science has grown exponentially. The growth, however, is primarily in physical and biological domains with human sciences lagging far behind. The asymmetry between the two is a cause of serious concern for those looking at the future of humans on this planet.

Humans are endowed with minds and consciousness that place them at the pinnacle of the evolutionary pyramid. They give them enormous advantage over the rest of the inhabitants of the earth to control not only their own destiny but also that of the entire planet for better or worse. What is this mighty thing called the mind, at once so important and yet so enigmatic? Is it merely a "pack of neurons" firing in synchrony, as physical sciences have increasingly inclined to assert? Are we no more than complex computers with outstanding parallel processing capabilities? Is ours no more than conditioned existence with little freedom beyond the deterministic web in which we are situated?

If the mind were without consciousness, if our knowing abilities were limited to what we perceive through our senses, and if one's freedom of will and choice were no more than chimerical hope of the human condition, then perhaps we could ungrudgingly settle for a mechanistic and reductionist conception of the mind as a complex, computing machine. However, the intrinsic subjectivity of consciousness, the not inconsiderable evidence for the existence of extraordinary human abilities such as ESP, and the notion of free-will so sacred to our species cry out loud and clear that we look beyond the neurological configurations to understand the nature of the human mind.

If we are simply brain-driven machines, what becomes then to our notions of freedom and responsibility, long cherished and nourished by civilized societies throughout ages in the East and the West? How about spiritual beliefs and practices that are the backbone of all major global traditions? Is the manifest conflict between private experiences of people and the public verifiability of truth real? Are there any alternatives to the neurocentric conception of consciousness and the mind that could conceivably bridge the epistemic asymmetry between objective science and subjective experience?

The above questions cry out for answers. Both yoga and parapsychology appear to suggest an alternate paradigm that may be seen as interesting as well as challenging in this context. The yoga tradition in the Indian subcontinent, so distinct and starkly different from the Western, is unique in many ways. It is unparalleled in its claimed success in cultivating and controlling the human mind and achieving higher states of consciousness, and greater degrees of achievement and happiness. Consequently, it has the potential for providing a new paradigm for studying the mind, one that would reconcile the scientific demands as well as spiritual aspirations. The theory and practices of yoga and the phenomena born of them could serve at a minimum as useful check posts to screen the current conceptions of the mind for their inclusiveness, consistency and validity; and at their best they may suggest new models and methods to investigate the mind.

Parapsychology, notwithstanding its self-imposed limits to work within the climatic constraints of Western "scientific culture", has provided during a century of effort impressive and in many ways unassailable evidence for the existence of cognitive anomalies. These anomalies seem prima facie to conflict with the so-called basic limiting principles that are considered sacrosanct in scientific establishments around the world. The irony of it all is that parapsychology is solemnly wedded to the scientific method absorbing all its positivist biases and commitments; and yet over the years it has accumulated massive evidence that questions the very assumptive base of science itself.

The unfortunate consequence of all this is that psychical research is disowned by the scientific establishments by and large and discarded in a large measure as blasphemous by the spiritual traditions in the West. It is pushed to the margins of science; and it is all but banished by the religious right. Few in the scientific establishment find for parapsychology a rightful place as a legitimate scientific endeavour and even fewer among the organized religions see psi as an integral aspect of our being.

From the perspective of yoga and the classical Indian tradition, the cognitive anomalies claimed by parapsychologists and ignored by the scientific establishment in general are no anomalies at all. Rather they are anticipated as natural consequences of development of the mind. Consequently, the belief in the validity and the veracity of psychic phenomena has persisted in the Indian subcontinent for centuries. Systematic treatises discussing them were compiled, as mentioned, beginning with Patañjali's *Yoga-Sūtra*s in 3rd century BCE. Along with other classical writings on the subject, it contains a mine of ideas, which could give psi research a rich hidden resource to excavate and exploit. In recent history, the life and writings of Sri Aurobindo are an inspiring example of the practice of yoga for psychic development and spiritual transformation.

We may not be oblivious, however, to the fact that yoga itself has come to be a much abused concept – confused, conflated and commercialized. Yoga is a billion dollar business in the US, where it is equated with physical and bodily culture. There is a felt need for bringing greater conceptual clarity to discourses on yoga, for developing yoga theory in the light of current advances in science, and for focusing on methodological rigor in yoga research so that its inherent potential for understanding the human mind in paradigmatically new ways could be fully realized.

Keeping this in view, a national conference and a workshop were organized during January 3-23, 2006 at Andhra University by the Institute for Human Science and Service with international participation. The present volume is a compilation of the major presentations at the conference and workshop, which are appropriately revised and edited in the light of the discussions.

The contents of the volume contain theoretical articles and reviews as well as experimental reports. Contributors come from different countries besides India, including the United States of America, Sri Lanka, United Kingdom, Germany and the Netherlands. Thus, the volume is international in scope and coverage.

We are honoured to have the Foreword for this volume from Dr. Karan Singh, a statesman philosopher, whose interest in drawing inspiration from classical Indian thought to address troubling contemporary issues and problems is well known. A leading scholar in Sri Aurobindo tradition, Dr. Singh is instrumental in promoting yoga as an academic discipline at the National Institute of Mental Health and Neurosciences (NIMHANS), Delhi and the All India Institute of Medical Sciences (AIIMS), Delhi during his tenure as cabinet minister in the Government of India. The community of Indian scholars interested in the scientific study of yoga look up to him to provide the much needed leadership and global initiative. I am grateful for the opportunity of knowing him and working with him.

The organization of the conference and the workshop and the publication of this volume are made possible by grants from Maurin Foundation for Parapsychology, U.S.A. and the Indian Council of Philosophical Research, Delhi. I acknowledge our indebtedness to both these organizations. Of course our greatest debt is to the contributors and other participants who came from countries listed earlier and also from France and Iran. Some of them travelled long distances to attend the conference and the workshop and gave a lot of their time in writing and revising their papers published here. I am personally grateful to all of them. I acknowledge also the help and assistance received from my colleagues at the Institute for Human Science and Service, especially Mr. Sadasiva Rao who provided the much appreciated secretarial services. I am grateful to Motilal Banarsidass Publishers and specially to Shri N.P. Jain for the care with which they have brought out this volume.

Last but no less important is the support I received from Dr. Sonali Bhatt Marwaha who shared the main burden of correspondence and other editorial chores. I am thankful and appreciative of her continued association and cooperation. If this volume would help to spur some interest in the scientific study of parapsychology in this part of the world and at the same time promote in the West an awareness of yoga, beyond *āsana*s and *prāṇāyāma*, as a discipline that has great relevance for enhancing human potentials and wellness, we would consider the efforts that went into bringing out this volume well their worth.

Parapsychology and Yoga

K. Ramakrishna Rao

Introduction

Yoga is widely known around the world; parapsychology is less so. However, both are equally misunderstood. For example, according to the *Compact Oxford Dictionary* (2001/2005) I have on my desk, parapsychology is "the study of mental phenomena which are outside the area of orthodox psychology." This hardly tells us anything about parapsychology except that it is outside the scope of conventional psychology. Again, the same dictionary says that yoga "is a Hindu spiritual discipline," which is also not the right description. Yoga is more than a Hindu discipline; and it is not limited to spiritual seekers. Parapsychology is the scientific discipline that studies psychic phenomena such as the ability to have information and to interact with environment by means that do not seem to involve no known energy transfer or exchange. In public perception parapsychology is often confused with spiritualism, ufology, astrology, palm-and tarot-card readings, hypnotic regression to "past lives," and a host of other occult practices. Similarly, for many yoga means no more than certain physical postures and breathing exercises. There is more to parapsychology and yoga than these popular misconceptions of them suggest.

While the subject matter of parapsychology appears to be the same in the East and the West, the orientation for studying it tends to be different. For example, from the Indian perspective parapsychology is the science of *siddhi*s; and *siddhi*s are natural phenomena, whereas in the western professional description it is the study of cognitive anomalies. The difference between the western and Indian descriptions has significant ramifications which are not always acknowledged and appreciated. It stems from the striking difference in the practice of science in the two cultures. In the western tradition science and religion/spirituality grew apart, often one standing in opposition to the other. In the Indian tradition, there is no intrinsic separation or antagonism between science and spirituality. In the west scientific discoveries were projected as revolutions displacing other beliefs. In India, they are seen as natural unfolding of physical laws without displacing other beliefs. Science and spirituality are complementary and not compartmentalized belief systems. Consequently we scarcely find in India such contentious and acrimonious debates like creationism/intelligence design versus evolution. Indian history is largely free from the practice of persecuting scientists for being blasphemous and irreverent.

What has all this to do with parapsychology or yoga? The story of parapsychology I am going to narrate will reveal why parapsychology as pursued in the West is likely to remain for ever a study of anomalies rather than a science with a specific subject matter; and why parapsychology may never gain scientific legitimacy as a respectable academic discipline if pursued within the western paradigm.

The difference between eastern and western perspectives is not due to differences in the belief in ostensible parapsychological phenomena. Surveys around the world show that significant majority of people in both East and West, educated professionals as well as illiterate masses, believe in the genuineness of psychic events such as precognition.

If such phenomena are indeed real, as the available evidence suggests, they not only have profound implications to our theoretical understanding of who we are and what our place in the universe is, but they also have almost limitless possibilities for practical application at various levels. This fact was not lost sight of in the West. For example, documents declassified a few years ago in USA reveal that the Central Intelligence Agency and the Pentagon had funded research into psychic abilities for a number of years at SRI, SRI International and SAIC (Utts, 2001).

PARAPSYCHOLOGY : THE WESTERN PERSPECTIVE

Background

The beginnings of parapsychological studies in the West may be traced back to antiquity. In fact one could argue that western attempts at controlled observation and study of extraordinary human experiences such as premonitions, knowing the future intuitively, are as old as in India. For example, it is reported that King Croesus of Lydia sent his agents to the oracles in Egypt and Greece to check on their allied psychic abilities. The agents were instructed to question the oracle at an appointed time what the King was doing. In order to fool the oracle, the King engaged himself in the unusual task of cooking in a kitchen at that time. However, the oracle at Delphi, it was reported, described accurately what the King was doing, convincing the King of her paranormal abilities (Dodds, 1973). Thus a field parapsychological experiment was successfully carried out some twenty-five centuries back.

The belief in the psychic phenomena persisted throughout the recorded history of the West. However, these beliefs spilled over soon into organized religion; and that meant an end to the empirical study of the phenomena. In fact, Christianity with its own claims of a multitude of miracles soon tended not only to discourage but also suppress the institution of oracles. Mediumstic practices and inspirational insights were attributed to devils. Thus, with the sole exception of St. Augustine, the early fathers of Christian church looked at parapsychological phenomena as the work of devils to be condemned.

There is little of note as far as psychic phenomena are concerned during the middle ages in Europe. During the Renaissance period and the following centuries the growing rationalism in Europe cast increasing skepticism on the very possibility of these extraordinary phenomena. Thus both the Church as well as the establishments of science stood together as powerful inhibitors of public discussion of the paranormal. The Church saw in it the evil spirits; and science considered them as a bunch of superstitions unworthy of inquiry.

One can discourage discussion of the phenomena, but cannot prevent their manifestation. Psychic phenomena continued occurring in various forms and in widely separate regions. Mesmer and his workers saw psychic phenomena in their studies of animal magnetism. Also spiritualism, which rapidly spread in Europe and America, provided copious trance phenomena with a lot of psychic component in the occult form. And these did not go unnoticed. For example, Sir Williams Crookes, Fellow and President of the Royal Society wrote in the *Quarterly Journal of Science* in 1870: "That certain physical phenomena, such as the movement of material substances, and the production of sounds resembling electrical charges, occur under circumstances in which they can not be explained by any physical law at present known, is a fact of which I am certain as I am of the most elementary fact in chemistry" (p.8).

Attempts to study psychic phenomena scientifically began well over a century ago with the establishment of the Society for Psychical Research (S.P.R.) in England in 1882. Since then sporadic studies of the phenomena were carried out in various parts of the world, some in universities and a few in other research establishments. Early experimental work at the S.P.R. was in the area of telepathy. For example, Henry and Eleanor Sidgwick and others (1889) carried out interesting experiments aimed at testing the possibility of telepathy under hypnosis. ESP (extrasensory perception) under hypnosis was also the subject of investigation in France by Pierre Janet

(Gurney, 1888) and in the U.S.S.R. by the physiologist L.L. Vasiliev (1963). Also in France, Charles Richet (1975/23) carried out ESP tests with playing cards and attempted to apply the calculus of probability to evaluate the significance of the results.

Among the first to experimentally study ESP in the U.S. was J.E. Coover (1975/17) at Stanford University. His studies were followed by studies of Troland (1917) and Estabrooks (1961/27) at Harvard University. About the same time, a group of psychologists in Germany carried out an ESP experiment, reported by H.J.F.W. Brugmans (1922), which is still cited as an important evidential experiment (Beloff, 1980).

Still, it was not until J.B. Rhine's arrival at Duke University that parapsychology as an experimental science was born. The scientific stage of parapsychology began, as Brian Mackenzie (1977) has noted, with the founding of the Parapsychology Laboratory at Duke University in 1927, or perhaps with the first major output of this laboratory, Rhine's *Extra-Sensory Perception* (1973/34). By 1940, when another major work entitled *Extrasensory Perception after Sixty Years* (Rhine et al., 1966/40) was published, 145 experimental studies of ESP had been carried out.

In the years following the publication of *Extrasensory Perception after Sixty Years*, a large body of experimental data has accumulated which is strongly supportive of the reality of psi. And with this support, the attention of research scientists in parapsychology has shifted from proving the existence of psi in its various forms to understanding its nature. By exploring the attitudes, moods, personality factors and states of mind of persons who participate in psi experiments, researchers hoped to see the psi process revealed. Also being studied for this purpose are cognitive processes such as memory and subliminal perception, as well as sex differences and the effects of motivation, feedback, distance, and target differences. The discovery of psi-missing, the tendency to significantly miss the target when attempting to hit it, has further led to a variety of research strategies and interesting results.

With the increase in the number and sophistication of psi experiments has come rigorous and critical scrutiny of them by sceptics. Indeed, a spate of critical books have appeared (Hansel, 1980; Marks and Kammann, 1980; Alcock, 1981; and Abell and Singer, 1981). Parapsychologists responded to the critics with improved research, reanalysis of data and rational defence of their research. In spite of a large data base (Rao and Palmer, 1987; Radin, 1997) and incontrovertible evidence for the existence of psi, parapsychology continues to be a controversial science.

There are many reasons for this state of affairs. First, the theoretical implications of these findings are unsettling to the assumptive base of science in general and the physical sciences in particular (MacKenzie and MacKenzie, 1980). They seem to question the basic principles that limit the extent of human information acquisition resources that are considered sacrosanct in science (Broad, 1953). In other words, psychic phenomena are of a kind that would not happen in a universe determined by physical laws. If the universe is entirely determined by physical causation, as is generally assumed, any claims of psychic phenomena that appear to call into question such determinism should be considered spurious and a priori unreal. It is so because the antecedent probability accorded to their occurrence is zero. Therefore, no amount of evidence is sufficient to prove their existence. They are assumed unreal, ex-hypothesis.

The second is the methodological problems of reliability and replication. Psychic abilities appear to be notoriously unreliable, creating difficult problems of prediction and control. There has been a degree of replication of laboratory effects involving psi (a generic term for psychic phenomena) but far less than what is required to convince critics with a preexisting prejudice against the possibility of these phenomena.

In the Indian context, the problem is somewhat different. The classical Indian tradition accords reality to psychic phenomena, which are presumed to exist like other human abilities. However, very little attention is given to the scientific study of these phenomena in our academic institutions. Not much credible research has been carried out in recent years. This is unfortunate for a number of reasons. First, the implications of the genuineness of psychic events are truly mind blowing. Second, there is already credible scientific evidence that strongly suggests their existence (Rao and Palmer, 1987). Third, the reality of the phenomena, unlike in the West, is not precluded and in fact is consistent with the national ethos and the long Indian intellectual tradition. Fourth, there are numerous claims in India of mastery of these abilities, the claims that deserve to be scientifically tested and verified. Indian folk psychology as well as classical texts of consciousness studies, such as *Yoga-Sūtras*, *Yoga Vāśiṣṭha and Viśuddhimāgga,* give us clear accounts and descriptions of practices that are believed to enable one to acquire these abilities. Therefore, it would seem, India is the natural place for a systematic study of psychic phenomena.

Psychic Phenomena as Cognitive Anomalies

Psychic phenomena refer to a broad range of phenomena that are often confused in the public mind. Any attempts to scientifically explore psychic events must clearly delineate the field, carefully define the core concepts, limit the scope of research to problems that permit observation and experiment. Again, early psychical research was guilty of spreading itself too thin, lacking in the focus on workable programs of research. If the past experience is any guide, researchable psychic events fall into two categories – (1) those that refer to anomalous acquisition of information and, (2) anomalous mind-body interactions. The first category includes phenomena that are generally classified under the term extrasensory perception (ESP). ESP includes telepathy, clairvoyance and precognition. Telepathy is mind reading. Clairvoyance is awareness of objects and events outside of ones sensory field. Precognition is noninferential knowledge of the future. The second category refers to what is called psychokinesis (PK) or direct action of mind over matter.

Rhine (1934) coined the word extrasensory perception, a concept that is extensively used in current parapsychological literature. There are, however, numerous other concepts, which refer to the same thing. They include remote viewing (Targ and Puthoff, 1977) remote perception (Jahn, 1982), anomalous cognition (May, Utts and Spottiswoode, 1995) traveling clairvoyance, out-of-body experiences and so on. Many of these terms are theoretically loaded. At this stage of relative ignorance as to the nature of the phenomena and the apparent transgression of the basic limiting principles, and currently accepted epistemological assumptions by the putative paranormal phenomena, cognitive anomalies is the favored term to refer to these ostensibly extra-sensory and extra-motor events. Cognitive because they deal with information acquisition and exchange and anomalies because they do not fit into any current conceptions of cognition.

The existence of cognitive anomalies in the form of ESP and PK is demonstrated beyond all reasonable doubt. This is not the same as saying that it is accepted as a scientific fact by the mainstream science. (Please see our target article and comments on it by over fifty scientists in the journal *Behavioral and Brain Sciences*, Rao and Palmer, 1987). I refer to two experiments, one by Rhine and Pratt (1954) and another by Helmut Schmidt (1973) and associates as providing overwhelming evidence for psi phenomena. These were replicated many times.

Space, Time and the Complexity of Psi Task

Parapsychological research has gone well beyond the question of the existence of psi. There has been experimental demonstration of various forms of psi such as ESP and PK and the discovery of lawful regularities between psi and other psychological and physical variables. One of the most important finding is that ESP, unlike any known physical phenomena, is apparently unconstrained by space/time variables or the complexity of the task (Stanford, 1977).

Quite early in his experimental investigations, J.B. Rhine found that the distance between the subject and the target in ESP experiments made no significant difference in the success rate of his subjects (Rhine, 1934). Similarly, Russian physiologist L.L. Vasiliev (1963) reported that he was able to hypnotize his subject telepathically during randomly determined periods of time from a distance of about 1,700 kilometers. He found also that his attempts to shield any possible electromagnetic wave transmission between the hypnotist and the subject by placing them in separate Farady cages did not diminish the success rate of the telepathic induction of hypnosis. Marilyn Schlitz and Elmar Gruber (1980) successfully carried out transcontinental remote viewing experiments in which the subject, totally unaware of it sensorially, attempted to describe a randomly selected location in another continent being visited by an experimenter.

There is also experimental evidence to support the precognition hypotheses. As in spontaneous cases in which people have reported their experiences of having information about future events apparently without any other means of knowing them, experimental studies have also shown that it is possible to have information about a target that does not exist now but will come into being at a time in the future. For example, it was found in some remote viewing experiments that the subjects were able to successfully describe the location where the experimenter will be at a predetermined future time (Jahn, 1982). Earlier, J.B. Rhine (1938) had reported significant results suggesting that his subjects were able to guess correctly the target order in a deck of ESP cards randomized after the subjects made their calls. In a meta-analysis of forced-choice experiments comparing clairvoyance, and precognition, F. Steinkasmp, J, Milton, and R.L. Morris (1998) found no significant difference in the success rate in precognition and clairvoyance studies, even though the cumulative overall effects is significant in both clairvoyance and precognition studies.

Another significant aspect of psi appears to be the relative ineffectiveness of task complexity in constraining it. Rex Stanford (1977) has reviewed the relevant literature ad concluded that the efficiency of PK function is not reduced by an increase in the complexity of the target system. Thus, psi, which is believed to involve no sensory mediation, is also found not to be constrained by the variables of space and time nor by the physical properties of the items of information. There is nothing to indicate from the research results available to date that any energy patterns emanating from the target objects reach the subject in ESP tests. It would seem that somehow the subject has access to information under conditions that simply do not permit any known physical energy transmission from the target. Such a possibility raises serious questions about the subject-object distinctions in cognitive processes and the representational theory of knowledge in general.

For example, if it is the case that a subject (S) in a telepathy experiment is able to know what an agent (A) is thinking at a particular time, what then is the cause of S's knowledge? One would normally assume that the cause of S's knowledge is the act of A's thinking. We know, however, that we are unable to discover any causal sequences connecting A's thinking and S's extrasensory knowledge of former's thoughts; and we also know that S could do the same thing even if A were not actually thinking at that time but were to do so at some time in the future.

Psi and Sensory Noise Reduction

Not only is there compelling data in support of the existence of such cognitive anomalies as ESP and PK and data suggesting that these abilities unlike normal abilities are unconstrained by time, space and the complexity of the task, but there is also a vast amount of experimental evidence suggesting that ESP occurrence is facilitated by the reduction of on going sensory stimuli.

Cortical Arousal, Extraversion and ESP

Several parapsychologists consider ESP "an ancient and primitive from of perception" (Eysenck, 1967). Therefore, it is suggested that conditions of high cortical arousal may inhibit ESP, whereas a state of relaxation and reduced sensory input may facilitate its occurrence. British psychologist H.J. Eysenck (1967) surveyed a surprisingly large number of studies that have bearing on this. Pointing out that introverts are habitually in a state of greater cortical arousal than extroverts, Eysenck hypothesized that extroverts would do better in ESP tests than introverts. Indeed, there is much evidence in support of this hypothesis. For over fifty years, extroversion-introversion has been one of the most widely explored dimensions of personality in relation to ESP. Carl Sargent (1981) reviewed all the English-language reports bearing on the extroversion-ESP hypothesis and found that significant confirmations of a positive relationship between ESP and extroversion occur at six times the chance error. Honorton, Ferrari, and Bem (1998) report a comprehensive meta-analysis of 60 independent studies of the ESP-extroversion relationship. Again there is significant evidence to suggest that extroverted subjects do better than introverted subjects.

There are a number of other studies, which shed direct light on the hypothesis of ESP facilitation via sensory noise reduction. There is substantial evidence to suggest that the occurrence of ESP may be enhanced by procedures that result in the reduction of meaningful sensory stimuli and proprioceptive input to the organism. In fact, many of the traditional psychic development techniques such as yoga appear to employ sensory noise reduction procedures, as do a variety of relaxation exercises and altered state of consciousness. Psi researchers have explored some of these.

Several subjects who have done well on psi tests have claimed that they did their best when they were physically relaxed and their minds were in a "blank" state. Mary Sinclair, whom her husband, novelist Upton Sinclair, found to be an outstanding subject, gave the following advice: "You first give yourself a 'suggestion' to the effect that you will relax your mind and your body, making the body insensitive and the mind a blank" (Sinclair, 1930, p. 180). Rhea White (1964), who reviewed the early literature on this topic, also concluded that attempts "to still the body and mind" are common among the techniques used by successful subjects.

Relaxation and ESP

According to one count, there are 33 ESP studies in which progressive relaxation procedures have been used. Seventeen of these gave significant results. William Braud and associates carried out the most extensive work in this area. In the first experiment (Braud and Braud, 1974) there were 16 subjects and the subjects self-rated their degree of relaxation. Braud and Braud report that those who performed well in the ESP tests rated themselves as more relaxed than the poor psi performers. The second experiment consisted of 20 volunteer subjects who were assigned randomly to "relaxation" or "tension" conditions. Those in the relaxation condition went through a taped, progressive-relaxation procedure (an adaptation of Jacobson's) before taking an ESP test, which was to guess the picture being "transmitted" by an agent in another room. The subjects in the other group were given taped, tension-inducing instructions before they did the same ESP test. Each subject's level of relaxation was assessed through electromyographic recordings. The EMG results showed a significant decrease in the EMG activity among the subjects in the "relaxation" group and a significant increase among those in the "tension" group. As predicted, the ESP scores of the subjects in the relaxation group were significantly higher than those of the subjects in the tension group.

Other reports of interest are Braud (1975), and Altom and Braud (1976). Confirmation of Braud's results may be found in Stanford and Mayer (1974). Honorton's (1977) summary of studies on relaxation and psi shows a 77 percent success rate. Ten of the 13 studies involving induced relaxation achieved statistical significance at the 5 percent level in support of psi.

ESP in Hypnotic States

The idea that the hypnotic state may be psi-conducive is as old as scientific parapsychology. A French physician, Azam, observed that one of his patients in a hypnotic state responded to an unspoken thought. Pierre Janet was reportedly successful in inducing a somnambulistic trance state 16 out of 20 times by mere mental suggestion (Podmore, 1984). Eleanor Sidgwick (Sidgwick et al., 1889), at the Society for Psychical Research in England, experimented with hypnotized subjects by using two digit numbers and colors are targets. The Russian physiologist Vasiliev (1963) was highly successful in inducing hypnotic trance by telepathy from a distance. There are a large number of controlled laboratory studies suggesting that hypnotic states are conducive for manifestation of ESP.

Within the card-calling paradigm, J.J. Grela (1945) reported the first ESP experiment with hypnosis. Jarl Fahler (1957) carried out experiments in Finland, which gave significant results when the subjects were under hypnosis. He replicated the results in experiments carried out at Rhine's laboratory at Duke University, with the involvement of other experimenters collaborating with him (Fahler and Cadoret, 1958). L. Casler (1962; 1964) also reported important work in the area of hypnosis and psi. Casler went a step further than Fahler by giving explicit suggestions to the subjects for improvements in their ESP scoring. Milan Ryzl (Ryzl and Ryzlova, 1962) claimed that he trained the outstanding subject Pavel Stepanek with the help of hypnosis. Charles Honorton's (1977) review lists 42-psi studies using hypnosis, 22 of which gave significant evidence of psi.

Ephraim Schechter (1984) published a review and meta-analysis of the experimental studies of ESP and hypnosis. The analysis confirms the hypothesis that subjects tend to obtain higher ESP scores in the hypnotic state than in a controlled waking state. That the hypnotic state is psi-conducive fits well with the observation that people who report spontaneous psychic experiences tend to have dissociative tendencies (Pekala, Kumar and Marcano, 1995). Hypnotic susceptibility, like psychological absorption, is a dimension of dissociative processes.

Another meta-analysis of ESP studies involving hypnosis and contrasting conditions is reported by Rex Stanford and Adam Stein (1994). Included in the analysis are 25 studies by 12 chief investigators. Claiming that their attempt was to extend and refine Schechter's work, Stanford and Stein also report cumulative ESP-test scores significant for hypnosis. They, however, caution that we may not draw any substantive conclusions from the current database, because the difference in ESP scores between hypnosis and contrast conditions is significant only when the comparison condition preceded hypnosis. They point out also that there is significant psi-missing in the contrasting condition.

Meditation and ESP

The practice of yoga, it is said, enables one to develop psychic abilities. In the third century before Christ, Patanjali wrote a treatise on Raja Yoga (Woods, 1927) detailing the processes and procedures involved and the varieties of supernormal abilities one may obtain by practicing this discipline. Meditation is the most important feature of yoga. It is pointed out that the practice of intensely focusing attention on a single object and following this by meditation enables the practitioner to hold his focus for an extended period of time, which results in a standstill state of the mind (*samādhi*). The *samādhi* state is the one in which psychic abilities are believed to manifest. Unfortunately, there are very few systematic studies of yogins to test for their psi, even though there is a vast amount of anecdotal material concerning their extraordinary psychic claims. However, a number of exploratory studies in which some kind of meditation procedure was used seem to suggest a positive relationship between meditation and ESP. Honorton (1977) reports a survey that shows 9 out of 16 experimental series involving meditation giving significant psi results.

At Andhra University we conducted a series of experiments to investigate the effect of meditation on ESP. In one study (Rao, Dukhan and Rao, 1978/2001) 59 subjects who had various degrees of proficiency in meditation took ESP tests before and immediately after they had meditated for half an hour or more. The ESP tests involved matching cards with ESP symbols and guessing concealed pictures. Both the tests yielded results that showed that the subjects obtained significantly better ESP scores in the post–meditation sessions than in the pre-meditation sessions. Other meditation–psi studies include those by Schmeidler (1970), Osis and Bokert (1971), and Schmidt and Pantas (1972). Honorton (1977) reports a survey that shows 9 out of 16 experimental series involving meditation to have given significant psi results.

ESP in the Ganzfeld

Finally, a number of well-designed experimental studies looked at the effects of reduced external stimulation on subject's ESP scoring by utilizing the ganzfeld. The ganzfeld is a homogeneous visual field produced, for instance, by taping two halves of a ping-pong ball over the eyes and focusing on them a uniform red light from about two feet. The subject may also be given "pink" noise through attached earphones. After being in the ganzfeld for about one half hour, subjects typically report being immersed in a sea of light. Some subjects report a total "black out" complete absence of visual experience (Avant, 1965). Continuous uniform and unpatterned stimulation in the ganzfeld, it is believed, produces a state that, in the absence of meaningful external stimulation, enhances the possibility of attention to internal states, which in turn facilitates the detection of ESP signals.

In a typical ganzfeld-ESP experiment, the subject while in the ganzfeld for about 30 minutes is asked to report whatever is going on in his/her mind at that time. The subject's mentation is monitored and recorded by an experimenter in another room via a microphone link. In most cases, a second experimenter, acting as an agent, located in a different room isolated from the subject and the experimenter monitoring the subject, looks at a picture for about 15 minutes, attempting to "transmit" it to the subject in the ganzfeld. At the end of the ganzfeld period, the monitoring experimenter gives the subject four pictures with a request to rank them 1 through 4 on the basis of their correspondence to the subject's mental images and impressions during the ganzfeld. The monitoring experimenter of course does not have any knowledge as to which one of the four pictures is the one looked at by the agent. After all the four pictures are ranked, the subject is shown the target picture. The rank the subject gives to the picture provides the score for a statistical analysis for matching the degree of subject's mentation with the target. Sometimes a judge, in addition to or in place of the subject, does the ranking.

Honorton and Harper (1974) reported the first ganzfeld-ESP experiment, which provided evidence that the subject's mentation during the ganzfeld matched significantly with the target pictures. Between 1974 and 1981 there were in all 42 published ganzfeld-ESP experiments of which 19 gave significant evidence of psi; it seemed that psi in ganzfeld is a highly replicable effect. However, at the joint conference of the Society for Psychical Research and the Parapsychological Association held at Cambridge University during August 1982, psychologist Ray Hyman made a presentation raising serious questions about the replicability of the ganzfeld psi experiment. Subsequently a comprehensive critical appraisal of ganzfeld ESP experiments was published in the *Journal of Parapsychology* (Hyman, 1985). In this paper Hyman (1) challenged the claimed success rate of replication, (2) argued that possible flaws involving inadequate randomization and insufficient documentation vitiate experiments reporting significant psi effects, and concluded that (3) the ganzfeld-ESP data base is "too weak to support any assertions about the existence of psi."

Charles Honorton, who responded to Hyman's critique, called attention to the inconsistent or inappropriate assignment of flaw ratings in Hyman's analysis. He presented his own meta-analysis that eliminated multiple analyses and other problems mentioned by Hyman. His analysis revealed that neither selective reporting not alleged procedural flaws account for significant psi effects reported in the ESP ganzfeld studies.

Hyman and Honorton (1986) issued a "joint communiqué" on the psi ganzfeld debate. In it they agree that such considerations as selective reporting or multiple analyses cannot reasonably explain away the overall significance of the effect. They disagree, however, on the degree to which the effect constitutes evidence for psi. More important are the recommendations they make for conducting future experiments in this area. These were followed in some of the subsequent experiments that provided significant evidence for ESP.

Very significant in ganzfeld-ESP research is a report of a replication of the psi ganzfeld effect by Cornell psychologist Daryl Bem and Honorton (1994), published in the mainstream psychology journal, *Psychological Bulletin.* This study, consisting of 11 experiments, utilized computer control of the experimental protocol. It complied with all the guidelines Hyman and Honorton recommended in their joint communiqué. The results from the new setup, called the autoganzfeld studies, strongly support the existence of a psi effect in the data and replicate the ESP-ganzfeld effect, meeting the "stringent standards" requirement as recommended by Hyman and Honorton in their joint communiqué of 1986.

Since the publication of Bem-Honorton experiment, there have been a number of other studies of ESP in the ganzfeld. Julie Milton and Richard Wiseman (1999) published a follow-up meta-analysis of 30 more ganzfeld ESP studies conducted between 1983 and 1997. Their analysis did not provide significant cumulative evidence for the ganzfeld effect, raising again the question of replicability of the ganzfeld experiment.

Subsequently, Bem, Palmer and Broughton (2001) further updated the ESP ganzfeld database by adding ten more studies published after 1997 and not included in the meta-analysis by Milton and Wiseman. When these 10 additional studies are included, the meta-analysis yields a mean effect size that is statistically significant, though smaller than the one observed in the earlier studies. Bem et al. observed, however, that some of the experiments included in the new database appeared to deviate significantly form the standard protocol of the ganzfeld experiment. Therefore, they arranged for three independent raters unfamiliar with the studies involved to rate the degree to which each of the 40 studies in the new database deviated from the standard protocol. As expected they found that "the effect size achieved by a replication is significantly correlated with the degree to which it adhered to the standard protocol." They point out: "Standard replications yield significant effect sizes comparable to those obtained in the past."

It seems reasonable, therefore, to say that we now have a broad range of replications of ganzfeld-ESP experiments covering over a period of 25 years. They involve over 90 experiments by a wide range of investigators scattered around the globe, showing a fairly robust effect comparable across studies that adhere to the standard ganzfeld protocol. It may also be noted that correlational studies have shown greater effect sizes when the subjects say that the ganzfeld produced an altered state of consciousness in them, further strengthening our argument that sensory noise reduction is conducive to the manifestation of ESP.

The results from ESP studies involving meditation, relaxation, hypnosis, and ganzfeld thus meaningfully converge to suggest that a reduction of ongoing sensorimotor activity may facilitate the manifestation of ESP in laboratory tests. Whatever may be the mechanism involved in ESP, it is reasonable to assume that ESP is a weak signal that must compete for the information processing resources of the organism. In this process, any reduction of ongoing sensory activity should improve the chances of detecting and registering the ESP signal. It would, therefore, seem reasonable to conclude that (a) psi exists; (b) psi effects are replicable, and (c) sensory noise reduction through such procedures as the ganzfeld is psi conducive.

Current Scene

There is a general consensus in the parapsychological community and among the research scientists involved in investigating psi phenomena that there is significant evidence in support of the existence of ESP and PK. However, there is a general lack of agreement as to what it all means. Very little progress has been made in finding meaningful physical correlates of ESP or PK. Over the past twenty-five years, several attempts were made to fit psi into quantum mechanics. Observational theories such as those proposed by Harris Walker (1975, 2000) and Helmut Schmidt (1975a, 1975b) and their modifications by others (Muttuck, 1984) did stimulate a significant amount of research. However, the validity of any of the versions of the observational theories of psi based on quantum physics is yet to be established (Irwin, 1999). Even in the liberal versions of quantum mechanics, it is highly controversial whether the collapse of the state vector involves consciousness in the sense observational theories require for explaining psi. Further, the question of what constitutes an "observation" that is involved in the collapse of state vector is not answered with any degree of clarity in physical terms.

The explanatory void haunting psi phenomena has resulted in labeling them as anomalous by those investigating it. Also, it breathed a lot of skepticism among the scientists watching psi researches from outside. We can hardly expect scientists to have interest in things that make little sense. Added to this is the confusion generated by the widespread observation of what is known as the "experimenter effect". Experimenter expectancy effects are not unknown in psychological literature (Rosenthal, 1966; Rosenthal and Rubin, 1978); but the experimenter effect in parapsychology has taken new turns and twists causing severe problems to the researchers in this field and making it an easy target to the skeptics to shoot at.

It has been observed from the early days of scientific research into psi that the experimenter is a relevant variable. It is now well known that some experimenters are more successful than others in obtaining results in support of psi hypothesis. Skeptics generally point to this as a weakness and argue that the evidential results could be due to slackness of experimental rigor and failure to control the artifacts. However, a strong case has been made that the experimenter effects observed in parapsychological research are themselves genuine psi effects and not artefactual out-comes of experimenter incompetence or unreliability.

In fact, careful studies were conducted under well controlled conditions to test whether one experimenter is consistently more successful than another in eliciting a psi response. For example, Wiseman and Marilyn Schlitz (1997) published an experimental study in which they both acted as independent experimenters to test whether psi is involved in the commonly experienced phenomena of being stared at. A feeling of being stared at, when no one is directly looking at them, is reported by a vast majority of the population. According to some surveys the percentage of people reporting such feelings is as high as 80% (Sheldrake, 1994). The experiment involved monitoring the electrodermal activity of the subjects during randomly dispersed periods of covert staring and nonstaring. It is hypothesized that there would be more electrodermal activity during the periods of covert staring, i.e., when the experimenter isolated from the subject stares at the video image of the subject. Each of the two experimenters carried out a separate experiment; but they conducted them in the same location and used the same equipment. Schlitz has a long track record of being a successful psi experimenter whereas Wiseman, who is a skeptic, has been consistently unsuccessful in the past. The results of the study showed that there is significant evidence for a psi effect in the data when Schlitz was the experimenter and no evidence of psi in the data of Wiseman. Thus the results of the study provide unambiguous evidence for experimenter psi effect, even though attempts to replicate them are not as successful for a variety of reasons.

The reality of genuine experimenter psi effects gives a new twist to psi controversy. If the experimenter is a relevant variable, his role in the experimental situation gains importance and needs clarification. In fact, serious questions as to who is the real source of psi are raised. It does seem parsimonious at least in some cases to consider the experimenter as the real source of psi rather than the subject.

YOGA: THE INDIAN PERSPECTIVE

Yoga is both a system of philosophy and a set of practices. The ultimate goal of yoga practice, however, is not development of psychic abilities but achieving *kaivalya*, self-realization. As one travels on the path of yoga, he passes through several stages of development that impact on the body and the mind of the practitioner. Patañjali in his *Yoga-Sūtra*s succinctly describes them. While Dasgupta (1922) dates Patañjali to 2nd Century BCE, Woods (1927) thinks that the *Yoga-Sūtra*s were written in 4th or 5th CE. Yoga did not originate with Patañjali. Nor is it confined to the Yoga system of philosophy. References to yoga practices go back to at least Upaniṣadic times. Explicit mention of yoga occurs in *Maitrāyaṇī*, *Śvetāśvatara*, and *Kaṭha Upaniṣad* among others. As Dasgupta (1922) says, Patañjali collected different yoga practices, systematized diverse ideas on the subject, and "grafted them on Sāṃkhya metaphysics" (p. 229). Also, yoga practices are not confined to Brahmanism; Buddhists as well as Jains perfected and practiced their own form of yoga. Therefore, yoga in a significant sense is pan Indian and coextensive with classical Indian tradition. As Mircea Eliade (1969) points out, "yoga constitutes a characteristic dimension of Indian thought to such a point that wherever Indian religion and culture have made their way we also find a more or less pure form of yoga" (p. 359). Yoga has much to offer for understanding parapsychological phenomena, both as theory as well as a set of techniques to enhance psi.

Yoga Theory

Yoga shares with Sāṃkhya a dualist worldview. The dualism of Yoga consists in its assertion that *prakṛti* and *puruṣa* are the two irreducible but complementary principles of reality. They enable us to understand the relative roles of permanence and change in our being. *Puruṣa* underscores permanence and *prakṛti* the changing phases of reality. The manifest world is a product of evolution of *prakṛti* with its three basic elements – *sattva*, *rajas* and *tamas*. Knowing may be mediated by and processed through the route of *prakṛti* or it may be directly accessed from the *puruṣa*.

Awareness is thus of two sorts, transcendental and phenomenal. Transcendental awareness ensues from directly accessing consciousness-as-such, which in the language of Sāṃkhya-Yoga is realization of *puruṣa*-hood. Phenomenal awareness consists in accessing the information content, the *sattva* component of the material objects through the mediation of the "knowledge" apparatus of the embodied mind. *Puruṣa* is consciousness-*as-such*, which in the human condition is masked by the manifestations of the mind (*vṛtti*s). The human mind is the centre of phenomenal awareness. At the same time it is also associated with *puruṣa* whose proximity bestows consciousness on the nonconscious contents of the mind. The embodied mind thus enjoys dual citizenship, as it were, in the domains of the physical world (*prakṛti*) as well as in the world of consciousness (*puruṣa*). It has the facility to access information from material objects and the potential to partake in consciousness-as-such.

The mind's dual engagement with *prakṛti* and *puruṣa* makes it the seat of a variety of awareness states between the sensory and the transcendental. These include (1) nonconscious states, (2) unconscious states, (3) normal phenomenal states, (4) altered phenomenal states, (5) transcendental states translated into or leading to phenomenal states, (6) transcendental states-as-such, and (7) anomalous mental states. Non-conscious states are those information states the mind is simply unaware of at all its levels, those that are devoid of *puruṣa* reflections. This may be so because the *sattva* or information content in them does not reach the threshold level to bask in the reflections of the *puruṣa* or because of the utter dominance of *tamas* that veils the information. The unconscious states are those, which were once conscious but now relegated to the region of the mind that is shielded from the light of *puruṣa* such as *saṃskāra*s and *vāsanā*s. They are, however, capable of influencing the mind without being noticed. The phenomenal states are what are generally regarded as conscious states. The light of the *puruṣa* shines on them with the result that their information content is *revealed* as subjective knowledge. Phenomenal knowledge is an image of consciousness but not consciousness-as-such. The image is set in an ever-flowing flux, which is subject to all kinds of distortions and alterations. Consequently, there is no finality to phenomenal awareness and no absolute phenomenal truth. Inasmuch as phenomenal states are mediated by several mechanisms of the mind (the knowledge apparatus, *antaḥkaraṇa*), any changes in the structure and functions of these mechanisms would have a corresponding effect on the processed image, i.e., the accessed information. The so-called altered states of consciousness are the sufficiently marked and distinguishable categories of alteration such as, for example, alterations that occur in dream states and states induced by hypnosis, drugs and other manipulations.

It would seem therefore that the phenomenal states mentioned so far are images of reality. Consciousness-as-such is reality itself. In transcendental states the reality is by assumption revealed in and of itself. The *puruṣa* detached completely from the mind in its sublime state of splendid isolation (*kaivalya*) is, of course, a state of supreme transcendence. How could such a state exist, however, in the human condition of the embodied mind? The answer, it seems to me, may be found in the inherent reflexivity of consciousness. Consciousness, which is the essence of reality, in the same sense the *sattva* component of material objects is their informational essence, reveals itself to the mind when the mind is in a *niruddha* state and is completely devoid of any content that could become transparent in the light of *puruṣa*. In such a situation consciousness instead of reflecting the contents of the mind reflects itself in the mind. The mind thus partakes in consciousness-as-such and experiences transcendental states. These are the states that highly evolved yogins are believed capable of achieving.

On this model, what the mystic experiences are transient states of transcendence in which consciousness-as-such is realized. Such a momentary realization may leave an indelible mark and manifest subsequently in the form of profound changes in the life-style, attitudes and personality of the individual experiencing such states. Inasmuch as the mystical experience occurs when the normal mental functions are in abeyance, it is not available to rational understanding and verbal descriptions. It is ineffable in this sense. Though ineffable, it is also infallible because it is consciousness-as-such. The mystic, therefore, struggles to translate his experience into common language for making sense to communicate to others. That is why the mystical utterances are often metaphorical and seldom convincingly empirical. What a mystic may not be able to communicate in words, he attempts to do so in his actions. Thus, nonrational forms of belief are formed. In attempting to express the ineffable experience in phenomenal terms, the mystic risks compromising infallibility for intelligibility.

Expanding the Sāṃkhya-Yoga epistemology further, one could argue that the source of intuitive knowledge is a state of transcendence, an experience with consciousness-as-such. Whereas a mystic reveals his wisdom in his actions, like a leader, or translates his experience in the form of metaphorical description as a poet does, or acts as a scientist who intuitively encounters a scientific truth and traces back stepwise from the generality of the intuitively grasped truth to the specific events contingent on it. In science one may go from fact to fact to weave a theory or begin with an intuitive hunch and gather relevant facts to make sense of the hunch and thus come to a discovery of a law or a relation. The former espouses the phenomenal or intellectual tradition whereas the latter is in line with the transcendental approach. Inasmuch as the image of reality is inlaid in the *sattva* component of the physical universe, the human mind with its knowledge apparatus has access to that image. It is the image we can share. It is reality in the third person. However, in its transcendental transactions the mind is capable of having truth-manifesting intuitions and first-person experience of reality.

Anomalous states (A-states) of awareness stand in between transcendental and phenomenal states. They are anomalous precisely because they do not fit into either of the two categories. They are different from phenomenal states (P-states) in that they appear to transcend sensory-motor and space-time constraints that bind phenomenal awareness. In this aspect they are more like the transcendental states (T-states). Anomalous states are, however, different from T-states because they are intentional and carry information like the P-states. A-states are mental *qua* mental states. The mind (*citta*) is different from consciousness, and it is physical, albeit subtle. The subtlety confers on it nonlocality in virtue of which it can relate to and interact with other minds and objects outside of it. By relating to other minds, it can acquire telepathic information. By relating to the *sattva* component of objects the minds may obtain clairvoyant information about them. The notion of the nonlocality of minds may also be seen in the concept of *mahat*, the collective mind that indeed is the first evolute of *prakṛti* and therefore has nexus to all minds and all objects in existence. The *sattva* component of material objects, whether of subtle thoughts or gross objects, is the link that makes a connection between minds and objects possible. This is succinctly expressed in *sūtra* 22 of *kaivalya pāda* in *Yoga-Sūtras*. Vācaspati Miśra commenting on this sutra says, "the soul's consciousness of its own cognition [obtains] when the mind takes its form."

Anomalous awareness seems to involve two stages. In Stage-I, anomalous information is received at the unconscious level. It is extrasensory in that the A-states are not processed by the sensory-motor apparatus. For that reason, on the one hand, they lack some phenomenal properties and, on the other hand, they are not subject to some of the phenomenal constraints. Stage-I anomalous states may make use of similar psychodynamic processes that are known to be involved in bringing unconscious states into overt behaviour and awareness. This is the Stage-II of the psi, the anomalous process.

In this model, anomalous awareness is different in kind from mystical awareness, which is believed to involve a glimpse of the transcendental, i.e., consciousness-as-such. It is intentional and conveys information about objects and events. Anomalous awareness is phenomenal awareness without some of the limitations of the latter. It is not sensory, but may affect sensory experience and may even be carried into the phenomenal field by means of what G.N.M. Tyrell (1946) called mediating vehicles, such as dreams, hallucinations and intuitive hunches. Anomalous awareness is not infallible even if it transcends some phenomenal limitations. Even though they are different from T-states, A-states bear some resemblance to them. Both of them are undermined by phenomenal states linked to sensory experience. The restriction and control of sensory noise appears to be conducive to the manifestation of anomalous states. The A-states are, however, considered an impediment for realizing *puruṣa*-hood (transcendence) or self-realization. Like the phenomenal states they are to be avoided if the goal is transcendence because they stand in the way of realizing that supreme state of splendid isolation (*kaivalya*), being one with consciousness-as-such.

To sum up, the mind is characterized by a stream of constantly changing thoughts, flowing through and constrained by subconscious and unconscious surrounds. Attention is "variously directed, discontinuous and diffused" (*Yoga-Sūtra*, III, 2). Thoughts, feelings and actions arise from the sensory inputs, memory and the unconscious determinants called *vāsanās* and *saṃskāras*. Empirical or phenomenal awareness arising thus is imperfect and incomplete because it is conditioned and biased by the processes involved. It is the existential predicament of humans, whose minds are driven by sensory inputs and unconscious impressions and impulses. Perfection in thought and action is within human reach. It consists in gaining control of the mind to transcend the limitations imposed by the senses and *saṃskāras*. Yoga is the method by which the fluctuating mind can be controlled and freed from the conditioning biases, prejudices and predispositions. In yoga practice, attention becomes the key to unlock the door that gives a direct access to consciousness.

Yoga Practice and *Siddhis*

A variety of practices go in the name of yoga. In common parlance yoga is synonymous with a set of physical exercises called *āsana*s. This, however, is a misconception. In Patañjali yoga, which is known as *Rāja Yoga*, there are eight distinguishable aspects to yoga practice. They are considered to be eight *anga*s or organs of yoga. They involve those that primarily focus on manipulating the physical and physiological states while the others are essentially psychological. The same appear in other forms of yoga, even though the emphasis on some of them varies. For example, in Haṭha yoga the emphasis is more on physical and physiological aspects rather than on the psychological processes. Since it is not possible to review in the space available the different forms of yoga in the Hindu and non-Hindu traditions the following discussion is confined to Patañjali yoga.

In the *Yoga-Sūtra*s, Patañjali describes how the mind can be restrained to achieve a state of quiescence, how the natural wanderings of the mind, called *vṛtti*s, can be controlled, and how a variety of *siddhi*s, extra-ordinary abilities, may be obtained by yoga practice. The first five steps in yoga are preliminary leading to the last three, which are the integral part of Rāja Yoga. *Yama* and *niyama* are characterlogical prescriptions intended to control emotions and desires that distract the mind. *Āsana*s and *prāṇāyāma* involve physical manipulations that are required to eliminate bodily disturbances that stand in the way of controlling the mind. The fifth step *pratyāhāra* is an exercise in detaching the mind from attending to the constantly impinging sensory inputs. Each of the five steps appear to be independent of each other. Also, one could attempt to practice meditation without going through the five-fold preliminaries. Patañjali (II.53), however, is clearly of the view that the preliminary steps should be followed before attempting concentration (*dhāraṇā*) and practice meditation (*dhyāna*).

Meditation is the most important feature of yoga. According to Patañjali, practice of focused attention on a single object (*dhāraṇā*) progressively leads the subject to a state of meditation (*dhyāna*).

Sustained meditation over a period of time results in a stand still state of the mind called *samādhi*. The triple-effect of *dhāraṇā-dhyāna-samādhi* is called *saṃyama*. *Saṃyama* is often accompanied by the manifestation of paranormal phenomena, *siddhis*. However, the goal of yoga practitioners, Patañjali tells us, is not the acquisition of *siddhis*, which are more of a distraction (III.37) leading one away from the main goal of *kaivalya*, self-realization. *Kaivalya* is possible only in a state of complete cessation (*nirodha*) of all mental states, including the paranormal ones.

One-pointed and unwavering mind is the pre-requisite to gain control of the disorderly and often turbulent stream of thought. *Ekāgratā*, focused attention on a single point, whether a physical object such as the tip of the nose or a thought (e.g., a metaphysical or religious dictum) is the recommended practice for controlling the perpetual fluctuations of the mind (*citta-vṛtti*s). Focused attention is like building a dam to control the flow of the mental stream and channel it in an orderly fashion toward the desired direction. The mental stream is fed by the sensory secretions and thoughts stimulated by external as well as proprioceptive inputs and conscious and unconscious motivations, propensities and habits. *Ekāgratā* gives volitional control over one's psycho-physiological activity.

The ability to focus attention on a single point, get absorbed, and stay undisturbed and mentally focused is dependent on various factors such as attitudinal, psychological and physiological variables. In Patañjali's system of Yoga there is a clear recognition of psycho-physiological interdependence, a recognition that physical conditions and bodily states influence psychic functions and vice-versa. Consequently yoga places specific emphasis on one's beliefs and observances and the exercises one should practice and the duties to perform as preliminaries to practicing focused attention which is believed to lead ultimately to a state of *saṃādhi*, a state of complete absorption in pure consciousness.

The essence of yoga is *saṃyama*. *Saṃyama* involves the triple effort of *dhāraṇā* (concentration), *dhyāna* (meditation), and *samādhi* (absorption) (III.6). The first three *sūtras* in the third chapter of *Yoga-Sūtras* describe them in the following way. Concentration involves focusing attention on an object (III.1), which progressively leads to the restraining of the natural wanderings of the mind. In the state of *dhyāna* there is an uninterrupted flow of the mind toward the object of meditation (III. 2) so that the practitioner can focus the attention totally on a single object for a prolonged period of time. Such prolonged one-pointed attention to a single object leads to *samādhi*, a state of absorption. In a state of *samādhi* there is the awareness of the object alone, without an awareness of self (III. 3). When the yogin thus loses self-awareness and enters a state of complete absorption in the object of meditation, he/she achieves a state of higher consciousness that enables him/her to grasp the essence of the objects in focus (III. 4). The yogin thus knows the things in their true state without the biasing influence of the senses or the presuppositions and predilections of the mind. Some of these experiences may appear anomalous to those who do not have similar experiences themselves. The final point of yogin's progress is complete liberation from all phenomenal constraints of the mind so that she may realize the state of *asamprajñāta samādhi*, an experience of consciousness-as-such with no sensory content.

Patañjali says that knowledge of past and future is gained by *saṃyama* on the three transformations, i.e., the changes in *dharma, lakshaṇa* and *avastha*. Bhoja (3.16) explains this thus: "In this possessor of attributes (*dharmi*) (i.e., a thing) this attribute (*dharma*), this characteristic (*lakshaṇa*) and this state (*avasthā*), having come from a path that has not yet come, and having fulfilled its function in the present path enters the past path. Like this rejecting all fluctuations(*vikṣepa*) if *saṃyama* is made on that which is yet to be and that which is, everything will be known, because the *citta* is of the form of the light of pure *sattva*, and it is capable of apprehending all things, but this capacity is obstructed by fluctuations like nescience. When by following such and such methods the fluctuations are suppressed, then like the capacity of a cleanly-wiped mirror to reflect, the mind's capacity to apprehend everything becomes manifest due to the force of concentration."

When *saṃyama* is done on the mind of another person by means of concentration on his *mukharāga* (facial expression) etc., then the knowledge of his mind is generated. To know the *citta* of others is to know whether there is love, fear, pride or truth or whatever it may be, but not the object of such thought or feeling. That, according to the Yoga, could be known only by a further *saṃyama*. It is possible to know another's *citta* with its *ālambana (*object), because the *ālambana* cannot be made an object of mediation by any sign. This is so because by *liṅga* (sign) the other's *citta* is alone grasped, and not whether that *citta* has for its object yellowness or blueness. As *saṃyama* is impossible to be performed upon that which is the object of another's *citta*, it cannot be known. Therefore, another's *citta* is not grasped along with the *ālambana*, but the attributes of another's *citta* are grasped. When, however, a man performs *praṇidhana*, i.e., concentration in the form, "what is the *ālambana* of this man's *citta*?" then, from that *saṃyama*, the knowledge of the thing also is generated (3.20.)

According to Yoga system, things seen by clairvoyance are more of the same kind as are seen by physical eyes. By *saṃyama* on an idea or thing a man can master it. Patañjali distinguishes between those two kinds of knowledge (i) sensuous and (ii) real knowledge or knowledge of the *puruṣa*. There is a fundamental difference between the two: the first is for another's sake, while the second is for the sake of itself. Knowledge which is called experience exists for the fulfillment of our purposes, and is not a living reality, but only an idea. On the other hand, knowledge of the self is, so to say, living knowledge, i.e., knowledge which knows itself as knowledge (*svasaṃvedya*).

Philosophers belonging to other schools may have disputed the theories of Sāṃkhya-Yoga, but few have questioned the merits of yoga practice. It should be mentioned also that as the practitioner of yoga reaches the *samādhi* state and is able to practice *saṃyama* he/she is likely to encounter a variety of paranormal phenomena. In fact, Patañjali devotes a major part of the third chapter of *Yoga-Sūtra*s to describing the *siddhi*s (paranormal powers) that one could obtain by doing *saṃyama*, such as knowledge of past and future, knowing other people's thoughts, becoming invisible, and so on. Thus, the anomalous states of awareness appear to be a natural consequence of yoga practice. They are, however, states that the yogin should ignore and move forward on the path to *kaivalya* to attain a state of consciousness-as-such, which ultimately results in self-realization.

Patañjali recognized that yoga and *saṃyama* are just one way of acquiring *siddhi*s. There are other factors such as genetics (birth), drugs, *mantra* (sacred incantation), and *tapas* (practice of austerities) (IV.1) that could result in the manifestation of paranormal phenomena. This observation is also consistent with the findings that there are some star performers in ESP tests, the so-called gifted subjects like Pearce tested by Rhine.

CONCLUDING SUMMARY

Parapsychology has travelled far since J.B. Rhine conducted the Pearce-Pratt experiment eighty years ago, which may be considered the first definitive study to provide solid evidence for the existence of ESP. It has crossed many milestones, overcoming many hurdles, and accumulated massive evidence. It has survived savage attacks from some of the most vociferous critics science has ever known. Researchers in this field have attempted to answer all reasonable questions. In response to criticism they have modified their experimental protocols, revised their analyses, and introduced additional safeguards. Yet in terms of achieving a broad consensus among scientists on the question of the existence or otherwise of psi we have come no further than when Rhine published his early ESP test results. Optimism that parapsychologists and their critics could carve out a common ground for communication and for evaluating psi research generated by the publication of the Hyman-Honorton (1986) joint statement has been eroded. The proponents and opponents of psi continue to live in two separate universes.

Part of the problem is due to lack of understanding what psi really is. We know very little about psi beyond that it is not mediated by our sensory system. There is no one theory that could provide a reasonable explanation of ESP and PK. However, there is no dearth of theories, but there is none that holds any promise to guide sustained systematic research beyond accumulating more and more evidence in favour of the existence of an anomaly (Rao, 1978; Radin, 2006). As C.T.K. Chari (1977) wrote some thirty years ago, parapsychology "is strewn with dead and dying hypotheses and desperate expedients" (p. 806). We are caught in a theoretical quagmire unable to understand the perceived absurdities of action at a distance, knowing without senses and awareness of events and objects nonexistent at the time. Thus lack of theoretical understanding of psi phenomena further adds to the scepticism about their reality.

The conundrums of cognitive anomalies, created by the available empirical evidence, which is massive and in many ways unassailable, and the equally strong resistance to accept it by the scientific community continue to clog the Western mindset on parapsychological phenomena. The mother of all of them is inherent in the very paradox of naturalization of the supernormal, the task parapsychology has set for itself from the very beginning. William McDougall commended J.B. Rhine for attempting to do just that (Rhine, 1973/34). This continuing riddle relates to how one may evaluate the scientific evidence for psi, which, if valid, would undermine science itself by raising fundamental questions about its very assumptive base. How can we have a science that does not share the basic assumptions of science about the nature of reality? Obsession to gain scientific credibility and acceptance led psi researchers more and more data-driven than theoretically guided. This has not helped either in gaining acceptance of their findings or the credibility of their research.

In an intellectual climate that accords zero subjective probability to the possibility of psychic phenomena, no amount of statistical data is sufficient to establish their existence. Parapsychology in the West started its journey, it would seem, on a dead-end road. Consequently the overwhelming evidence for the existence of psi by the work of serious researchers for over one hundred years amounted to no more than discovering an anomaly. Stranded at the end of a closed road, staring at the wild scenario, they are straining their minds seeking new avenues to reach the goal of acceptance and recognition. These include repeated attempts to rediscover the same phenomena by employing new methodologies and techniques and improved technologies, to answer rationally and with fresh data the persistent criticisms of sceptical colleagues, by attempting replications and conducting extensive meta-analyses of all known studies. All these efforts proved valuable in some respects and clearly revealed the solid data base, and gave some interesting insights into the nuances and peculiarities of the phenomena being investigated. There is no question that we learned something from them. However, the goal of gaining recognition to the results and acceptance of the claims of the researchers as genuine is not within sight and certainly no closer than fifty years ago when I enthusiastically entered this field.

After fifty years of first-hand participation in parapsychological research, I have grown to be a little wiser. I am convinced now, more than ever, that we in parapsychology need a strategic shift and acknowledge at once with courage and conviction that psi is neither a theoretical anomaly nor a methodological artefact. Rather its existence is implied in a more inclusive psychological model as to who we are and where our destiny lies. Thus the goal of parapsychology may not be one of naturalizing the supernatural, but studying exceptional phenomena as natural phenomena. We should attempt doing this by bringing out the relevance of psi to life by exploring the methods for developing it. This should not scare any of us in India. We have had a long and continuing tradition that accords primacy to consciousness, regards psi and *siddhi*s as natural phenomena and has available psycho-physical techniques to develop psychic abilities. Here then is the relevance of yoga, in its secular sense, to psi research.

The reality of psi poses severe explanatory challenges within the western paradigm of science. Psi phenomena refer to events that cannot simply occur in the physical universe as we know it. The basic limiting principles, as C.D. Broad (1953) labeled them, governing the assumptive base of science rule out the possibility of mind-to-mind communication that does not involve meaningful transformation of energy between minds. Similarly noninferential precognition is a theoretical absurdity. All attempts to naturalize the supernatural result in a paradox. It is the paradox of using science to demolish the very assumptive base of science itself. Once a dichotomy of natural and supernatural is postulated, we confront the "paradox of naturalizing the supernatural" in studying such phenomena as psi. Similarly the subject-object distinction so basic to western epistemology is at the root of the confusion caused by psi experimenter effects and the difficulty in tracing the source of psi.

In the classical Indian tradition no sharp distinction is made between the natural and the supernatural, the scientific and the spiritual. At some level of awareness, even the subject-object dichotomy disappears. Consequently, neither the paradox of naturalizing the supernormal nor the perplexities of the experimenter effects in psi research pose any serious threat for an understanding of the psi process within the Indian paradigm.

I am inclined to argue that parapsychology is unlikely to make much headway if the research continues to employ the disjunctive western conceptual categories. The most that could be established within western paradigm is to provide extensive and even compelling evidence for the existence of cognitive anomalies. Beyond this, I venture to hazard, few insights into the nature of the phenomena themselves could be gained by methods that basically assume their nonexistence.

In this context, Indian psychology has much to offer to give a new direction and a fresh impetus to parapsychological research. Not only is the native Indian culture hospitable for studying these phenomena, but we also have here concepts, methods and models that could make a difference. In the Indian tradition, humans enjoy dual citizenship in the physical world of sense, reason and objectivity, on the one hand, and in the realm of consciousness, subjectivity and intuition on the other. Itself a material form, the mind's citizenship in the material world is by birth as it were. Its naturalization in the domain of consciousness is a matter of choice and an outcome of significant effort.

Normal and paranormal processes aid the mind in its dual roles. The sensory-motor processes are those that come under the category of the normal. The paranormal process involves accessing consciousness-as-such. In normal processes consciousness is *reflected* in the mind. By the paranormal process, consciousness is *realized* in the mind. *Nididhyāsana* is meditating on the truth for realizing it in one's being.

Indian psychology is not opposed to science, even though it leaves room for understanding the spiritual side of human nature. First-person methodologies have extensive application in Indian psychology. Second-person mediation provides a way of bridging the explanatory gap between first and third-person perspectives. Employing first-person and second-person methodologies and applying the mind controlling techniques such as yoga to develop psychic abilities, I believe, it would be possible to advance parapsychological research to the levels that western approaches are simply unable to achieve.

REFERENCES

Abell, G.O. & Singer, B. (Eds.) (1981). *Science and the Paranormal*. NewYork: Charles Scribner's Sons.

Alcock, J.E. (1981). *Parapsychology: Science or Magic*? New York: Pergamon Press.

Altom, K. & Braud, W.G. (1976). Clairvoyant and telepathic impressions of musical targets. In J.D. Morris, W.G. Roll, & R.L. Morris (Eds.), *Research in Parapsychology* (pp. 171-174). Metuchen, NJ: Scarecrow Press.

Avant, L.L. (1965). Vision in the ganzfeld. *Psychological Bulletin,* 64, 246-258.

Beloff, J. (1980). Seven evidential experiments. *Zetetic Scholar*, July, 91-94, 116-120.

Bem, D.J. & Honorton, C. (1994). Does Psi exist? Replicable evidence for anomalous process of information transfer. *Psychological Bulletin,* 115, 4-18.

Bem, D.J., Palmer, J. & Broughton, R.S. (2001). Updating the ganzfeld database: A victim of its own success. *Journal of Parapsychology,* 65.

Braud, L.W. & Braud, W.G. (1974). Further studies of relaxation as a psi-conducive state. *Journal of the American Society for Psychical Research, 68*, 229-245.

Braud, W.G. (1975). Psi-conducive states. *Journal of Communication*, 25, 142-152.

Broad, C.D. (1953). *Religion Philosophy and Psychical Research.* New York: Harcourt Brace.

Brugmans, H.J.F.W. (1922). Une communication sur des experiences telepathique au laboratoire de psychologie a Groningon faites por M. Heymans, Docteur Weinberg, et Docteur H.J.F.W. Brugmans. Le compete Rends official du Premier Congres International des Researches Psychiques. Copenhagen. (For a free translation from the French into English see G. Murphy (1961) *Challenge of Psychical Research*, New York: Harper).

Casler, L. (1962). The improvement of clairvoyance scores by means of hypnotic suggestion. *Journal of Parapsychology,* 26, 77-87.

Casler, L. (1964). The effects of hypnosis on GESP. *Journal of Parapsychology*, 28, 126-134.

Chari, C.T.K. (1977). Some generalized theories and models of psi: A critical evaluation. In B. Wolman (Ed.), *Handbook of Parapsychology*, New York: Van Nostrand Reinhold.

Coover, J.E. (1975). *Experiments in Psychical Research.* New York: Arno Press.

Dasgupta, S. (1922). *History of Indian Philosophy,* Vol. I. London: George Allen and Unwin.

Dodds, E.R. (1973). Supernormal phenomena in classical antiquity. In, *The Ancient Concept of Progress* (pp. 156-210). Oxford : Clarendon Press.

Eliade, M. (1969). *Yoga: Immortality and Freedom.* Bollingon Series LVI Princeton, NJ: Princeton University Press.

Estabrooks, G. (1961). A contribution to experimental telepathy. *Journal of Parapsychology.*

Eysenck, H.J. (1967). Personality and extra-sensory perception. *Journal of Parapsychology,* 21, 179-185.

Fahler, J. (1957). ESP card tests with and without hypnosis. *Journal of Parapsychology*, 31, 93-98.

— & Cadoret, R.J. (1958). ESP card tests of college students with and without hypnosis. *Journal of Parapsychology*, 22, 125-136.

Grela, J.J. (1945). Effect on ESP scoring of hypnotically induced attitudes. *Journal of Parapsychology*, 9, 194-202.

Gurney, E. (1888) Recent experiments in hypnotism. *Proceedings of the Society for Psychical Research.*

Hansel, C.E.M. (1980). *ESP and Parapsychology: A Critical Re-evaluation.* Buffalo, NY: Prometheus Books.

Honorton, C. (1977). Psi and internal attention states. In B.B. Wolman (Ed.), *Handbook of Parapsychology.* New York: Van Nostrand Reinhold.

—, Ferrari, D.C. & Bem, D.J. (1998). Extroversion and ESP performance: A meta-analysis and new confirmation. *Journal of Parapsychology,* 62, 255-276.

— & Harper, S. (1974). Psi-mediated imagery and ideation in an experimental procedure for regulating perceptual input. *Journal of the American Society for Psychical Research,* 68, 156-168.

Hyman, R. (1985). The ganzfeld psi experiment: A critical appraisal. *Journal of Parapsychology*, 49, 3-49.

— & Honorton, C. (1986). A joint communiqué: The psi ganzfeld controversy. *Journal of Parapsychology,* 50, 351-364.

Irwin, H.J. (1999). *An Introduction to Parapsychology* (3rd edn.) Jefferson, NC: McFarland & Co.

Jahn, R.G. (1982). The persistent paradox of psychic phenomena: An engineering perspective. *Proceedings of the IEEE,* 70, 136-170.

Mackenzie, B. (1977). Three stages in the history of parapsychology. Paper presented at the Quadrennial Congress on History of Science, Edinburgh, Scotland.

— & Mackenzie, L. (1980). Whence the enchanted boundary? Sources and significance of the parapsychological tradition. *Journal of Parapsychology,* 44, 125-166.

Marks, D. & Kammann, R. (1980). *The Psychology of the Psychic*. Buffalo, NY: Prometheus Books.

Mattuck, R.D. (1984). A quantum mechanical theory of the interaction of consciousness with matter. In M. Cazenave (Ed.), *Science and Consciousness* (pp. 45-65). New York: Pergamon Press.

May, E.C., Utts, J.M., & Spottiswoode, S.J.P. (1995). Decision augmentation theory: Applications to the random number generator database. *Journal of Scientific Exploration*, 9:4, 453.

Milton, J. & Wiseman, R. (1999). Does psi exist? Lack of replication of an anomalous process of information transfer. *Psychological Bulletin*, 125, 387-391.

Osis, K. & Bokert, E. (1971). ESP and changed states of consciousness induced by meditation. *Journal of the American Society for Psychical Research,* 58, 158-185.

Pekala, R., Kumar, V.K. & Marcano, G. (1995). Anomalous/paranormal experiences, hypnotic susceptibility, and dissociation. *Journal of the American Society for Psychical Research*, 89, 313-332.

Podmore, F. (1984). *Apparitions and Thought-transference*. London: Scott.

Radin, D.I. (1997). *The Conscious Universe: The Scientific Truth of Psychic Phenomena*. San Francisco: Harper Edge.

— (2006). *Entangled Minds: Extrasensory Experiences in a Quantum Reality*. New York: Paraview Pocket Books.

Rao, K.R. & Palmer, J. (1987). The anomaly called psi: Recent research and criticism. *Behavioral and Brain Sciences,* 10, 539-555.

—(1978). Theories of psi. In Stanley Krippner (Ed.), *Advances in Parapsychological Research, Vol. 2, Extrasensory Perception*. New York: Plenum Press.

Rhine, J.B. (1934). Extra-sensory perception. In B.B. Wolman (Ed.), *Handbook of Parapsychology.* New York: Van Nostrand Reinhold.

— (1938). Experiments bearing on the precognition hypothesis. *Journal of Parapsychology,* 2, 38-54.

— (1973). *Extra-sensory Perception*. Brookline Village, Mass.: Branden Press.

— Pratt, J.G., Smith, B.M., Stuart, C.E. & Greenwood, J.A. (1966). *Extra-sensory Perception after Sixty Years*. Boston: Bruce Humphries.

Richet, C. (1975). *Thirty Years of Psychical Research.* New York: Arno Press.

Ryzl, M. & Ryzlova, J. (1962). A case of high-scoring ESP performance in the hypnotic state. *Journal of Parapsychology*, 26, 153-171.

Sargent, C.L. (1981). Extraversion and performance in "extra-sensory perception" tasks. *Personality and Individual Differences,* 2, 137-143.

Schechter, E.I. (1984). Hypnotic induction vs. control conditions. Illustrating an approach to the evaluation of replicability in parapsychological data. *Journal of the American Society for Psychical Research,* 78, 1-27.

Schlitz, M.J. & Gruber, E.R. (1980). Transcontinental remote viewing. *Journal of Parapsychology, 44, 305-317.*

Schmeidler, G.R. (1970). High ESP scores after a swami's brief instruction in meditation and breathing. *Journal of the Society for Psychical Research*, 64, 100-103.

Schmidt, H. (1975a). A logically consistent model of a world with psi interaction. In L. Oteri (Ed.), *Quantum Physics and Parapsychology* (pp. 205-228). New York: Parapsychology Foundation.

— (1975b). Toward a mathematical theory of psi. *Journal of the American Society for Psychical Research*, 69, 301-319.

— & Pantas, L. (1972). Psi tests with internally different machines. *Journal of Parapsychology*, 36, 222-232.

Sheldrake, R. (1994). *Seven Experiments That Could Change the World.* London: Fourth Estate.

Sidgwick, H., Sidgwick, E.M. & Smith, G.A. (1889). Experiments in thought transference. *Proceedings of the Society for Psychical Research,* 6, 128-170.

Sinclair, U. (1930). *Mental Radio.* Monrovia, CA: Sinclair.

Stanford, R.G. & Mayer, B. (1974). Relaxation as a psi-conducive state: A replication and exploration of parameters. *Journal of the American Society for Psychical Research*, 68, 182-191.

Stanford, R.G. (1977). Experimental psychokinesis: A review from diverse perspectives. In B.B. Wolman (Ed.), *Handbook of Parapsychology* (pp. 324-381). New York: Van Nostrand Reinhold.

— & Stein, A.G. (1994). A meta-analysis of ESP studies contrasting hypnosis and a comparison condition. *Journal of Parapsychology*, 58, 235-269.

Steinkasmp, F., Milton, J. & Morris, R.L. (1998). A meta-analysis of forced-choice experiments comparing clairvoyance and precognition. *Journal of Parapsychology*, 62, 193-218.

Targ, R. & Puthoff, H.E. (1977). *Mind Reach.* New York: Delcorte Press/Eleanor Friede.

Troland, L.T. (1917). *A Technique for the Study of Telepathy and Other Alleged Clairvoyant Processes*. Albany: Brandow Publishing Co.

Tyrrell, G.N.M. (1946-49). The modus operandi of paranormal cognition. *Proceedings of the Society for Psychical Research*, 48, 65-120.

Utts, J. (2001). An assessment of the evidence of psychic functioning. In K.R. Rao (Ed.), *Basic Research in Parapsychology* (pp. 110-141). Jefferson, NC: McFarland.

Vasiliev, L.L. (1963). *Experiments in Mental Suggestion.* Church Crookham: Institute for the Study of Mental Images.

Walker, E.H. (1975). Foundations of paraphysical and parapsychological phenomena. In L. Oteri (Ed.), *Quantum Physics and Parapsychology* (pp. 1-53). New York: Parapsychology Foundation.

— (2000). *The Physics of Consciousness.* Cambridge, MA: Perseus Books.

White, R.A. (1964). A comparison of old and new methods of response to targets in ESP experiments. *Journal of the American Society for Psychical Research*, 58, 21-56.

Wiseman, R. & Schlitz, M. (1997). Experimenter effects and the remote detecting of staring. *Journal of Parapsychology*, 61, 197-207.

Woods, J.H. (1927). *The Yoga System of Patañjali*. Cambridge, MA: Harvard University Press.

Spirituality and the Capricious, Evasive Nature of Psi

J.E. Kennedy

The inability to demonstrate consistent, sustained paranormal effects is the most significant characteristic of experimental parapsychology. The discussions of this failure have often implied an active agency that prevents sustained psi effects. Beloff (1994) described psi as “actively evasive”, Braud (1985) described it as “self-obscuring”, Hansen (2001) as a “trickster”, Batcheldor (1994, p. 93) as seeming “to avoid those positions in space and time when we are actively looking for it”, McClenon (1994) as acting “capriciously, as if…to resist complete verification”, and William James (1909/1982, p. 310) as “intended ... to remain *baffling*”. In addition, other writers such as Eisenbud (1992), White (1994), and Lucadou (2001, 2002) have suggested that psi cannot be controlled in the manner required for experimental research.

The purpose of the present paper is to summarize the key evidence for the capricious, evasive nature of psi and to discuss the implications of this property of psi.

Evidence for Capricious, Evasive Psi

Psi Missing

Psi effects that are significantly opposite to what is desired and intended in an experiment are called psi missing and have occurred frequently throughout the history of parapsychology. A shift to psi missing can occur within or between studies. In describing the evolution of ESP research at the Duke laboratory, Palmer (1981, p. 31) noted "more typical of the new trend was the performance of a teenage boy identified as P.H., whose promising psi-hitting when tested informally reverted to significant psi-missing when better controls were applied (Russell and Rhine, 1942)."

Rao used terms like "bidirectionality" and "differential effect" to characterize the property that "shifts the mode of psi response from hitting to missing in a rather capricious manner" (Rao, 1965, p. 245). He summarized numerous examples and described this characteristic as preventing the useful application of psi. Bierman (1980) pointed out that the frequently observed shift between psi hitting and psi missing is not just low reliability, but negative reliability. Psi seems to be almost defiant when the results are the opposite from what is intended and from what occurred previously.

Unintended Secondary Effects

Another seemingly capricious or defiant psi manifestation is when the overall intended effect becomes nonsignificant, but unintended secondary effects provide evidence for psi. The Princeton Engineering Anomalies Research (PEAR) laboratory provides a recent example. Studies with electronic REGs had small, but significant effects for a decade. A recent large scale replication effort obtained nonsignificant results overall, but Jahn, *et al.* (2000) reported unintended internal structural effects that appeared to indicate psi. The analyses for these effects were based on findings in the previous data and the effects were reported as significant after adjusting for multiple analyses. However, the effects had different patterns than the earlier results and were not consistent across the 3 laboratories participating in the project. Jahn and Dunne

(2001) summarized the situation as: "At the end of the day, we are confronted with an archive of irregular, irrational, yet indismissable data that testifies, almost impishly, to our enduring lack of comprehension of the basic nature of these phenomena" (p. 300).

The evolution of research at the Princeton laboratory is notably similar to the earlier experience at the Duke laboratory. At Duke the initial research was remarkably successful in demonstrating the intended effects. However, a decade later, unintended, internal effects were increasingly being reported as the primary finding.

In fact, Rhine (1974) argued that these internal effects were some of the best evidence for psi because the lack of motivation, intention, and expectation for their occurrence reduced the likelihood of fraud or errors. Of course, skeptics would argue that the internal effects were (are) simply post hoc data selection in an effort to salvage nonsignificant results. However, the internal effects were remarkably consistent in the early studies — at least when they were not intended or expected.

Loss of Effects

The consistent loss of psi effects also indicates the evasiveness and unsustainability of psi. The loss of psi effects occurs for individual subjects, experimenters, and lines of research. Pratt (1975) summarized the universal loss of psi effects with individual subjects: "we must recognize what has been the most serious limitation on psi research with outstanding subjects. This is the unexplained loss of ability that has always brought their successful performance in the test situation to an end" (p. 159). Houtkooper (1994, 2002; Haraldsson and Houtkooper, 1995) proposed the term "meta-analysis demolition" to describe the loss of effect for an experimenter or experimenter group. His evaluation of 7 different series of studies found that a summary evaluation was followed by an average of 90% reduction in effect size. Kennedy and Taddonio (1976) noted other examples of declining effects for experimenters. In early parapsychological research, Taves and Dale (1943) used the term experimenter "Midas touch in reverse" to describe the tendency for effects to decline within a study.

Bierman (2001) showed that declines in effect are typical for most lines of research in parapsychology. His evaluation used several meta-analysis databases. Throughout the history of parapsychology, new lines of research have initially had exciting results and great promise, but then the results became evasive. Beloff (1994, p. 71) described this pattern as a "succession of false dawns and frustrated hopes."

In spite of these various declines, the overall significance level for most of these subjects, experimental series, and lines of research remain significant. There is evidence for psi, but the effects seem systematically unstable.

Lack of Practical Application of Psi

The inability to practically apply psi provides some of the clearest evidence for the capricious or unsustainable nature of psi. Even minimal reliability of psi could be leveraged into money-making operations. The fact that parapsychological research is not financed by entrepreneurs profiting from successful applications of psi is a clear indication of the unsustainable nature of psi and lack of tangible progress.

Efforts to develop applications of psi have occurred throughout the history of parapsychology, but the capricious, evasive effects did not maintain the interest of those supporting the research. Several exploratory experiments have been carried out to predict the outcomes of casino games (Brier and Tyminski, 1970a, 1970b; Dean and Taetzsch, 1970, Puthoff, May, and Thompson, 1986). These studies provided statistically significant outcomes but failed to develop into useful applications. Such applications presumably would put gambling industries like casinos, lotteries, and races out of business. However, there is no realistic evidence that parapsychology poses a threat to the gambling industries, even though there is a strong financial incentive to develop such applications. A contracted project to investigate using ESP to find land mines produced statistically significant results in the first few sessions, but the later sessions declined to chance (Rhine, 1971). J.B. Rhine terminated the study because he thought it unlikely that the positive results would resume. Targ described another case: "we did a series of trials some time ago where we had nine successes in a row forecasting silver futures changes, and then I tried to replicate that ...and got eight out of nine hits... I then sought for replication to take advantage of this mechanical psi machine we had created and I got eight out of nine failures. That has really stopped my personal psi investigation for a couple of years while I have tried to meditate on what the problem is here" (Targ, Braud, Stanford, Schlitz, and Honorton, 1991, pp. 76-77).

The U.S. government funded Star Gate project to investigate using psi in government intelligence work is probably the most well funded effort to develop applications of psi. After 24 years of effort with controversial results, the project was dropped. The use of psychics in police investigations is another situation that has produced some striking anecdotal successes within a larger domain of unreliable results (Lyons and Truzzi, 1991; Truzzi, 1995). Similarly, the initial research with intercessory prayer for healing appears to have the same issues of unreliability as other type of psi studies (Kennedy, 2002). Two large, well funded, carefully designed studies at prestigious research institutions both failed to support the efficacy of prayer (Benson, *et al.* 2006; Krucoff, *et al.*, 2005).

The great majority of spontaneous psi cases also have not involved a practical benefit. This is obvious from examining the cases in any case collection. For example, McClenon (2002a) reported that his case collection did not support the hypothesis that psi experiences generally provide direct benefits. Eisenbud (1992, p. 13) similarly commented "that psi-derived information is on the whole quite useless in the ordinary sense of the word is one of the most obvious facts of parapsychology."

The lack of practical use has been apparent throughout the history of paranormal phenomena. Inglis (1992) argued that interest in research on spiritualism declined due to a lack of meaningful explanation and utility for the phenomena more than a lack of evidence. For example, he quoted Maeterlinck (1914) describing the "strange, inconsistent, whimsical, and disconcerting" character of the phenomena that seem to be "without rhyme or reason, and keep to the providence of supernaturally vain and puerile recreations" (Inglis, 1992, p. 437). Historically, some of the most common spirit entities in shamanism were thought to be tricksters whose role was "to show how egocentric, selfish behavior resulted in humiliation and bad outcomes, or how the spirit world could play unpredictable tricks on people and thus prevent them from becoming too self-confident or haughty" (Hayden, 2003, p. 119). Hansen (2001) argued that paranormal phenomena in general are best characterized as an irrational, disruptive trickster.

Inconsistent with Statistical Research Methods

These results suggest that the desired outcomes in experiments become actively avoided and are not just a signal in noise as assumed for statistical research. A signal in noise would be expected to produce results approaching chance, not avoidance of the desired outcome or unintended internal effects in the absence of primary, intended effects. A signal in noise would be expected to produce improved experimental results over time if relevant variables were controlled or relatively uniform results if no progress was made in understanding the phenomenon. The declines in parapsychology are not consistent with this expectation. Statistical signal enhancement methods can be used to develop useful applications for a signal in noise, but attempts to develop useful applications of psi have not been successful.

Perhaps most important, a signal in noise produces more reliable results with larger sample sizes as assumed by statistical theory. Meta-analyses consistently show that psi experiments do not have this property (Kennedy, 2003b, 2004). The failure to obtain more reliable results with larger sample sizes undermines the use of normal statistical methods, including meta-analyses.

Traditional Explanation for Evasive Psi

The usual explanations in parapsychology for the evasive properties of psi involve psychoanalytic speculations about unconscious, instinctive fear of psi and suppression of psi to prevent information overload. However, the widespread interest in psi and extensive efforts of some people to cultivate psi abilities are not consistent with these speculations about fear of psi. It may be true that some people fear psi, but there is very strong evidence that many others do not and, in fact, some people strongly desire to develop useful psi abilities. Similarly, the speculations about information overload overlook the fact that instances of striking psi occur without information overload. These speculations do not explain why instances of striking psi do not occur more frequently and with greater control.

The speculations about fear and information overload, combined with the unreliable, unuseful nature of psi effects, imply that psi has more adverse effects than benefits. Experimental parapsychology assumes that psi is a widespread human ability; however, psi would not be expected to evolve as a human ability if it caused substantial adverse effects and little benefits. The instinctive propensity to fear snakes (Tallis, 2002, pp. 135-138) provides a useful comparison. Such instinctive fears make sense for reacting to external threats like snakes, but do not offer a rationale for the evolution of an ability that appears to have negligible material benefit and serious adverse effects that need to be suppressed. The arguments about unconscious fear of psi imply that the source of psi is external to people rather than psi being a human ability.

Attempts to understand psi must recognize both the striking results in some cases and the capricious, evasive properties overall. Most models of psi have focused on either the striking cases or the evasive properties, without integrating or explaining the overall observed characteristics of psi.

What Does Psi Do?

Research on the effects of psi experiences has found that the primary effect is to alter the person's world view and increase his or her sense of spirituality, connectedness, and meaning in life (Kennedy and Kanthamani, 1995; McClenon, 1994, 2002b; Palmer, 1979; Palmer and Braud, 2002; White, 1997a). In a survey of people with psychic or transcendent experiences, 72% agreed with the statement "As a result of my paranormal or transcendent experience, I believe my life is guided or watched over by a higher force or being" (Kennedy and Kanthamani, 1995). White (1997a, 1997b) has devoted the greatest effort to collecting and summarizing the effects of psychic and other exceptional experiences, and describing the transformative after effects. Paranormal experiences are frequently reported in surveys of mystical experiences and are generally found to be a component of a single mystical experience factor (Hood, Spilka, Hunsberger and Gorsuch, 1996, p. 248; Thalbourne and Delin, 1994).

The relatively few spontaneous psi cases that appear to have direct benefits related to motivation may actually serve as vehicles for this transformative aspect of psi. For example, I previously described a personal experience that in retrospect appeared to have been contrived to be a dramatic exceptional experience (Kennedy, 2000). The apparent psi experience had a significant practical benefit, but the benefit could have been achieved much more easily in a less dramatic and less conspicuously paranormal manner. However, that would have had little impact on my world view. Similarly, spontaneous psi experiences of awareness of a traumatic event happening to a loved one affects the recipient's world view pertaining to the event, but rarely allows the event to be avoided as would be expected if psi were guided by the motivations and needs of the people involved.

Throughout eastern and western spiritual writings, paranormal miracles are reported and interpreted as evidence for a nonphysical, transcendent level of reality (McClenon, 1994; Woodward, 2000). Paranormal phenomena and interpretations have been frequently described for eastern spiritual teachers or masters (e.g., McClenon, 1994; Rama, 1978; Yogananda, 1946). In Christianity, various paranormal effects were specifically described as having a decisive role in convincing people that Jesus was a great or unique spiritual teacher. The occurrence of miracles in later centuries had a key role in the proliferation of Christianity (McClenon, 1994; Woodward, 2000). McClenon (1994) argued that the formation and initial growth of religious groups has hinged on demonstrations of paranormal effects that were more impressive than those by competing religious groups.

These findings suggest that the primary purpose of psi experiences may be transformative. Spontaneous experiences may be intended to be noticed as exceptional experiences that expand a person's sense of connectedness, meaning in life, and spirituality. Belief in paranormal phenomena is associated with spirituality, particularly for people with the strongest beliefs (Kennedy, 2003a).

The instances of striking psi draw attention away from the material world and the capricious, actively evasive characteristics of psi prevent using psi for material self-interest. Both aspects of psi are important for promoting spiritual awareness. Enhanced consciousness appears to be the self-evident result of biological evolution, the ultimate goal of spirituality, and the primary effect of paranormal experiences.

Common Source for Psi and Mystical Experiences

Psi and mystical experiences have several common characteristics that strongly suggest they derive from a common source.

Personality

Psi and mystical experiences are associated with the same personality characteristics. Absorption and fantasy proneness are strongly associated with both paranormal and mystical experiences (summarized in Kennedy, Kanthamani and Palmer, 1994; Thalbourne, 1998; Lange, Thalbourne, Houran and Storm, 2000). The Myers-Briggs intuitive (N) and feeling (F) personality types are also associated with belief in psi (Arcangel, 1997; Gow, Lurie, Coppin, Popper, Powell and Basterfield, 2001; Lester, Thinschmidt and Trautman, 1987; Murphy and Lester, 1976). Keirsey (1998) stated that people with an NF personality type are mystical in outlook and often explore occultism, parapsychology, and esoteric metaphysical systems. (The Appendix provides a short overview of the Myers-Briggs personality model.) As noted above, the occurrence of psi and transcendent experiences are correlated with each other and are found to be part of one common factor (Hood, Spilka, Hunsberger and Gorsuch, 1996, p. 248; Thalbourne and Delin, 1994).

Unconscious

Psi and mystical experiences are both thought to arise from an unconscious or higher part of the mind and to be facilitated by efforts to still the conscious mind and reduce superficial unconscious activity. Both types of experience are viewed as a link or doorway to a higher realm of interconnectedness. In fact, the primary difference is that psi experiences provide information about the material world whereas mystical experiences provide information about the higher realm of interconnectedness itself. William James (1902/1982) noted that the knowledge revealed in mystical experiences may pertain to sensory events (e.g., precognition or clairvoyance) or to metaphysics.

Lack of Control

Both psi and mystical experiences are spontaneous and normally outside of direct conscious control. At best, one can create conditions that set the stage for the experiences. Claims for direct, sustained, consistent control of mystical or transcendent experiences are very rare and very controversial (Kornfield, 2000). Likewise, claims for sustained, consistent control of psi involve misinterpretation and/or deception in the great majority, and perhaps all, of such cases. This is true for shamans, mediums, psychics, and experimental researchers (Hansen, 2001; Markwick, 1978; McClenon, 1994; Rhine, 1975).

After-Effects

The primary effects of both mystical and psi experiences are increased sense of meaning in life, interconne-ctedness, and spirituality. Mystical experiences and paranormal miracles have both had major roles in most spiritual traditions.

Inconsistent with Biological Evolution

According to the prevailing scientific perspective, humans have emerged through biological evolution, which is driven by self-serving enhancement of reproductive and associated material success. However, transcendent and psi experiences both have characteristics that seem inconsistent with the properties of biological evolution. The pursuit of transcendence in the form of monastery traditions inhibits reproductive success and has the specific goal of eliminating the motivations for material self-interest, success and status. These conditions are in direct opposition to the assumed driving forces of biological evolution and would not be expected to emerge from evolution. Similarly, the capricious, actively evasive nature of psi prevents its use for material self-interest and would not be expected to emerge from biological evolution.

The inconsistency with biological evolution may be evidence for a spiritual realm that is distinct from the material world of biological evolution. The only person I have known who appeared to have sustained, consistent psi ability viewed her psychic gifts entirely as God acting through her to help people on their spiritual paths (Kennedy, 2000). She did not believe that she directly controlled psi or that she should or could use psi for material self-interest. For those who believe in an active spiritual realm, contact with that realm is a paranormal process. From that perspective, paranormal phenomena and spirituality are inextricably interlinked.

Cautions

People appear to have strong motivations to believe in psi for self-serving reasons and this greatly complicates research. These motivations appear to cause many people to misinterpret normal experiences as paranormal. Broughton (1991, p. 10) noted that surveys typically find that over half of the population report having had a psi experience, but closer examination of the cases suggests that only about 10% to 15% of the population have had experiences that appear to be possible psi. This estimate is consistent with early surveys (Rhine, 1934/1973, p. 17) and with later studies (Haight, 1979; Schmiedler, 1964). Apparently, at least 70% to 80% of the people reporting psychic experiences are likely misinterpreting the experiences.

Understanding the motivations for incorrect beliefs about psi is important for parapsychology, and for psychology in general. Two of the more conspicuous motivations are discussed below.

Need for Efficacy

Baumeister (1991) described the need for efficacy, or to control the environment and to have an impact on the world. The drive to impress one's self on the world manifests in various forms, including creating technology, building construction projects, climbing or conquering mountains "because they are there," writing books, and creating various forms of entertainment. Conflicts with other people are another way of impressing themselves on the world. This includes various forms of competition in sports, business, and politics, as well as war, gangs, and sometimes crime. The development of computer viruses is some of the clearest evidence for this drive and demonstrates that this drive sometimes is stronger than ethical motivations. This drive tends to be stronger in males than in females.

Attempts to obtain instrumental control over psi for personal benefit is a basic premise of occultism, new age beliefs, experimental parapsychology, and commercial psychics and fortune tellers. These belief systems basically view psi as a magical power that can be controlled to fulfill a person's wants or to provide information about the future.

Belief in instrumental control of psi occurs in spite of the pervasive evidence that psi is capricious and defies reliable manifestations. Several authors have proposed that belief in psi is motivated by a need for an illusion of control of uncertain events (see Irwin, 1993; 2000).

Need for Superiority

Humans have an innate motivation to have self worth, which often manifests as a need to feel superior (Baumeister, 1991). Judging oneself as better off than others is a significant factor in human happiness, and comparing oneself to less fortunate persons is a standard technique for coping with unfortunate events (Baumeister,

1991; Myers, 1992). Membership in elite social groups also provides feelings of superiority. Human males in particular tend to have an innate drive to compete for power and status (Campbell, 2002; Geary, 1998). Of course, there is variability in these tendencies. Some men have this drive to a lesser degree and some women have it to a high degree. Men tend to overlay dominance and superiority on hierarchical systems. This is particularly conspicuous in military and corporate organizations, and government bureaucracies. The organizations are often in conflict or competition with other organizations and even the lower level members feel superior to those outside the organization.

Religion can provide a sense of self-worth and superiority, particularly for those who cannot achieve it in a more material form. For example, the religions of slaves have commonly included belief in meritorious rewards in an afterlife and punishment of oppressors (Baumeister, 1991). Members of fundamentalist religions believe they have a special relationship with God that makes them superior to others. Unfortunately, this sense of superiority has a long history of hostility and violence toward those who are viewed as being inferior and deserving of punishment (Baumeister, 1991). Fundamentalism places emphasis on religious authority and dominance rather than on internal transcendent experiences. Altemeyer (1996) argued that fundamentalism is a religious manifestation of the authoritarian personality.

More subjective forms of spirituality can also provide a means for establishing a hierarchy of superiority. Characteristics and criteria for determining who is more spiritually advanced are often proposed. These characteristics often reflect the temperaments and values associated with different personality types. The particular personality type of the person developing the criteria is set as the highest state. The claim to be among a small minority of highly evolved people and that everyone should strive to be like him or her is a common symptom of the drive to achieve a sense of superiority.

Psi experiences are sometimes presented as associated with an advanced state of consciousness or spiritual development (Grosso,

1992; Murphy, 1992; Ring, 1984; Thalbourne, in press). Traditional yoga writings similarly proposed that paranormal abilities are associated with developing spirituality (Prabhavananda and Isherwood, 1981).

Mystical or transcendent experiences are widely interpreted as evidence of high spirituality and are sought through practices such as meditation (Kornfield, 2000). As noted above, psi experiences are frequently reported as a form of mystical experience. The occurrence of these experiences is taken as a sign of spiritual superiority by some people (usually males). For example, Gopi Krishna (1974) claimed that his kundalini experiences (which resembled a mental health breakdown) made him a highly evolved "genius" and gave him psychic powers. However, that was a self-evaluation with no objective or tangible evidence to support his high opinion of himself.

It is now widely recognized that the occurrence of transcendent experiences does not necessarily indicate ethical behavior, compassion, wisdom, integration, or other characteristics normally associated with spirituality (Kornfield, 2000; Zweig, 2003). In fact, the sense of superiority from such experiences may promote self-serving abuse of power. The most conspicuous evidence for this point comes from the numerous cases of spiritual leaders who claim many transcendent experiences, but have a lavish lifestyle and use their position of authority for sexual activity with people they are supposedly spiritually guiding. This has happened much more widely than is generally acknowledged in both eastern and western spiritual organizations (Gonsiorek, 1995; Kornfield, 2000; Neimark, 1998; Roemischer, 2004; Zweig, 2003). Such behavior appears to have occurred in the majority of prominent yoga and meditation organizations in the U.S. The sexual exploitation has resulted in numerous lawsuits, but even when consensual, it still appears to be an abuse of authority and trust. In an important discussion of the realities of spiritual pursuits, Kornfield (2000) described the common error of mistaking charisma for wisdom.

In short, some people build superiority hierarchies in the material world and some build them in their minds. Unfortunately, psi and mystical experiences appear to sometimes be pursued or claimed in an effort to achieve a sense of superiority.

Personality and Skepticism:

The evidence that belief in psi is associated with certain personality types implies that skepticism may be associated with other personalities. Although there has been virtually no research focusing on the personalities of skeptics of paranormal phenomena, it is a safe bet that the Myers-Briggs STJ (sensing, thinking, judging) dispositions predominate. This is implied in the evidence that NF is associated with psi beliefs. Keirsey (1998) describes the SJ disposition as materialistic, distrusting of fantasy and abstract ideas, and tending to feel a duty to maintain traditional authority and to enforce rules of right and wrong. Skeptics tend to place great value on rational thinking and control (Kennedy, 2003a), which is consistent with the T disposition. Gow, *et al.* (2001) found that paranormal beliefs were negatively correlated with S and T personality factors, but not significantly with J.

People with an STJ disposition tend to rise to positions of leadership and authority (Keirsey, 1998; Kroeger, Thuesen and Rutledge, 2002). Kroeger, Thuesen, and Rutledge (2002) administered the Myers-Briggs personality test to over 20,000 people in all levels of a wide variety of corporate, government, and military organizations. Across these diverse organizations, they found that 60% of 2,245 people in top executive positions had STJ personalities. On the other hand, only about 1% were the opposite personality types (NFP), which are more prone to interest in mystical and psychic experiences.

This personality bias in the upper echelons of power and status may be a major factor in the institutional skepticism and resistance to psi. For example, the strong skepticism of high status scientists has been documented (McClenon, 1982). Fudjack and Dinkelaker (1994) question whether the masculine "extraverted / rational - empirical/pragmatic/materialist" bias that predominates in western culture is healthy for organizations or for society. Research with twins indicates that these personality dispositions have significant genetic components (Bouchard and Hur, 1998; Tellegen, *et al.*, 1988).

Skepticism may also be related to the need for superiority. The hostility of extreme skeptics toward those who believe in paranormal phenomena appears to be a manifestation of the drive for dominance and superiority, and has noteworthy similarities with religious fundamentalism (Kennedy, 2003a).

Conclusions

The human needs for superiority and efficacy appear to contaminate both science and spirituality. These motivations can prevent proponents of science from being objective and rational, and prevent proponents of spirituality from being compassionate and ethical.

Experimental parapsychology is largely driven by a motivation and implicit bias for efficacy and control. This bias has not produced significant scientific progress. When the phenomena are examined without this bias, the relationship with transcendence emerges as the central organizing factor. The primary function of psi appears to be spiritual transformation or growth. Reliable use of psi for material self-interest has not occurred and, at this point, does not seem feasible.

The evidence that most cases interpreted as psi are not actually psi, combined with the motivations to believe in psi to achieve feelings of efficacy and superiority make it difficult to identify actual instances of psi. The slowness in acknowledging the capricious, evasive property of psi even though that has been the dominant characteristic of psychical research for over a century typifies the challenges.

It is not surprising that those who are by disposition materialistic, pragmatic, rational, and wanting closure find the evidence for psi to be not remotely convincing. At this point, they consider psi research to be a well established waste of time and effort.

At the same time, people with dispositions more inwardly focused continue to have experiences that they describe as providing absolutely certain knowledge that there is a spiritual realm (James, 1902/1982; Miller and C'de Baca, 2001; Ring, 1984). These people find substantial commonalities among their experiences and the after-effects. The fact that others with more externally focused, materialistic dispositions do not have such experiences and are skeptical is irrelevant to the interpretation of their experiences. They feel that they are dealing with direct experience and knowledge, not philosophical theories, academic rationalizations, or speculations.

For many people the motivation for spiritual beliefs and experiences appears to be much stronger and more focused than would be expected from misplaced motivations for efficacy and superiority. Setting aside scientific parsimony, the most straightforward explanation may be a deep recognition that there is a spiritual realm that is the ultimate goal of life and that may supersede the drives for reproductive and material success.

I believe that science can do much to sort out the various motivations and to create better understanding among people with different dispositions. There seems to be a natural tendency for people to assume that everyone has or should have the same basic motivations and values as they have. This assumption is a major source of conflicts. Research on personality and individual differences clearly shows that this assumption is not correct.

A good starting point would be to identify and measure the personality factors associated with (a) experiences that could be actual psi, (b) experiences that appear to be misinterpreted as psi, and (c) skepticism about psi. Personality models and measures that deal with all relevant factors need to be developed, including motivations for transcendence as well as efficacy and superiority. The need for superiority, in particular, has been under appreciated in research – perhaps because many scientists prefer to overlook that aspect of their own personality.

Cross-cultural comparisons may be particularly valuable for identifying the limitations resulting from the masculine extraverted/

rational-empirical/pragmatic/materialist bias that predominates in western culture. Understanding the diversity of personalities and motivations is a prerequisite for addressing questions about when and if psi actually occurs.

Psi appears to be intrinsically and virtually exclusively spiritual. The tangible lesson from the capricious, evasive nature of psi is that the human motivations for self-serving efficacy and superiority are not applicable in this domain. One of the best strategies for research may be to investigate the relationship between psi and spirituality-related factors such as humility and gratitude. In addition, further exploration of the relationship between spirituality and psi may find that the most appropriate model is to view the source of psi as largely external to living persons.

Appendix

Overview of the Myers-Briggs Personality Model. The Myers-Briggs personality model (Myers and Myers, 1995) was developed for practical use in occupational settings and interpersonal relationships, and has been widely used in those contexts for several decades. It is based on the writings of Carl Jung. The model utilizes 16 personality categories based on the combinations of four factors. The summary below was taken from Keirsey (1998), whose concepts are largely the same as the original Myers-Briggs model, but more clearly separate the E/I and S/N factors that conceptually overlap in the original Myers-Briggs model.

Extroverted/introverted (E/I) indicates whether a person feels energized (E) or drained (I) from being with a group of people;

Sensing/intuitive (S/N) indicates whether a person focuses their awareness and attention more on the external, material world and prefers concrete, observable facts (S) or focuses internally on the self and imagination, and prefers abstract ideas (N);

Thinking/feeling (T/F) indicates whether a person tends to value rational thinking and self-control (T) or emotional expression (F);

Judging/perceiving (J/P) indicates whether a person prefers setting and achieving goals and having a sense of closure (J) or spontaneously exploring open-ended possibilities and keeping options open (P). For example, ESTJ is one personality type and INFP is the most different personality type. The primary sex difference in personality types is for the T/F factor. About two-thirds of males are T (thinking) and about two-thirds of females are F (feeling) for U.S. data (Macdaid, McCaulley and Kainz, 1986).

The Myers-Briggs model describes all personality types as being valuable in some circumstances. Presumably, the different personality types have been maintained throughout evolution because they had adaptive value, or at least did not inhibit reproductive success.

REFERENCES

Altemeyer, B. (1996). *The Authoritarian Spector*. Cambridge, MA: Harvard University Press.

Archangel, D. (1997). Investigating the relationship between Myers-Briggs Type Indicator and facilitated reunion experiences. *Journal of the American Society for Psychical Research*, 91, 82-95.

Batcheldor, K.J. (1994). Notes on the elusiveness problem in relation to a radical view of paranormality. *Journal of the American Society for Psychical Research*, 88, 90-115.

Baumeister, R.F. (1991). *Meanings of Life*. New York: Guilford.

Beloff, J. (1994). Lessons of history. *Journal of the American Society for Psychical Research*, 88, 7-22.

Benson, H., Dusk, J.A., Sherwood, J.B., Lam, P., Bethe, C.F., Carpenter, W., Levisky, S., Hill, P.C., Clem, D.W., Jain, M.K., Drumel, D., Kopecky, S.L., Mueller, P.S., Marek, D., Rollins, S. & Hibberd, P.L. (2006). Study of the Therapeutic Effects of Intercessory Prayer (STEP) in cardiac bypass patients: A multicenter randomized trial of uncertainty and certainty of receiving intercessory prayer. *American Heart Journal,* 151, 934-942.

Bierman, D.J. (1980). Negative Reliability: The ignored Rule. In W.G. Roll & J. Beloff (Eds.), *Research in Parapsychology* (pp. 14-15). Metuchen, NJ: Scarecrow Press. (Longer summary available at: http://rea3140.fmg.uva.nl/PUBS/1981/).

— (2001). On the nature of anomalous phenomena: Another reality between the world of subjective consciousness and the objective work of physics? In P. van Locke (Ed.) *The Physical Nature of Consciousness* (pp. 269-292). New York: Benjamins. (Also available at: http://rea3140.fmg.uva.nl/PUBS/2001/).

Bouchard, T.J. & Hur, Y.M. (1998). Genetic and environmental influences on the continuous scales of the Myers-Briggs Type Indicator: An analysis based on twins reared apart. *Journal of Personality*, 66, 135-149.

Braud, W.G. (1985). The two faces of psi: Psi revealed and psi obscured. In B. Shapin & L. Coly (Eds.), *The Repeatability Problem in Parapsychology* (pp.150-175). New York: Parapsychology Foundation.

Brier, R.M. & Tyminski, W.V. (1970a). Psi application: Part I. A preliminary attempt. *Journal of Parapsychology,* 34, 1-25.

— (1970b). Psi application: Part II. The majority-vote technique-analysis and observations. *Journal of Parapsychology,* 34, 26-36.

Broughton, R.S. (1991). *Parapsychology: The Controversial Science*. New York: Ballantine Books.

Campbell, A. (2002). *A Mind of Her Own: The Evolutionary Psychology of Women*. Oxford, Oxford University Press.

Dean, D. & Taetzsch, R. (1970). Psi in the casino: Taetzsch Method. In W.G. Roll, R.L. Morris & J.D. Morris (Eds.), *Proceedings of the Parapsychological Association,* 7:14-15. Durham, NC: Parapsychological Association.

Eisenbud, J. (1992). *Parapsychology and the Unconscious.* Berkeley, CA: North Atlantic Books.

Fudjack, J. & Dinkelaker, P. (1994). Toward a diversity of psychological type in organization: Part three. Paper presented at the First Annual Antioch University Management Faculty Conference, October, (Retrieved January 3, 2005, from http://tap3x.net/ENSEMBLE/mpage1c.html).

Geary, D.C. (1998). *Male, Female: The Evolution of Human Sex Differences*. Washington, DC: American Psychological Association.

Gonsiorek, J.C. (1995). (Ed.) *Breach of Trust: Sexual Exploitation by Health Care Professionals and Clergy*. Thousand Oaks, CA: Sage Publications.

Gow, K., Lurie, J., Coppin, S. Popper, A., Powell, A. & Basterfield, K. (2001). Fantasy proneness and other psychological correlates of UFO experiences. Queensland University of Technology, Brisbane, Queensland, Australia. (Retrieved October 5, 2005, from http://www.anomalistik.de/gow.pdf).

Grosso, M. (1992). *Frontiers of the Soul: Exploring Psychic Evolution*. Wheaton, IL: Quest Books.

Haight, J. (1979). Spontaneous psi cases: A survey and preliminary study of ESP, attitude, and personality relationship. *Journal of Parapsychology*, 43, 179-203.

Hansen, G.P. (2001). *The Trickster and the Paranormal*. Philadelphia: Xlibris Corporation.

Haraldsson, E. & Houtkooper, J.M. (1995). Meta-analyses of 10 experiments on perceptual defensiveness and ESP: ESP scoring patterns and experimenter and decline effects. *Journal of Parapsychology*, 59, 251-271.

Hayden, B. (2003). *A Prehistory of Religion: Shamans, Sorcerers, and Saints*. Washington, D.C.: Smithsonian Books.

Hood, R.W., Spilka, B., Hunsberger, B. & Gorsuch, R. (1996). *The Psychology of Religion: An Empirical Approach* (2nd edn.). New York: Guilford Press.

Houtkooper, J.M. (1994). Does a meta-analysis demolition effect exist? *Abstracts of the 18th International Conference of the Society for Psychical Research* (Bournemouth, England, September 2-4, 14-15.

— (2002). Letter to the editor. *Journal of Parapsychology,* 66, 329-333.

Inglis, B. (1992). *Natural and Supernatural: A History of the Paranormal from Earliest Times to 1914* (rev. edn.). Garden City Park, NY: Avery Publishing Group.

Irwin, H.J. (1993). Belief in the paranormal: A review of the empirical literature. *Journal of the American Society for Psychical Research,* 87, 1-39

— (2000). Belief in the paranormal and a sense of control over life. *European Journal of Parapsychology,* 15, 68-78.

Jahn, R. & Dunne, B. (2001). A modular model of mind/matter manifestations (M5). *Journal of Scientific Exploration,* 15, 299-329.

—, Bradish, G., Dobyns, Y., Lettieri, A., Nelson, R., Mischo, J., Boller, E., Bosch, H., Vaitl, D., Houtkooper, J. & Walter, B. (2000). Mind/machine interaction consortium: PortREG replication experiments. *Journal of Scientific Exploration,* 14, 499-555.

James, W. (1960). The final impressions of a psychical researcher. In G. Murphy & R.D. Ballou (Eds.), *William James on Psychical Research* (pp. 309-325). New York: Viking. (Original work published in 1909)

— (1982). *The Varieties of Religious Experience.* New York: Penguin. (Original work published in 1902)

Keirsey, D. (1998). *Please Understand Me II.* Del Mar, CA: Prometheus Nemesis Book Company.

Kennedy, J.E. (2000). Do people guide psi or does psi guide people? Evidence and implications from life and lab. *Journal of the American Society for Psychical Research,* 94, 130-150.

— (2002). Commentary on "Experiments on distant intercessory prayer" in Archives of Internal Medicine. *Journal of Parapsychology,* 66, 177-182.

—- (2003a). The polarization of psi beliefs: Rational controlling masculine skepticism versus interconnected, spiritual, feminine belief. *Journal of the American Society for Psychical Research.* 97, Pages 27-42.

— (2003b). Letter to the editor. *Journal of Parapsychology,* 67, 406-408.

— (2004). A proposal and challenge for proponents and skeptics of psi. *Journal of Parapsychology,* 68, 57-67.

— (2005) Personality and motivations to believe, misbelieve, and disbelieve in psi. *Journal of Parapsychology*, 69, 263-292.

— & Kanthamani, H. (1995). An exploratory study of the effects of paranormal and spiritual experiences on peoples' lives and well-being. *Journal of the American Society for Psychical Research,* 89, 249-264.

—, Kanthamani, H. & Palmer, J. (1994). Psychic and spiritual experiences, health, well-being, and meaning in life. *Journal of Parapsychology,* 58, 353-383.

— & Taddonio, J.L. (1976). Experimenter effects in parapsychological Research. *Journal of Parapsychology,* 40, 1-33.

Kornfield, J. (2000). *After the Ecstasy, the Laundry.* New York: Bantam Books.

Krishna, G. (1974). *Higher Consciousness and Kundalini.* Norton Heights, CT: The Kundalini Research Foundation.

Kroeger, O., Thuesen, J.M., & Rutledge, H. (2002). *Type Talk at Work: How the 16 Personality Types Determine Your Success on the Job* (rev. edn.). New York: Random House.

Krucoff, M.W.,Crater, S.W., Gallup, D., Blankenship, J.C., Cuffe, M., Guarneri, M.Krieger, R.A., Kshettry, V.R., Morris, K., Oz, M.,

Pichard, A., Sketch, M.H., Koenig, H.G., Mark, D. & Lee, K.L. (2005). Music, imagery, touch, and prayer as adjuncts to interventional cardiac care: The monitoring and actualization of noetic trainings (MANTRA) II randomized study. *Lancet*, 366(9481), 211-217.

Lange, R., Thalbourne, M.A., Houran, J. & Storm, L. (2000). The Revised Transliminality Scale: Reliability and validity data from a Rasch top-down purification procedure. *Consciousness and Cognition*, 9, 591-617.

Lester, D., Thinschmidt, J. & Trautman, L. (1987). Paranormal belief and Jungian dimensions of personality. *Psychological Reports*, 61, 182.

Lucadou, W. v. (2001). Hans in luck: The currency of evidence in parapsychology. *Journal of Parapsychology*, 65, 3-16.

(2002). Theoretical contributions to psi: Does parapsychology go mainstream? In V. G. Rammohan (Ed.) *New Frontiers of Human Science* (pp. 79-94). Jefferson, NC: McFarland.

Lyons, A. & Truzzi, M. (1991). *The Blue Sense: Psychic Detectives and Crime*. New York: Mysterious Press.

Macdaid, G.P., McCaulley, M.H. & Kainz, R.I. (1986). *Myers-Briggs Type Indicator Atlas of Type Tables*. Gainesville, FL: Center for Applications of Psychological Types.

Maeterlinck, M. (1914). *The Unknown Guest*. London: Methuen and Co.

Markwick, B. (1978). The Soal-Goldney experiments with Basil Shackleton: New evidence of data manipulation. *Proceedings of the Society for Psychical Research*, 56, 250-277.

McClenon, J. (1982). A survey of elite scientists: Their attitudes toward ESP and parapsychology. *Journal of Parapsychology*, 46, 127-152.

— (1994). *Wondrous Events: Foundations of Religious beliefs*. Philadelphia: University of Pennsylvania Press.

— (2002a). Content analysis of an anomalous experience collection: Evaluating evolutionary perspectives. *Journal of Parapsychology*, 66, 291-316.

— (2002b). *Wondrous Healing: Shamanism, Human Evolution, and the Origin of Religion*. DeKalb, IL: Northern Illinois University Press.

Miller, W.R. & C'de Baca, J. (2001). *Quantum Changes: When Epiphanies and Sudden Insights Transform Ordinary Lives*. New York: Guilford.

Murphy, M. (1992). *The Future of the Body: Explorations into the Future Evolution of Human Nature*. Los Angeles, CA: Jeremy P. Tarcher.

Murphy, K. & Lester, D. (1976). A search for correlates of belief in psi. *Psychological Reports*, 38, 82.

Myers, D.G. (1992). *The Pursuit of Happiness*. New York: William Morrow.

Neimark, J. (1998). Crimes of the soul. *Psychology Today*. (Retrieved November 2, 2005, from http://cms.psychologytoday.com/articles/index.php?term=pto-19980301-000043.xml 19980301-000043.xml).

Palmer, J. (1979). A community mail survey of psychic experiences. *Journal of the American Society for Psychical Research*, 73, 221-251.

— (1981). Review of J.B. Rhine's research findings: I. Extrasensory perception. *Journal of Parapsychology*, 45, 25-39.

Palmer, G. & Braud, W. (2002). Exceptional human experiences, disclosure, and a more inclusive view of physical, psychological, and spiritual well-being. *Journal of Transpersonal Psychology*, 34, 29-61.

Pratt, J.G. (1975). Outstanding subjects in ESP. *Journal of the American Society for Psychical Research*, 69, 151-160.

Prabhavananda & Isherwood, J. (1981). *How to Know God: The Yoga Aphorisms of Patanjali.* Hollywood, CA: The Vedanta Society of Southern California.

Puthoff, H.E., May, E.C. & Thompson, M.J. (1986). Calculator-assisted psi amplification II: Use of the sequential-sampling technique as a variable-length majority-vote procedure. In D.H. Weiner & D.I. Radin (Eds.) *Research In Parapsychology,* (pp.73-77). Metuchen, NJ: Scarecrow Press.

Rama, S. (1978). *Living with the Himalayan Masters.* Honesdale, PA: Himalayan International Institute.

Rao, K.R. (1965). The bidirectionality of psi. *Journal of Parapsychology*, 29, 230-250.

Rhine, J.B. (1971). Location of hidden objects by a man-dog team. *Journal of Parapsychology*, 35, 18-33.

— (1973). *Extra-sensory Perception*. Boston: Branden Press. (Original work published 1934)

— (1974). Security versus deception in parapsychology. *Journal of Parapsychology*, 38, 99-121.

— (1975). Comments: "Second report on a case of experimenter fraud." *Journal of Parapsychology*, 39, 306-325.

Ring, K. (1984). *Heading toward Omega: In Search of the Meaning of Near-death Experiences.* New York: William Morrow.

Roemischer, J. (2004). Women who sleep with their gurus – and why they love it. *What is Enlightenment*, Issue 26. (Retrieved October 20, 2005, from http://www.wie.org/i26/women-who-sleep.asp).

Russell, W. & Rhine, J.B. (1942). A single subject in a variety of ESP test conditions. *Journal of Parapsychology*, 6, 284-311.

Schmiedler, G.R. (1964). An experiment of precognitive clairvoyance: Part V. Precognition scores related to feelings of success. *Journal of Parapsychology,* 28, 109-125.

Tallis, F. (2002). *Hidden minds: A History of the Unconscious.* New York: Arcade Publishing.

Targ, R., Braud, W.G., Stanford, R.G., Schlitz, M.J. & Honorton, C. (1991). Increasing psychic reliability. *Journal of Parapsychology,* 55, 59-83.

Taves, E., & Dale, L.A. (1943). The Midas touch in psychical research. *Journal of the American Society for Psychical Research,* 37, 57-83.

Tellegen, A., Lykken, D.T., Bouchard, T.J., Wilcox, K.J., Segal, N.L. & Rich, S. (1988). Personality similarity of twins reared apart and together. *Journal of Personality and Social Psychology,* 54, 1031-1039.

Thalbourne, M.A. (1998). Transliminality: Further correlates and a short measure. *Journal of the American Society for Psychical Research,* 92, 402-419.

— (in press). The transhumanation hypothesis. *Journal of the American Society for Psychical Research.*

— & Delin, P.S. (1994). A common thread underlying belief in the paranormal, creative personality, mystical experience and psychopathology. *Journal of Parapsychology,* 58, 3-38.

Truzzi, M. (1995). Reflections on *The Blue Sense* and its critics. *Journal of Parapsychology,* 59, 99-128.

White, R.A. (1994). Seek ye first the kingdom of heaven: What are EHEs and what can we do about them. In R.A. White (Ed.), *Exceptional Human Experience: Background Papers: I,* (pp. 34-46). Dix Hills, NY: Exceptional Human Experience Network.

— (Ed.) (1997a) Background Papers II. The EHE Network, 1995-1998: Progress and Possibilities. *Exceptional Human Experience: Special Issue,* 15.

— (1997b). Exceptional human experiences and the experiential paradigm. In C.T. Tart (Ed.), *Body, Mind, Spirit: Exploring the Parapsychology of Spirituality* (pp. 83-100). Charlottesville, VA.: Hampton Roads.

Woodward, K.L. (2000). *The Book of Miracles: The Meaning of the Miracle Stories in Christianity, Judaism, Buddhism, Hinduism, Islam*. New York: Simon and Schuster.

Yogananda, P. (1946). *Autobiography of a Yogi.* Los Angeles, CA: Self-Realization Fellowship.

Zweig, C. (2003). *The Holy Longing: The Hidden Power of Spiritual Yearning*. New York: Tarcher/Putnam.

First Sight: Elaborations and Implications of a Model of Psi and the Mind

JAMES C. CARPENTER

A Model of Psi and the Mind

The model holds that psi processes are an ordinary and continuous part of the psychological functioning of all organisms. In fact, they are the leading edge of the formation of all experience and all volition. Preconscious psychological processes that are intrinsically unconscious precede and condition the development of all experience. Cognitive psychologists speak of these as providing the *context* of consciousness (Baars, 1997, pp. 115-129).These processes typically function very rapidly and transiently. Studies of perception without awareness demonstrate that unattended stimuli serve to arouse nexi of meaning and feeling that serve to channel the development of perceptual experience. The model assumes that the development of all other forms of experience in addition to perceptual, as well as all volitional action, are similarly preceded by preconscious orienting processes. Psi processes initiate these series of activity. Prior to the action of a subliminal stimulus, an extrasensory apprehension of its general nature and significance serves to orient the mind toward the development of the meaning to come. Prior to the commencement of any deliberate action, psychokinetic influence acts to begin the physical processes in the body that will enact the decision, and may begin to exert some influence on the object of intention beyond the body as well.

For this conception to be sensible, we will need to assume that each organism exists, by its nature, beyond its own physical boundaries, in some sort of commerce with the larger surround of space and time. A phenomenological/existential model of the nature of conscious being is employed. One implication of this is that the problem of the connection between body and mind is not solved, rather the split between them is not assumed to begin with. Another implication is that it is assumed that even preconscious processes are best understood in terms of personal meaning and choice rather than impersonal biological mechanism.

Psi information is not kept from awareness by some sort of screen, and is not rendered into analogical form by any secondary, disguising process. Its intrinsic ambiguity is a function of the fact that with it alone there is no sensory information available, and sensory information is required to clarify the impression into a perception that can be construed. Anything which comes to consciousness must go through four steps: 1) an unconscious surround, 2) an impression, 3) conscious material, and 4) construal or understanding. This is true whether the experience is a matter of memory, immediate sensory experience, feeling, or cognition. First there is an unconscious, orienting surround, then a vague semi-conscious impression, then conscious material upon which one can focus (stimulus, memory, feeling or idea), then an interpretation or construal of that material. At the point of construal we have some idea of what it is that we are seeing, hearing, remembering, thinking, feeling, or beginning to do. Without the conscious material to construe, no conscious experience can be grasped.

The initial psi stage of the process involves an access to potential knowledge that is indefinite in extent. We cannot know its boundaries, or anything else about it directly, since it is thoroughly unconscious.

Psi in its normal, everyday functioning is presumed to be continuous, extremely efficient and invisible to conscious awareness. Like the effects of subliminal stimulations, extrasensory apprehensions can be inferred by examining non-deliberate expressions of the orienting nexi of meaning and feeling which they arouse. Both subliminal and extrasensory apprehensions can be seen most clearly in such inadvertent behaviours as dreams, slips of the tongue and other errors, associational processes, expressions of feeling and meaning in projective tests, the flow of spontaneous social behaviour, shifts in mood, and the development of spontaneous imagery. The actual psi processes themselves are intrinsically unconscious. They are neither knowing nor acting, as we ordinarily use the terms, since these phenomena belong to the province of consciousness. Rather they serve as bridges toward the efficient development of these phenomena. Of course, if the development of a conscious experience is impeded by the removal of the thing from the sensory field before it can be consciously known, then only the inadvertent expressions of the anticipatory arousal can be seen.

Psi functioning is presumed to be bi-modal. In terms of extrasensory perception, the mind either elects to orient toward the object of potential awareness or away from it. This capacity of the mind to pre-consciously orient toward or away-from as befits the needs of the organism, is called *the Hypothesis of Directional Intention*, as it is proposed that the primary determinant of the direction of orientation is conscious and unconscious intention. These bimodal tendencies may be relatively stable in regard to some meaning, or may be relatively unstable, switching rapidly. In an ESP test, a stable orientation toward the potential meaning is expressed as psi-hitting, and a stable orientation away from it is expressed as psi-missing. A relatively stable tendency is shown by a large deviation from chance expectation, while a rapid switching of tendencies produces small deviations from chance expectation. Switching directional tendencies is presumed to be a function of mixed or shifting intentions in regard to the potential meaning. This is what is meant by *the Hypothesis of Intentional Stability.* In ordinary experience beyond the laboratory, a stable tendency toward knowing the potential meaning facilitates our rapid and accurate experience of it. On the other hand, a stable orientation away from the meaning will facilitate the development of some alternative experience and behaviour instead. Since (as we assume) the mind always strives to experience the one most useful thing at any given moment in terms of a shifting fabric of needs and intentions, the movement away from many potential experiences is very functional. A stable orientation away-from some meaning also may serve to avoid pre-consciously apprehended danger in an efficient manner. In general, a stable orientation serves to assure that the behaviour of the organism will reflect some response to the potential meaning, while rapidly shifting orientations will act to assure that no apparent response at all will be reflected in behaviour.

When anticipational networks have been aroused by some extrasensory or suboptimal-sensory information, and validating sensory experience is *not forthcoming*, then the mind ordinarily adjusts to this situation by turning away from the original concern in favour of something else which may be more importantly incipient to an experience-to-come. The turning-away is effected by movement to a rapidly-shifting pattern of intention, which acts to "bind" the concern safely out of awareness. If ESP testing is kept up in relation to such a "bound" concern, consistent chance-level performance will result. In the preconscious part of our mind we wish to form and understand meaningful experience, and will ordinarily move on to where it is actually developing. ESP testing sustained past this point may be in accord with conscious intention, but will probably run counter to the unconscious intention of moving on efficiently to actual experience.

Cognitive closure, or a situation in which one is committed to some construction of experience, is presumed to trigger unconscious tendential switching in regard to alternative meanings or potential experiences. At such a moment, I know what I am concerned with experiencing, and I am engaged with understanding it or working with it. In favour of this concern, other potential issues are held in abeyance.

On the other hand, brief or prolonged states in which closure is delayed, and uncertainty is sustained, are presumed to facilitate the consulting of inadvertency, a sustained concern with the unknown meaning, and a relatively stable psi-hitting or psi-missing orientation. States of sustained uncertainty and absence of clear cognitive work have been found to be psi-conducive as well as conducive to the expression of subliminal stimulation. Persons who are more prone than most to psi-expressive behaviour, are likely to be able to sustain cognitive uncertainty, or for some reason to be relatively unable to achieve clear closure (as in the case of persons with certain brain or nervous system injuries). Relatively more "psychic" persons are also expected to be generally positively oriented to express such extrasensory meanings, to be relatively free of anxiety and self-defeating tendencies, and to be relatively skilled in the interpretation of their own inadvertent psychological expressions, as in understanding their dream life, or personal imagery.

In terms of observed performance on an ESP task, this model offers these interpretations for different possible findings:

- When significant hitting is observed in a subject's performance, it indicates the action of a consistent unconscious intention to approach the potential experience and possibly to come to be aware of it.

- When significant missing is observed in a subject's performance, it indicates the action of a consistent unconscious intention to avoid the potential experience and knowledge of it.

- When no overall directional trend is present in a subject's performance, but the scores show an extra-chance extremity of scoring (large variance), this expresses the action of an unconscious sense that the potential experience is salient, but that the intention to approach or avoid it is switching across runs of guessing effort.

- When significantly consistent chance-level performance is observed in a subject's performance (small variance), it expresses the intention to not be distracted by the potential experience by moving either toward or away from it.

- While this very brief summary should be of some usefulness in grounding the discussion to follow, the interested reader may wish to refer to the prior paper (Carpenter, 2005b) where these and related points are spelled out in more detail.

Since psi, in its normal, unconscious functioning is presumed to work alongside other preconscious psychological processes, the next issue to be considered is how they might be expected to interact, and to examine pertinent evidence about this that has been reported.

The Co-Mingling of Psi and Other Preconscious Processes

This model implies that in its preconscious functioning the mind democratically draws from all its potential sources to solve its problems of finding the most adaptive response to a situation or bringing the most important issue to the stage of consciousness. In the previous paper this was referred to as *the Hypothesis of Functional Equivalence.* Psi apprehensions are expected to be used along with all other material available, such as that from ongoing sensations, or from memory, or from the imaginative resources of the creative process. However, it is only when uncertainty is sustained for a time, and the solution is not readily at hand, that we would expect to see the traces of the psi process. If something is clearly seen, or readily remembered, or some problem easily solved, the issue will be quickly closed, and we will see only the clear working of consciousness. Therefore, it is when something is uncertainly remembered, or unclearly perceived, or when some creative production is not quite within reach, that preconscious processes, including psi, may be visible.[1] In such cases, this model predicts that extrasensory information will be combined with

[1] In the context of normal, sensory psychology, this is congruent with the Zeigarnik (1927, 1967) effect, in which it was shown that the failure to cognitively complete a task led to prolonged motivation that in turn led to an enhancement of memory of the uncompleted problem. (Lewin, 1935; Martin, Tesser, and McIntosh, 1993)

information from other sources, frequently additively but sometimes subtractively.

In general terms, I propose that the extrasensory information combines additively with sensory information when it is preconsciously understood to be contextually useful in the interpretation of the sensory information. When it is preconsciously judged to be irrelevant to the sensory material, or otherwise contrary to the task of most fruitfully understanding it, the effect of the extrasensory material will initially be subtractive (i.e., it will tend to be expressed by some sort of behavioural reference less often than chance would expect), and subsequently, through the mechanism of rapid directional switching, it will come to have no apparent behavioural reference at all. What is judged to be useful may be a matter of categorical relevancy, or bear on other matters of intentions and goals. In this context, it is helpful to refer to the social psychological literature on the formation of judgments of other persons. Sometimes subliminal primes have been found to have the effect of biasing responses in the direction of their content (called *assimilation*), but sometimes they show the opposite biasing effect (called *contrast*). Schwartz and Bless (1992) proposed an *inclusion-exclusion* model, proposing that the influence of a prime depends on the ease with which it can be incorporated in a target impression. A prime that can be easily included with the target becomes assimilated, biasing the impression toward its suggestion. A prime that cannot be included may be expected to have the opposite effect, causing contrast and biasing the result away from the prime. This principle may be a very general one, effecting psi-hitting and psi-missing as well as subliminal and unattended sensory material. This contrast effect and psi-missing appear to be very similar processes. This is discussed further below under the topic of the sheep-goat effect.

Three major areas of experience that involve a sustained lack of cognitive closure are the interpretation of subliminal or unattended sensory information, the retrieval of memory, and the achievement of some creative production. All of them would seem to be fruitful areas in which to study the confluence of psi information with other preconscious information. The following are findings that already bear upon this question.

Psi and Ambiguous Sensory Information

When sensory information is clear and unambiguous, conscious perceptions spring quickly to mind, and the influence of psi processes are not expected to be visible. However, when sensory information is so attenuated that it is difficult to perceive, one must struggle some to understand it, "guessing around" the cues until a perception is formed. If the stimulation is so attenuated or unnoticed that it is subliminal and in no way conscious, then even the effort to construe ambiguous cues does not obtain, and any effects of the stimulation may be experienced only as inadvertency, or misattributed to something else. It is in this situation of subliminal, or "suboptimal priming", (Murphy and Zajonc, 1993) that an interaction between suboptimal-sensory and extrasensory processes may be sought and seen. The expectation that effects frequently will be additive when they are acting together is supported by the fact that subliminal stimuli themselves often have been found to show additive effects (Bargh and Tota, 1988; Fulcher and Hammeri, 2002; Jaskowski and Skalska, 2003; Murphy, Monahan and Zajonc, 1995).

Extrasensory Perception and Subliminal Perception as Correlated Capacities

A number of studies have been done in which scores have been obtained from both extrasensory and subliminal-sensory paradigms on the same participants. Schmeidler (1986, 1988) has carried out an analysis of 24 reported experimental series of this type, dividing them into two groups: weak subliminal or suboptimal stimulation (well below the conscious threshold), and strong stimulation (near the threshold). She expected, and found, that of the 22 series with weak stimulation, 17 showed a positive relation between subliminal and ESP scores. Nine of those were statistically significant. There were no significant relationships in the opposite direction. The 2 series with stronger subliminal stimulation produced significant negative relationships. Schmeidler concluded from this that truly subliminal stimulation functions in a way very similar to ESP, but that stronger stimuli are processed differently. In another series of studies, a high-scoring special subject was found to process information similarly in subliminal and extrasensory responding, relying on cues of visual similarity in both cases (Kelly, Kanthamani, Child, and Young, Kanthamani and Kelly, 1974). These findings support the idea that when persons are producing responses based upon preconscious apprehensions, extrasensory and subliminal-sensory information is accessed (or not) in generally similar ways. Persons who are relatively prone to successfully consult pure inadvertency when uncertain, may demonstrate this tendency whether the inadvertencies imply extrasensory or subliminal material, while persons who are prone to focus more exclusively on more tangible sources of information may be more successful when such information is at hand, like the subjects in Schmeidler's review who were better at interpreting marginally subliminal stimulations. In terms of the *First Sight* model, one would say that a person's tendency to make positive use of preconscious information for whatever reason will be expressed with extrasensory and subliminal-sensory information alike; whereas a tendency to avoid such material, and express it subtractively, will tend to be shown with both as well.

Subliminal Effects on a Psi Task

When extrasensory and subliminal-sensory information are both controlled in an experiment, the *First Sight* model predicts that they should interact meaningfully with one another in influencing behaviour. Palmer and his colleagues have carried out a relevant series of studies in which they attempted to effect the mood of the percipient with a subliminal stimulus and thereby influence the effort at guessing an extrasensory target (the correct element among several in a visual field). The studies were exploratory and the results sometimes surprised them. An attempt to control high and low scoring by accompanying targets with subliminal primes intended to be either reassuring or threatening resulted instead in overall tight variance of scores (Palmer and Johnson, 1991) a finding which was successfully replicated (Palmer, 1992). A subsequent attempt to heighten the reassurance effect with a combination of incidental and subliminal cues resulted in overall psi-missing (Palmer, 1998).

The next study (Palmer, 1994) examined the effect of a reassuring prime (a suggestion of merger) which was sometimes presented immediately before another subliminal prime involving a threatening face. The condition considered most propitious for psi-hitting (subliminal merger/no threat) did yield psi hitting in the first series in the subjects were tested, but not the second. None of these studies employed manipulation checks for mood, so one cannot say whether or not the subliminal primes had the desired effects upon the subjects' state.

All of these findings suggest that the effects of affectively charged subliminal stimuli do enter into the preconscious processing that leads to the ESP response, but that more precise conceptualization is needed to anticipate the nature of the effects. The repetitive presentation of subliminal faces may evoke a vigilant state in which the ESP test feels irrelevant or distracting, resulting in tendential switching and small variance. It may also be that primes intended to evoke a mood of safety had the opposite effect in some cases, resulting in psi missing. This possibility is suggested by the finding of Sohlberg and her colleagues (Sohlberg, Billinghurst and Nylen, 1998; Sohlberg, Samuelberg, Siden and Thorn, 1998) in which they report a tendency of subjects to experience a change in mood in a negative direction when a stimulus ordinarily found to elicit positive mood was shown too many times. This sort of negative "over-dosage" might have been present in Palmer's studies, in which the stimulus intended to be reassuring was presented over and over. This negative effect may have been less marked in the first series of the study in which psi hitting was observed, as in that condition fewer exposures had accumulated.

Psi Effects on a Subliminal Task

Another approach to studying the patterns of interaction of subliminal and extrasensory information was taken by Kreitler and Kreitler (1972), who exposed their subjects to letters projected on a screen at an intensity and duration that had been found in pre-testing to permit correct identification 40% of the time. They were told that the letter identification was the sole task, and no extrasensory element was mentioned. In half the cases, however, an agent added an "extrasensory stimulus" to the situation by telepathically trying to transmit the correct letter to the subject as they were viewing the exposure, while in the other half looking at an irrelevant picture. The extrasensory "transmission" was effective in boosting the rate of identification, as shown by a significant difference between the conditions. Another series involved an examination of the influence of both subliminal and extrasensory material upon the perception of ambiguous optical illusions. There was no overall evidence of an extrasensory influence, however an interaction was observed in this study, in that when the ESP "prime" was contrary to that of the subliminal exposure surrounding the supraliminal figure presented to the subject (the optical illusion), the subjects' judgments showed more influence of the ESP information than in the case in which no subliminal information was present. When the extrasensory "prime" competed with a subliminal prime, the extrasensory information predominated, and was also expressed more strongly than when no competing subliminal information was present. The authors interpret this rather odd finding as suggesting that extrasensory information may be especially salient when it contradicts other low-intensity (e.g., subliminal) stimulation. Other interpretations that the authors make of these and 2 other series appear to be vitiated by problems of design (Child, 1977). These findings appear to suggest that psi may interact with subliminal information sometimes in an additive way, and sometimes in a competing manner (i.e., sometimes with assimilation, and sometimes with contrast).

Psi and Remembered Information

Important preconscious processes contribute to the act of remembering, and these have been studied extensively by cognitive psychologists (Schacter, 1997). The *First Sight* model would predict that the preconscious processes of memory and psi processes should often interact.

Memory as a Factor Influencing an ESP Task

Theories of psi offered by Roll (1966) and Irwin (1979) have emphasized the importance of memory traces as the vehicles for psi expression. Partly because of these ideas, there have been a number of studies on the relationship between memory ability and psi scores, and between the degrees of familiarity (or strength of association) of targets with the psi performance expressed using them. Results of both lines of work have been complex and generally mixed, and they appear to be difficult to synthesize. As Palmer has said (1978, 1982), the many significant relationships reported make this appear to be an area of research of some potential importance, but little conceptual clarity has been offered. The model proposed here suggests three things: First, as Stanford has argued (1974, 1975), learned associations should be more available to an individual than unlearned material as vehicles for expressing the influence of extrasensory apprehensions (learned material is more meaningful than unfamiliar material, and is also more available for the construction of experience). Secondly, familiar target material should be more pertinent to an individual's interests and intentions, and tend to elicit more interest and positive unconscious motivation so long as the familiar content is not for some reason undesirable to the subject. Thus, familiar material should generally tend to produce a more positive direction of scoring than unfamiliar material. Some findings support this idea (Kanthamani, 1965; Nash and Nash, 1968; Rao, 1963; 1964, 1965; Rao, Kanthamani and Palmer, 1990). The model would also predict that when remembered material is so well learned as to produce clear conscious construal and stereotyped patterns of response, null scoring and tight variance would be expected, while somewhat less familiar material permitting more impulsive or spontaneous responding should yield more extreme scoring deviations (in situations otherwise conducive to psi-hitting, expressed as stronger hitting). Some studies have tended to support these ideas as well (Cadoret, 1952; Stanford, 1973; Stanford and Stio, 1976)

Psi as a Factor Influencing Memory Tests

Several studies have been carried out in this area. Some tests of memory were administered, and a "psi stimulus" was also present somewhere in the experimental context. In some studies, subjects were told of the extrasensory dimension of the task, in others they were not. In general terms the *First Sight* model would predict that the psi information should function additively with the memory information in cases in which memory is uncertain, but might show no effect or perhaps a contrary effect when memory is strong.

Johnson (1973) tested the power of an extrasensory "stimulus" to enhance memory performance by attaching hidden answers to some questions to the answer sheets given to students in an academic exam. Half the hidden answers were correct, and half were incorrect. He found that when memory was "primed" by the hidden answers, memory performance was significantly better than unprimed responses when the hidden answers were correct, and was significantly poorer when the answers were wrong. Some confirmations of this effect have been reported by Braud (1975) and Schechter (1997).

Kreiman (1978) gave subjects a short time to memorize a list of words, then asked them to write down all they could remember. Twenty of the 50 words were randomly picked as ESP targets. He reasoned that subjects should write down their most strongly remembered words first, and the ones remembered with more difficulty should be given last. He divided each subject's response list in half, and predicted psi-missing in the first halves, and psi-hitting in the second. His predictions were confirmed. Non-significant trends toward confirming this effect were reported by Weiner and Haight (1980) and Schmeidler (1980), and Schmeidler also found that when she carried out a study with subjects most like Kreiman's (persons who believed that ESP was not impossible in the task, and who found it interesting) the effect was confirmed significantly.

Taken together, these studies suggest that psi effects may enter into the act of remembering, particularly when relatively poorly learned but still relevant material is involved. More study is needed to understand more clearly the patterns of interaction.

Psi and Creative Acts

Psi Ability in Creative People

Several writers have pointed out many similarities that appear to exist between psi processes and creativity (e.g., Murphy, 1963,

Myers, 1903/1961). In line with the expectation that they are related, several reports have described unusually good ESP performance on the part of persons who are seriously engaged in one of the arts (Dalton, 1997; Morris, Summers and Yin, 2003; Moss, 1969; Schlitz and Honorton, 1992). Less consistent but still largely positive results have been reported with measures of cognitive skills or styles thought to contribute to creativity (see Schmeidler, 1988, for a review of this material).

The Contribution of Psi to Creative Acts

The *First Sight* model predicts that extrasensory factors participate with other preconscious processes in the construction of creative acts. I could locate no studies in which there was an attempt to influence the outcome of some creative act by serious artists, such as writing a poem or interpreting a piece of music, by some extrasensory intention. There are a number of studies, however, that examine responses that are somewhat like a creative act. The free-association task of the ganzfeld study elicits an uncensored flow of ideas; and it has generally produced significant evidence of psi influence (Bem and Honorton, 1994). Other studies have examined more restrictive forms of free-association (Stanford, 1973; Stanford and Schroeter, 1978). Dreaming may be thought of as a generically "creative" act in which almost everyone engages; and dreams have often been found to express extrasensory intrusion (Child, 1985; Dunne 1927). Other creative-like activities that have been shown to express such intrusion includes producing hypnotic dreams (Honorton, 1969, 1972; Honorton and Stump, 1969; Krippner, 1968), freely drawing (Bevan, 1947; Humphrey, 1946; Shrager, 1978; Targ, 2004), engaging in spontaneous social interaction in a congenial, unstructured group (Carpenter, 2002), moving a ouiji board planchette (Palmer, 2001; Sargent, 1977), and making up stories in response to cards from the Thematic Apperception Test (Kreitler and Kreitler, 1972). There is a general trend for such "creative-expression" tasks to show either relatively high or relatively extreme ESP scoring. The effect on extremity may be the more essential relationship.

The Effect of More Creative Approaches to the Psi Task

In terms of our model, subjects who respond to an ESP task in a more creative way should produce scoring that is more extreme and/or higher than that of persons responding less creatively. By "more creative", I mean an approach that permits the generation of relatively more inadvertent, preconscious material, and that also displays the act of consulting that inadvertency. Many studies have generally confirmed this expectation. In ganzfeld studies, post-session reports have often found that subjects who experienced a state with more "altered" imagery, body-experience, and mood during their sessions scored more strongly than others reporting less of these qualities (Harley and Sargent, 1980; Palmer, Khamashta, and Israelson, 1979; Parker, 1975; Sargent, Bartlet, and Moss, 1982). Stanford (1979) has examined actual session transcripts and found that the variability of the length of time making up discrete blocks of speech, or utterances, related positively to hitting. He interpreted this variability as reflecting the fluidity or spontaneity of the response. Another approach to the analysis of session transcripts was taken by Carpenter (2001), who analyzed data from several laboratories and found that when persons expressed a more active involvement in their own imagery and more emotional openness towards it, they scored well. On the other hand, those whose imagery showed signs of intellectualization and cognitive analysis scored poorly. A measure of creativity modelled after Holt's (1970) Rorschach score (involving primary process material and tolerance for irrational content) found that this measure predicted scoring successfully when high scores were not accompanied by many signs of anxiety. In these same data, he also found (unreported relationships) that scores on the measures of intellectualization and cognitive analysis were associated with tight variance, while profiles indicating emotional openness predicted large deviation scores. In still other ganzfeld studies, Sondow (1979) found that asking subjects to free-associate to the various target alternatives after they had gone through the ganzfeld session improved their scores relative to other subjects who did not carry out the free-association; and she (Sondow, 1987) also found that subjects who reported making a slight effort in producing their material scored better than those who described their imagery as completely uncontrolled. Free association is a technique that would be expected to facilitate consulting the implications of imagery in a creative way, and making a bit of effort in generating the material would seem likely to show that the subject was creatively engaged in the task, and not simply being a passive self-observer. In a related study Braud, Shafer, and Mulgrew (1983) asked subjects to project meanings onto a looping audio tape of the word "cogitate", and found that those who drew upon larger numbers of independent associations showed more positive intrusion of the ESP targets. A greater number of associates seem plausibly related to the aggressiveness and facility with which the subjects searched their inner material. In the behaviour of an unstructured group, Carpenter (2002) found significant evidence of implicit, behavioural reference to the ESP target when sessions were relatively light-hearted and spontaneous, and found psi-missing when the group was extremely serious and focused on difficult emotional material. Palmer (1994) found that subjects scored most highly when they reported having "felt drawn" to their choices, as opposed to when they chose them more rationally.

Even forced-choice ESP guessing tends to show more positive evidence of psi influence when the task is carried out more "creatively", in the sense of being more spontaneous, or being more free of rigid, intellectualized patterns (Cadoret, 1952; Ross, Murphy and Schmeidler, 1952; Scherer, 1948; Stanford, 1966a, 1966b, 1968; Tart, 1976). Finally, some reports have indicated that very high ESP performance may be found when persons with special facility for creatively consulting inner inadvertencies (such as professional artists or trained meditators) are observed to be approaching their task in measurably more creative ways (Carpenter, 2001, 2005a; Watt, 1996).

The general trend of these findings supports the idea that psi processes and the creative process are indeed related. Psi may influence the outcome of creative efforts, and psi tasks may be especially likely to express the intrusion of the target material when the subjects engage in them in more creative ways. Sometimes the greater psi effect is shown as hitting, sometimes as extreme scoring in both directions. It may be that the more general effect of creative inner searching is a tendency toward greater scoring extremity, frequently expressed as high scoring.

The Utility of the Model

Criteria for a Model

To be useful, a model for parapsychological phenomena must address issues on at least three fronts. It must be useful to working parapsychologists by coherently organizing current findings and suggesting fruitful new directions for research. For the many people not knowledgeable about this field, and not prone themselves to paranormal experiences, it must help make the phenomena described by parapsychologists seem sensible and congruent with everyday experience. For scientists in other disciplines who may suspect that anti-scientific motives may hide behind the well-scrubbed methods of parapsychologists, the model must help show that psi phenomena may be understood as part of nature, cogently connected to other areas of knowledge.

Congruence of the Model with Some Major Parapsychological Findings

The Sheep-Goat Effect

Using Schmeidler's (Schmeidler and McConnell, 1958) basic definition: that "goats" believe that ESP is not possible under the conditions of the experiment, and "sheep" are all others, it appears that this criterion is a rough operationalisation of the subject's unconscious motivation in the study. One who declares that the task is impossible probably has an unconscious intention to not-know the target, even though this is belied consciously by taking the test and apparently trying to succeed at it. On the contrary, declaring that the ability in the test conditions is at least possible suggests an unconscious intention to express the material accurately. Unconscious intention to know or not-know (or approach or avoid) the material is presumed to be an important determinant of scoring direction.

In better understanding this differential motivation, it may be helpful to recall the social psychological literature on assimilation and contrast of subliminal primes in the perception of other persons (Fazio, Powell and Herr, 1983; Higgins, 1996; Srull and Wyer, 1980; for a meta-analytic review, see DeCoster and Claypool, 2004), and presumably in many other sorts of judgments as well. As stated earlier, a prime is assimilated when it apparently is judged pre-consciously to be relevant to a target, and it then biases perception of the target in the direction of the prime. A subliminal prime shows the phenomenon of contrast when it is pre-consciously judged to be irrelevant to the target, and this is expressed by a lowered probability that the prime will be expressed in the perception (analogous to psi-missing). It has also been found that contrast effects may be a result of more conscious processing, in which subjects are aware that they may be influenced by a prime (perhaps a supraliminal, semantic term), and try to correct for this bias by avoiding the use of the prime (often over-correcting in the process). On a conscious level, persons may form "naive theories" in which they believe themselves to be biased by some information, and then they will tend to decline to use that information and use alternatives to it instead (Wegener and Petty, 1997). In the ESP experiment, "sheep", who are comfortable with the idea that emerging ideas and images may express ESP target material, would be expected to consult that imagery directly and use it trustingly; goats, on the other hand, might consider such inner material to be only a source of error, and tend to "over-correct" by calling in directions different than their naive impressions. This might happen both at preconscious and more conscious levels of processing.

Since attitude about ESP is not likely to be a highly salient, highly stable characteristic for most people, it is probably wise to assume that it is made more active by the prime of the sheep-goat question itself in the context of the study. Testing which quickly follows the administration of the question would thus be expected to more strongly express the action of this prime than would testing carried out later. Some evidence for this has been found by Carpenter (1991) who found a strong correlation between attitude and performance for testing at the sitting in which the response was elicited, only a marginal trend in the next sitting, and zero correlations in two later sittings of effort.

The Effect of Anxiety

As discussed earlier, more anxious people typically score below chance expectation (Palmer, 1977). The *First Sight* model leads one to expect that more fearful people would be more likely to find the potential event in some way dangerous and have an unconscious intention of avoiding it. Again, unconscious intention determines scoring direction.

The Psi-facilitating Effect of Hypnosis

While flaws in design make some matters of interpretation uncertain (Schechter 1984, Stanford and Stein, 1994), many studies have shown above-chance scoring in subjects who are hypnotized and chance or below-chance scoring in control groups. Hypnosis, particularly in persons inclined to be especially responsive to it, would seem to be a good situation for securing a positive unconscious intention to score well when that is suggested by the hypnotist and is generally acceptable to the subject. Hypnosis should also tend to produce a manner of effort characterized by an absence of cognitive analysis and planning, selective inattention, heightened access to memory and fantasy, as opposed to ongoing realities and an absence of the kind of reality testing that ordinarily characterizes waking consciousness. These are all characteristics described by Hilgard (1965) as typifying the hypnotic state. The positive intention would be expected to make an inclination toward psi-hitting generally likely, and the manner of effort would be likely to assure a tendency toward relatively large scoring deviations, while providing access to an inner stream of inadvertent material of the sort that expresses preconscious activity. This is the combination most likely to result in strong overall positive scoring.

Dreams as a Vehicle for Psi

The dreaming state of awareness is noted both for its lack of reflectiveness and for the absence of conscious, rational processing (Boss, 1977).Thus a shifting of intentions and cognitive tack, with consequent shifting of directional tendency, would be unlikely to occur. Like the hypnosis situation, both these things, a pro-knowing orientation with little directional switching, together with the particularly inadvertent material of the dream, would be expected to lead to strongly positive performance. Confirming this, a review by Child (1985) has shown that dreaming sleep has been found to be especially propitious in conveying ESP information about target material which the dreamer is desiring to perceive. Going to the trouble of participating in an ESP dream study would seem to make it likely that a person intends, at both a conscious and unconscious level, to come to consciously engage the intended information.

The Ganzfeld as a Psi-conducive Situation

The ganzfeld protocol's combination of mild sensory deprivation, the provision of an undifferentiated visual and auditory field, and relaxation, provides the same combination of ideal conditions just described for hypnosis and dreaming, and it has often been reported to show positive scoring (Bem and Honorton, 1994). Our model would predict that these factors would be especially propitious for participants whose manner of verbalizing suggests a positive implicit approach to the situation and an absence of anxiety and cognitive analysis. This is the pattern that has been found (Carpenter, 2001).

Creativeness as a Psi-conducive Trait

This model holds that an unconscious wish to realize the meaning of extrasensory material, coupled with an invariant attention to inadvertent phenomena should make the expression of such material more likely. Creative persons who are engaged in the psi task would be expected to display these things. Persons who are more creative, particularly those who are seriously and actively artistic, have been found to display higher levels of psi performance in several studies. At least two factors may be at work. First, such persons tend to be highly motivated and successful at producing effective performances when called upon to do so. Because of that, we may assume that their conscious motivation to perform is generally matched as well by an unconscious intention to do well. This unconscious wish to succeed should result in a tendency to construct allusions-toward the potential meaning at the psi level. Also, one requirement of successful artistic work is that one suspends rational analysis at times and consults an inner field of sensed preferences, impulses and incipient understandings. How does the poet find the next image, or the cellist sense the right emotional interpretation of a solo, or the actor's body find the right posture for a character? They must "feel their way", suspending clear decisions and cognitive analysis long enough for an implicit sense to emerge and declare itself. This sustained openness to the "felt sense" (Gendlin, 1997) and suspension of premature cognitive closure should allow a relatively stable directional tendency at the psi level of engagement, and show itself as extreme scoring deviations.

The Importance of Caring about the Information

An unconscious intention to know about something should tend to produce a psi orientation in the toward-direction when some pertinent event about that thing is impending. Something or someone of central emotional importance to the person will be expected to be associated with a relatively invariant intention to know, hence producing a stable directional orientation, or a relatively large deviation in response from chance expectation. Many lines of work support this assumption. Examination of collections of reports of spontaneous psychic experiences has typically shown that cases involving personally important information are statistically over-represented. Information about beloved other persons is particularly common (Feather and Schmicker, 2005; Gurney, Myers and Podmore, 1886; Rhine, 1962a, 1962b; Schwartz, 1971; Stevenson, 1970). While reporting bias may account for some of this trend, it is congruent with several experimental findings. When targets are more meaningful, scoring has been found to be higher (Dean, 1962; Kanthamani and Rao, 1975; Nash and Nash, 1968; Rao, 1962; Skibinsky, 1950). When the testing itself feels more meaningful, scoring is stronger (Rogers, 1966, 1967). The more meaningful interpersonal context provided by an agent or sender with whom one is emotionally close is associated with higher performance (Broughton and Alexander, 1997; Stuart, 1946), and this is similar to the finding that a reciprocity of liking between agent and percipient often helps performance (Anderson and White, 1956, 1957; Nash, 1960). Having a more satisfying and meaningful outcome of good performance has been found to help performance (Stanford, Stio, et. al., 1976). When the sought information is more need-relevant in the context of the interpersonal testing situation, those targets are perceived more accurately (Roll, Morris, et. al., 1973). Even targets that are associated with unknown material that is potentially more emotionally meaningful to the percipient has been found to boost scores (Carpenter, 1971). It would seem that it is what we most care about that we most learn about, in the arena of pre-sensory apprehensions, as well as in sensory experience. Perhaps, again it might be fruitful to consider that paranormal phenomena are rather like creative ones. In that case, these words of Amadeus Mozart are pertinent: "Neither a lofty degree of intelligence nor imagination nor both together go to the making of genius. Love, love, love, that is the soul of genius."

The Decline Effect

The *First Sight* model holds that the mind normally and preconsciously employs extrasensory information in the anticipation of its developing experience. However, these are normally very rapid and transient processes, and in ESP testing there is normally no quick development of an experience of the sought material. When effort continues and no sensory experience is forthcoming, our model predicts that the mind will obey its ordinary pattern of moving away from the extrasensory "prime" toward other sources of incipient experience. Initially, this may tend toward a switch in direction to a tendency to misidentify, or significantly miss the target. Thus, we would predict a decline in scoring as testing proceeds. The decline effect has been described as perhaps the most consistent finding in parapsychology (Palmer, 1978). Three major types of declines have been reported: long term declines of high-scoring subjects to a chance level (e.g., Banham, 1966; Brugmans, 1922; Pratt, 1973; Rhine, 1934/1973), within-session declines of hitting (e.g., Dean and Taetzsch, 1963; Humphrey, 1945; Parker and Beloff, 1970; Schmeidler, 1968; Roll and Klein, 1972), and declines of scoring extremity (Carpenter, 1966, 1968, 1969; Carpenter and Carpenter, 1967; Rogers and Carpenter, 1966; Sailaja and Rao, 1973). Since almost all reports of scoring declines have been drops from psi-hitting to chance performance (in one case from psi-missing to chance performance – Schmeidler, 1964), the decline of scoring extremity may be the more general phenomenon.

There are comparisons one may draw between findings in parapsychology and in work on Perception Without Awareness (PWA). As mentioned above, Sohlberg, Billinghurst and Nylen (1998) have reported that an "overdosage" of too many subliminal exposures of a stimulus normally evocative of a good mood, gives a reverse effect of a bad mood. Bem (2005), in his "precognitive boredom effect," has found that a relatively large number of exposures of an emotionally neutral stimulus leads toward a precognitive aversion in regard to that target. Smaller numbers of exposures had no effect at all. Apparently the mind tends to preconsciously choose to move away from any stimulus which is too-often presented without the development of any accompanying sensory material. This is the contrast effect mentioned above as a basic mechanism for psi missing. Tease it too much, with no experience forthcoming, and the mind will lose interest and turn away. It may then be the case that if testing effort is kept up even past this point, one preconsciously will wish to avoid the material still more decisively, by having no consistent direction of interest at all. In order that the now-abandoned material not be distracting by any sort of referential tendency, a rapidly-shifting pattern of intention will come into play, which will be expressed as chance-level performance. If effort is still maintained, the mind's "binding" action will be expressed by a chance level of performance so consistent across runs that it is extra-chance!

Ordinary Non-Psychic Experience and the Model

It is desirable for our model to make the constructs of parapsychology more sensible to the many persons who do not easily find them so. Even if the model has some utility for accounting for psychic experiences, these events are still odd or perhaps even dangerous aberrations from the point of view of everyday experience for most people. Is the model helpful in accounting for this discrepancy between normal experience and the constructs of parapsychology?

Evidence for ESP and the Absence of Psychic Knowledge in Everyday Life

When first confronted with what appears to be evidence for the reality of ESP, common sense is offended. Everyday experience tells us that we cannot see around corners or read next week's newspaper. As a professor of mine once quipped: "If people could do that, don't you think someone would have noticed by now?" We are all initially sceptical when very reliable assumptions appear to be violated. It seems as if we are being asked to choose between an understanding of human nature as we understand it to be from our experience, and another version endowed with magical powers of knowledge and action. This model implies that we are not forced into any such choice. It suggests that the apparent, predominant absence of paranormal phenomena and their occasional, unbidden intrusions are all part of a sensible whole. A person is not endowed with magical powers of knowing because, according to this model, ESP is not knowledge at all. It is the mind's capacity to unconsciously anticipate knowledge at a point prior to any actual sensory experience. In everyday experience, consciousness is occupied by knowledge that is the result of all active pre-conscious processes, including psi, and which is often validated and given closure by interpretable sensory experience. The preconscious processes themselves are not available to awareness. This is not belied by the fact that accurate *guesses* may often be made about events not sensorily available (or only subliminally available). For example, Emanuel Swedenborg's famous vision of a fire 300 miles distant from him (Sigstedt, 1952), as remarkably accurate as it was, was not *knowing*, in the sense that knowledge was available to those near the fire. It was an accurate interpretation of fantasy images provoked by extrasensory apprehensions experienced in a state of reverie. As another example, the gifted remote viewer is not assumed by this model to *know* the location of a sought missing person. Rather, the place of the missing person, which the viewer desires to know, arouses an anticipational network of preconscious feelings and meanings that serve to orient her attention. If someone were about to simply tell her what she wants to know, this anticipation would merely make her slightly quicker and more efficient in understanding what she is about to be told. She would never consciously know of having anticipated it. However, if this information is not available to the viewer, this anticipational arousal must "hover" on the edge of awareness, without cognitive closure, because no validating sensory information is available. The skilled and practiced viewer tolerates this suspended uncertainty, consults the inadvertent feelings and images issuing from the "hovering" anticipational activation, and draws out a collection of allusive chunks of content containing measurable truth.

In everyday life, we do not ordinarily search out the possible connection between inadvertent psychological phenomena and distant realities; nor are situations generally conducive to doing so. Many truth-implying experiences probably flow by uninterpreted and unremembered. We pass most of our hours sensibly intending to understand what is close at hand for us, in good critical touch with reality, and in states of mind other than those most suited to glimpsing the activity of preconscious processes. Those processes are not inactive at such moments, but they are invisible.

Thus, by this model, the general absence of psi experience and the occasional occurrence of psi experience may be understood in the same terms, all as sensible parts of normal functioning. This reasoning may not be compelling to someone who has never felt the need to seriously confront the possible reality of psi phenomena, but it may at least encourage an open-minded attitude about the possibility.

The Fear of Psi

Besides thinking of psi as unusual and improbable, many people also find the possibility of psi experiences a frightening idea. There are probably many sources of this apprehension. Three important ones would appear to be the popular association of psychic claims with mental illness, fears of being influenced or controlled by extra-personal forces, and the moral proscription against delving into such questions by major religious traditions. This model may offer some help in regard to each of these matters.

Psi and Mental Illness

Experiences which people construe as psychic, or "Subjective Paranormal Experiences" (Neppe, 1983), are popularly associated with madness, and indeed, they may characterize psychotic break-downs of either a manic or schizophrenic sort (American Psychiatric Association, 2004), as well as less malignant conditions, such as schizotypal personality disorder and dissociative identity disorder. Many people are fearful of apparently paranormal experiences for this reason, and many who believe they may have had such experiences are fearful that others will think that they are insane. In my role as a clinical psychologist, I have often found that it is reassuring to authoritatively tell such persons that they are perfectly sane, when I am sure that they are. Assuming that the premises of this model are correct, it might be even more reassuring to inform them that psi is not only normal, it is probably universal among human beings, although its normal mode of functioning is almost entirely preconscious. It might be most reassuring if we could say that there is absolutely no connection in reality between genuine psi and psychosis, but reality may be more complex than our constructs would have it. The *First Sight* model suggests that persons who are suffering from prolonged confusion or disorientation might in fact be open to experiencing a plethora of preconscious processes, including psi, but their ability to interpret the experiences accurately and use them constructively would be severely compromised. However, persons who appear to be able to exercise some control over their psi productions, and make constructive use of them present a very different picture. Their openness to preconscious material represents a positive adaptation, not a breakdown of functioning. In this way, they are like the creative persons described by Kris (1952) who have the capacity of "regression in the service of the ego". Like persons who have developed their sensibilities in art or music, or cultivated their powers of memory or attention to detail, many such persons seem to have gone to the trouble of developing the skill to make use of cues that are probably available to all of us – cues that are useless and quickly forgotten without the requisite skill in employing them.

Fear of Extra-Personal Influence

This fear arises not only in regard to extrasensory phenomena, but with the idea of subliminal influence as well. To say that some activity is unconscious or preconscious seems mystifying, and gives us the sense that the activity might be done somehow by something separate from our conscious intentions. If such influences occur, perhaps we all really slaves to impersonal, physical processes that control us.

However, these "influences" are actually our own (preconscious) activity in which we engage in pursuing the construction and meaning of our experience. They are not done *to us*, but are done *by us*. This is one reason I have grounded this model in an existential context, that is to say, attempted to look at it in terms of life as is actually lived altogether, as opposed to seeing it in the context of some abstraction about some aspect of life. Existentially, we are active, whole beings; we press forward with our lives. We are not simply the products of mechanical processes impinging upon us, but we *use* those processes for our becoming. Some important aspects of this using are unconscious and preconscious. The fact that part of my using is unconscious does not mean that this part is being done by someone or something else. It is still being done by me. When I walk from one place to another, I am not conscious of all the myriad of muscular actions that make the walking work. They are unconscious constituents to my action of walking. However unconscious, they are still being done by me, they are part of my walking, and are serving my intention of getting to the new place. Now adding reference to the observations of parapsychology, we may say that at the outermost edge of all of our pressing forward, we use psi processes, which is to say, we make use of the fact that we exist always a little beyond ourselves in space and ahead of ourselves in time (actually, we can make use of bigger spans ahead and beyond if that meets our needs, but ordinarily a little ahead and beyond is most useful for us).

Scientists frequently contribute inadvertently to this fear of being impersonally driven. Since many scientists presume (preconsciously) that the best account of something is one which is impersonal and does not refer to any sort of intention, they often gravitate to ways of thinking about unconscious processes that imply that the processes are purely physical actions, like chemical reactions. This may feel comfortable to the scientist since it seems to be accounting for something on a basic level. It also adds to the mystifying sense that somehow we might all be robots, in spite of our experience of intention and consciousness. Even more oddly, given the findings of parapsychology, we might be robots driven by distant influences![2] However, if a scientific account of the person is to be adequate to its subject, it must take account of the existential fact that life-as-lived is much more a *project* than a *process*. Impersonal processes like chemical reactions are certainly constituent parts of the project of life, but they are not the whole story. To proceed as if they are mystifying, and is a failure to avoid the reductionistic fallacy (Rychlak, 2003). For psychology to be adequate to its subject matter, our model suggests that it must take account of the fact that preconscious processes are used by each individual in the pursuit of meaningful experience, not inflicted upon him or her. Conveying this sort of understanding to the general public should help dispel the fantasies and fears of external control.

Moral Proscriptions against the Paranormal

The *Holy Bible* and the *Koran,* along with many other texts of the monotheistic faiths, contain numerous references to paranormal

[2] Many acutely paranoid individuals have inhabited this terrifying possibility.

phenomena such as prophecies, blessings, curses, and miracles. Sometimes these are seen as sacred events, and are viewed with great reverence. At other times they are seen as evil and condemned severely. Similarly, great texts of Eastern wisdom, such as the *Yoga-Sutras* of Patañjali (Satchidananda, 1990) speak of the various *siddhis*, or paranormal powers, that accompany the highest levels of spiritual development, but caution that they must not be sought for their own sake, but should be experienced only within the context of utter compassion and reverence for the Supreme. Perhaps a common theme for all of these traditions of spiritual life is that paranormal abilities may be real, but if they are sought for their own sake, and developed toward the end of personal power and aggrandizement over others, they are destructive and should be avoided. If held in the context of loving reverence for all creation, and for the transcendent powers behind creation, they may lead in the positive directions of healing, enlightenment and self-transcendence. The *First Sight* model has no theological commitments, but it does stress a conception of human nature in which each person is not contained within personal, physical boundaries, but ontologically and epistemologically extends beyond that into intimate commerce with all the rest of reality, including all other persons. To pursue paranormal experiences selfishly, over-against the interests of others, would therefore be self-contradictory, and by the logic of the model, probably doomed to failure. If the model is basically correct, it implies that as we learn more about the functioning of psi processes, we will in turn learn more about our profound interconnectedness and the inseparability of our interests from those of all beings. Seeking such knowledge is in tune with the great traditions of wisdom and faith, not contrary to them.

Harmonizing Parapsychology with other Branches of Science

This model offers a view of psychological functioning that includes a sensible place for psi processes. It shows how the errant anomalies described by parapsychologists may actually represent tirelessly active and normally unconscious capacities utilized in our ongoing adjustments to the circumstances of our lives. This model does not prove that psi processes actually occur. However, developing a picture of the mind in which psi can fit together with the other facts of psychological process should make it easier for scientists of other disciplines to attend with more interest to all of the research which does prove that psi phenomena are genuine occurrences. At least two other things are necessary, however, before many scientists will take seriously the possibility of that reality. They want from parapsychologists a replicable phenomenon, and they want a mechanism for how a mind may interact with distant matter or with other minds.

The Problem of Replication

For some parapsychologists this problem has already been solved. The replicability of an effect is a matter of degree, and many parapsychological hypotheses in broad terms have been shown by meta-analysis to be reliable enough, and free enough of apparent error, to be considered real (Utts, 1996). Still, no parapsychological phenomenon is perfectly reliable, and no parapsychologist, no matter how many successful studies he or she may have conducted, presently is able to toss a coin into the air and either will or predict with absolute accuracy the face on which it will land. Can this model hasten the day in which such reliability is achieved? It may, since it suggests a direction for understanding not only the sporadic anomalies of apparent psi but also the countless moments of apparent absence of psychic process, all in the same terms. Understanding the true scope of a phenomenon, in its implicit as well as its explicit expressions, will provide a firmer basis for comprehension and prediction. Even if this model should prove to be basically wrong, the research disproving it should lead us in the direction of greater understanding, and as the understanding of psi phenomena improves, the replicability of operations demonstrating it will as well.

A Mechanism for Psi

I have presented this model in the context of a phenomenological approach to the basic ontological and metaphysical problems that appear to beset the psi hypothesis. In a phenomenological approach, a dualistic split between the subjective and objective aspects of experience is eschewed, and the need for providing some sort of physical mechanism linking mind to world or present to future event is avoided. The facts as observed are left to speak for themselves. I believe that this is a sufficient basis for grounding meaningful psychological scientific work. This will not seem satisfying, however, to scientists who are deeply committed to a physicalist conception of the mind. Most scientists probably assume that all mental events are ultimately reducible to physical events, the "promissory materialism" of Popper and Eccles (1977, p. 96). As stated earlier, this derivative and reductionistic idea of the mind also leads to the assumption that mere consciousness should have no reach beyond the physical body, and mere intention should have no immediate grip of its own upon physical events. For many scientists, such assumptions are so deeply held as to seem to be given realities. From such a base, psi phenomena will always seem unreal because they will feel impossible.

Developments during the last century in basic theoretical physics call into question this structure of assumptions. Current research in physics is heavily involved with the study of what David Bohm (1993) calls "quantum interconnectedness". The theorem of J.S. Bell (1964) specified this expectation of non-local correlation between separated quanta of light under certain circumstances. The theorem has been empirically proven (Freedman and Clauser, 1972). While it cannot be said that a mechanism for psychic connections between mental events and distant physical events has been established by these means, several physicists have argued that these and other aspects of quantum mechanics have opened a door that may lead in that direction (e.g., Bohm, 1990, Josephson and Fotini, 1991, Targ, 2004, Walker, 1975; Whiteman, 1977). As physics broadens to encompass consciousness, the parapsychologist's phenomena may find a warm home. The model of psi developed in this paper should be ultimately congruent with such an expanded conception of reality.

Even if a scientist is not a reductionist in regard to mental processes, he or she may reasonably want an account of psi phenomena which is elaborated in terms of known psychophysiological processes. This model should be eminently congruent with such psychophysiological accounts as they develop and become available to our use.

Many contributions in this area have been made already (e.g., Broughton, 2002, Ehrenwald, 1976, 1977, Kelly, Kelly, Crabtree, et. al. 2006). The *First Sight* model of psi, as it is developed further, may provide a useful structure to which accounts of relevant nervous system activity can be related. Analogous work is already being done that relates preconscious perceptual processes with various aspects of psychophysiological activity (e.g., Shevrin, 1988; Shevrin, Bond, et. al., 1996).

Suggested Directions for Future Research

Various features of this model suggest particular directions for study. The following are examples.

Study the inadvertent expression of psi processes in situations not understood as parapsychological experiments

Since psi processes are presumed to be active all the time, and their typical expression is in the form of inadvertencies, more study should be done to elucidate the functioning of psi in situations in which persons are carrying on "normal" activities, and not attempting to express some paranormal effect. This suggestion has been made before by Stanford (1974a), and I wish to second it here. Schechter (1997) has summarized research that has looked for unconscious extrasensory effects in such situations as academic tests, and Carpenter (2002), Ehrenwald (1948) and Eisenbud (1969, 1970) have examined the expressions of ESP in psychotherapy. Psi effects in what would otherwise appear to be "normal" experiments on psychological phenomena have been reported also, such as Klintman's (1984) study of reaction times to the presentations of colours, and Bem's (2004) examination of relative preference between matched pairs of pictures. Such work suggests directions that we may take, but, assuming that psi functions ubiquitously, we can extend such investigation into almost any behavioural context.

Analyze Scoring Direction and Scoring Extremity Separately and Routinely

This model emphasizes that these two parameters of performance are expected to be influenced by different factors, and that both are important and continuous aspects of ongoing psi process. Both aspects of performance should be analyzed regularly in studies of ESP and PK performance, with attention paid to variables that affect each of them. It is important to avoid any analyses such as the use of the "direct hit" in ganzfeld research that confound the two parameters, since this creates unnecessary confusion. The rank of number one represents both the most extreme score of psi-hitting and one of the higher values of scoring extremity. Any correlations between some other variable and this binary psi variable (one versus all other ranks) thus confound these two basic parameters of psi process, and cannot be clearly interpreted. Palmer (1997) has also addressed this problem. In assessing relevant patterns of performance in rank-order data, the methods of Solfvin, Kelly and Burdick (1978) are particularly helpful.

Focus on inadvertent aspects of response that are especially likely to be sensitive expressions of psi

Since psi functioning is intrinsically preconscious, it is reasonable to operationalize it by examining inadvertent expressions of its orienting action, rather than asking subjects to try to generate an approximation of conscious knowledge. Aspects of response that are generally known to reflect preconscious processes are likely to yield fruitful results. Examples of this useful approach are already available, such as the use of unconscious physiological responses (Braud, 2003; Dean, 1962; Radin, 2003; Radin, Taylor and Taylor, 1995; Spottiswoode and May, 2003), spontaneous social behaviour (Carpenter, 2002), perceptual judgments (Kreitler and Kreitler, 1972, 1973), involuntary pupillary fixations (Palmer, 1994), word associations (Stanford, 1973) and affective reactions (Bem, 2003).

Employ implicit measures of psychological independent variables

Since the variables effecting psi functioning (directional orientation and directional switching) act on an unconscious level, it should be more useful to study them with implicit or behavioural methods such as projective techniques than with self-report measures such as questionnaires. Such implicit measures tend to be more valid indicators of preconscious processes. As McClelland, Koestner, and Weinberger (1989) point out, self-report measures appear to be most effective at predicting future self-conscious self-representation, as in the responses to future questionnaires. Projective measures on the other hand, or other implicit measures which sample behaviours presumed to implicitly express the unconscious issues being studied, are superior in predicting behaviour in future situations where the behaviour is not self-conscious (i.e. most of the time, and probably always in regard to psi functioning) (see Dauber, 1984, and Weinberger, Kellner and McClelland, 1997). Examples of other measures which would be expected to be more valid include defining as "creative" those persons who successfully do creative work, and assessing a percipient's "defensiveness" by his or her choice of carrying out a task in a chair that was either fully or partially reclined (Stanford and Schroeter's, 1978).

Study the action of psi processes in the context of other preconscious phenomena

This is perhaps the major "action item" of the present paper. In carrying out parapsychological studies it would be wise to borrow aggressively and collaboratively from mainstream psychologists who are working with preconscious phenomena. Psychologists have been ingenious in recent decades at developing methods for gaining experimental access to some unconscious and pre-conscious mental processes. Perception-without-awareness, implicit memory, implicit social perception, perceptual defensiveness, and subliminal psychodynamic activation are examples of the fertile work being done. Psi phenomena do not represent disguised knowledge, but the functioning of pre-knowledge, pre-perceptual apprehensive mental processes at a point beyond the physical impingement of a stimulus upon the organism. In consciously collaborative work, parapsychologists will have new contributions from their own tradition. For example, although there is some notice of the phenomenon of significant missing in the perception-without-awareness literature (e.g., Bonnano and Stillings, 1986, Grosz and Zimmerman, 1965, Merikle and Reingold, 1991), they have paid less systematic attention to this matter than parapsychologists have.

Two studies from the laboratory of the Rhine Research Center demonstrate some of the forms such integrative work might take. In a recent study, the research team examined the effect of an attempted suboptimal manipulation of the subject's merger-motivation, mood of security, and cognitive approach on their ESP performance in the ganzfeld. We expected heightened levels of scoring in the condition intended to facilitate a sense of secure merger and a non-intellectual approach to the task. We also examined the effects of the manipulation by analyzing the transcripts of the sessions and the post-session state reports of the percipients. Unfortunately, our condition did not succeed in changing the state and implicit attitude of the percipient in the ways that we had hoped, and perhaps for that reason did not alter ESP performance either. In another study soon to begin, a first series will examine the effect of a subliminal manipulation of mild moods of insecurity and security on both an ESP task and a replication of the "mere exposure" effect (in which a false sense of familiarity is engendered by subliminal exposure). In the second series, the subliminal stimuli engendering feelings of insecurity and security will be "delivered" only by an extrasensory agent. We will then examine whether this action leads to an extrasensory "mere exposure" effect, and to indirectly measured changes in mood. Thus, in these studies we are examining the commingling of psi and other preconscious processes as expressed in ganzfeld mentation and in a different inadvertent ESP response. The first study examined the effect of subliminal stimulation on an extrasensory task. The second examines the action of an extrasensory intention upon a classical PWA effect. Through such beginning steps as these, and others to follow, we hope to shed more light upon the ways in which "first sight" interacts with other preconscious psychological processes in the development of the stream of consciousness.

Conclusion

How is it that consciousness takes the form that it does? I am proposing a model in the context of which answers to this perennial, psychological question might be sought. In so doing, I am also suggesting that what have been considered psychic phenomena actually represent continuously ongoing and normally unconscious processes that contribute to the construction of experience and action. Since they are presumed to begin the sequences of events leading to experience, they may fairly be referred to as *First Sight.* The model also suggests basic ways in which the mind may utilize its pre-sensory apprehensions in the context of developing sensory experience, and ways in which its anticipatory effects may be surmised indirectly.

The model is intended to be useful in several different ways. It develops an understanding of psi functioning which places it in the context of normal, preconscious psychological processes. It suggests that the mind uses psi apprehensions in the anticipation and construction of its experiences and actions, much as it uses subliminal, or suboptimal, perceptual information. Curiously, some researchers in the field of suboptimal perception have attributed little utility to their phenomena in everyday life. One prominent scientist has even suggested that subliminal perception may be only a kind of laboratory freak, with no practical importance and only rare occurrence in everyday life (Bargh, 1992). To the contrary, this model proposes that the mind continually uses suboptimal and extrasensory information in anticipating, constructing and understanding its own developing experience. If psi processes function in everyday experience in a continuously active, if normally implicit way, then they cannot be omitted by any psychologist attempting to understand the basic problem of the field according to William James (1890): how experience comes to be what it is.

It is a propitious time. Serious parapsychological work has proceeded for over 100 years, and findings are now numerous enough and secure enough that implicit patterns are more clearly emerging. Psychology, after its long focus on the publicly behavioural, has rediscovered consciousness, and at the same time has found a very fruitful field in the preconscious processes that contextualize consciousness. It is time to think scientifically of all these things at once. An understanding of psychological reality cannot be adequate without the anomalies of parapsychology. Walt Whitman (1900) proclaimed, "I... am not contain'd between my hat and boots." Since this seems literally to be true, scientifically understanding our larger selves should lead us to larger possibilities of knowledge and action. The *First Sight* model is intended to help in this effort, but if not, then some other one with similar intentions must arise.

REFERENCES

American Psychiatric Association (1994). *Diagnostic and Statistical Manual of Mental Disorders.* Washington, DC: American Psychiatric Association.

Anderson, M. & White, R. (1956). Teacher-pupil attitudes and clairvoyance test results. *Journal of Parapsychology,* 20, 141-167.

Anderson, M. & White, R. (1957). A further investigation of teacher-pupil attitudes and clairvoyance test results. *Journal of Parapsychology,* 21, 81-97.

Baars, B.J. (1997). *In the Theatre of Consciousness.* New York: Oxford University Press.

Banham, K.M. (1966). Temporary high scoring by a child subject. *Journal of Parapsychology,* 30, 106-113.

Bargh, J.A. (1992). Does subliminality matter to social psychology? Awareness of the stimulus vs. awareness of its influence. In R. F. Bornstein & T. S. Pittman (Eds.), *Perception Without Awareness.* New York: The Guilford Press.

— & Tota, M.E. (1988). Context-dependent automatic processing in depression: Accessibility of negative constructs with regard to self but not others. *Journal of Personality and Social Psychology,* 54, 925-939.

Bell, J.S. (1964). On the Einstein-Podolsky-Rosen paradox. *Physics I: 195-200.*

Bem, D.J. (2003). Precognitive habituation: Replicable evidence for a process of anomalous cognition. *Journal of Parapsychology,* 67, 249-250 (abstract).

— (2004). Precognitive avoidance and precognitive déjà vu. *The Parapsychological Association 47th Annual Convention.*

— Bem, D.J. (2005). Precognitive aversion. Proceedings of Presented Papers: The *Parapsychological Association 48th Annual Convention.*

— & Honorton, C. (1994). Does psi exist? Replicable evidence for an anomalous process of information transfer. *Psychological Bulletin,* 115, 4-18.

Bevan, J.M. (1947). The relation of attitude to success in ESP scoring. *Journal of Parapsychology,* 11, 296-309.

Bohm, D. (1990). A new theory of the relationship of mind and matter. *Philosophical Psychology*, 3, 271-286.

— & Hiley, B.J. (1993). *The Undivided Universe*. London: Routledge.

Bonnano, G.A. & Stillings, N.A. (1986). Preference, familiarity and recognition after repeated brief exposures to random geometric shapes. *American Journal of Psychology,* 99, 403-415.

Boss, M. (1977). *I Dreamt Last Night.* New York: Gardner Press.

Braud, W.G. (1975). Conscious versus unconscious clairvoyance in the context of an academic examination. *Journal of Parapsychology*, 39, 277-288.

Braud, W. (2003). *Distant Mental Influence*. Charlottesville, VA: Hampton Roads Publishing.

— Shafer, D. & Mulgrew, D. (1983). Psi functioning and assessed cognitive lability. *Journal of the American Society for Psychical Research,* 77, 193-208.

Broughton, R.S. (2002). Telepathy: Revisiting its roots. *4°Simposio da Fundação Bial: Behind and Beyond the Brain.* Porto: Casa do Médico.

Broughton, R.S. & Alexander, C.H. (1997). Autoganzfeld II: An attempted replication of the PRL ganzfeld research. *Journal of Parapsychology,* 61, 209-226.

Brugmans, H.J.F.W. (1922). Une communication sur des experiences telepathiques au Laboratoire de Psychologie a Groninque faites par M.Heymans. Docteur Weinberg, et Docteur H.J.F. Brugmans. In *Le Compte Rendu Officiel du Premier Congres International des Ressearches Psychiques.*Copenhagen.

Cadoret, R.J. (1952). The effect of novelty in test conditions on ESP performance. *Journal of Parapsychology,* 16, 192-203.

Carpenter, J.C. (1966). Scoring effects within the run. *Journal of Parapsychology,* 30, 73-83.

— (1968). Two related studies on mood and precognition run-score variance. *Journal of Parapsychology,* 32, 75-89.

— (1969). Further study on a mood adjective check list and ESP run-score variance. *Journal of Parapsychology,* 33, 48-56.

— (1971). The differential effect and hidden target differences consisting of erotic and neutral stimuli. *Journal of the American Society for Psychical Research,* 65, 204-214.

— (1991). Prediction of forced-choice ESP performance: Part III: three attempt to retrieve coded information using mood reports and repeated-guessing technique. *Journal of Parapsychology,* 55, 227-280.

— (2001). A psychological analysis of ganzfeld protocols. *Journal of Parapsychology,* 65, 358-359.

— (2002). The intrusion of anomalous communication in group and individual psychotherapy: clinical observations and a research project. *4° Simposio da Fundação Bial: Behind and Beyond the Brain.* Porto: Casa do Médico.

— (2005a). Implicit measures of participants' experiences in the ganzfeld: Confirmation of previous relationships in a new sample. *Proceedings of Presented Papers: The Parapsychological Association 48th Annual Convention,* 36-45.

— (2005b). First Sight: Part one. A model of psi and the mind. *Journal of Parapsychology,*

Carpenter, James, & Carpenter, Josephine. (1967). Decline of variability of ESP scoring across a period of effort. *Journal of Parapsychology,* 31, 179-191.

Child, I.L. (1977). Statistical regression artifact in parapsychology. *Journal of Parapsychology,* 41, 10-22.

— (1985). Psychology and anomalous observations: The question of ESP in dreams. *American Psychologist,* 40, 1219-1230.

Dalton, K. (1997). Exploring the links: Creativity and psi in the ganzfeld. *Proceedings of Presented Papers: The Parapsychological Association 40th Annual Convention,* 119-134.

Dauber, R.B. (1984). Subliminal psychodynamic activation in depression: On the role of autonomy in depressed college women. *Journal of Abnormal and Social Psychology,* 93, 9-18.

Dean, E.D. (1962). The plethysmograph as an indicator of ESP. *Journal of the Society for Psychical Research,* 41, 351-353.

— & Taetzsch, R. (1963). An ESP test for speakers using computer scoring. *Journal of Parapsychology,* 27, 275-276.

DeCoster, J. & Claypool, H.M. (2004). A meta-analysis of priming effects on impression formation supporting a general model of information biases. *Personality and Social Psychology Review,* 8, 2-27.

Dunne, J.W. (1927). *An Experiment with Time.* New York: Macmillan.

Ehrenwald, J. (1948). *Telepathy and Medical Psychology.* New York: Norton.

— (1976). Parapsychology and the seven dragons: A neuropsychiatric model of psi phenomena. In G.R. Schmeidler (Ed.), *Parapsychology: Its Relation to Physics, Biology, Psychology and Psychiatry.* Metuchen, N.J.: Scarecrow Press.

— (1977). Psi phenomena and brain research. In Benjamin Wolman (Ed.), *Handbook of Parapsychology* (pp.716-729). New York: Van Nostrand Reinhold.

Eisenbud, J. (1969). Chronologically extraordinary psi correspondences in the psychoanalytic setting. *Psychoanalytic Quarterly,* 56.9-27.

— (1970). *Psi and Psychoanalysis.* New York: Grune and Stratton.

Fazio, R.H., Powell, M.C. & Herr, P.M. (1983). Toward a process model of the attitude-behavior relation: Accessing one's attitude upon mere observation of the attitude object. *Journal of Personality and Social Psychology,* 44, 723-735.

Feather, S.R. & Schmicker, M. (2005). *The Gift: ESP-Extraordinary Experiences of Ordinary People.* New York: St. Martin's Press.

Freedman, S. & Clauser, J. (1972). Experimental test of local hidden variables theories. *Physical Review Letters,* 28, 934-941.

Fulcher, E.P. & Hammeri, M. (2002). When all is revealed: A dissociation between evaluative learning and contingency awareness. *Consciousness and Cognition,* 10, 524-549.

Gendlin, E. (1997). *Experiencing and the Creation of Meaning: A Philosophical and Psychological Approach to the Subjective.* Chicago: Northwestern University Press.

Grosz, H.J. & Zimmerman, J.A. (1965). Experimental analysis of hysterical blindness: A follow-up report and new experimental data. *Archives of General Psychiatry,* 13, 255-260.

Gurney, E., Myers, F.W.H. & Podmore, F. (1886). *Phantasms of the Living* (Vol.1). London: Trubner.

Harley, T.A., & Sargent, C.L. (1980). Trait and state factors influencing ESP performance in the ganzfeld. In *Research in Parapsychology* (pp.126-127). Metuchen, NJ: Scarecrow Press.

Higgins, E.T. (1996). Knowledge activation: Accessibility, applicability, and salience. In E.T. Higgins & A.W. Kruglanski (Eds.), *Social Psychology: Handbook of Basic Principles (*pp.133-168). New York: Guilford.

Hilgard, E. (1965). *Hypnotic Susceptibility.* New York: Harcourt, Brace & World.

Holt, R.R. (1970). Artistic creativity and Rorschach measures of adaptive regression. In Klopfer, Meyer & Brown (Eds.), *Developments in the Rorschach Technique, Vol.III: Aspects of Personality Structure.* New York: Harcourt Brace Javonovich.

Honorton, C.A. (1969). A combination of techniques for the separation of high and low-scoring ESP subjects. *Journal of the American Society for Psychical Research,* 63, 69-82.

— (1972). Significant factors in hypnotically-induced clairvoyant dreams. *Journal of the American Society for Psychical Research,* 66, 86-102.

— & Stump, J.P. (1969). A preliminary study of hypnotically-induced clairvoyant dreams. *Journal of the American Society for Psychical Research,* 63, 175-184.

Humphrey, B.M. (1945). Further position effects in the Earlham College series. *Journal of Parapsychology,* 9, 26-31.

— (1946). Success in ESP as related to form of response drawings: I. Clairvoyance experiments. *Journal of Parapsychology,* 10, 78-106.

Irwin, H.J. (1979). *Psi and the Mind.* Metuchen, NJ: Scarecrow Press.

James, W. (1890). *The Principles of Psychology.* New York: Henry Holt and Company.

Jaskowski, P. & Skalska, B. (2003). How the self controls its "automatic pilot" when processing subliminal information. *Journal of Cognitive Neuroscience,* 15, 911-920.

Johnson, M. (1973). A written academic exam as a disguised test of clairvoyance. In W.G. Roll, J.D. Morris & R.L. Morris (Eds.) *Research in Parapsychology* (pp. 28-30). Metuchen, NJ: Scarecrow Press.

Josephson, B.D. & Fotini Pallikari-Viras (1991). Biological utilisation of quantum non-locality. *Foundations of Physics*, 21, 197-207.

Kanthamani, B.K. (H.) (1965). A study of the differential response in language ESP tests. *Journal of Parapsychology,* 29, 27-34.

Kanthamani, H., & Kelly, E.F. (1974). Awareness of success in an exceptional subject. *Journal of Parapsychology,* 38, 355-382.

— & Rao, H.H. (1975). The role of association strength in memory-ESP interaction. *Journal of Parapsychology,* 39, 1-11.

Kelly, E.F., Kanthamani, H., Child, I.L., & Young, F.W. (1975). On the relation between visual and ESP confusion structures in an exceptional ESP subject. *Journal of the American Society for Psychical Research,* 69, 1-31.

Kelly, E.F. & Kelly, E.W., Crabtree, A., Gauld, A., Grosso, M. & Greyson, B. (Eds.) (2006). *Irreducible Mind: Toward a Psychology for the 21st Century.* Lanham, MD.: Rowman and Littlefield.

Klintman, H. (1984). Is there a paranormal (precognitive) influence in certain types of perceptual sequences? Part II. *European Journal of Parapsychology,* 5, 129-140.

Kreiman, N. (1978). (The function of psi in a test with university students.) *Cuadernos de parapsychologia, 1976,* 9, 1, 3-12. (Abstract in *Journal of Parapsychology,* 1978, 42, 15-155.)

Kreitler, H. & Kreitler, S. (1972). Does extrasensory perception affect psychological experiments? *Journal of Parapsychology,* 36, 1-45.

— (1973). Subliminal perceptionand extrasensory perception. *Journal of Parapsychology*, 37, 163-188.

Krippner, S. (1968). Experimentally-induced telepathic effects in hypnosis and non-hypnosis groups. *Journal of the American Society for Psychical Research,* 62, 387-398.

Kris, E. (1952). *Psychoanalytic Explorations in Art.* New York: International Universities Press.

Lewin, K. (1935). *A Dynamic Theory of Personality.* New York: McGraw Hill.

Martin, L.L., Tesser, A. & McIntosh, W.D. (1993). Wanting but not having: the effects of unattained goals on thoughts and feelings. In D.M. Wegner & J.W. Pennebaker (Eds.), *Handbook of Mental Control* (pp. 552-572). Englewood Cliffs, NJ: Prentice Hall.

McClelland, D.C., Koestner, R. & Weinberger, J. (1989). How do self-attributed and implicit motives differ? *Psychological Review,* 96, 690-702.

Merikle, P.M. & Reingold, E.M. (1991). Comparing direct (explicit) and indirect (implicit) measures to study unconscious memory. *Journal of Experimental Psychology: Learning, Memory, and Cognition,* 17, 224-233.

Morris, R.W., Summers, J. & Yim, S. (2003). Evidence of anomalous information transfer with a creative population in ganzfeld stimulation. *Journal of Parapsychology,* 67, 256-257 (abstract).

Moss, T. (1969). ESP effects in "artists" compared with "non-artists". *Journal of Parapsychology,* 33, 57-69.

Murphy, C. (1963). Creativity and its relation to extrasensory perception. *Journal of the American Society for Psychical Research*, 57, 203-214.

Murphy, S.T., Monahan, J.L. & Zajonc, R.B. (1995). Additivity of nonconscious affect: Combined effects of priming and exposure. *Journal of Personality and Social Psychology*, 69, 589-602.

— & Zajonc, R.B. (1993). Affect, cognition and awareness: Affective priming with optimal and suboptimal stimulus exposures. *Journal of Personality and Social Psychology*, 64, 723-739.

Myers, F.W.H. (1903/1961). *Human Personality and Its Survival of Bodily Death.* New York: University Books.

Nash, C.B. (1960). The effect of subject-experimenter attitudes on clairvoyance scores. *Journal of Parapsychology*, 24, 189-198.

Nash, C.B. & Nash, C.S. (1968). Effect of target selection, field dependence, and body concept on ESP performance. *Journal of Parapsychology*, 32, 249-257.

Neppe, V. (1983). Temporal lobe symptomatology in subjective paranormal experiences. *Journal of the American Society for Psychical Research*, 77, 1-30.

Palmer, J. (1977). Attitudes and personality traits in experimental ESP research. In Benjamin Wolman (Ed.), *Handbook of Parapsychology* (pp.175-201). New York: Van Nostrand Reinhold.

— (1978). Extrasensory perception: Research findings. In Stanley Krippner (Ed.), *Advances in Parapsychological Research. Volume 2*. New York: Plenum Press.

— (1982). ESP research findings: 1976-1978. In Stanley Krippner (Ed.), *Advances in Parapsychological Research. Volume 3.* New York: Plenum Press.

— (1992). Effect of a threatening subliminal stimulus on the perceptual ESP test: A partial replication. *Journal of Parapsychology*, 56, 189-204.

— (1994). Explorations with the perceptual ESP Test. *Journal of Parapsychology*, 58, 115-148.

— (1997). Correlates of ESP magnitude and direction in the PRL and RRC autoganzfeld data bases. *Proceedings of the Parapsychological Association,* 40 : 283-298.

— (1998). The perceptual ESP test in a religious context. In M.J. Schlitz & N.L. Zingrone (Eds.), *Research in Parapsychology 1993.* Lanham, MD: Scarecrow Press, 115-119.

— (2001). Motor automatisms as a vehicle of ESP expression. *Journal of Parapsychology,* 65, 372-373 (abstract).

— & Johnson, M. (1991). Defensiveness and brain hemisphere stimulation in a perceptually mediated ESP task. *Journal of Parapsychology,* 55, 329-348.

— Khamashta, K. & Israelson, K. (1979). An ESP ganzfeld experiment with transcendental meditators. *Journal of the American Society for Psychical Research*, 73, 333-348.

Parker, A. (1975). Some findings relevant to the change in state hypothesis. In J.D. Morris, W.G. Roll & R.L. Morris (Eds.), *Research in Parapsychology* (pp. 40-42). Metuchen, NJ: Scarecrow Press.

— & Beloff, J. (1970). Hypnotically-induced clairvoyant dreams: A partial replication and attempted confirmation. *Journal of the American Society for Psychical Research,* 64, 432-442.

Popper, K.R. & Eccles, J.C. (1977). *The Self and Its Brain.* Berlin: Springer-Verlag.

Pratt, J.G. (1973). A decade of research with a selected ESP subject: An overview and reappraisal of the work with Pavel Stepanek. *Proceedings of the American Society for Psychical Research,* 30.

Radin, D.I. (2003). Electrodermal presentiment of future emotions. Paper presented at the Parapsychological Association 46th annual convention, Vancouver, Canada.

— Taylor, R.D. & Taylor, W. (1995). Remote mental influence of human electrodermal activity: A pilot replication. *European Journal of Parapsychology,* 11, 19-34.

Rao, K.R. (1962). The preferential effect in ESP. *Journal of Parapsychology,* 26, 252-259.

— (1963). Studies in the preferential effect. I. Target preference with types of targets unknown. *Journal of Parapsychology,* 27, 23-32.

— (1964). The differential response in three new situations. *Journal of Parapsychology,* 28, 81-92.

— (1965). The bidirectionality of psi. *Journal of Parapsychology,* 29, 230-250.

—, Kanthamani, H. & Palmer, J. (1990). Exploring normal/ paranormal interaction within a memory-ESP testing paradigm. *Journal of Parapsychology*, 54, 245-259.

Rhine, L.E. (1962a). Psychological processes in ESP experiences. Part I. Waking experiences. *Journal of Parapsychology*, 26, 88-111.

— (1962b). Psychological processes in ESP experiences. Part II. Dreams. *Journal of Parapsychology*, 26, 172-199.

Rhine, J.B. (1934/1973). *Extra-sensory Perception* (rev. edn.). Boston: Bruce Humphries.

Rogers, D.P. (1966). Negative and positive affect and ESP run-score variance. *Journal of Parapsychology,* 30, 151-159.

— (1967). Negative and positive affect and ESP run-score variance. Study II. *Journal of Parapsychology,* 31, 290-296.

— & Carpenter, J.C. (1966). The decline of variance of ESP scores within a testing session. *Journal of Parapsychology,* 30, 141-150.

Roll, W.G. (1966). ESP and memory. *International Journal of Neuropsychiatry,* 2, 505-521.

— & Klein, J. (1972). Further forced-choice ESP experiments with Lalsingh Harribance. *Journal of the American Society for Psychical Research,* 66, 103-112.

— Morris, R.L., Damgaard, J.A., Klein, J. & Roll, M. (1973). Free verbal response experiments with Lalsingh Harribance. *Journal of the American Society for Psychical Research,* 67, 197-207.

Ross, A.O., Murphy, G. & Schmeidler, G. R. (1952). The spontaneity factor in extrasensory perception. *Journal of the American Society for Psychical Research,* 46, 14-16.

Rothermund, K. (2003). Automatic vigilance for task-related information: Perseverance after failure and inhibition after success. *Memory & Cognition,* 31, 343-352.

Rychlak, J.F. (2003). *The Human Image in Postmodern America.* Washington, DC: American Psychological Association.

Sailaja, P. & Rao, K.R. (1973). *Experimental Studies of the Differential Effect in Life Settings (Parapsychological Monographs No.13).* New York: Parapsychology Foundation.

Sargent, C.L. (1977). An experiment involving a novel precognition task. *Journal of Parapsychology,* 41, 275-293.

Sargent, C., Bartlet, H. & Moss, S. (1982). Response structure and temporal incline in ganzfeld free-response GESP testing. *Research in Parapsychology* 1981 (pp.79-81). Metuchen, NJ: Scarecrow Press.

Satchidananda, Sri S. (1990). *The Yoga-Sutras of Patanjali.* New York: Integral Yoga Publications.

Schacter, D.L. (1997). *Searching for Memory: The Brain, the Mind, and the Past.* New York: Basic Books.

Schechter, E.I. (1984). Hypnotic induction vs. control conditions: Illustrating an approach to the evaluation of replicability in parapsychological data. *Journal of the American Society for Psychical Research,* 78, 1-27.

— (1997). Nonintentional ESP: A review and replication. *Journal of the American Society for Psychical Research*, 71, 337-374.

Scherer, W.B. (1948). Spontaneity as a factor in ESP. *Journal of Parapsychology*, 12, 126-147.

Schilder, P. (1942). *Mind: Perception and Thought in Their Constructive Aspects.* New York: Columbia University Press.

Schmeidler, G.R. (1964). An experiment on precognitive clairvoyance: Part II. The reliability of the scores. *Journal of Parapsychology*, 28, 15-27.

— (1968). A search for feedback in ESP: Part I. Session salience and stimulus preference. *Journal of the American Society for Psychical Research*, 62, 130-141.

— (1980). Does ESP influence the recall of partially learned words? In W.G. Roll (Ed.), *Research in Parapsychology* (pp. 54-57). Metuchen, NJ: Scarecrow Press.

— (1986). Subliminal perception and ESP: Order in diversity? *Journal of the American Society for Psychical Research*, 80, 241-264.

— (1988). *Parapsychology and Psychology: Matches and Mismatches.* Jefferson, NC: McFarland, Inc.

Schmeidler, G.S. & McConnell, R.A. (1958). *ESP and personality patterns.* New Haven: Yale University Press.

Schlitz, M.J. & Honorton, C. (1992). Ganzfeld ESP performance within an artistically gifted population. *Journal of the American Society for Psychical Research*, 86, 83-98.

Schwartz, B.E. (1971). *Parent-Child Telepathy.* New York: Garrett Publications.

Schwartz, N. & Bless, H. (1992). Constructing reality and its alternatives: An inclusion/exclusion model of assimilation and contrast effects in social judgments. In L.L. Martin & A. Tesser

(Eds.), *The Construction of Social Judgments* (pp. 217-245). Hillsdale, NJ: Lawrence Erlbaum Associates, Inc.

Shevrin, H. (1988). Unconscious conflict: A convergent psychodynamic and electrophysiological approach. In M. Horowitz (Ed.), *Psychodynamics and Cognition* (pp.117-167). Chicago: University of Chicago Press.

—, Bond, J.A., Brakel, L.A., Hertel, R.K. & Williams, W.J. (1996). *Conscious and Unconscious Processes.* New York: Guilford Press.

Shrager, E.F. (1978). The effect of sender-receiver relationship and associated personality variables on ESP scoring in young children. *Journal of the American Society for Psychical Research,* 72, 35-47.

Sigstedt, C.O. (1952). *The Swedenborg Epic: The Life and Works of Emanuel Swedenborg.* New York: Bookman Associates.

Skibinsky, M. (1950). A comparison of names and symbols in a distance ESP test. *Journal of Parapsychology*, 14, 140-156.

Sohlberg, S., Billinghurst, A. & Nylen, S. (1998). Moderation of mood change after subliminal symbiotic stimulation: Four experiments contributing to the further demystification of Silverman's "mommy and I are one" findings. *Journal of Research in Personality,* 32, 33-54.

—, Samuelberg, P., Siden, Y. & Thorn, C. (1998). Let the healer beware: Two experiments suggesting conditions when the effects of Silverman's "Mommy and I are One" phrase are negative. *Psychoanalytic Psychology,* 15, 93-114.

Solfvin, G.F., Kelly, E.F. & Burdick, D.S. (1978). Some new methods of analysis for preferential-ranking data. *Journal of the American Society for Psychical Research,* 72, 93-110.

Sondow, N. (1979). Effects of associations and feedback on psi in the ganzfeld: Is there more than meets the judge's eye? *Journal of the American Society for Psychical Research,* 73, 123-150.

— (1987). Exploring hypnotizability, creativity, and psi: Conscious and unconscious components to psi success in the ganzfeld. In Debra Weiner & Roger Nelson (Eds.), *Research in Parapsychology* (pp. 42-47). Metuchen, NJ: Scarecrow Press.

Spottiswoode, S.J. & May, E.C. (2003). Skin conductance prestimulus response: Analyses, artifacts and a pilot study. *Journal of Scientific Exploration,* 17(4), 617-641.

Srull, T.K. & Wyer, R.S, Jr. (1980). Category Accessibility and social perception: Some implications for the study of person memory and interpersonal judgments. *Journal of Personality and Social Psychology*, 38, 841-856.

Stanford, R.G. (1966a). The effect of restriction of calling upon run-score variance. *Journal of Parapsychology,* 30, 161-171.

— (1966b). A study of the cause of low run-score variance. *Journal of Parapsychology,* 30, 236-242.

— (1968). An effect of restricted spontaneity on ESP run scores. In J.B. Rhine & R. Brier (Eds.), *Parapsychology Today* (pp. 104-113). New York: Citadel.

— (1973). Extrasensory effects upon associative processes in a directed free-response task. *Journal of the American Society for Psychical Research*, 67, 147-190.

— (1974). An experimentally testable model for spontaneous psi events. I. Extrasensory events. *Journal of the American Society for Psychical Research.* 68, 34-57.

— (1975). Response factors in extrasensory performance. *Journal of Communication,* 25, 153-162.

— (1979). Cognitive factors in ESP performance. In Merging of humanistic and laboratory traditions in parapsychology. A symposium sponsored by Div. 32 at the 87th Annual Convention of the American Psychological Association, New York.

— & Schroeter, W. (1978). Extrasensory effects upon associative processes in a directed free-response task: an attempted replication and extension. In W. G. Roll (Ed.), *Research in Parapsychology* (pp. 52-64). Metuchen, N.J.: Scarecrow Press.

— & Stein, A.G. (1994). A meta-analysis of ESP studies contrasting hypnosis and a comparison condition. *Journal of Parapsychology,* 58, 235-270.

— & Stio, A. (1976). A study of associated mediation in psi-mediated instrumental response. *Journal of the American Society for Psychical Research,* 70, 55-64.

—, O'Rourke, D., Barile, F., Wolyniec, J., Bianco, J. & Rumore, C. (1976). A study of motivational arousal and self-concept in psi-mediated instrumental response. *Journal of the American Society for Psychical Research,* 70, 167-178.

Stevenson, I. (1970). *Telepathic Impressions.* Charlottesville: University of Virginia Press.

Stuart, C.E. (1946). GESP experiments with the free-response method. *Journal of Parapsychology,* 10, 21-35.

Targ, R. (2004). *Limitless Mind.* Novato, CA: New World Library.

Tart, C.T. (1976). *Learning to Use Extrasensory Perception.* Chicago: University of Chicago Press.

Utts, J.M. (1996). An assessment of the evidence for psychic functioning. *Journal of Scientific Exploration,* 10, 3-30.

Walker, E.H. (1975). Foundations of parapsychological phenomena. In L. Oteri (Ed.), *Quantum Physics and Parapsychology.* New York: Parapsychology Foundation.

Watt, C.A. (1996). Knowing the unknown: Participants' insight in three forced-choice ESP studies. *Journal of the American Society for Psychical Research,* 90, 97-114.

Weggener, D.T. & Petty, R.E. (1995). Flexible correction processes in social judgment: The role naive theories in corrections for perceived bias. *Journal of Personality and Social Psychology,* 68, 36-51.

Weinberger, J., Kelner, S. & McClelland, D. (1997). The effects of subliminal symbiotic stimulation on free-response and self-report mood. *The Journal of Nervous and Mental Disease,* 185, 599-605.

Weiner, D.H. & Haight, J. (1980). Psi within a test of memory: A partial replication. In W. G. Roll (Ed.), *Research in Parapsychology.* Metuchen, NJ: Scarecrow Press.

Whiteman, J.H.M. (1977). Parapsychology and physics. In Benjamin Wolman (Ed.), *Handbook of Parapsychology* (pp.730-756), New York: Van Nostrand Reinhold.

Whitman, W. (1900). *Leaves of Grass.* Philadelphia: David McKay.

Zeigarnik, B. (1927). Das Behalten erledigter und unerledigter Handlungen. *Psychologische Forschung*, 9, 1-85.

— (1967). On finished and unfinished tasks. In W.D. Ellis (Ed.), *A Sourcebook of Gestalt Psychology*. New York: Humanities Press.

Anomalous Cognition in the Light of Sri Aurobindo's Theory of Knowledge

MATTHIJS CORNELISSEN

> "Nothing can be taught to the mind which is not already concealed as potential knowledge in the unfolding soul of the creature. ...We know the Divine and become the Divine, because we are That already in our secret nature. All teaching is a revealing, all becoming is an unfolding."
>
> *-Sri Aurobindo*

Like Virochanā[1], mainstream science takes matter as the ultimate reality and objective, sense-based observation as the ultimate assayer of truth. According to Sri Aurobindo, our dependence on the senses is not more than a habit, formed during our gradual and as yet incomplete development out of the ignorance. Like many great mystics before him, he holds that knowledge comes essentially from within. In a short essay on education he says that the "first principle of true teaching is that nothing can be taught" (Aurobindo, 2003) and throughout his works one can find passages in which he

[1] See the *Chāndogya Upaniṣad* (8. 7-12)

indicates that even knowledge which seems to come from outside is actually the reactivation of a deep pre-existent inner knowledge. What should we understand under this inner knowledge, this knowledge of the Self ? Does it, indeed, as the Upaniṣads say, make us immortal? Does it, indeed, make everything known? Is such a thing really possible? And if it is, how could it be developed? Could we base a new approach to psychology on it?

Two Concepts of Consciousness

In itself there is nothing new in the idea that knowledge comes from within. The very word education means to bring out, and certainly in the mystical domain, apparently new realisations tend to feel subjectively more like the recovery of a knowledge which had always been part of oneself, than like the acquisition of something entirely new. In the Vedic literature, on which Sri Aurobindo builds, there is frequent mention of a secret knowledge by which everything is known, *yasmin vijñāte sarvam vijñātam*. In principle one could take this "knowledge by which everything is known" in the weak sense of the self-awareness which is implicitly present in all human knowledge. Sri Aurobindo takes it however, in line with the tradition, in the strong sense of a core-knowledge, which is not only the essence and foundation of all other knowledge but which can even provide the detailed content of all other forms of knowing. The key to understanding how this, at first sight rather amazing claim, might actually be possible rests in the Vedic conceptualisation of consciousness and its relation to the basic structure of reality.

Modern science has had a difficult time with consciousness. For most of the twentieth century consciousness was simply taboo in science and even now the new interdisciplinary field of consciousness studies is plagued by what Chalmers calls the "hard problem" how the (objective) brain can cause (subjective) awareness. The issues involved are complex, but simplifying things drastically, one could perhaps say that the historical origin of the problem can be traced to the protracted civil war in post-medieval Europe between the scientific enterprise and the Roman Catholic Church. Their struggle for epistemic hegemony was never fully settled, but it did lead to a truce which divided the knowledge territory into two separate realms with the objective outer half of reality allotted to science and the subjective inner half to the Church. Both science and religion have basically kept to the terms of the settlement and science has focussed its attention primarily on the objective external reality, adopting a "view from nowhere" which studiously ignores the subjective side of the knowledge process. Recent progress in the fields of artificial intelligence, neurophysiology, and biotechnology has, however, forced consciousness back into scientific focus as it seems to be the main difference left between man and machine[2].

There is little consensus within the field of consciousness studies, but the view that in the prestigious *Journal of Consciousness Studies* is most commonly described as mainstream is probably John Searle's *Emergentism* (e.g., Searle, 2006). There are actually not that many philosophers of science who subscribe to all details of it, but it forms the starting point for most practical research projects and it is a convenient viewpoint to contrast other views with, as we all know it so well. Searle's way of looking at consciousness is entirely based on the way consciousness appears to humans in their ordinary waking state.

The main differences between the present mainstream view as presented by Searle and the Vedic view as presented by Aurobindo are as follows:

- The mainstream view is based on the appearance of consciousness in the ordinary waking state. The Vedic view is based on the spiritual experience of consciousness in which self and world are seen as one with the transcendent Absolute.
- As a result the mainstream view identifies consciousness with mind, or rather only with the small portion of all mental processes of which we are aware in our ordinary waking state. The Vedic tradition sees consciousness as that core-element of reality that

[2] On a more personal level the increasing use of both yoga and drugs to produce altered states of consciousness amongst scientists may also have played a role in increasing the interest in consciousness.

is responsible for "name and form", and it sees our mental consciousness as just one particular type of consciousness approximately halfway in an extensive hierarchy of different types of conscious existence ranging from spirit to matter.

- In our ordinary waking state, matter looks subconscious and spirit superconscious. In the Vedic view both are manifestations of consciousness, though in entirely different ways.

- In the mainstream view, consciousness is an exception, occurring only in the complex nervous systems of mammals and perhaps a few other types of animals. (Some restrict it to humans, and others extend it even to sufficiently complex machines.) In the Vedic view, consciousness is pervasive throughout existence: it manifests subjectively as *puruṣa* (self) and objectively as *prakṛti* (nature).[3] In the ultimate Transcendent it is still there as an integral part of the indivisible unity of *sat*, *chit* and *ānanda* (existence, consciousness and joy).

- In the mainstream view, consciousness is a late entrant in the play: it is a (difficult to explain) result emerging[4] from an essentially chance-driven evolution. In the Vedic view, consciousness is there from before time.

---

[3] In contrast to the Tāntric literature, in which Śiva and Śaktī imply and include each other, Sāṃkhya takes its division between *puruṣa* and *prakṛti* (Self and Nature) as almost absolute: it sees consciousness as the central power of the *puruṣa*, and nature as empty of consciousness. The idea that matter is void of consciousness is common even amongst Vedāntins, but it goes against many passages in the Vedas and older Upaniṣads, which assert that everything is a manifestation of consciousness.

[4] In this context it may be noted that "emergence" is not a valid explanatory category, but simply a poorly concealed admission of ignorance. Searle's *Emergentism* states that consciousness is different from matter and yet, in an entirely unknown fashion, arises from it. The two examples he uses to buttress his position, fluidity and higher order patterns in the game of life, are both poorly chosen. While nobody has the faintest idea how objective phenomena in the physical world could give rise to subjective awareness, the laws of fluid mechanics can be derived entirely from the properties of the molecules making up the fluids concerned. Within physics, fluidity is in fact a standard example to support the idea that physicalist reductionism, to which Searle is opposed, actually does work. Similarly, the appearance of higher order structures (like lines and triangles)

- In the mainstream view, consciousness is basically one-dimensional: there is essentially only one type of consciousness, of which one can have more or less (leading to the states of wakefulness, dream, sleep and coma). In the Vedic view there are many different varieties of consciousness, which form together a complex spectrum of different worlds, each representing a different type of relationship between *puruṣa* and *prakṛti*.

- In the mainstream view, consciousness is centred in the ego and identified with the mind. As such it is intrinsically intentional: it always maintains a difference between subject and object.[5] In the Vedic view, consciousness can be centred in the ego, in the atman, the Brahman or even nowhere at all; as such it can be dual, biune, unitary, or even "empty".

- In the mainstream view, consciousness is limited to awareness. In the Vedic view, at least the way Sri Aurobindo interprets it, consciousness is also a power: *chit* is also *chit-shakti* (or *chit-tapas*).[6]

- In the mainstream view, consciousness is nothing more than an epiphenomenon caused by physical processes, but without any possibility of affecting the physical world.

  In the Vedic view, consciousness is the essential nature of reality. As long as our consciousness is tied to its physical

---

in the game of life, proves the opposite of what Searle thinks. The higher order phenomena he mentions do not actually occur within the world of the game of life itself, as the automata that make up the game of life have no way to detect them. They occur only in the minds of human observers who recognise them as such, exactly because they have these patterns already as pre-existent structures within themselves.

[5] Searle acknowledges that there are non-intentional states of consciousness even in the waking state, but in this he seems to be the exception (Searle, 2005).

[6] There are other schools of Vedānta that limit consciousness to its witness aspect. In Sri Aurobindo's view this is a useful, even necessary device in the earlier stages of Sādhanā, but it cannot be the ultimate truth, as the manifestation could not have come into existence unless power was an essential element of the ultimate nature of Brahman.

> embodiment, we are, indeed, the puppets of the (seemingly) unconscious processes of nature. However, when we free ourselves from those bonds, we attain the state of a pure witness, and when we take one further step and identify with the cosmic consciousness supporting and inhabiting the manifestation, we can affect events out of a genuine freedom, not from without, but from within.

Considering these differences one could get the impression that naming both concepts as "consciousness" is simply a mistake, but looking closer it becomes clear that the mainstream conceptualisation of consciousness simply covers one amongst many forms of consciousness recognised as such in the Vedic view. For the rest of this paper I will use the word "consciousness" systematically in the wider, more comprehensive Vedic sense.

TABLE 1. TWO CONCEPTUALISATIONS OF CONSCIOUSNESS

Mainstream view	**Vedic view**
derived from mind as experienced in the ordinary waking state	derived from *cit* as experienced in a state of cosmic consciousness
consciousness is less than mind: only a few mental processes are conscious	consciousness is more than mind: mind is only one type of consciousness
an exception	pervasive, in & beyond space
a late arrival	from before time
one-dimensional	many types and levels
centred in the ego	centred in the *ātman* (Self)
only awareness	awareness as well as power: *cit* as well as *cit-tapas*
an epiphenomenon	the essence of self & world

Types of Consciousness in Nature

Before we come back to the possibility of knowledge from within, we need to discuss a little further the different types of consciousness (and knowledge) that occur in nature, and especially look at Sri Aurobindo's concept of an ongoing evolution of consciousness.

One can divide the different types of consciousness in nature in various ways, but for our present purpose, a simple division into three major layers is sufficient. Within this threefold system, the layer we recognise most easily as consciousness is the mental consciousness, which occurs in humans and probably in some other mammals. In its most typical form this type of consciousness is psychologically dualistic and philosophically intentional in the sense that it maintains a strict separation between the knower as subject and the known as object, with in between these two the knowing process and the resultant knowledge. Its typical *guṇa* (quality) is *sattva* (harmony). At its best, this mental plane (the *manomaya kośa*) allows one to rise above oneself and look with a certain detachment, "objectively", at oneself and at the world. In practice, however, one tends to identify with the ego (*ahaṃkāra*), a bio-social construct in the surface nature, rather than with one's deeper Self (*puruṣa* or *ātman*), and the result is that one's perceptions are not genuinely objective but biased by one's mental and vital preferences and predispositions. The *manomaya kośa* is typical for humans, but many other mammals share at least its simpler forms (e.g., most mammals seem to share with humans the sense-mind, *manas*, though not the intellect, *buddhi*).

The second layer we can still easily recognise as conscious is the layer of the emotions, feelings, and the life force.[7] Sri Aurobindo calls this layer "the vital", and in the Vedic tradition it is called the *prāṇamaya kośa*. Consciousness on this plane is typically interac-

---

[7] It may be noted that in the human surface consciousness these different types of consciousness are all mixed up: emotions for example are clad in words from the mental plane as well as in bodily phenomena from the physical plane (like hormonal changes, a faster heartbeat, etc.). It is only on a deeper, inner level that one can clearly distinguish their separate characteristics. One discovers then, for example, that emotions and desires are by themselves entirely non-verbal.

tive. In humans, it is the plane of I-and-thou. At its best, this is the layer of genuine love and delight arising from the soul. However, its typical *guṇa* is *rajas*, and the energy that this layer provides to the human enterprise is more commonly steered by ego-based desires, likes and dislikes, with all the disharmony and pain these bring with them. In nature, this is also considered to be the realm of the plants and simpler animals.

The third layer, which in the Vedic tradition is called the *annamaya kośa*, consists in human beings and animals of their physical body, and in general nature of inanimate matter. As it is difficult for most people to imagine a type of consciousness that is entirely non-verbal, non-emotional, and unsupported by a complex nervous system, matter is widely considered to be unconscious. The typical *guṇa* of matter is *tamas*, inertia, and matter certainly does look unconscious, but this lack of consciousness might be apparent only and no more than an anthropocentric misconception. The laws nature obeys can well be conceived as expressions of a built-in knowledge. As Sri Aurobindo writes:

> "Everywhere we see Law founded in self-being and, when we penetrate within into the rationale of its process, we find that Law is the expression of an innate knowledge, a knowledge inherent in the existence which is expressing itself and implied in the force that expresses it."
>
> -Sri Aurobindo, *The Life Divine,* p. 120

To recognise consciousness in matter, one could think of consciousness on this level as an entirely implicit, involved habit of form and action. Just as our body can learn how to ride a bicycle, even if our mind has no clue about the complicated physics involved in this amazing skill, so one could say that an electron needs to know (in a completely implicit manner) how to behave like an electron, even though it has no nervous system to support the explicit, symbolic type of knowledge that guides some of our human behaviour. It is quite clear that the electron cannot have the same type of knowledge and consciousness humans have with their complex brain-based minds, but still, one can look at the ability of an electron to behave like an electron as a peculiar, involved type of know-how. One can even argue that for the electron to work perfectly in harmony with the laws of nature and the forces that are impinging on it, it should have a complete knowledge of 1) all the laws of nature (as they are all interconnected) and 2) the entire surrounding universe (as forces work at infinite distances, however diminished their influence may be). This may look like rather far-fetched speculation but mystics have always claimed to see nothing less than the Divine in each little part of nature, and a concealed omnipresent omniscience might actually be the aspect of reality that is needed to understand "anomalous cognition".

There are not only types of consciousness and knowledge below the human mind, but also above it. We need not go deeply into them as they are perhaps more relevant to spiritual development than to anomalous cognition as such, but three aspects of these higher planes are probably good to mention. The first is that there are many layers of consciousness that are far beyond the ordinary human mind, but that still belong to the basic principle of Mind. Sri Aurobindo distinguishes the Higher Mind, Illumined Mind, Intuition and Overmind, as a series of increasingly non-dual, true, non-egoic and ultimately cosmic forms of consciousness. Second, humans, or at least some humans, seem to have the ability to transcend the mental consciousness entirely, rise above the *manomaya kośa* and the whole manifestation based on it, and enter into a state of pure consciousness, pure bliss, pure existence, *mokṣa, śunya, nirvāṇa*, or whatever other names have been given to members of this family of experiences. Third, according to Sri Aurobindo, the layer of consciousness above the *manomaya kośa*, the *vijñānamaya kośa*, is a layer of genuinely gnostic consciousness, where there is no trace whatsoever of ignorance, incapacity, falsehood, suffering or separation and where each entity is a fully conscious manifestation of the Divine. It is the progressive manifestation of this type of consciousness within the physical reality that according to Sri Aurobindo will make a truly divine life on earth possible.

TABLE 2: TYPES OF CONSCIOUSNESS IN NATURE

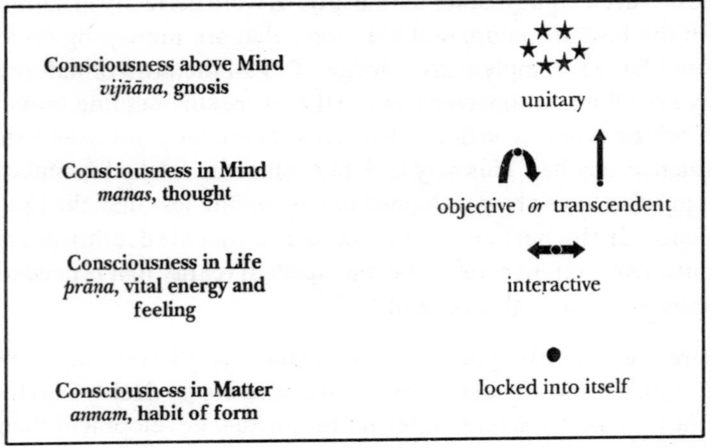

Consciousness above Mind
vijñāna, gnosis
unitary
Consciousness in Mind
manas, thought
objective *or* transcendent
Consciousness in Life
prāṇa, vital energy and feeling
interactive
Consciousness in Matter
annam, habit of form
locked into itself

Involution and Evolution

The picture sketched so far is static, but Sri Aurobindo's vision of the world is far from static. In fact, the way he conceptualises the dynamics involved in the ongoing evolution of consciousness might well be his greatest contribution to philosophy. Sri Aurobindo takes evolution primarily as the gradual manifestation of increasingly emancipated forms of consciousness. In contrast with contemporary biology, however, his primary focus is not on the earliest stages of this evolution, but on the next step, for which he finds the key in his psychological interpretation of the *Vedas*. To understand the ontological basis for anomalous cognition, it is however crucial to get a good grasp of his essentially Vedic ideas on the earlier stages of the manifestation.

Just as modern consciousness studies are faced with the "hard question how matter can give rise to consciousness" (Chalmers, 1995), the Vedic tradition has had a difficult time with the equally hard question how the infinite, omniscient, omnipotent and blissful consciousness of Brahman could give rise to the limitations, ignorance, incapacity and suffering that are so obviously part of the material creation we inhabit. Many schools of Vedānta solve the problem by looking at the manifestation as an at most semi-real, dream-like imposition on the blissful Reality of Brahman. Sri Aurobindo, however, considers this unacceptable for a truly *advâitic* (non-dual) philosophy, and insists that if all is Brahman, the *saguṇa* (the world of name and form) must be as real as the *nirguṇa* (the formless).

Sri Aurobindo gives at different places slightly different explanations for the origin of imperfection, ignorance and pain, but the common thread behind these perspectives is a double movement of involution and evolution of which the second half, the evolution, is as yet incomplete.[8] The core of Sri Aurobindo's theory of the involution is his notion of Exclusive Concentration. In *The Life Divine* (1990, p. 342) he describes the process by which the absolute unity of *saccidānanda* manifests the manifold world out of itself by a triple process of self-multiplication followed by self-variation and self-oblivion. By self-multiplication the Divine creates many instances of itself. By self-variation these different entities begin to manifest different qualities, and by self-oblivion these different entities achieve some degree of independence and lose track of their oneness with the whole. He attributes the processes of self-variation and self-oblivion to a faculty that is very much part of our ordinary mental consciousness: the ability to concentrate on one thing at a time. When you read this text, for example, your consciousness is concentrated exclusively on what is written here, while everything else you know is temporarily relegated to the background. Similarly all that the Divine needs in order to manifest one specific material object out of its own all-comprehensive magnificence is to exclude from this instance of itself everything that is not part of the *svabhāva*, the essential nature, of that particular object.

Though all I can do here is present a rough outline of the detailed and well-argued case Sri Aurobindo makes for this theory, a few things need to be noted. First of all, Sri Aurobindo holds that not only the manifestation of the physical world has taken place in this

[8] The painter Vincent van Gogh expressed a similar idea very neatly when he reportedly said that one should not blame God for the state of the world, as it was as yet only a draft!

way, but that in the process a whole series of occult, typal planes has been created which forms a kind of bridge between the Supreme and the material world. These inner worlds are entirely ignored by modern science, but virtually all mystical traditions agree that they actually do play an extensive role in the affairs of the world. Sri Aurobindo holds that most so-called paranormal phenomena are to be explained by the existence of these subtle worlds, and that even the evolution is to some extent guided by them.

Second, the evolution is not a simple mirror of the process of involution. If that had been the case, butterflies and tigers would be little wafts and whirlwinds of life-energy, *prāṇa*. What we have instead are physical creatures that express as much of the basic characteristics of the vital consciousness as their material substrate allows. Similarly the mental stage of the evolution has not only produced free-floating ideas, but also our hapless race of semi-intelligent bipeds. It appears that at every level evolution takes place through a process of transcendence and integration: the newly evolved higher forms of consciousness transform the physical structure in which they manifest.[9]

Third, in the Indian tradition it has often been asserted that desire is the cause of the manifestation, and that a complete silencing of the mind will not only lead to the merger of the individual back into Brahman (or into the Buddhist *śūnya*, the void), but also to a complete dissolution of manifest reality. According to Sri Aurobindo, this overestimates both the powers of the mind and the illusionary character of the world. Desires and mental activity may be responsible for the exact form and prolongation of one's individual *saṃskāra*-s, but they cannot be the origin of creation, all was it only because there cannot have been *karma* at the beginning of time. The mind is only a derivative deformation of the original creative force, which is the genuine truth-consciousness known as the *vijñānamaya kośa* in Vedānta and as the *maharloka* in the

[9] Ken Wilber is often given credit for the idea of transcendence and integration, but it had already been worked out in great detail by Sri Aurobindo much before Wilber (e.g., see Aurobindo, 1990, p. 702, Chapter XVIII "The Evolutionary Process — Ascent and Integration")

Purāṇas. This is important, because if the mind had been the origin of the manifestation, the world would be irredeemably mired in ignorance and pain. In that case, escape into *nirvāṇa* or heavens beyond would indeed be the only way out, as most religions and spiritual traditions assert. But if the origin of the manifestation is the *vijnanamaya kośa*, where there is variety but no trace of ignorance and pain, then the logical next step of the evolution might be an embodied, genuinely Gnostic Truth-consciousness. In that case, a full manifestation of "Truth, Light and Immortality" right here in matter might not only be actually possible, but the inevitable next step of the evolution.

Diagrammatically, Sri Aurobindo's vision of involution and evolution runs then something like this:

TABLE 3. INVOLUTION AND EVOLUTION

INVOLUTION	EVOLUTION
Sat	
Chit	
Ananda	
Vijnanamaya kosa	**Supermind**
Manomaya kosa	**Mind**
Pranamaya kosa	**Life**
Annamaya kosa	**Matter**

Implications

All this may look like a rather massive pile of metaphysical speculation which should not be needed to explain a few anomalous phenomena, but if these phenomena are genuine, which they seem to be, then the reason they have to be called anomalous must rest in the limitations of the theoretical framework in which they are studied, and if these limitations are deep and structural, then they need a thorough overhaul to be overcome. The long period during which science has neglected the subjective domain has led to a conceptualization of reality that is almost unbelievably one-sided,[10] and compared to the Indian viewpoint, its understanding of consciousness is amazingly naïve. Theories like the one I have presented above as the mainstream view occur in the Indian tradition mainly as the viewpoint of the beginning aspirant before he undertakes a serious study of the subject. Though it may be difficult for the modern Eurocentric mind to accept the superiority of an ancient worldview of Asian origin, one could well argue that the present mainstream view relates to the Vedic view more or less like the Flat Earth theory relates to modern theories about the structure of the universe: just as the Flat Earth view took the little patch of land on which we stand as the centre of the physical universe, so the contemporary mainstream view presumes that consciousness is limited to how consciousness occurs in our human brains. That science endorses such a narrow view of consciousness is remarkable as modern science otherwise prides itself on the assumption that the laws, particles and forces we discover on earth function equally throughout the cosmos. It seems unreasonable to exempt consciousness from this demand of universality, and even more so because some of the most fundamental elements of life, like love; beauty, truth and even scientific understanding, depend on it. If in actuality consciousness is pervasive, then the "Flat Earth" concept of consciousness is likely to present a serious stumbling block on the way to further progress in consciousness studies as well as psychology. In the rest of this section, I will outline a few practical implications that follow from specific aspects of the view of matter and consciousness that I have presented in the previous sections.

If Sri Aurobindo is right, then evolution is primarily the development of higher levels of embodied consciousness. He argues: (1) that the

[10] I mean one-sided here in the purely pragmatic sense that science ignores the inner half of the story: it ignores what happens inside the observing and theorizing scientist, and makes models of "reality", without taking into serious consideration that what we see as reality is not reality as it is in itself, but an *interaction* between what we see as ourselves and what we see as not-ourselves. The post-modern schools acknowledge social influences on our thinking but without a subtle, psycho-spiritual cosmology, this can only lead to a paralyzing, agnostic relativism.

human mind is too imperfect a type of consciousness to be the final resting point of such an evolution, (2) that we should consider man as a transitional being and (3) that we can expect a higher, Gnostic truth-consciousness to supervene on our present mentality (1990, e.g., p. 1-5). If the radical transformation of consciousness he predicts is not something nature will work out slowly during millions of years, but something of which the first beginnings can be effected in individuals right now, then this would have far-reaching implications for the possibilities of inner growth, spiritual development, therapy, education and many other aspects of our individual and social life. It might also imply that the most effective line of research in "anomalous cognition" would be to develop a better understanding of the subtler levels of consciousness and being that according to Sri Aurobindo make "anomalous cognition" possible. One of the most sophisticated systems to do so is yoga. Yoga is nowadays looked at mainly in the context of stress-management and personal well-being, but in the Vedic tradition yoga was also (or perhaps even primarily) seen as a method to engender reliable knowledge and right action. One could well argue that yoga relates to psychology somewhat like technology to science: on the one hand, yoga works by making a sophisticated and specialized use of psychological processes, and on the other hand yoga is an essential tool to develop a deeper insight into these same psychological processes.

In the Vedic view as interpreted by Sri Aurobindo, matter is the last stage in a gradual condensation of the infinite conscious-existence of *sachchidananda*. This gradual materialization of consciousness takes place through a process of exclusive concentration which produces on the way several intermediate layers of more subtle forms of conscious existence. As this is a process in time, what happens in the physical reality has generally happened already on these subtle planes some time before it becomes manifest on the physical plane. This might explain the experience of déjà vus and the fact that so many new discoveries give the feeling of

[11] There are people who at times experience the entire physical reality as a film which they have already seen. Though some such phenomena may be due to

remembrance.[11] Contact with these layers could also explain why so many forms of anomalous cognition involve time-shifts and elements of pre-cognition.

An interesting detail of this "layering in time", which is directly relevant to anomalous cognition, is that the physical reality sometimes seems to follow the subtle chain of events exactly, while at other times it doesn't. This can make it difficult to distinguish between genuine prevision, in which one sees the future exactly as it will happen, and the perception of mere tendencies or possibilities. Some guidance in this area can be gathered from the characteristics of what one sees, as they can indicate from where the prevision comes. If, for example, a predictive vision comes from a subtle physical plane just "behind" the physical, what one sees is generally very precise: it looks almost real, or even more than real, and the physical event is likely to happen within a few days exactly as seen. If, on the other hand, the prevision comes from a deeper plane, the vision is likely to have a more symbolic character, to happen after a longer time-interval, and the actual event may differ from what was pre-seen, possibly due to intervening forces. Sri Aurobindo spent considerable time and effort to find out how to distinguish between these different possibilities and to develop the more advanced *siddhi* of seeing the actual physical past, present and future at the same time.[12]

According to the Vedic tradition, all beings are ultimately instances of the original oneness of *saccidānanda*, and our deepest innermost self is ultimately one with the self of the All, as well as with all other individual beings and things. This is the fundamental principle that allows us in potentiality to know everyone and everything that exists in the universe as if from within, through a type of knowledge which Sri Aurobindo calls "Knowledge by identity".[13] The hitch hides, of

errors in the communication between different parts of the brain, this does not seem to explain all cases. It is conceivable that such people might be living in contact with one of these more subtle layers where things happen before they percolate to the surface reality.

[12] As this would introduce a whole new layer of practical and philosophical issues, we will not take up this issue in this paper.

[13] If then we can extend our faculty of mental self-awareness to awareness of

course, in the phrase "in potentiality". There is a very long road between our surface being and our innermost self, and the ordinary individual is not only separated from the Divine and all other individuals, but also from his own deeper Self by a thick coat of "self-oblivion". The whole question is how and to what extent we can free ourselves from these intervening veils of ignorance (*avidyā*).

What nature has arranged so far is an incredibly complicated nervous system that through a sophisticated web of interactions with its environment provides the self with an amazingly detailed (and rather fancy) multimedia representation of that environment. The knowledge this mechanism provides is, however, compromised by the defects and limitations of the physical senses and the nervous system, which are only partially compensated for by our individual intellect and the tremendous collective effort of science. Sri Aurobindo holds that the knowledge that we construct with the help of our intellect and sense organs is easy to access but because of its indirect nature intrinsically defective, while the intuitive knowledge by identity, which knows the world directly from within, is difficult to reach, but in its own realm intrinsically true. In this view, what makes it in practice difficult to rely on intuitive knowledge is not due to defects in the intuitive knowledge itself, but due to defects in the transmission of this knowledge from the depths of our being to the surface.

It may be noted that Sri Aurobindo does not think that all forms of anomalous cognition are based on knowledge by identity. In fact, he ascribes most anomalous phenomena to a direct contact between the consciousness of the subject and the consciousness of the object on any one of the intermediary, subtle planes that exist between the physical surface reality and the innermost self. The deeper the layer on which this contact takes place, the closer the cognition comes to

---

the Self beyond and outside us, the Ātman or Brahman of the Upaniṣads, we may become possessors in experience of the truths which form the contents of the Ātman or Brahman in the universe. It is on this possibility that Indian Vedānta has based itself. It has sought through knowledge of the Self the knowledge of the universe. — Sri Aurobindo, *The Life Divine*, p. 60

what he calls knowledge by identity and the more reliable the knowledge is. The erratic nature of anomalous phenomena is due to the fact that these deeper layers are ordinarily subliminal to the surface consciousness of the individual: most people are hardly aware of the intimations and influences that rise up from their own depths, and the little they do receive consciously, gets distorted by desires and mental preferences. Sri Aurobindo ascribes the erratic nature of paranormal phenomena thus largely to internal errors in the communication between the deeper layers of our nature, where this type of knowledge originates, and the surface being where it is erratically recorded. If this is true, then the most effective way forward in parapsychology should involve methods to purify the physical, vital and mental parts of our nature. An essential condition to turn our inner nature into a more reliable instrument of knowledge would then be to silence the mind, and to free it from its preoccupation with the outer senses.

The last aspect of Sri Aurobindo's theoretical framework for psychology that I would like to mention here is the distinction he makes between three different aspects of the Self:

- The immutable self, the *jivātman*, which in experience is reached by rising entirely "above" the individual nature and its adventures in time.
- The group of distinct *puruṣas* which one finds on each level of consciousness in the centre of one's individual being (e.g., the *manomaya puruṣa, prāṇamaya puruṣa*, etc.).
- The *caitya puruṣa* or *antarātman*, behind these and supporting them, which is reached by going deep within at the level of the heart. Sri Aurobindo calls this the *psychic being*, our divine essence at the centre of our evolving, incarnate existence.

What is interesting about these three different aspects of the Self in the context of anomalous cognition is that the type of "occult", inner knowledge one develops through yoga seems to depend, at least to some extent, on the path one follows from the surface consciousness to these three different aspects of one's deepest, innermost Self.

The *jivātman* is reached by a shift upwards of the centre of one's consciousness. It is our cosmic and transcendent Self and it is experienced as one with the *paramātman*, the Self of the Divine itself. While on the highest levels one reaches realms that are far beyond the mental dualities between self and other, emptiness and Being, personal and impersonal, on the way upwards the aspect of impersonality seems to predominate. It is as if the shift from personal feelings to impersonal thought that one finds between the heart and the mind pursues one in the higher realms. Immediately above the ordinary mind there is, for example, a realm of global ideas, where one immediately senses the interconnectedness of concepts that at lower levels seem to oppose each other. As one rises further up into still higher ranges of consciousness there is a growing sense of eternal, immutable Truth and the knowledge one receives comes more and more in the form of images and intensities of light that are increasingly difficult to express in words. The further the sense of immediacy, truth, lucidity increases, the further the feeling of a separate individual self disappears, and with that many dichotomies that seem acute on the mental level, begin to be experienced as mutually dependent complementarities. The non-self and the all-comprehensive self, for example, which are philosophically each other's opposite, become so close to each other in experience that they appear as half-truths representing something ineffable beyond both. Interestingly the element of impersonality which one encounters in these higher realms, is also there in the intuitions that one can receive from these higher planes while remaining otherwise on a lower level: intuitions that come "from above" tend to be impersonal truths concerning the nature of reality and the workings of nature.

The path leading to the second "group of selves" brings in its wake a different type of cognitive experiences. Our individual *puruṣa* on each level of consciousness is the very essence of our being on that specific level. One can reach these different aspects of the Self interestingly by two seemingly opposite movements: either by going deep inside on any of the various levels of one's subtle being, or by widening oneself within any of them beyond one's egoic boundaries.

The essential common element between both approaches is the dissolution of the small separative ego. What one experiences on these journeys depends on the level on which one moves. On the mental plane for example, one may initially get in contact with the thoughts of others, but ultimately one ends in a state of an absolutely pure, silent witness consciousness, the *sākṣī*. Similarly, as one goes deeper or wider on the various life-planes, one can first get in contact with the feelings of others, but if one goes further, one gets in contact with intensities of delight, peace, love and power that are far beyond what one can ever experience on the surface of one's nature. And finally, if the border of one's separative ego becomes more permeable on the material plane, one can feel with an amazing precision the physical sensations of others as if they occur in one's own body.

The third type of self and knowledge, which Sri Aurobindo calls the psychic, is perhaps the most important entry point for a gradual divinization of life on earth. The psychic being, which one finds by going deep within at the level of the heart, is the very essence of our incarnate existence, and the centre of our evolving soul. Here again, the ultimate state is beyond the division between personal and impersonal, but on the way the personal element remains present, even if not in an egoic sense. In terms of feeling one may experience an immense love for the personal Divine, a total child-like trust, an utter nearness of the Eternal's presence, or even an absolute identity between oneself and one's *iṣṭa devatā*. If one receives in one's ordinary consciousness intimations from this inner core of one's being, they tend to come as a soft, short, and perfectly to the point description of exactly what one needs to know about one's immediate situation, or as a clear indication of right action, of the thing to do.

A fascinating aspect of these three different forms of intuitive knowledge is that they come in two flavours: in the first the knowledge pops up in one's own awareness as if from nowhere; one simply knows what is to be known. In the second type, one has the clear impression that the knowledge is offered to one by someone, by one's guide, one's guru or even by the Divine him or herself.[14] Though some aspects of these experiences, the cladding so to say, are likely to be projections from below up, the experience as a whole does not seem to have that character. It appears rather as if all experience is in the end just a play between the Divine and his/her/itself which can be taken in a more personal or a more impersonal way, and in which it is fairly arbitrary what we experience as "ourselves" and what as "other".

Conclusion

If Sri Aurobindo and the Vedic tradition on which he bases himself are right, then this amazing world in which we live is far more complicated and far more beautiful than what science and even most religions present to us. The main differences are that there is a whole hierarchy of subtle worlds supporting and even guiding the physical world; that there is not only a horizontal connection exerting an influence from past to future, but also a vertical one, from spirit to matter; that there is consciousness and knowledge throughout the universe, in each little particle, force, or entity; and finally that there is a power in nature that pushes not only towards increasing complexity, but also towards the embodiment of increasingly sophisticated forms of consciousness.

The Vedic worldview and the technology of yoga are relevant to parapsychology for several reasons: The anomalous phenomena parapsychology studies are anomalous only because they cannot be explained within the parameters of the present scientific worldview, which takes only the outer physical reality into account, while the anomalous phenomena seem to depend on the more subtle aspects of reality which all mystical traditions attest to. As a consequence they will stop being anomalous the moment one adopts a more comprehensive theory about the basic nature of reality. In the Vedic conceptualisation of reality, the anomalous cognition become less erratic and more reliable, if we perfect and purify the

[14] A beautiful description of all the different guises the inner Guide can take in individual experience can be found at the end of the chapter "The Maste Work" in Sri Aurobindo's *The Synthesis of Yoga* (Aurobindo, 1999).

inner instrument of knowledge, the *antaḥkaraṇa*. The most appropriate technology to do so is yoga, which is in its essence a time-tested psychological method to arrive at reliable knowledge about the whole of reality, inclusive of the subtle domains that are not accessible to the physical senses on which modern science so far exclusively relies.

REFERENCES

Aurobindo, Sri (1910/2003). A system of national education: Some preliminary ideas. In *Early Cultural Writings*. Pondicherry: Sri Aurobindo Ashram Publication Department.

Aurobindo, Sri (1990). *The Life Divine*. Pondicherry: Sri Aurobindo Ashram Publication Department. (First published in the monthly review *Arya*, 1914-19).

Aurobindo, Sri (1999). *The Synthesis of Yoga*, Pondicherry: Sri Aurobindo Ashram Publication Department. (First published in the monthly review *Arya*, 1914-21).

Chalmers, D.J. (1995). Facing up to the problem of consciousness. *Journal of Consciousness Studies*, 2 (3): 200-219.

Searle, J.R. (2005). *The Problem of Consciousness*. (Retrieved on December 1, 2005, from http:// www.ecs.soton.ac.uk/ ~harnad/ Papers/ Py104/ searle.prob.html).

The Normality of the Supernormal: *Siddhis* in Sri Aurobindo's *Record of Yoga*

RICHARD HARTZ

The *Record of Yoga* and Parapsychology

Sri Aurobindo is a rare example of an accomplished yogi who had received his education in the West, where he imbibed the essence of the modern scientific attitude. Through an original synthesis of yogic methods, he developed psychic, intuitive and spiritual faculties and realizations of the highest order without any loss of intellectual clarity and capacity for systematic observation. This gives an unusual interest to the diary he kept for many years, which lay unknown among his manuscripts for some decades after his passing and has only recently been published under the title *Record of Yoga*.[1]

[1] Sri Aurobindo (Aurobindo Ghose, 1872-1950) was born in Calcutta, but was educated mostly in England, where he lived between 1879 and 1893, attending St. Paul's School, London, and King's College, Cambridge. Returning to India, at first he worked for the Maharaja of Baroda and was a professor in the Baroda

The experiments and experiences documented in this diary include many that pertain to the types of phenomena studied in parapsychology. Since the publication of the *Record of Yoga*, therefore, Sri Aurobindo's relevance to psychical research has begun to be apparent. He was ideally suited for what William Braud has called the experiential approach to psi inquiry, in which investigators study their own paranormal experiences. This approach involves "careful introspection and reflections on one's own experiences, their circumstances and possible triggers, their accompaniments and outcomes, and their interpretations and meanings for the experiencer" (Braud, 2008). All these kinds of introspection can be found in the *Record of Yoga*, where the inevitable subjectivity of this approach is compensated by the wealth of experiences described, by the experimenter's conscientious efforts to detect and remove all sources of self-deception and error, by the subtlety of his powers of observation and discrimination, and by the depth of his reflections on the significance of what he observed.

Yoga in all its forms, however it is defined, implies an extension of the range and powers of consciousness. It involves, as Sri Aurobindo puts it, "the supernormal becoming normal to us" (Aurobindo, 1994, p. 339). If psychology fails to explore such exceptional possibilities, its investigations of the nature of consciousness may remain at a level comparable to the stage reached by astronomy before the invention of the telescope. It may be worthwhile, therefore, to see what a yogi like Sri Aurobindo has to say about our supernormal potential.

College. In 1906 he went to Bengal and emerged as one of the first leaders of the Indian independence movement. Meanwhile he had begun to practice yoga. In January 1908 he was shown by a yogi how to silence his mind. The powerful realisation that resulted was followed by other spiritual experiences during a year in Alipore Jail undergoing trial for conspiracy charges of which he was finally acquitted. In 1910 he went to the French colony of Pondicherry in south India, where he remained for the rest of his life. Among his major works, covering a wide range of subjects, *The Synthesis of Yoga* and *The Life Divine* explain his Integral Yoga and the philosophy based on it. Sri Aurobindo kept his diary, the *Record of Yoga*, mainly from 1912 to 1920, with some earlier and later entries mostly in 1909, 1911 and 1927.

Siddhis and Skepticism

Siddhi, meaning perfection or attainment, is the general Sanskrit word for the state of being that is sought by the various psycho-spiritual disciplines of yoga. Understood in somewhat different ways in different systems, this term covers the whole field of the super-normal in its broadest and highest sense. It is also used in a more restricted sense in the plural, *siddhi*s, where it sometimes refers to certain specific psychic abilities or extraordinary powers that are said to emerge in the course of yogic practice. These belong to the relatively limited province of the supernormal that we call paranormal, thus forming a link between yoga and parapsychology.

*Siddhi*s, in the latter sense, have been dismissed or disparaged for opposite reasons from materialistic and spiritual standpoints. "The sceptic disbelieves in them," Sri Aurobindo notes, "and holds them to be impostures, fables or hallucinations, as a clever animal might disbelieve in the reasoning powers of man. The saint discourages them because they seem to him to lead away from God; he shuns them just as he shuns the riches, power and attainments of this world and for the same reason" (Aurobindo, 2001, p. 14). Sri Aurobindo found elements of truth in both of these attitudes, but accepted neither of them.

The spiritual objection to cultivating *siddhi*s – that they inflate the ego and distract from higher aims – is valid so long as the ego has not been transcended. But beyond that point, it cannot be binding on an integral yoga whose goal is not only inner liberation, but terrestrial transformation. On the other hand, some scepticism with respect to claims about such phenomena may be justified, as Sri Aurobindo acknowledges, because of "the credulity of ordinary men who regard these things as miracles and invent them where they do not exist" (Aurobindo, 2001, p. 15). His daily experience convinced him, however, that *siddhi*s are real and are part of the natural action of the suprarational faculty which he called *vijñāna*.

Sri Aurobindo advocates a balanced and disciplined ap[illegible] these matters. He points out that "in the psychic[illegible] there is a very large room for the possibility of misleading and often captivating error, and here even a certain amount of positive scepticism has its use and at all events a great caution and scrupulous intellectual rectitude" (Aurobindo, 1914-21/2002, p. 778). It is when scepticism "amounts to a disabling denial" that it becomes an obstacle to knowledge. The rigorous methods of the physical sciences, Sri Aurobindo believed, could be a preparation for recovering the knowledge of the supraphysical and establishing it on a sounder basis than before:

> For that vast field of evidence and experience which now begins to reopen its gates to us, can only be safely entered when the intellect has been severely trained to a clear austerity; seized on by unripe minds, it lends itself to the most perilous distortions and misleading imaginations and actually in the past encrusted a real nucleus of truth with such an accretion of perverting superstitions and irrationalising dogmas that all advance in true knowledge was rendered impossible. It became necessary for a time to make a clean sweep at once of the truth and its disguise in order that the road might be clear for a new departure and a surer advance. The rationalistic tendency of Materialism has done mankind this great service.
>
> (Aurobindo, 1914-19/2004, p. 15)

The Mechanism of Telepathy

Shortly after Sri Aurobindo began to keep a regular diary of his yogic progress, near the end of 1912 when he happened to be following news from the Balkans with interest, he wrote in the *Record of Yoga*:

> Yesterday there came in the mind the positive idea that Turkey had asked to be included in the Balkan Confederacy; today the same is given (in yesterday's evening paper reaching here this morning), as a strange piece of news from Constantinople and Sofia. This is striking as there was neither data nor probability & the knowledge, of the

> fact or rumour, came suddenly without previous thinking in that direction.
>
> (Aurobindo, 2001, p. 120)

Although Sri Aurobindo considered this to be a striking instance of the working of the telepathic faculties that were developing in him, it was not an isolated case. He recorded it as an example of the "continual proofs of vyapti prakamya" he had been seeing for some time.

In the terminology of the *Record of Yoga*, *vyāpti prākāmya* means telepathy. The words *vyāpti* and *prākāmya* also occur separately as the terms for two processes distinguished by Sri Aurobindo in his analysis of how telepathy works. The first of these he defines as follows:

> Vyapti is when the thoughts, feelings etc. of others or any kind of knowledge of things outside yourself are felt coming to the mind from those things or persons. This is the power of receptive Vyapti. There is also a power of communicative Vyapti, when you can send or put your own thought, feeling etc. into someone else.
>
> (Aurobindo, 2001, p. 1474)[2]

The idea about Turkey and the Balkan Confederacy was evidently an instance of "receptive Vyapti", where knowledge seems to come into the mind from an outside source. A more everyday example is: "Vyapti from Saurin of the idea of making the tea. Immediately after I heard him talk of it, and a minute after he came and made it" (Aurobindo, 2001, p. 45). During Sri Aurobindo's first years in Pondicherry, as we see in other entries, the making of tea by the young men in his household was an irregular affair that gave him many opportunities for experimenting with *siddhis*. He similarly

---

[2] Sri Aurobindo's explanations of the Sanskrit terms he used for various *siddhis* are quoted, here and elsewhere in this paper, from a text published in an appendix to the *Record of Yoga*. Unlike the diary itself, there is no manuscript of this text in his handwriting. But the substance, if not the wording, of the available transcripts (possibly based on talks) is consistent and appears to be authentic.

took advantage of other trivial circumstances of his daily life and immediate surroundings for testing and perfecting psychic abilities which he hoped to employ eventually for the benefit of the world at large.

His study of what he called *vyāpti* led him to conclude that this *siddhi* is simply the conscious mastery of a process that is going on unconsciously all the time. "For every thought, feeling, sensation or other movement of consciousness in us creates a wave or current which carries it out into the world-consciousness around" (Aurobindo, 2001, p. 20). There it may enter, often in a disguised form, into anyone who is receptive to it. A thought received in this way may, for instance, be "entertained by the mind not as a perception of thought in another's mind, but as an impression registered as a thought in one's own mind, yet vaguely but uncertainly associated, perhaps as a speculation of the other's conduct, with another mind." This is illustrated by the following example:

> B brings tea. Mind thinks of B looking for a cigarette, seeing none & possibly bringing one. There is no such look or action in B's body, but only a vague idea of such a thought, possibly, in his mind. The next minute B brings a cigarette and looks to see whether or not there were any left, showing that this had actually been in his mind and he was now verifying by his senses an idea the mind had arrived at in thought only.
>
> (Aurobindo, 2001, pp. 399-400)

An alternative explanation had to be considered, however (here the terms effective *vyāpti* and *śrauta* [inspired] *vyāpti* are substituted for what is elsewhere called communicative and receptive *vyāpti*):

> At the same time it is possible that the thought went from my mind to his and produced the action or went to another's who gave the cigarette to be placed there and then only B looked to see if there were no cigarettes already. In the latter case the thought was an effective vyapti from my

mind to his or another's; in the former a srauta vyapti from his to mine.

(Aurobindo, 2001, p. 400)[3]

In receptive vyāpti, spontaneous telepathic knowledge can arise without any deliberate focusing of attention on the object of knowledge. But there is also a more active type of telepathic perception, involving the exercise of a power of concentration that enables the mind to work unimpeded by the limits normally imposed by the body. Sri Aurobindo calls this *prākāmya.* He uses the same term for extra sensory perception of various kinds, such as clairvoyance. He explains the two kinds of *prākāmya* in this way:

> Prakamya is when you look mentally or physically at somebody or something and perceive what is in that person or thing, thoughts, feelings, facts about them etc. There is also another kind of Prakamya which is not of the mind but of the senses. It is the power of perceiving smells, sounds, contacts, tastes, lights, colours and other objects of sense which are either not at all perceptible to ordinary men or beyond the range of your ordinary senses.
>
> (Aurobindo, 2001, p. 1474)

Prākāmya of the senses interested Sri Aurobindo mainly as a means of contact with planes of reality that are otherwise inaccessible to us. This is an important subject in his diary, but is most often referred to as *viṣayadṛṣṭi* (perception of subtle sense-objects), not as *prākāmya.* In the *Record of Yoga,* what is almost always meant by *prākāmya* is the *prākāmya* of the mind, the faculty of telepathic perception which is a companion faculty to that of telepathic reception or *vyāpti.*

---

[3] This and other examples have been selected because they illustrate Sri Aurobindo's terminology and his theories about the working of various *siddhi*s, not because they are necessarily the best evidence that phenomena were occurring for which there is no other possible explanation. A text written early in the last century is in any case likely to be of more value for process-oriented than proof-oriented studies.

At an early stage in his cultivation of these *siddhi*s, Sri Aurobindo did many experiments with animals, birds and insects, noticing that he could often read their minds and thus predict their actions somewhat more easily than those of human beings. He observed the "internal motions of animals and to a less extent of men" and found his perceptions "usually justified by the attendant or subsequent action" (Aurobindo, 2001, p. 67). On 30 December 1912, for example, he wrote:

> A squirrel on the roof-ridge descends the angle of the tiles, leaps on to the wall of the next house, runs along it and ascends its roof. The first motion seen in the squirrel's mind (prakamya) before it is executed, the second d[itt]o, the third by trikaldrishti without any data objective or subjective.
>
> (Aurobindo, 2001, p. 169)

Trikāladṛṣṭi is literally "the vision of the three times", i.e., the past, present and future, but in the *Record of Yoga* it refers most often to the future. This example illustrates the distinction between two types of prevision sometimes referred to by Sri Aurobindo as telepathic and non-telepathic *trikāladṛṣṭi*. According to his own account, he could predict the first two movements of the squirrel by perceiving its impulses before they were translated into action; this would be an instance of telepathic *trikāladṛṣṭi.* But the reliability of this way of knowing the future is limited by the fact that telepathy "only brings to the knowledge actual forces, thoughts, states, tendencies, intentions etc." Therefore, if the mind "comes to take any & every vyapti & prakamya as an indication of actual event,...it falls into numberless errors" (Aurobindo, 2001, pp. 363-64).

The squirrel's last movement, on the other hand, is said to have been foreseen by a more direct precognition. A full discussion of Sri Aurobindo's attempts to achieve this kind of foreknowledge would take us beyond the scope of the present paper. But in passing we may note his comment, applicable to all such faculties, that the "condition of success appears to be perfect passivity. If there is any arambha [initiation], any setting about to know, mental activity with its tangled web of error starts again" (Aurobindo, 2001, p. 81).

But passivity does not mean inertia. To be precise, there must be a complete freedom from both "the haste of intellectual decision & error of intellectual hesitation, –the Scylla & Charybdis of prophetic thought" (Aurobindo, 2001, p. 140).

Even with regard to the reading of human minds, early in 1913 Sri Aurobindo summed up his recent progress:

> Prakamya of the thoughts of others which so often came & went, in a half-clear half-confused movement, has...become clear & luminous & its objective sign in the corresponding movement, pause or *ingita* [gesture] is so clearly shown that even the intellect cannot doubt the truth and accuracy of the siddhi.
>
> (Aurobindo, 2001, p. 189)

He added, however: "There is still confusion as to the time, place & order of circumstance of the event foreseen."

Though Sri Aurobindo made an important distinction between *prākāmya* and *vyāpti*, these two sides of telepathy were closely connected in his experience. In the *Record of Yoga* they are usually mentioned together as *vyāpti prākāmya* or *prākāmya vyāpti*; either of these compound expressions can be considered equivalent to the English word "telepathy". One reason for combining the terms is suggested by the observation, "Prakamya generally turns into a vyapti" (Aurobindo, 2001, p. 122). Once mental contact is made by an intentional act of concentration, it tends to generate currents of more spontaneous communication.

Sri Aurobindo's diary shows that the *siddhi*s relating to telepathy were among the first *siddhi*s developed by him to a level that left no doubt in his mind about the reality of such supernormal powers. The initial manifestation of these powers in him had probably taken place during his year in jail and is not documented. But within a few weeks after beginning to record his yogic progress in what he hoped would be a systematic and regular form, he was able to write:

> The truth of telepathy is now thoroughly established; the proofs of its correctness when received from persons in the house or town [occur] daily, as by it I know when one is coming from one room to another, what an animal is about to do, when someone is returning to the house & often who it is...Also the proofs of it, when it comes from hundreds or thousands of miles away, are now coming in.
>
> (Aurobindo, 2001, pp. 150-51)

Nevertheless, imperfections remained which caused him to write a year or so later:

> The nature of the difficulty in telepathy,—the mutual confusion of the retrospective, prospective, near present & distant present in addition to errors of placement in patra [object], desha [place], kala [time] etc is now being fully displayed & worked out.
>
> (Aurobindo, 2001, p. 379)

The *Aṣṭasiddhi* and the *Sapta Catuṣṭaya*

Vyāpti and *prākāmya* are two of the eight powers or *aṣṭasiddhi* that were Sri Aurobindo's adaptation of a traditional list of *siddhi*s found in yogic texts.[4] The *aṣṭasiddhi* is part of the *vijñāna catuṣṭaya* or quaternary of the supra-intellectual faculty in the system to which he related most of the experiences he recorded.

In that system, the *vijñāna catuṣṭaya* is the third of seven sets of four terms each – the *sapta catuṣṭaya* – that form an outline of the integral perfection or transformation of human nature envisaged by Sri Aurobindo during the period of his diary. During the same period, he described this system as the "Yoga of self-perfection" in Part Four of *The Synthesis of Yoga.*

---

[4]Some variations are found in the enumeration of the eight *siddhi*s in traditional sources. But Sri Aurobindo's list is unusual – for example, he substitutes *vyāpti* for the standard *prāpti* – and his interpretations of some *siddhi*s seem original even when he uses the same terms. At the same time, he considered the *siddhi*s to be part of an ancient knowledge and did not regard his own version of them as essentially new.

He grouped his list of eight *siddhi*s into two "siddhis of knowledge", three "siddhis of power" and three "siddhis of being". This grouping sheds light on his conception of these *siddhi*s in relation to the fundamental nature of reality and the deeper aims of yoga.

Beginning with the "siddhis of being", which he calls elsewhere "siddhis of the body", he explains:

> The three siddhis of being are siddhis of the Sat or pure substance. In matter, Sat uses these siddhis according to fixed laws but in itself it is free to use them as it chooses. If one can get partly or entirely this freedom, one is said to have these three siddhis.
>
> (Aurobindo, 2001, p. 1473)

Sri Aurobindo adopted the traditional names *mahimā*, *laghimā* and *aṇimā* for these *siddhi*s, but interpreted the terms in his own way in the light of his personal experience. By *mahimā*, he understood an "unhampered force" that may be mental or physical. *Laghimā* meant for him "a similar power of lightness, that is to say of freedom from all pressure or weighing down in the mental, *pranic* [vital] or physical being" by which "it is possible to get rid of weariness and exhaustion and to overcome gravitation". *Aṇimā* involved bringing the nature of the subtle body into the gross body, making it possible, among other things, to "get free of physical strain or pain" (Aurobindo, 2001, p. 1475).

These three *siddhi*s, then, are at least partially physical in nature. They are mentioned throughout the *Record of Yoga* in connection with Sri Aurobindo's exercises for the development of what he called *utthāpanā*, which in the system of the *sapta catuṣṭaya* was a member of the fourth or *śarīra catuṣṭaya*, the quaternary of the body. A possible translation of *utthāpanā* is levitation. This is undoubtedly part of what he meant by it, since the idea of overcoming gravitation is present in the concept of *laghimā*. His experiences seemed to him to support the theoretical possibility of "tertiary utthapana [complete levitation]...of the whole body raised from the earth" (Aurobindo, 2001, p. 727), though this was not actually achieved during the period of the *Record of Yoga* (or later, as far as we know). He admitted at one point that "tertiary utthapana has been unable to emerge out of the pranic into the physical being" (Aurobindo, 2001, p. 527). But more important for practical purposes was the elimination of fatigue from the body and brain so that "the faculty of constant luminous work & activity" (Aurobindo, 2001, p. 572) could be perfected. This was called "primary utthapana". His exercise for developing it consisted of walking – sometimes for as much as twelve to sixteen hours a day – and had no obvious connection with levitation.

In his explanation of the eight *siddhi*s Sri Aurobindo goes on from the *siddhi*s of being to those of knowledge and power. He relates these, also, to basic principles of reality which to a mystic are much more than metaphysical abstractions: "Sat," he says, "manifests as Chit, pure consciousness, and Chit has two sides—consciousness and energy, that is to say knowledge and power" (Aurobindo, 2001, p. 1473). When these two aspects of the all-pervading *cit* (also called *cit-tapas* or consciousness-force) are freed in us from the habitual limitations caused by our normal state of subjection to the body, we acquire the *siddhi*s of knowledge and power and become able to communicate with and act upon other beings without physical means.

The possession of the eight *siddhi*s can thus be regarded as a natural result of realizing the omnipresent spirit or Brahman in two of the aspects – being and consciousness –designated by the term Sachchidananda (*sat-cit-ānanda*, the infinite existence-consciousness-bliss that is considered in Vedanta to be the source of all manifestation). The third principle, *ānanda* or delight of being, also has its *siddhi*s and these figure prominently in the *Record of Yoga*. They are not included in the *aṣṭasiddhi*, however, but occur elsewhere in the scheme of the *sapta catuṣṭaya*.[5]

[5] Some form of *ānanda* appears in almost every division of the *sapta catuṣṭaya*, often as its last member. These forms of *ānanda* include *sama ānanda* (equal delight), *sukha* (happiness) and *hāsya* (laughter) in the first or *samatā catuṣṭaya*, the quaternary of equality; *ānanda* or *vividhānanda* (various delight) in the fourth or *śarīra catuṣṭaya*, the quaternary of the body; *kāma* ("divine enjoyment") in the fifth or *karma catuṣṭaya*, the quaternary of action; *ānandam brahma* (the realisation

The *siddhi*s of knowledge are *vyāpti* and *prākāmya*, which we have already seen to be the components of telepathy. These faculties could be expected to come easily to those who are able to enter by yoga into a universal consciousness. Likewise, there is said to be a universal energy – *cit* in its aspect of force – with corresponding *siddhi*s. With regard to these Sri Aurobindo says:

> To have these siddhis of power is to have the conscious and voluntary use of this force of Chit. The three powers are Aishwarya, Ishita, Vashita. These powers can only be entirely acquired or safely used when we have got rid of Egoism and identified ourselves with the infinite Will and the infinite Consciousness.
>
> Aurobindo, (2001, p.1474)

The difference between these three *siddhi*s can be explained most clearly by beginning with *vaśitā*, which occurs "when you concentrate your will on a person or object so as to control it." *Aiśvarya*, on the other hand, "is when you merely use the will without any such concentration or control and things happen or people act according to that will." *Īśitā* depends even less on deliberate effort; with this *siddhi*, "you do not will but merely have a want or need or a sense that something ought to be and that thing comes to you or happens" (Aurobindo, 2001, p.1475).

The "force of Chit" or energy of consciousness that acts through the *siddhi*s of power is called *tapas*. The word *tapas* (or *tapas-siddhi*) is also used in the *Record of Yoga* for the combined working of these three *siddhi*s themselves, in much the same way as the joint operation of the *siddhi*s of knowledge is called telepathy. On 8 May 1914, for example, under the heading *Tapas-siddhi*, Sri Aurobindo described several experiments in what might now be termed distant mental influence, without specifying which *siddhi* or *siddhi*s he exercised in each case. The first was one of his innumerable experiments with birds:

---

of "the delight in all things") in the sixth or *brahma catuṣṭaya*, the quaternary of Brahman; and *bhukti* ("integral beatitude") in the seventh or *siddhi catuṣṭaya*, the quaternary of perfection.

> Doves flying along the roof & past were made to turn towards it, but alighted on the edge not on the ridge to which they were directed; at first resisting & meditating a downward flight, they turned suddenly & flew on to the spot indicated.

Another attempt in the same series was slightly less successful:

> The spy near the corner willed to go to the corner & turn it, went & stood at the turn & looked down the other road but then sat down near it.[6]
>
> (Aurobindo, 2001, p. 467)

At times Sri Aurobindo saw his will being "fulfilled at the very moment, almost with the act of going out"; at other times there were signs that it was working, but against a more or less effective resistance. Seeing a crow sitting on a branch, he sent it the suggestion of going to the end of the branch. The crow apparently received the suggestion, but was unwilling to obey it. It went a little way, then

> came rapidly back, & for some minutes began dancing on the branch this way & that, towards the end when the force was applied, away from it when it was relaxed, until it reached the point as if driven suddenly by physical force, seeming several times about to fall off the tree, & then fluttered off to another bough.
>
> (Aurobindo, 2001, p.135)

At the end of the same morning he wrote without giving details, referring to *tapas* as "power": "The power is now being applied to movements in the mass where a number of agents are concerned. An effect is produced, especially at the beginning, but afterwards the resistance stiffens and is successful." After dealing with other subjects, in the afternoon the entry for this day continues: "The Power is now in small things fulfilling itself in exact circumstance

---

[6] As a former national leader, Sri Aurobindo was watched by spies hired by the British police during his first few years in French India.

of place & order of circumstance, in isolated cases, frequently, although always with a resistance." The resistance ranged from "entirely ineffective or effective only to delay" to "wholly effective...to prevent any tangible result." But by the evening, the only *siddhi* that seemed at least partially intact was that of maintaining equanimity in the face of repeated failures – an attainment belonging not to the *aṣṭasiddhi* in the *vijñāna catuṣṭaya*, but to the first or *samatā catuṣṭaya*, the quaternary of equality:

> During the rest of the day there was a strong force of the obstruction and no progress. The attempt at exact trikaldrishti of time failed entirely; the Power also failed signally to act several times and only succeeded at close quarters. There fell from outside reflections of the old anger of impatience & to a less extent of tamasic tyaga [inert renunciation] almost amounting to depression. There was, however, no settled ashanti [disquiet] & no duhkha [unhappiness].
>
> (Aurobindo, 2001, pp. 136-38)

Of the specific *siddhis* of power, the one most often mentioned in the *Record of Yoga* is *aiśvarya*. In pure *aiśvarya*, the will is exerted and then left to work itself out. But Sri Aurobindo observed early in 1914: "Hitherto aishwarya has usually had to take the help of vashita; this dependence is now disappearing. Ishita is still slow & uncertain in its results" (Aurobindo, 2001, p. 373).

He recorded many examples of the exercise of *aiśvarya*, beginning with some as modest as "Aishwaryam on ant to give up its object and go back, done after a short persistence in the forward movement" (Aurobindo, 2001, p. 42). Eventually he was able to write:

> Successive movements of birds & ants etc can now often be determined for some minutes together with less resistance than formerly & fewer deviations, but in the end the object escapes from control, often however with an after effect inducing the sudden fulfilment of unfulfilled aishwaryas when the actual pressure was withdrawn.
>
> (Aurobindo, 2001, pp. 382-83)

One of his most elaborately recorded experiments, this time with a human subject, is found in the entry of 8 July 1914 under the heading *Typical aishwarya*. First the "materials" for the experiment are listed: "the house & shop at the distant corner, the door of the house in one street, the door of the shop in the other. A child of about four going round the corner from the house to the shop. Two bamboo mats at the corner of the pavement." Next the object of the exercise is stated: "Aishwarya for the child not to go to the shop, but turn aside to the mats." The effect of the *aiśvarya* is then described:

> The child first turned the corner, took two paces, then stopped dead under the influence of the aishwarya, uncertain for a time whether to go on or return. Then it drew back to the corner & stayed there fronting the shop. After a while one of the mats was blown on to the road by the wind, but this was not observed by the child, as its eyes were turned elsewhere. (Contributory circumstance created by pressure of Aishwarya on Prakriti [nature]). It finally turned the corner & went some way to the house then paused & turned again in the direction of the mats, but without observing them. It was seen that it would go into the house, not [to] the mats.

To bring the experiment to a successful conclusion required an exercise of communicative *vyāpti* and a renewed application of *aiśvarya*:

> Sent vyapti to suggest to the mind the idea of the mats. The vyapti had effect; the child observed the mats & began to get the idea that they were not in the right place. After a long hesitation it went on towards the house in obedience to the prior impulse & then, overcome by fresh aishwarya, turned, went to the mats & brought them one by one to the door of the house.
>
> (Aurobindo, 2001, p. 539)

Sri Aurobindo seems to have conducted countless such experiments, only a fraction of which he noted down. These had a serious purpose despite their frequently playful appearance, which perhaps reflected his vision of the *līlā* (cosmic game) of Krishna (the personality of the Divine associated especially with the *ānanda* aspect of Sachchidananda). The aim of his experimentation was partly theoretical – he spoke of proving "the theory of the Yoga" (Aurobindo, 2001, p. 173), if only to himself – but there was also the practical motive of perfecting the *siddhis* as means of action. At one point he wrote: "Aishwarya increases considerably & rapidly in force & effectiveness, no longer in the old field of exercise mainly (movements of birds, beasts, insects, people around) but in the wider range of life." (Aurobindo, 2001, p. 280)

His applications of *aiśvarya* and other *siddhis* to life included distant healing, the transmission of spiritual experiences to others, and the influencing of world events. Not surprisingly, it was in the attempt to influence large-scale events at a distance that failures were most often recorded. In one entry in 1913 we come across the statement: "The two great disappointments of the aishwarya have been the fall of Janina & Adrianople & the outrages in Bengal; the aishwarya has failed to avoid these disasters" (Aurobindo, 2001, p. 241). On a "day of baffled aiswaryasiddhi", Sri Aurobindo observed: "The siddhis of power acted in small things with partial effectiveness, but failed in great" (Aurobindo, 2001, pp. 250-51). Nevertheless, during a certain period we also find him recording many instances of what he regarded as the fulfilment of *aiśvarya* even in public matters.

In any case, the exercise of this *siddhi* was always subject to the condition: "Aishwarya has to be utilised only where there is perception of the Divine Will behind." In the same entry, Sri Aurobindo described his state as one of complete surrender (*dāsya*) "whether in motion, speech, emotion or thought", extending even to "such involuntary motions as the closing or blinking of the eyelids". He added, using the formula of the sixth or *brahma catuṣṭaya*: "sarvam anantam jnanam anandam Brahma is seen everywhere" (Aurobindo, 2001, pp. 206-7).

The realization expressed by the words *sarvam anantam jñānam ānandam brahma* is the perception of Brahman, the spirit, in its four aspects, by which one experiences

> ...all the universe as the manifestation of the One [*sarvam brahma*], all quality and action as the play of his universal and infinite energy [*anantam brahma*], all knowledge and conscious experience as the outflowing of that consciousness [*jñānam brahma*], and all in the terms of that one Ananda [*ānandam brahma*].
>
> (Aurobindo, 1914-21/2002, pp. 696-97)

This is another way of describing the realization that all is Sachchidananda, with *sat* represented by *sarvam brahma* and the two sides of *cit* as energy and consciousness represented by *anantam* and *jñānam brahma*.

In Sri Aurobindo's experience, such a spiritual realization made the flowering of *siddhi*s virtually inevitable. An especially close connection between *jñānam brahma* and the *siddhi*s involved in telepathy is indicated by statements in the *Record of Yoga* such as: "It is the firm basing of the Jnanam Brahma which admits of a more & more complete telepathy" (p. 574). In another entry we read:

> The whole day has been devoted to a struggle, attended by revived asiddhi [imperfection, the contradiction of *siddhi*]...to establish the organisation of the ritam [truth] in trikaldrishti, telepathy etc on the basis of entire Brahmabodha [Brahman-consciousness] including especially the jnanam Brahma. (p. 332)

In the awareness of Brahman, if it could be made complete and constant, evidently the separative mentality that is the normal human condition might be replaced by a unity of consciousness in which obstacles to the direct communication and interaction of mind with mind could be largely abolished.

Brahman, Vijñāna and *Siddhi*s

If Sri Aurobindo's diary is taken to be a reasonably accurate account of his experiences, it may lend some support to certain trends that have recently emerged in the field of parapsychology; it may also suggest potentially fruitful directions for long-term future investigation, especially in view of the gradual weakening of Eurocentric biases and a growing willingness to learn from other cultures. Already we find the concept of Brahman invoked by parapsychologists such as Dean Radin (1997), who writes:

> The idea that consciousness may be fieldlike is not new. William James wrote about this idea in 1898, and more recently the British biologist Rupert Sheldrake proposed a similar idea with his concept of morphogenetic fields. The conceptual roots of field consciousness can be traced back to Eastern philosophy, especially the *Upanishads*, the mystical scriptures of Hinduism, which express the idea of a single underlying reality embodied in "Brahman," the absolute Self. (p. 159)

Sri Aurobindo joins the yogis of the entire Indian tradition in affirming the possibility of developing psychic abilities, while cautioning us at the same time against pursuing *siddhi*s for the wrong reasons. Ideally their awakening should be part of a total change of consciousness based on a discovery of our inner or higher self, which must replace the ego if we are to be free from the temptation to misuse our enhanced powers.

Admittedly this is a tall order in our impatient age. Yet the theory of evolution has accustomed the modern mind to the idea that radical change is possible over time. Sri Aurobindo was a pioneer of philosophical thinking on the evolution of consciousness. It was in this context that he proposed an integral yoga as a way of accelerating the process. The next step in evolution, he believed, would depend on transferring the centre of our being and action from the mind to a higher plane he called *vijñāna*, gnosis or supermind. His interest in *siddhi*s and his conviction that they can become a normal part of a transformed human nature was connected with this primary goal of his yoga.

This does not mean that he considered all *siddhi*s to be inherently "supramental". On the contrary, for the most part he took them to be manifestations of

> ...powers of the mind we do not ordinarily use or develop; they remain subliminal and emerge sometimes in an irregular and fitful action, more readily in some minds than in others, or come to the surface in abnormal states of the being.
> (Aurobindo, 1914-21/2002, p. 651)

Vijñāna – defined most concisely by Sri Aurobindo as "the knowledge of the One and the Many, by which the Many are seen in the terms of the One" (Aurobindo, 1914-21/2002, p. 414) – is "suprapsychic" as well as suprarational. But one result of the change it could effectuate would be

> ...to base the phenomena of the psychical consciousness on their true foundation by bringing into it the permanent sense, the complete realisation, the secure possession of the oneness of our mind and soul with the minds and souls of others and the mind and soul of universal Nature.
> (Aurobindo, 1914-21/2002, p. 880)

For most of us, such a transformation may seem a distant prospect at best. Sri Aurobindo never claimed that it could be achieved overnight or by a simple technique, however powerful the methods of yogic and other traditions might be for reducing mental agitation, increasing concentration and otherwise preparing our consciousness to shed its present disabilities. But a great step forward is taken when we arrive at a condition "in which the mind seeks for its source of knowledge rather within than without". Sri Aurobindo calls this the intuitive mind and says of it:

> This mind is conscious that the knowledge of all things is hidden within it or at least somewhere in the being, but as if veiled and forgotten, and the knowledge comes to it not as a thing acquired from outside, but always secretly there and now remembered and known at once to be true, – each thing in its own place, degree, manner and measure.
> (Aurobindo, 1914-21/2002, p. 887)

There are researchers in parapsychology who already seem to be aware that this is the kind of knowledge they are dealing with. Russell Targ (1994) remarks:

> A common experience associated with trying to psychically create visual pictures associated with a psi target is that it is just like searching for a memory. When you try to remember a forgotten name, you may struggle and struggle, and then give up. Only then will the name appear, upon your release of effort...The process feels the same.

In proposing hypotheses that might account for such observations, it would be arbitrary to exclude the yogic position represented by Sri Aurobindo among others. According to this view, the "true mind is the universal within us and the individual is only a projection on the surface";[7] the first stage in the "inner enlightening and transformation of the mind of ignorance" comes, therefore, "when the individual mind goes more and more inward and is always consciously or subconsciously near and sensitive to the touches of the universal mentality in which all is contained, received, capable of being made manifest" (Aurobindo, 1914-21/2002, pp. 887-88).

Sri Aurobindo was a yogi whose mental outlook owed much to his Western education. He tried to perfect his distinctive synthesis of yogic knowledge through a meticulously documented process that had something in common with the methods of experimental science. Today more and more people in the West, including some scientists, seem ready to expand their horizons by learning from the East, as the East has for the last two centuries been learning from the West. Parapsychology is a field where such mutual enrichment might be especially rewarding. Under such circumstances, Sri Aurobindo's writings could well serve as a natural bridge between different approaches to the exploration of our supernormal potential.

---

[7] Cf. Vivekananda (2002): "The mind is universal. Your mind, my mind, all these little minds, are fragments of that universal mind, little waves in the ocean; and on account of this continuity, we can convey our thoughts directly to one another" (vol. 2, p. 13).

REFERENCES

Aurobindo, Sri (1994). *Essays Divine and Human*. Pondicherry, India: Sri Aurobindo Ashram.

Aurobindo, Sri (2001). *Record of Yoga*. Pondicherry, India: Sri Aurobindo Ashram.

Aurobindo, Sri (2002). *The Synthesis of Yoga*. Pondicherry, India: Sri Aurobindo Ashram. (First published in the monthly review *Arya*, 1914-21).

Aurobindo, Sri (2004). *The Life Divine*. Pondicherry, India: Sri Aurobindo Ashram. (First published in the monthly review *Arya*, 1914-19).

Braud, W. (2008). Patanjali yoga and siddhis: Their relevance to parapsychological theory and research. In K. Ramakrishna Rao, Anand Paranjpe and Ajit Dalal, (Eds.) *Handbook of Indian Psychology*. New Delhi: Foundation Books, Cambridge University Press (India).

Radin, D. (1997). *The Conscious Universe: The Scientific Truth of Psychic Phenomena*. San Francisco: Harper Edge.

Targ, R. (1994). Psi, sight and awareness. *Noetic Sciences Review, 30*. (Retrieved December 5, 2005, from http://www.noetic.org/publications/archive.cfm).

Vivekananda, Swami (2002). *The Complete Works of Swami Vivekananda*. Kolkata, India: Advaita Ashrama.

The Rain clouds of Mind-Modifications and the Shower of Transcendence: Yoga and *Samādhi* in Patañjali *Yoga-Sūtras*

SANGEETHA MENON

The *Yoga-Sutra* of Patañjali presents a rigorous system of *rāja yoga*. The four chapters of the text deal with meditation, the steps to *yoga*, psychic powers (*siddhi*) attained, and, the nature of, *kaivalya*, the final result of *yoga*. This paper will focus on three major ideas that Patañjali presents in his text: (i) different modifications and states of mind, (ii) how the modifications are restrained and transcended, (iii) the nature of *saṃyama,* a refined spiritual tool that combines concentration (*dhāraṇā*), contemplation (*dhyāna*), and meditation (*samādhi*).

THE TRADITION

It is estimated that Patañjali lived some time between 400 BCE and 200 CE. Since this work has been transmitted for centuries by oral tradition there is controversy amongst scholars on the date and authorship (whether Patañjali is the name of a single person or the name of a lineage) of the *Yoga-Sutra.* However, archaeological evidences and ancient scriptures tell us that the practices of the *Yoga-Sutrā* have continuously been implemented in ancient India since as early as 3000 BCE. Patañjali systematized the various strands of Yoga and laid the foundation of rajā yoga. Amongst the classic commentaries of *Yoga-Sutra* the most significant are *Yoga Bhāśya* by Vyāsa, *Tattva Vaiśāradī* by Vācaspacti Miśrȧ, *Yogavārttika* by Vijñāna Bhikṣu, *Rāja-Mārtanḍa* by Bhojaraja, *Bhāsavatī* by Hariharananda Aranya, and *Patañjala Rahasya* by Raghavanada Saraswati. There have been several commentaries on the text in the modern times.

The *Yoga-Sutra* is written in the *sūtra* style. It is a style that captures the essence of the idea in a terse and cryptic manner. The word '*sūtra*' is derived from the Sanskrit root '*siv*' meaning to sew. Literally *sūtra* means a rope or thread. In the literary style it means an aphorism or a collection of aphorisms in the form of a manual. The style of *sūtra* is defined thus in the *Padma Purāṇa*:

> *alpaksaram asandigdham saravad viṣvatomukham*
> *aṣtobhyamānavādyam ca sūtra m sūtra vido vidhu?*

A *sūtra* and one who knows a *sūtra* must be brief, certain, firm and unambiguous in stating what is in the mind and is wise. The *sūtra* should use least possible number of words and syllables. There should be lack of ambiguity about the statement made. Explanation should be only of essential bases. There should be the capacity for universal application. There should be precise denotation neither more nor less than required for the statement.

The *Yoga-Sutra* has 196 *sūtras* arranged in four chapters. The first chapter *Samādhi Pāda* has fifty-one *sūtras* and deals with the ultimate goal of yoga and different levels of *samādhi*. The second chapter with fifty-five *sūtras* is *Sādhanā Pāda* and deals with the means to realize yoga and attain *samādhi*. The third chapter is *Vibhuti Yoga* has fifty-six *sūtras* and deals with extraordinary powers gained through yogic practices. The last chapter *Kaivalya Pāda* has thirty-four *sūtras* and deals with the experience and characteristics of *kaivalya* the fruit of yoga.

Philosophical Foundations of *Sāṃkhya*-Yoga

Yoga psychology of Patañjali is founded on Sāṃkhya metaphysics. Sāṃkhya of Kapila presents reality in dual terms. Consciousness (*puruṣa*) and matter (*prakṛti*) are the twin, primal, independent entities which explain the world. Neither is consciousness dependent on matter nor matter on consciousness. Nothing but *puruṣa* and *prakṛti* are eternal. They appear as the subject and the object, the knower and the known. Heinrich Zimmer (1951, p.326) says, "The two principles *prakṛti* (composed of the *guṇas*) and *puruṣa* (the collectivity of radiant but inactive life-monads), are accepted as eternal and real on the basis of the fact that in all acts and theories of knowledge a distinction exists between subject and object, no explanation of experience being possible without the recognition of a knowing self as well as of an object known."

Puruṣa – the Static Consciousness

Puruṣa is pure consciousness. But it is non-active. *Puruṣa* is distinct from *prakṛti* and is untouched by the *guṇas*. It is entirely different from the insentient *prakṛti*. The existence of *puruṣa* as consciousness is indubitable. As stated in verse 17 *Sāṃkhya Kārikā* of Īśvara Kṛṣṇa "Spirit exists (as distinct from matter)....since there must be an enjoyer...." for whom *prakṛti* and its evolvents exist (Shastri, 1973). There must be a conscious *puruṣa* besides the composite *prakṛti*.

By itself *puruṣa* is inactive. But it is that which excites the activity of *prakṛti*, upsetting the equilibrium of *guṇas*. Haribhadra says in his *Saḍ-darśana Samuccaya* that *puruṣa* is "… eternal consciousness, who is a non-doer, devoid of *guṇas* and enjoyer" (Murty, 1986). The qualities like knowledge, pleasure, pain, desire etc. which are accepted as the qualities of the Self by Nyāya are deprived of from the *puruṣa* in Sāṃkhya. Nyāya attributes both doership and enjoyership to the Self. Sāṃkhya differs in giving doership to the *prakṛti* and enjoyership to the *puruṣa*. *Puruṣa* is only a perceiver, remaining as a witness (*Sāṃkhya Kārikā*: 19). *Puruṣa* is not a substance in the form of the substratum of consciousness. *Puruṣa* itself is of the nature of consciousness. According to Vācaspati Miśra, the conscious nature of *puruṣa* is natural and not adventitious as regarded by Nyāya. "Consciousness....according to Sāṃkhya refers to an existent that is different from the tripartite process and thus differentiated from all of the transactions of awareness (intellect and so forth), transcending all objectivity whether specific or unspecific, utterly unique or uncharacterisable, sentient or intelligent and incapable of producing anything" (Potter, 1987, p.79).

The individual according to Sāṃkhya is a composite of *puruṣa* and *prakṛti*. The self-sense of *puruṣa* appears due to its association with *prakṛti*. "Hence from their association, the non-intelligent *linga* (comprising the intellect, individuation etc.) becomes intelligent as it were....becomes agent, as it were" (*Sāṃkhya Kārikā*: 20). Each *jīva* possesses a gross material body which suffers dissolution at death, and a subtle body which transmigrates. And due to the multiplicity of *jīva* there is the multiplicity of *puruṣa* also. "The plurality of spirits certainly follows the distributive (nature) of the incidence of birth and death and of (the endowment of) the instruments (of cognition and action), from (bodies) engaging in action…" (*Sāṃkhya Kārikā*: 18).

Prakṛti – The Dynamic Matter

Prakṛti is the primordial matter. It is the cosmic substance and is the first cause of the universe, which is uncaused. It is the active principle. "The *prakṛti* is eternal, one and non-intelligent" (*Sāṃkhya Kārikā*: 11). It consists of three constituents called *guṇas*. The complexity of *guṇas* explains the diversity of objects. The potential consciousness or "*sattva* is considered to the buoyant and illuminating, *rajas* to be stimulating and mobile; *tamas* alone is heavy and enveloping" (*Sāṃkhya Kārikā*: 13). *Guṇas* support one another, intermingle with one another and are intimately connected. When one *guṇa* becomes predominant, the others remain latent.

Thus, whenever there is disturbance of equilibrium of *guṇas*, manifestation occurs. The return to the quiescent state of *guṇas* is called *pralaya* of the *prakṛti*. According to Sāṃkhya the material *guṇas* are the basis of all emotions and actions. *Sattva* gives rise to pleasure, but by itself cannot produce any impulsion to action without *rajas*. *Tamas* functions for inhibiting activity. Activity is a process confined to the realm of *prakṛti*. *Puruṣa* or consciousness has no role in determining actions, since it is inactive.

Interaction of Matter and Consciousness

For Sāṃkhya, the universe owes its existence to the interaction of *prakṛti* and *puruṣa*, the principles of materiality and consciousness. The *Sāṃkhya Kārikā* uses the word *samyoga* and Sāṃkhya *pravacanasūtra* uses *sānnidhya* to indicate the interaction. It is the presence of *puruṣa* that upsets the equilibrium of the *guṇas* and thus passively starts the evolutionary process in *prakṛti*. *Samyoga* is a key concept in Yoga psychology. Sāṃkhya recognises the mutual association of consciousness and matter as essential for creation. It is said in *Sarvasiddhānta Saṁgraha* that, "Through the association (of *prakṛti*) with that (*ātman*) possessed of consciousness there arises creation" (*Sarva-Siddhānta Sangraha*: IX.15-16). Metaphorically illustrated, the 'lame *puruṣa* cannot operate without the blind *prakṛti*.' "The association of the two, which is like that of a lame man and a blind one, is for the purpose of primal nature being contemplated (as such) by the spirit" (*Sāṃkhya Kārikā:* 21).

Creation, for Sāṃkhya, is not a new formation, but a transformation of the already existent. "The effect subsists (even prior to the operation of the cause) since what is non-existent cannot be brought into existence by the operation of a cause" (*Sāṃkhya Kārikā:* 9). Transformation (*pariṇama*) proceeds from an unmanifest (*avyakta*) cause to a manifest (*vyakta*) effect. World is real and is the actual transformation of the material *prakṛti*. Since the effect is pre-existent in the unmanifest *prakṛti* it can be said that cause and effect are identical. But in the manifest *prakṛti*, there is the difference as the cause and effect. Hence, to Sāṃkhyas, the relation between cause and effect is neither of pure identity nor of pure difference — it is identity in difference.

Creation is teleological. It is for the experience of *prakṛti* and its evolutes by *puruṣa*, and for the release of *puruṣa* from the consequent bondage. "Primordial materiality, therefore provides both ordinary experience and the extraordinary knowledge that consciousness exists" (Potter, 1987, p. 83). The *Sāṃkhya Kārikā* makes the purpose singular, when it says that the ultimate aim is the release of each spirit. "Creation from the intellect down to the gross elements is brought about by primal nature, to the end of the release of each spirit" (*Sāṃkhya Kārikā:* 56).

To the question how long is the evolution, Sāṃkhya answers with the help of the famous analogy. When *puruṣa* has enjoyed all manifestations of *prakṛti*, *prakṛti* ceases to act. It is like "a dancer [who] desists from dancing, having exhibited herself to the audience" (*Sāṃkhya Kārikā:* 59).

Through the cosmological evolution of *prakṛti*, Sāṃkhya presents a list of psychic principles. *Mahat* or cosmic intelligence is cited as the first evolute. In the individual it functions as *buddhi*, for ascertainment and decision (*adhyavasāya*) (*Sāṃkhya Kārikā:* 23). *Ahaṃkāra* is spoken of as the individuating principle and *manas* as the principle of cognition. Sāṃkhya, in total, enumerates twenty four principles and *puruṇa* as the twenty fifth principle which is "neither the evolvent nor the evolute" (*Sāṃkhya Kārikā:* 3).

Sāṃkhya accepts *buddhi* as the first evolute, which mediates between *puruṣa* and *prakṛti*. Knowledge is the cognitive modification of *buddhi*. On a realistic ground, Sāṃkhya views that knowledge is characterized by both truth and error. Nothing new is produced at any time. Hence error consists not in misapprehension but in non-apprehension (*akhyāti*). If both validity and invalidity belong to knowledge, then no knowing is possible as a valid cognition or invalid cognition. If it is said that circumstances reveal the nature of knowledge, that will again depend on something else to prove its validity.

Knowledge and Release

For Sāṃkhya, bondage is due to the ignorance of consciousness and matter as dual realities. The inactive *puruṣa* can have no real bondage. *Puruṣa* is neither bound nor liberated. It is *prakṛti* itself attached to different *puruṣas* that migrates. "....it is Primal Nature, abiding in manifold forms that is bound, is liberated and migrates" (*Sāṃkhya Kārikā:* 62). Bondage and release are superimposed on consciousness, since it is not discriminated from matter. Hence bondage ends by the proper discrimination of *puruṣa* and *prakṛti*. Due to the proximity of *puruṣa* and *prakṛti*, *prakṛti* which is insentient appears as if sentient and *puruṣa* which is inactive appears as if active. This contact of the discrete principles and the enjoyed-enjoyer relation is due to beginningless ignorance. Therefore release consists in the discriminative knowledge of *prakṛti* as inert and *puruṣa* as conscious. It is "the separation of *prakṛti* by *puruṣa's* discriminative knowledge" (*Saḍ-darśana Samuccaya*: III. 43). On this conception of Sāṃkhya, A.B. Keith (1975, p. 99) remarks, "The spirit not being really connected with the nature there is no ground on which there can be produced the lack of discrimination of spirit form nature which causes bondage.... a non-existing connection cannot create a lack of distinction which produces a connection."

The realistic schism between *puruṣa* and *prakṛti* confronts many objections. A.B. Keith and Karl Potter make similar observances on the dualistic psychology of Sāṃkhya. "Sāṃkhya designates....a dualism between a closed, causal system of reductive materialism.... and a non-intentional and contentless consciousness" (Potter, 1987, p. 77). "Starting from the fact of normal consciousness the whole content of consciousness is attributed to nature" (Keith, 1975, p. 87).

By emphasizing the mutual dependence of *puruṣa* and *prakṛti* Sāṃkhya lands in a position that to understand one the other is necessary. Either *puruṣa* and *prakṛti* come into contact or they do not. If they contact then the contact is mediated by *buddhi*. But it can be asked how *buddhi*, which is a material evolute, can mediate the relation. "If the second alternative that *puruṣa* and *prakṛti* do not come into contact is taken, then consciousness will be reduced to mere epiphenomenona" (Ranade, 1970, pp. 50-51). Max Müller (1973, p. xxiii) says, "The reality of matter reduces the purity of consciousness....Once this relational nexus is achieved the *puruṣa* loses its pristine purity,....its non-relational, structureless character."

YOGA OF PATAÑJALI

The concept of consciousness as dealt by the Yoga of Patañjali is similar to the major tenets expounded by Sāṃkhya. But unlike Kapila, the founder of Sāṃkhya, Patañjali believes in the existence of god. He brings forth the concept of god to explain the initiation of contact between *puruṣa* and *prakṛti*. *Puruṣa* is consciousness attributed of enjoyership and *prakṛti* is matter, which is the active principle. "The states of the mind are always known, because the Lord of the mind, the *puruṣa* is unchangeable" (Vivekanand, 1990, p. 259). Patañjali describes consciousness as the witness of all mental modifications. Commenting on the *Yoga-Sūtra* Archie J. Bahm notes, "Whereas a thing may be either known or unknown, the functions of the mind which knows consist in its conscious activities which are wholly apparent to the soul, since the awareness constituting consciousness is supplied by the soul. Without the presence of the soul's awareness, the mind not only would neither know itself nor objects but would not even exist as an evolute of *prakṛti*" (1978, p. 153).

According to Patañjali, yoga is the control of thoughts (*citta vṛtti*). "Yoga is restraining the mind-stuff (*citta*) from taking various forms (*vṛttis*)" (Vivekanand, 1990, p. 115). "The object of Yoga is to divest mind of all its impurities, so that the stream of consciousness is clear as a crystal capable of reflecting whole reality" (Safaya, 1976, p. 270). As the preliminary step to Yoga, Patañjali gives the *aśṭāṇga yoga* or the eight-fold path that includes *yama*, *niyama*, *āsana*, *prāṇāyama*, *pratyahāra*, *dhāraṇā*, *dhyāna* and *samādhi*.

Yoga and Wellbeing

According to Patañjali mind-modifications is the cause of bondage. And the restraint of them is yoga. Three *sūtras* of the first chapter and the seventeenth *sūtra* in the fourth chapter, in a brief but profound manner, encapsulate the nature of mind and the possibility for it to transcend its modifications. (YS: 1.2).[1]

Yoga is the restraint of mind-modifications.[2] *Nirodhe* implies *yojane* (uniting with the Self), *viyojane* (disuniting), *samyamne* (restraining) and *nirodhe* (stopping). *Citta* can be described as mind with all its properties including the conscious and subconscious dimensions. It corresponds to the *antaḥkaraṇa* of Vedānta and includes *manas*, *buddhi* and *ahaṃkāra*.

When the modifications of mind are restrained, the seer abides in its true nature. The restrained mind, *sāttvic* mind, abides in the real nature of the seer without being distracted by thought or sensations or memories. In other cases, when there is no restraint, mind identifies with modifications and not pure consciousness.[3] (YS: 1.3, 1.4).

When mental modifications have been almost disappeared and the mind becomes like a transparent crystal and takes the colour of what it rests on, whether it is the cognizer, the cognised or the act of cognition, there is total oneness between mind, world and *puruṣa*. (YS: 1.41).

The knowing and unknowing of an object depend upon its coloring of the mind. Whether or not something is known is a function of whether and how the human mind is coloured by it. Knowledge of an object is a function of how that object affects *citta*. The percep-

---

[1] The acronym YS is used for *Yoga-Sūtras of Patañjali*

[2] I translate *citta-vṛtti* as mind-modifications and include both cognitive and emotive modifications of mind.

[3] The translations (if not otherwise specified) and the interpretative meanings throughout this paper are taken from the following unpublished manuscript: Swami Bodhananda, *Yogasutras of Patanjali*, Sambodh Foundation, (New Delhi: 2008)

tion of the mind is a consequence of the interaction of the object and the *citta*. Without such an interaction there cannot be knowledge. (YS: 4.17).

Patañjali gives a holistic concept of mind incorporating physical, emotional and ethical aspects. His Yoga psychology is woven around the discussion of five mental planes according to Vyāsa (*citta bhūmi*) (YS: 1.2), five cognitive modes (*citta vṛtti*) (YS: 1.6-11), nine mental afflictions/impediments (*antarāya*) (YS: 1.30) and five causes of existential and ontological pain (*citta kleśa*) (YS: 2.3).

Five Mental Planes

In his commentary to the second *sūtra* Vyāsa talks about *citta bhumayaḥ* – five planes of mind: (i) *kṣipta* (unstable), (ii) *mudha* (confused and obscure), (iii) *vikṣipta* (distracted —stable and unstable), (iv) *ekāgra* (attentive — attention fixed on a single point), and (v) *niruddha* (absorbed – completely restrained).

The various modifications and afflictions of mind happen within the larger space of these five planes. The first two planes belong to an ordinary mind. It is the nature of mind to be unstable at some point, and confused. It is also the nature of an ordinary mind to be distracted with periodicity of stability and instability. Examples given by Mircea Eliade for the third plane are: in an effort of memory, for example, or on a problem in mathematics (1975, p. 52). The third and fourth planes are reached through the exercise of attention and concentration. While the first three planes are undesirable though given, the last two planes are desirable and positive. Their invoking will restrain the first three negative planes. To restrain the first three *citta bhūmi* the last two have to be cultivated.

When the mind is in its earliest stage of disturbance, it lacks judgment and is generally hyperactive, unable to ignore external stimuli. The next stage of the *mudha* or stupefied state of mind is distinguished by inertia, lethargy, sluggishness, vice, ignorance and sleep. The state of *vikṣipta* is an advanced stage of the *kṣipta* mind. It still lacks stability and is unable to reflect.

Ekāgra and *niruddha* are the mental levels at which the mind ceases to be affected by the *kleśas* (causes of pain). They are the calm peaceful states of mind. *Ekāgra* or the attentive mind is very near to reaching *samādhi. Niruddha* is the plane where there are no modifications at all and the mind is ready for *samādhi*.

The first task is to invoke more of the last two planes of *citta* – *ekāgra* and *niruddha* – and reduce the first three.

Five Cognitive Modes

Patañjali classifies modifications of mind into five. These five can produce either or both painful and painless (neutral experiences). The five cognitive modes (*citta vṛtti*) are valid cognition, erroneous cognition, imaginary cognition, sleep and memory. All these mind-modifications are present in the *kṣipta*, *mudha* and *vikṣipta* planes of mind. In *ekāgra* and *niruddha* planes of mind these modifications have been almost restrained.

Pramāṇa and *viparyaya* comprise all those images which are formed by some kind of direct contact through the sense organs with the outer world of objects. *Vikalpa* and *smṛti* comprise all those images or modifications of the mind which are produced without any kind of direct contact with the outer world (Taimini, 1974, p.19; YS: 1.6).

Pramāṇa

Pramāṇa is valid cognition and comprehension. How does valid comprehension happen? There are three means of valid comprehension. Valid cognition is received through perception, inference and verbal testimony. The cognition resultant of these means is still a modification of mind and can invoke either painful or neutral experience. This would mean that valid cognition not only is of perceptual objects but also thoughts, events and contexts that are capable of invoking feelings and emotions (YS: 1.7).

Viparyaya

Viparyaya is also based on some kind of contact with an external object but the mental image does not correspond with the object.

Wrong cognition does not have correspondence with the real object, thought or event. In this modification of mind there is no congruence between the *vṛtti* and the object. Our concept of the object does not correspond with the real object. (YS: 1.8).

Smṛti

The first two categories (*pramāṇa* and *viparyaya*) of mental modifications exhaust all kinds of experiences in which there is some kind of contact with an object outside the mind. If there is no such contact then the mental image is an imagination of the mind. If the mental modification is based upon a previous experience and the mind merely reproduces it, it is *smṛti* (memory). *Smṛti* is not forgetting objects experienced before. It is not allowing an experienced object to escape (YS:1.11).

Vikalpa

If it is not based upon an actual experience in the past or has nothing to correspond to in the field of actual experience but is a figment of the mind then it is *vikalpa* (imaginary cognition). What we know as a result of the interaction between our mind and the object, thought or context, can not only by right and wrong but also result in cognition that is of an imaginary nature. The classic example for this is imagining a flower in the sky. *Vikalpa* is cognition without correspondence to any object. The object exists only in the individual's imagination and that too until s/he gets the valid cognition. It is an image conjured up by words without any actual content (YS: 1.9).

Nidrā

Sleep is the modification of the mind that is based on the absence of any content (*pratyaya*). Even sleep is a modification of the mind, though there is no content to it. Yet, it is not to be mistaken to *nirbīja samādhi*. The contentlessness in sleep is temporary and because of lack of contact with the actual world of objects (YS: 1.10).

Taimni explains this: "During the time a person is in this state his mind is, as it were, a blank or a void. There is no *Pratyaya* in the field of consciousness. This state outwardly appears to be the same as that of *Citta-Vṛtti-Nirodha* in which also there is complete suppression of mental modifications. How does this state then differ from the condition of *Nirbīja-Samādhi* for the two are poles apart? The difference lies in the fact that in the state of *Nidrā* or deep sleep the mental activity does not stop at all, only the brain is disconnected from the mind and so does not record the activities which are going on in the mind. When the person wakes up and the contact is established again, the brain again becomes the seat of mental activity as before. When a car is put out of gear the engine does not stop, only the effect of the running of the engine on the car disappears and so there is no motion of the car. In the same way, in deep sleep although there is no *Pratyaya* in the brain the mental activity is transferred to a subtler vehicle and goes on as before. Only the brain has been put out of gear. Experiments in hypnotism and mesmerism partly corroborate this view" (Taimni, 1974, pp.23-24).

Samādhi and Preliminaries for Restraining Mind-Modifications

Patañjali after discussing the five mind-modifications talks about two disciplines by which the restraint of mind-modifications (*citta-vṛtti-nirodha*) can be attained. They are *abhyāsa* and *vairāgya* (YS: 1.12).

Abhyāsa is the continuous and consistent effort to restraint mind-modifications. It is to abide in the restrained mind (YS: 1.13). It becomes firm with long term and uninterrupted practise of positive attitude (YS: 1.14).

Vairāgya is dispassion towards objects of enjoyment. It is detachment from desire for objects. Patañjali qualifies *vairāgya* as mastery of mind achieved through desirelessness towards objects heard or seen. Desirelessness for *guṇa* (objects) is the knowledge of supreme *puruṣa*. With the knowledge of *puruṣa* there will be no mind-modifications at all (YS:1.15-16).

Steps Leading to Samādhi

Puruṣa is elsewhere defined as *Īśvara* and *Ātman*. *Īśvara* is a 'special *puruṣa*' (*puruṣa viśeṣa*) untouched by the afflictions of life, actions and the results and impressions produced by these actions. *Abhyāsa* is surrendering to this *Īśvara* by the chanting of aum and meditating on the meaning of *aum*. (YS: 1.24, 28).

Abyāsa includes philosophical reflection (*vitarka*) upon objects of the outside world (*viṣaya*) and introspection (*vicāra*) upon objects of inner world. Reflection and introspection upon the objects of the gross world outside and the subtle inner world (mental and causal) creates certain happiness (*ānanda*) and a new identity (*asmitā*). This stage is *asamprajñāta samādhi* (YS: 1.17).

Reflection upon the objects of gross world will lead to *savitarka samādhi*. Introspection upon objects of inner world will lead to *savicāra samādhi*. These two together constitute *samprajñāta samādhi*.

Savitarka samādhi is mixed with disturbances of knowledge of meaning of words. Continued practise of *savitarka samādhi* leads to *nirvitarka samādhi*. In *nirvitarka samādhi* memory is pure there is no intervention of ego. The individual at this stage becomes more perceptive, less verbal and will have less likes and dislikes. The object of meditation alone shines. (YS: 1.42, 1.43, 3.3).

Continued practice of *savicāra samādhi* leads to *nirvicāra samādhi*. Continued practice of *nirvicāra samādhi* leads to the causal state, and stays without any impressions. (YS:1.45).

These three together constitute *asamprajñāta samādhi*. *Asamprajñāta samādhi* is attained as a result of long practice and when all mental modifications have ceased by *vitarka* and *vicāra*. (YS1.18).

Both *samprajñāta* and *asamprajñāta* are with seeds for future bodies (*sabīja*) and hence *sabīja samādhi*. The yogi at this stage will be untouched by the effects of the five elements. Yet, this state of consciousness would still have the seeds of past impressions (*saṃskāra*), though the ego is almost absent. S/he is totally detached from passions of body, but *saṃskāra* for future bodies (*bhāva pratyaya*) remain. The seeds of *vṛtti*, *kleśa* and *antaraya* persist. (YS: 1.19).

At this stage of *samādhi*, though the mind-modifications have ceased, the *saṃskāras* for future lives are still present. Evolutionary change is caused by change in sequence/order. A thing cannot be understood fully by looking at its present nature alone. What evolves is already involved, i.e., potential present. Only that which exists potentially manifests. (YS: 3.15).

For those who want to remove the *saṃskāras* as well they should continue *abhyāsa* with faith, energy and memory of what has been learnt from the teacher, and an inner wisdom that is resultant of all these. The continuous practice will lead to *nirbīja samādhi*. When you come to a point of absolute effort, surrender to *Īśvara* (*Īśvara praṇidānat*) since the final *samādhi* has to come due to grace of *Īśvara*. (YS: 1.20, 23).

Continued practice of *nirvicāra samādhi* leads to where the grace from *puruṣa* dawns upon the yogi and s/he experiences *nirbīja samādhi*. One who is not excited even about psychic powers gains discriminatory knowledge under all conditions and receives the shower of bliss and *samādhi*. Purity gained from the practice of *nirvicāra samādhi* causes cheerfulness of mind. Then the mind becomes saturated with the Truth (*ṛtamabhara prajñā*). *Saṃskāra* borne of *ṛtamabhara prajñā* destroys all other potencies. When the new *saṃskāra* borne of *ṛtamabhara prajñā* are also restrained there is total calmness and *nirbija samādhi* is attained. (YS: 4.29, 1.47, 1.48, 1.50, 1.51).

Potencies and Afflictions of Mind

It was discussed earlier that until *nirbīja samādhi* is attained there is the presence of latent potencies. When a mental activity ceases to be operative, it does not completely die out but leaves behind in the mind a potency that manifests itself again under suitable conditions. Such residual potencies are known as *saṃskāras*. *Saṃskāras* are generated from mental activities. But mental activities themselves are partly the products of pre-existent *saṃskāras*. In this way the potencies and activities form a causal series that is beginningless (Mishra, 1953, pp. 308). *Saṃskāras* are of two kinds: those that bind the individual to the sensory world, and those that liberate the individual from the sensate world. The latter type is produced as a result of *nirvicāra samādhi*. *Saṃskāras* borne of *nirvicāra samādhi* destroy the *saṃskāras* borne of interaction with the sensate world. (YS: 1.48, 1.50).

The binding *saṃskāras* are of two types: those that cause the afflictions (or afflicting activities) and those, which are the latent residual potencies of the various actions, performed. The former are *saṃskāras* of affliction, and the latter are *kārmasayas*, or 'vehicles of action'. The vehicles of action are of two types, virtue and vice, the former being the residuum of good actions and the latter of bad actions. Virtue and vice determine one's type of life, period of life, and type of experiences. In this ethical aspect, *saṃskāras* are popularly known as karmas and fall within the scope of the law of karma (Mishra, 1953, pp. 309).

Afflictions

Kleśa is a key concept in Yoga psychology. *Kleśa* is the mental affliction and causes mind-modifications that are pleasurable (*kliṣṭa vṛtti*) or unpleasant (*akliṣṭa-vṛtti*)[4]. Patañjali enumerates five afflictions: *avidyā* (self-ignorance), *asmitā* (I-sense), *rāga* (likes and dislikes), *dveṣa* (attachment to body), *abhiniveśa* (attachment to life). What is interesting here is that the nature of these five afflictions is not wholly mental but also includes attributes that concern the person as an individual. It relates to existential and ontological pains. Afflictions arise from the person as a whole.

Likes and dislikes depend on the I-sense (*asmitā*), attachment to one's body and life (*abhiniveśa*) and all these are based on the primal affliction (avidyā) which is lack of knowledge about the true

[4] *kliṣṭa vṛtti* are those states of mind, we are told in the *Yoga-bhāsya*, which are caused by *kleśa* (*kleśa-hetūkah*), whereas the *Yogavarttika* describes them as those which lead to suffering (*kleśa*).

nature of the self. From self-ignorance comes an insecure and false identity (which is the meaning of desire) (Bodhananda, 2004). From likes and dislikes arise *pravṛtti* and *nivṛtti*, the disposition to attain pleasurable objects and give up painful objects. And, the greatest attachment (*abhiniveśa*) is the attachment to the body. Hence fear of death is the greatest fear. These five afflictions (*pañca kleśa*) lead the mind towards the sensate world and block discriminative knowledge (*viveka khyāti*). Hence they also lead to erroneous cognitions (*pañca viparyaya*).

In conventional use the word *kleśa* is a synonym of *dukkha* (suffering). *Kleśa* is not an antonym of pleasure but is suffering in the technical sense. *Kleśa* is that which is responsible for the bondage of self. In this sense both *kliṣṭa* (pleasurable) and (*akliṣṭaḥ*) neutral/non-pleasurable *vṛttis* are to be restrained. This significant idea is clear in Vyāsa's commentary on YS: 1.14, when he says that even at the time of enjoyment of pleasure (*viṣaya sukkha kale'pi*) the yogi discerns it as painful and as a hindrance (*pratikūlātmakam*) to self-realisation.

Five Pains

Patañjali discusses in detail five mental afflictions in the second chapter enumerating its nature, implications and ways to eliminate them. Of the list of five, *avidyā* holds a significant place in that the rest of *kleśas* are founded on *avidyā*.

Ground of Pain: Self-ignorance is the ground on which all other afflictions manifest. Self-ignorance is therefore the greatest and foremost ontological pain that need to be avoided. Patañjali gives a grade for the intensity of self-ignorance such as that which is dormant, feeble (pertains more to the causal and subtle body), spasmodic and full blown (pertains to gross body). (YS:2.4).

What is self-ignorance? Avidyā is wrong knowledge (*khyāti*) by misapprehending the permanent, pure (indivisible), blissful, limitless self (*ātman*) to be the impermanent, impure and unhappy self (*anātman*). It is confounding pure consciousness and content of consciousness. (YS: 2.5).

What is I-ness? Asmitā is homogenising the power of seer and power of cognition. It is confounding pure consciousness with intentional consciusness (*citta* and its modifications). (YS: 2.6).

What is Like and Dislike? Rāga is mind dwelling on pleasurable objects, persons or relations. *Dveśa* is mind dwelling upon unpleasant objects, persons or relations. (YS: 2.7, 2.8).

What is Attachment? Abhiniveśa is primarily the deep rooted and compulsive attachment to body, which is present even amongst scholars. (YS: 2.9).

All the five afflictions constitute pain (suffering) in its entirety.

River that Flows in Two Directions

But then the saving grace is that 'the river called mind flows in two directions'. Vyāsa comments to the *sūtra* (YS: 1.12) on the two steps for restraint of mind, *abhyāsa* and *vairāgya*, describing the twin nature of mind. Mind can flow towards good and evil (*vahati kalyāṇāya vahati pāpāya ca*). It can flow towards the sensate world and the spiritual world. It can cause further modifications owing to the sensate world. It could also initiate restraint of its modifications that is needed for discriminative knowledge. Vyāsa uses an allegorical style to describe the twin possibilities hidden in mind. When it is borne onward to *kaivalya*, downward towards discrimination, then it is flowing unto good; when it is borne onward to the whirlpool-of-existence, downward towards non-discrimination, then it is flowing unto evil. In these cases the stream towards objects is dammed by passionlessness (*vairāgya*) and the stream towards discrimination has its floodgate opened by practice in discriminatory knowledge (Woods, 1914). Vācaspati further qualifies that 'borne onward to' means a continuous connection (to the sensate world), and 'downward towards' suggest depth (Woods, 1914). The mind-river (*citta-nadī*) can have a continuous connection and depth in both directions — the sensate world as well as *kaivalya*.

Why Pain?

Why pain? Pain is due to the false association, union (*samyoga*) of seer and seen. Though the seer is always pure consciousness it is perceived through mind-modifications (*pratyāya anupasya*). The disassociation of pure consciousness and mind-modifications is the only way to remove union and thereby pain. That is the only way for the seer to be alone – *kaivalyam.* (YS: 2.17, 2.20, 2.25).

The root of afflictions is the result of past deeds, which in effect is the reservoir of *saṃskāra* responsible for the body in the present life and those awaiting in future births. *Saṃskāra* is the cause for the experiences (afflictions). As long as this cause exists until then its evolutes such as birth, life span and enjoyment happens. *Saṃskāra* has its lasting effect on life (present and future). Life experiences can be of pleasure and pain according to the nature of acts. But for a wise person even pleasurable acts are painful since s/he knows the root cause and ground of such enjoyments. Because of anxiety caused by change and uncertainty, fear of the need for repeated experiences (habit formations) and contradictions involved in modifications of *guṇa* (mood changes), for a person who sees things discriminately everything is pain. Hence even pains that are going to come in the future are to be avoided.

Ways to remove pain

Patañjali, at various points of the text, suggests various techniques meant for a beginner as well as advanced person for restraining mind-modifications. Most significant of these are the techniques of *pratiprasavam, pratipakṣa bhāvana, vivekakhyāti, dhyānam,* and *kriyā* yoga).

Pratiprasavam : According to the idea behind the technique of *pratiprasavam* all the five pains can be rolled back. The five pains are to be treated in their dual form, such as the subtle and gross form. The gross form is the fully blown reflected existentially in the attitudes, responses and behaviours of the person. The subtle form is still in an ontological unconscious level and not expressed.

Patañjali introduces a very significant method called '*pratiprasavam*' in healing the unconscious tendencies. The subtle form of the five pains can be destroyed by a process of self-regression, by going forth (*prasavam*), and going back (*prati-prasavam*).

Hence, first the *kleśa* that are spasmodic and full blown (*vicchinam, udaram*) have to be reduced to their subtle form (*tanū* and *praśuptam*). Habits have to be traced to their causes.

The four pains in their subtle form can be resolved to the respective causes. Attachment to body (*abhiniveśa*) can be rolled back to likes and dislikes (*rāga dveśa*). Likes and dislikes can be rolled back to I-ness (*asmitā*). I-ness can be rolled back to self-ignorance (*avidyā*). (YS: 2.10).

Viveka Khyāti : Avidyā is removed by *viveka khyāti* (discriminative knowledge of pure consciousness and its content) between the *anātman* and *ātman*. It is the unbroken knowledge borne of discrimination between *dṛk* and *dṛṣya* and is the contemplative wisdom (*prajñā*). For one who is discriminating there is absence of seeing the mind as self. Then the mind soaked in discriminating knowledge gravitates towards liberation (*kaivalya*). (YS: 2.26, 2.27, 4.25, 4.26).

Dhyānam : The full-blown pains, that have become habits and attitudes, are destroyed by contemplation (*dhyāna*). And the six steps of *aṣṭāṅga* yoga precede *dhyāna*. The first seven steps of *aṣṭāṅga* yoga together will help destroy the full-blown habits and dispositions. (YS: 2.11).

Kriyā Yogam : In the second chapter Patañjali suggests *kriyā* yoga as well for the pulverization (*kleśa tanū karanat*) of afflictions, and that in turn will lead to *samādhi*. *Kriyā yoga* is composed of *tapas*, *svādhyāyam*, and *Īśvara praṇīdhāna*. (YS: 2.1, 2.2).

Tapas is extreme austerity like fasting, keeping silence, stand on one leg, sit surrounded by fire or stay naked in extreme cold. According to the *Gītā* (17:14-15), tapas is of three kinds: *śāriram* (physical), *vangamayam* (verbal), and *manasam* (mental). *Tapas* involves the disciplining of body, mind and intellect in pursuit of higher goals.

Svādhyāyam is the study of scriptures; reflect (*ikṣaṇam*) upon one's intentions, motives and physical states. The third component of *kriyā* yoga is *Īśvara-praṇidhānam* (surrender to god).

Systemic Healing

It is significant to note here the subtle and systemic way by which Patañjali gives the prognosis for both gross and subtle, expressed and germinal form of pain. The fully expressed forms such as our habits, attitudes, mental dispositions and physical diseases can be removed only by combining a medley of steps such as *yama, niyama, āsana, prāṇāyāma, pratyāhāra, dhāraṇā* and *dhyāna*. These cater to the physical (postures, breathing), ethical (societal interactions), and mental dimensions of the habit to be removed. The subtle forms of pain have to have a deeper method, and its healing lies in its being consciously rolled back to its cause.

The concept of *pratiprasavam* also brings back the key Yoga concept of *saṃskāra* and potencies. Any *vṛtti* or mind-modification leaves behind a *saṃskāra*, a potency or trace which in turn can provoke and reinforce a similar modification. A *saṃskāra* is not merely a memory or trace but also a latent tendency, a propensity, which is often compared to a seed that germinates under favourable conditions. Thus, the Yoga literature speaks of the perpetual wheel of modifications and traces. The theory also maintains that the *vṛttis* (mind-modifications) are always known, but that does not hold true for *saṃskāra* (Balslev, 1991, pp.77-88). The subliminal impressions remain unwatched and are therefore unconscious. But a yogi who has mastery over *citta vṛtti* through *nirodha* has access to even *saṃskāra*. S/he can perceive the unconscious *saṃskāra*. In the third chapter Patañjali talks about *saṃskāra sākṣātkara* (the perception of impressions). He adds that by directing *saṃyama* (see under *the master key of saṃyama and its magic* in this paper) on the heart one gains knowledge of memories and the unconscious. (YS: 3.18).

Nine Impediments to Wellbeing

The impediments to the restraint of mind and *samādhi* that follows are nine in number according to Patañjali. These could be considered as the dysfunctions of mind (*antarāya*). All the nine dysfunctions are accompanied by symptoms such as pain (discomfort), despair, trembling of body and heavy breathing. These symptoms are the features of a distracted mind (*vikṣepah*). (YS: 1.31).

The nine dysfunctions are: (i) physical and mental illness (*vyādhi*), (ii) disinterest, depression (*sthyanam*), (iii) doubt, lack of trust (*samśaya*), (iv) carelessness (*pramāda*), (v) laziness (*ālasyam*), (vi) continued indulgence, inability to restraint (*avirati*), (vii) delusion, hallucination (*bhrānti darśanam*), (viii) lack of progress, plateau feeling (*alabdha bhumigatvam*), (ix) digression (*anavastitatvam*). (YS: 1.30).

How to Overcome the Nine Dysfunctions?

In the first chapter of the *Yoga-Sūtras* Patañjali talks about two benefits that accrue from the practice of chanting *aum* and meditating upon its meaning. These two benefits are the inward turning (*pratyak cetanā*) of consciousness and the removal of the nine dysfunctions of mind. The person becomes more contemplative and introspective. There is an exhaustive list of practices that Patañjali continues to suggest in the first chapter for the removal of dysfunctions.

(i) Practice of one truth, like meditating upon a *mantra*, *devatā*, *cakra*, *bhrūmādya*, lotus, breath, one power that activate whole universe. (YS: 1.32).

(ii) Cultivating attitudes of friendliness (*maitrī*), compassion (*karuṇā*), cheerfulness (*muditam*), forgiveness (*upekṣā*), the mind becomes cheerful (*citta prasādam*) by *bhāvanā;* cultivating attitude of friendliness towards happy people, compassion towards unhappy people, cheerfulness towards good people, forgiveness/indifference bad/sinful people, and such matters. (YS: 1.33).

(iii) Breathing discipline, retention of inhalation and exhalation. (YS: 1.34).

(iv) Concentration, by which the mind becomes calm and steady as a result of engaging in concentrated activities.[5] (YS: 1.35).

(v) Concentrating upon the inner light free from grief. (YS: 1.36).

(vi) Concentrating upon a dispassionate mind, upon a person whose is mind free from attachments to objects – a passionless mind. (YS: 1.37).

(vii) Concentrating on the basis (nature) of sleep and dream. Fixing your attention upon the knowledge derived from dream and dreamless sleep. (YS: 1.38).

(viii) Concentrating on any ennobling object. (YS: 1.39).

What Can Change Mind?

Patañjali conceives discriminative knowledge (*viveka khyāti*) not as an event that happens at a certain occasion or as that invoked only for self-knowledge. The discriminative knowledge of the distinction between *dṛk* and *dṛśya*, *puruṣa* and *prakṛti* (*viveka jñāna*) is to be considered as accompanying one's awareness at all times. When discrimination weakens, in those gaps arise distracting thoughts impelled by old tendencies. (YS: 4.27).

These distracting thoughts are to be destroyed with the same discipline used for destroying *kleśas*. Negative thoughts, or any thought that identifies one with the sensate self or just the mind modification, have to be destroyed through the practices of *dhyānam*, *prati prasavam*, *pratipakṣa bhāvanam*, and *vivekakhyāti* gained through practice of eightfold yoga. (YS: 4.28).

How to Remove Negativities

Patañjali makes two major recommendations: one for the dawn of self-knowledge and the other the removal of all negativities of mind so as to attune the mind for self-knowledge. *Aṣṭāṅga-yoga* or the eight limbed yoga and *pratipakṣa bhāvanā* will remove all kinds of negativities. When discriminative knowledge (between *puruṣa*

---

[5] Vyāsa's commentary says the object of meditation can be *candra* (moon), *āditya* (sun), *graha* (other stars) *maṇī* (crystal), *pratīpa* (flame), *raśmi* (rays from stones), *jīhvā mule* (root of tongue), *jīhvā agre* (tip of tongue) *jīhvā madhye* (middle of tongue) and *taluṇi* (palate).

and *prakṛti*; *dṛk* and *dṛśya*; *ātman* and *anātman*) is perfect there will be the luminance of self-knowledge. (YS: 2.28).

Pratipakṣa Bhāvanam

Negative thoughts can lead to violent thoughts and deeds and will produce infinite pain. Negative thoughts, emotions (and actions) such as those of violence etc., whether they are done (indulged in), caused to be done or abetted, whether caused by greed, anger or delusion, whether present in mild, medium or intense degree, result in endless pain and ignorance. Hence, the need to cultivate positive thoughts. When negativities manifest in the mind opposite (positive) thoughts have to be activated. Positive thoughts neutralise negative thoughts. This is *pratipakṣa bhāvanam.* (YS: 2.33, 2.34).

Aṣṭāṅga Yoga

The eightfold yoga includes external, mental and spiritual exercises so as to suggest a comprehensive method for the final goal of *kaivalyam*. The eightfold path and their respective results in a synoptic manner are:

(1). *Yama* (restraint; ethical percepts regulating the social life).

Values such as non-violence, truthfulness, non-stealing, celibacy and non-possession are universal great disciplines regardless of caste, country, chronological time and occasion. (YS: 2.30, 2.31).

Result: When one is established in nonviolence in his/her presence there is absence of hostility. In the presence of nonviolent people, violent shed their hostile nature. The presence of a contemplative person quietens the mind of a disturbed person. (YS: 2.35).

When one is established in truthfulness s/he becomes the abode of all success. Whatever s/he does will be successful. Whatever s/he says will be accomplished. (YS: 2.36).

When one is established in non-stealing s/he becomes the abode of all wealth. (YS: 2.37).

When one is established in continence there is gain of energy. (YS: 2.38).

When one is established in non-possession knowledge of past lives arise. (YS: 2.39).

(2). *Niyama* (observance; ethical percepts with regard to the inner life).

Observances such as cleanliness, contentment, discipline, self-study, and surrender to the supreme god. (YS: 2.32).

Result: As a result of cleanliness one detests one's own body and avoids association with other bodies. (YS: 2.40).

As a result of practise of cleanliness, purity of mind and cheerfulness/good nature, one-pointedness mastery of senses and fitness for self-realisation are gained. (YS: 2.41).

When you are contented you gain incomparable joy. (YS: 2.42).

Austerity reduces impurities and creates physical and mental powers. *Tapas* is denying comforts to body. (YS: 2.43).

Union with one's chosen deity is gained through study and contemplation. (YS: 2.44).

Samādhi is attained through total surrender to god. (YS: 2.45).

(3). *Āsana* (seat or bodily posture).

Posture for meditation is that which is firm and comfortable. *Āsana* is a position of sitting which is firm and comfortable. The commonly recommended postures are *padmāsanam*, *virāsanam*, *bhadrāsanam*, *śucāsanam* and *śavāsanam*. When the mind is fixed on the infinite, effortless in posture is attained. (YS: 2.46).

Result: As a result of *āsana siddhi*, mastery of postures, one gains mastery over pairs of opposites and will be unaffected by the pairs of opposites. (YS: 2.48).

(4). *Prāṇāyāma* (regulation of breath; control of life-energy)

When one has mastered the posture then one moves to *prāṇāyāma*. *Prāṇāyāma* is stopping of inhaling and exhaling, holding breath after inhaling and holding breath after exhaling. With the practice of *prāṇāyāma*, the mind becomes fit for the advanced practices of contemplation beginning with *dhāraṇā* (concentration). (YS: 2.49, 2.53).

Result: As a result of *prāṇāyāma* there is thinning of the veil covering the self. The mind becomes quiet and the light of *puruṣa* manifests. (YS: 2.52).

(5). *Pratyāhāra* (sublimation or withdrawal from the senses).

When mind is detached from its objects following the detached nature of mind, the sense organs also naturally withdraw. (YS: 2.54).

Result: Then there is supreme control over the sense and motor organs. (YS: 2.55).

The Master Key of *Saṃyama* and its Magic

The three steps of *aṣṭānga* yoga that follows constitute a key concept in *Yoga-Sūtras*. *Dhāraṇā*, *dhyāna* and *samādhi* are together addressed as *saṇyama*.

Exclusive attention on an object is *dhāraṇā* (concentration). *Dhāraṇā* is focusing mind on a chosen limited space. Any act of concentration is *dhāraṇā*. Vyāsa in his commentary suggests concentration on the navel *cakra* (*nābhi cakra*), the lotus-heart (*hṛdya puṇḍarika*), between the eyebrows (*murdhini*), inner light (*jyotir*), tip of nose (*nāsikāgre*), tip of tongue (*jīhvāgare*), or any other external object (*bāhye va viṣaye*). (YS: 3.1).

Continued concentration on an object is *dhyānam* (contemplation). Flow of similar thoughts about the same object is *dhyānam*. It is the ability to continuously focus on a single object. Vyāsa describes *dhyānam* as objectless consciousness. (YS: 3.2).

Seeing the pure object alone (without the intervention of the ego) is *samādhi*. It is the egoless perception of the object, when the object alone shines without intervention of memory and ego, which will be the form of object of meditation. (YS: 3.3, 1.43, 2.25).

World of Magic Opens

As a result of mastery of *saṃyama*, light (*āloka*) of intelligence manifests. Of this ability (*viniyoga*) there are many applications (*bhūmiṣu*) on many domains. (YS: 3.5).

When many pointedness of mind ends and one pointedness arises, then by that practise one's mind permanently evolves to a state of *samādhi*. A stage comes when whether the mind is quiet or active it enjoys the same quietude. In that state you can say that the mind is in a state of total one-pointedness and concentration. For the yogi, then activity and passivity will be the same. The *Bhagavad-Gītā* describes a yogi as equanimous and who sees actionlessness in action (*karmāṇi akarma darśanam*). (YS: 3.11, 3.12).

By directing *saṃyama* on a respective field knowledge of that field is possible. Thus, by focusing on the various modes of manifestation of an object – past manifestation, present manifestation and future manifestation (*śānta*, *udita* and *avyapadeśa*) – one gains the knowledge of the past, present and future (of the object). (YS: 3.16).

If *saṃyama* is directed on another individual's thought, then the knowledge of his/her mind is gained. (YS: 3.19).

When *saṃyama* is directed on one's own body, its form, then there is cessation of its visibility. There is no contact with light from another's eyes and s/he will become. Through the same process of *saṃyama* on each sense organ the respective functions become inaccessible to others. By directing *saṃyama* on each of the sense organ the respective powers of being unseen, unheard, untouched etc. can be achieved. (YS: 3.21, 3.22).

Patañjali continues to enlist a series of magical powers that is resultant of directing *saṃyama* on various physical, vital (like breath) and inner objects, as well as mental attitudes such as friendliness, cheerfulness etc. For instance he says that by directing *saṃyama* on *maitrī, karuṇa, mudida* and *upekṣā* one gains mental powers. Yet another mention is that by focusing on the artery, one gains stability. By focusing on the heart, one gains knowledge of memories and the unconscious. (YS: 3.32, 3.24, 3.35, 1.33).

Patañjali suggests that psychic powers are gained either by birth, drugs, mantras, by austerities or deep meditation. Alteration of consciousness can arise as an inborn gift, through deep concentration, austerities or chanting of mantras. (YS: 4.1).

The Final Shower of Transcendence

The final or most important goal of *saṃyama* is *kaivalyam. Siddhi* is only a stage in the process. When one is detached even from the *siddhis* (magical powers) all limitations end and total freedom is attained. (YS: 3.51).

One who is not excited even about psychic powers enjoys discriminatory knowledge under all conditions and receives the shower of bliss and *samādhi*. When the mind is very quiet the light of self radiates. *Kaivalya* is attained when the mind becomes as pure as consciousness. (YS: 4.29, 3.56).

As a result of the shower from beyond, there is complete washing away of ignorance and ignorance prompted activities. Consciousness, which is free from all veiling defects, becomes infinite and the objective world, other than the subject, disappears. The outside world gets integrated with the subject. Thereafter, *guṇas* having fulfilled their purpose end their modifications. *Guṇas* without any purpose of serving the *puruṣa* fold back and become quiescent and the power of consciousness remains in itself. This is *kaivalyam.*

Henceforth there is nothing to be known or to be manipulated. The yogi experiences pure and all encompassing love. (YS: 4.30, 4.31, 4.32, 4.34).

CONCLUSION

Yoga philosophy leads to a systematic approach to human health and wellbeing. The four chapters of the *Yoga-Sūtra* comprehensively deal with physical, emotional and spiritual wellbeing. Yoga psychology differs radically from more recent, especially post-Freudian, schools of thought in its emphasis on self-emancipation rather than on self-acceptance (Iyer, 2004). According to Patañjali, thoughts, feelings, intentions, motives and desires (conscious and unconscious) are mental modifications (*citta vṛttis*). Transcending the mental modifications enables the luminance of *puruṣa* in its aloneness.

The eightfold yoga is one of the significant steps Patañjali recommends for the restraint of mind-modifications. The eightfold yoga includes physical, mental, ethical and spiritual practices that will lead to total health and wellbeing. It is also interesting to note that Patañjali is able to see the human mind from an inclusive context and that too situated in a sociocultural context. This is evident from his discussion on conflicts and negative attitudes of mind and how they can be removed by attitudinal changes. Patañjali's yoga is interested in changing people's lives and attitudes in order to gain mental refinement, and via mental refinement to spiritual realisation. This is made clear by his definition of yoga in the first *sūtra*. There can be no doubt that yoga begins its quest – a quest to change people, and not, as philosophy, to change merely the way they think – with an effort to understand one's self (Kesarcodi-Watson, 1982).

The South East Asian or pan-Indian concept of 'mind' is different from the Western concept of mind constitutionally and soteriologically. This is evidenced clearly in the *Yoga-Sūtra*. *Citta*, though for linguistic ease is translated as 'mind', is much more than mental and emotive content. From the various structures and typologies that Patañjali uses, we can understand that '*citta*' is a term that houses collective features of an individual that pertain to his/her existential, phenomenological, pragmatic, ethical, psychological and spiritual aspects. Patañjali's is a systemic approach to analyse the personality. For this reason, healing and therapy also addresses the person as a whole and not by part. Moreover the entire discussion on the limitations of mind (and the person as a whole) and possibilities for freedom is founded on the major premise that the ultimate goal is to understand and abide in the true nature of one's self which is pure consciousness.

Acknowledgement

Praṇāma to my Guru Swami Bodhananda Sarasvati, who taught me Patañjali *Yoga-Sūtra* with immense patience and compassion. My thanks to him for permitting me to use extensively from the unpublished manuscript of his book *Yoga-Sutra of Patañjali*, Sambodh Foundation, (New Delhi: 2008). I profusely thank Prof. K Ramkrishna Rao for his consistent encouragement to write this paper.

REFERENCES

Bahm A.J. (1978). *Yoga: Union with the Ultimate*. New Delhi: Arnold Heinemann Publishers.

Balslev, A.N. (1991). The notion of kleśa and its bearing on the Yoga analysis of mind. *Philosophy East and West*, 41(1), 'Emotion East and West', January, 77-88.

Bodhananda, Sw. (2004). *Lectures on* Yogasutra. New Delhi: Sambodh Foundation

Eliade, M. (1975). *Patanjali and Yoga*, New York: Charles Lam Markmann Tr. Schocken Books.

Haribhadra (K. Satchidananda Murty, Tr.) (1986). *Sad-Darsana Samuccaya*. (2nd rev. edn.). Delhi: Eastern Book Linkers

Iyer, R. (2004). *A Commentary on the* Yogasutras. Atmajyoti Ashram. www.atmajyoti.org/sw_commentary_on_yoga_sutras.asp

Keith, A.B. (1975). *A History of the Samkhya Philosophy*. Delhi: Nag Publishers.

Kesarcodi-Watson, I. (1982). Samadhi in Patanjali's *Yoga-Sutras*. *Philosophy East and West*, 32(1), pp. 77-90.

Max-Müller, F. (1973). *The Six Systems of Indian philosophy*. New Delhi: Associated Publishing House.

Mishra, N. (1953). Samskāras in Yoga philosophy and Western psychology. *Philosophy East and West*, 2(4), January, 308.

Potter, K. (Gen. Ed.). (1987). *Encyclopaedia of Indian Philosophies Vol. IV., Samkhya: A Dualist Tradition in Indian Philosophy*, Gerald James Larson and Ramshankar Bhattacharya (Eds). Delhi: Motilal Banarsidass.

Ranade, R.D. (1970). *Vedanta: The culmination of Indian thought.* Bombay: Bharatiya Vidya Bhavan.

Safaya, R. (1976). *Indian psychology.* New Delhi: Munshiram Manoharlal.

Suryanarayana Sastri, S.S. (Ed. and Tr.). (1973). *The Sankhya Karika of Isvara Krsna* (2nd rev. edn.). Madras: University of Madras.

Taimini, I.K. (1974). *The Science of Yoga: The Yoga-Sutras of Patanjali in Sanskrit.* Adyar: Theosophical Publishing House.

Vivekananda, Sw. (1990). *RajaYoga*, (19th imp.). Mayavati: Advaita Ashrama.

Woods, J.H. (1914). *The Yoga-system of Patanjali: Or the ancient Bindu Doctrine of Concentration of Mind.* Delhi: Motilal Banarsidass.

Zimmer, H. (1951). *Philosophies of India*. Joseph Campbell, Ed.. London: Routledge and Kegan Paul.

Self, Non-Self and Rebirth : The Buddhist Outlook

ARJUNA DE ZOYSA

Anicca (Transience)

Anicca or transience is central to the Buddhist doctrine. It is based on the simple fact that in this very life, the observation of transience is ubiquitous and inescapable. The seed grows to be a tree, and the tree withers and dies, another seed from the same tree may also give rise to a new shoot. So is mortal life, and so are the great mountains, it is only a matter of time scales – a human life may last a century, a mountain may last a geologically significant time span, but permanency is not observed.

This transience, when accompanied by a conscious self, clings to changing objects and views; seeking a sense of permanency, and is anguished by the apparent observation of transience. It thereby constructs metaphysical states of permanence for this self. Thus, one may speculate on a soul, which exists after death in a permanent state of bliss (heaven) or degeneration (hell). There are many variants to the crude hell/heaven dichotomy of post-mortem existence (Rahula, 1996). In this paper I deal primarily with the phenomena of re-birth as explained by the Buddha rather than present a discussion of these subtle attempts at a permanency of self.

Time and the Search for Absolutes

The observation of transience is *a-priori* to the concept of time, in that we derive 'time' as the interval between two observed events occurring in this transient cosmos. As example we could take the observation of light signals coming from the hands of a clock and record the time difference, as Einstein explained in his Special Theory of Relativity, in 1905 (De Zoysa, 2001). This concept of time is the same in Buddhism. The alternative conception of time is commonsensical and Newtonian (as in conventional physics), and observed change occurs in an absolute time scale. The concept of time, it is to be emphasized, is a derivative of the observation of change. This different conception on time has wide implications. Thus, in Buddhism although various heavenly states of being have long time spans; they are so only in earth time and not in their own relative time. The soteriological goal in Buddhism thus, is not taking birth in one of these relatively pleasant states of existence, but to transcend *saṃsāra* or the '*angst* of clinging to transience' known as *dukkha*.

Modern science, even in its most advanced disciplines (physics), observes transience. However, science *in praxis*, is accompanied by its cultural underpinnings, and as a result does not escape this tendency to seek a sense of permanency. Its theoretical constructs range from fundamental particles such as quarks and superstrings which attempt to form an unchanging essence to an experience of an ever changing materiality. Its construction of a transient self in genetic material (genome) is another such attempt at permanency. The genome becomes an all powerful essence, remaining unchanged during a whole life span; and determining our actions, even supposedly voluntary ethical choices. Many scientists do not agree with such a position, and call it bio-reductionism; however its modern attraction lies in this desire to perpetuate self, even in our offspring.

Human cloning is an extreme expression of such a desire. Self, as metaphor, has now become a clinging grasping entity, in search of an elusive immortality.

Self, Non-Self and Re-Becoming

The Buddha categorically denied any unchanging essence to the phenomena of *being*. No soul, no *ātman* and hence a denial of an afterlife metaphysic. However, he observationally rejected the secular idea of facing an 'abyss of nothingness' at death. Thus, death was *not* a final termination; it is followed by a re-becoming (popularly termed rebirth). The Buddha on the final night-watch before his enlightenment; supposedly had 'seen' the passing away and arising of many beings in all corners of the cosmos. This observation was common knowledge amongst numerous *brahmin* recluses through paranormal sight acquired through meditation. The Buddha, however, denied the discovery of any essence (*ātman*) which passed from one life to another, observing only a causal chain of events, governed by natural laws, just as it occurred in this very life (Bodhi, 1978).

Such a Re-becoming is depicted well by the following Japanese Zen poem,

With empty hands I came into this world,
Bare foot I leave it,
my coming and my going,
two simple events,
an End and a beginning
Woven into each other

Kozan Ichikyo (Zen master)

There is without denial a unique history to each one of us. This, in effect, gives us an instantaneous 'self', a uniqueness which is not fully shared by another. But this uniqueness has no essence to it, just its historical narrative; and re-becoming through *saṃsāra* means that we are formed by journeys which may have experienced many corners of this vast cosmos, and touched the lives of a countless others.

There is in the *Milindapanha* (Mendis and Horner, 1993), a discourse between King Milinda, a Bactrian king (Afghan of Greek origin) and an *arahant* (those who have reached the final stage of liberation) named Nagasena. At one point, the *arahant* responds to the King's query on the reality of a person thus: he says that it is, "Neither the same nor another (*na ca so na ca anno)*". He goes on to explain by similes that continuity establishes identity and not an essence such as a soul. I will here cite a simile given by Nagasena:

> "*It is as if, sire, some person might light a lamp. Would it burn all night?*"
>
> "*Yes, revered sir, it might burn all night.*"
>
> "*Is the flame of the first watch same as the middle watch?*"
>
> "*No, revered sir, it was burning all through the night in dependence on itself.*"
>
> "*Even so, sire, a continuity of phenomena is linked together. It up-rises as one and ceases as another, linked together as though were no before and no after. Hence it is neither the same nor another, but the subsequent consciousness is reckoned (together with) the preceding consciousness.*"

[The above is descriptive of youth, middle age and old age, in a single life span].

On the question of who takes rebirth, the conversation goes thus;

> "*Revered Nagasena, who takes rebirth?*"
>
> "*Mind-and-matter (nāma-rūpa), sire, takes rebirth.*"
>
> "*What, is it this same mind-matter itself that takes rebirth?*"
>
> "*This same mind-matter does not itself take rebirth, sire; but sire, by means of this mind-matter one does a good or bad deed and, because of this deed, another mind-matter takes rebirth.*"

"If revered sir, this mind-matter itself does not take rebirth would not one be freed from evil deeds?"

"If, sire, it did not take rebirth one would be freed from evil deeds. But because, sire, it takes rebirth one is not freed from evil deeds."

"Make a simile."

"Suppose, sire, some man were to steal another man's mangoes and the owner of the mangoes were to seize him and bring him before the king, saying, 'Your majesty, my mangoes were stolen by this man,' and he were to say, 'Your majesty, I did not steal his mangoes; the mangoes he planted were different from these that I now possess; I do not deserve punishments.' Would he, sire, not deserve punishment?"

"Yes, revered sir, he would deserve punishment."

"For what reason?"

"Whatever he may say, the mangoes he stole resulted from the mangoes which, he admits, the other man planted."

"Even so, sire, by means of this mind-matter one does a good or bad deed and, because of this deed, another mind-matter takes rebirth; therefore, one is not freed of evil deeds."

"You are dexterous, revered Nagasena."

(Mendis and Horner, 1993, 40, 44-50)[1]

Existence or Simply Being

There is yet another aspect which is unique to the Buddhist theory of rebirth. There is an intermediary state known as 'existence', where *vinñāna* (an unconscious stream of being), with a record of the state of the former being persists and then gives rise to birth. In the law of dependent origination (*paṭiccasamuppāda*), credited to

[1] Effects of *kamma* pass on through successive lives and this forms the basis of Buddhist ethics.

a discourse given directly by the Buddha, a state termed 'existence' precedes birth (Bodhi, 1995).

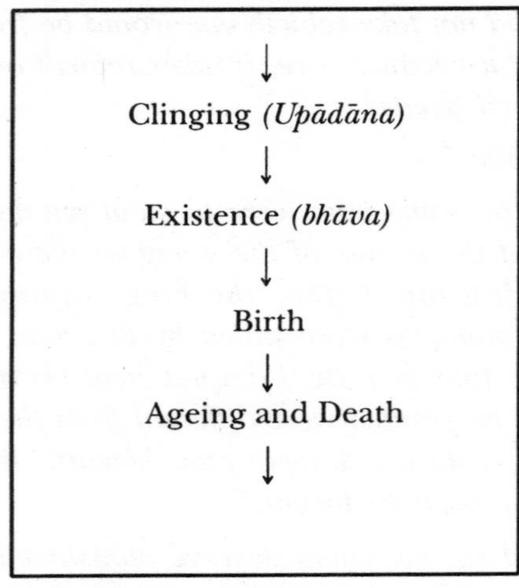

Section from the *Pattica Samuppada* (Bodhi, 1995)

The states of 'existence' (in Pāli – *bhāva*) are three fold: sensuous, fine material and immaterial. As for the *being* experiencing such states 'time' has stopped, in that *no activity* occurs, neither mental or physical, and any activity begins only after *vinñāna* is re-linked to some material form and rebirth occurs. The relativity of time, justifies the view that rebirth is instantaneous for the individual who has expired; as the next conscious event that could even potentially be recorded by him/her, is at birth. Rebirth memories seem to justify a break in conscious mental activity (Story, 1988) (see case histories below). I use the term re-becoming to include both existence and conscious birth (re-birth). This gives rise to the speculation that the immaterial state is only a *bhāva,* with no birth, and hence no ageing and death, simply an arising and passing away. A metaphor could be drawn to an arrow which has left the bow; travelling on potential alone. There are many speculative discussions on this, which is not relevant at this stage.

The concept of time as discussed in Buddhist texts makes it relative, as in modern physics, and the rather long periods of life or existence described in all religions are both impermanent and lengthy only in earthly terms, but not in their time frames.

Case Histories of Rebirth

I have chosen four rebirth investigations from the research studies done by Ian Stevenson (2000) of the University of Virginia, USA; two from Sri Lanka and two others from, Thailand and Myanamar. Stevenson has studied and reported over 600 cases, even from societies that do not have a philosophy of or belief in re-birth; in the case of those countries with a belief in rebirth, verifications have been possible for some through investigation, while the others have a conjectural quality to them. The particular four cases cited here are chosen to highlight different aspects of these phenomena. Some of these cases have been studied and reported in Sri Lanka by Francis Story (1975).

Rebirth Memories of Disna Samarasingha: Disna was born in a village off Kandy Sri Lanka, on the 29th of April 1959. She began recalling memories of her previous life, spontaneously at the age of three. From her description, the previous life was traced to be that of Tilakarachige Babanona who had died 15 months before at the age of 68, on the 15th of January 1958 at Wettewa a nearby village. No indication was given to the daughter and son of Babanona of this claim, they came to know of it only after Disna was taken to them. On the way to Wettewa, Disna was even able to indicate a short cut to her former abode. Apparently some traits were shared by Babanona and Disna, while others were not, as expected. This case is interesting because of the very thorough investigation done of it, and also the time gap of around five months between the death of the former person, and probable conception of the other (15-10 months) (Stevenson, 2000). This is indicative of the state of what is indicated in the sequence of dependent origination (*paṭiccasamuppāda*) *(P-S) as* 'existence', a state without consciousness before re-birth occurs

Siamese Twins: A second case reported by Stevenson, comes from unpublished proceedings of the Annual Sessions of the University of Peradeniya, Medical Faculty. He reported the case of identical twins in a southern village in Sri Lanka. Both twins recalled their previous existence, one claimed to have been a JVP activist who had been killed by the Sri Lankan armed forces, the other a Buddhist priest who had succumbed to a disease. Being identical twins they showed similar physical form, but had two widely different personalities. The twin who had been an activist, had an angry personality and at a very young age, he showed an interest in politics, the other who claimed to have been a priest, had a calm temperament and was interested in religion. Both the claimed past lives were traced by Stevenson. The interesting factor here is that they came from the same genome, and were brought up in the same family and society. Why then was there such a difference in personalities?

THAI SERGEANT: This case is of an army sergeant in Thailand, Thiang San Kla. A small wry man, with a large disfiguring birthmark, a capillary naevus, which spread from above his left ear to the base of his skull. He recalled his previous life as his own father's brother, who had been wrongly suspected of cattle-stealing and killed by a mob. The poor man had been knifed at a spot close to the ugly birth mark of the sergeant. Thiang remembered seeing his own body on the ground; subsequently he felt strongly attracted to his brother's wife who was already pregnant. The mother in this life had had a dream in which Thiang, her husband's brother appeared and was asking to be reborn in her womb. The interesting fact here is the passing down of traumatic markings during rebirth and the fact that strong desire with regards destination seem to have had an effect.

METAMORPHOSES OF A MOTHER: This case begins with U Khin Nyunt dreaming of his mother's death, and correctly identifying even the clothes she had been wearing at the time. The mother thereafter is recorded to have been reborn to her daughter-in law twice, once as a boy who lived up to the age of five and died, and then the boy reborn once again as a daughter three years later. This case of multiple rebirths is interesting from several angles, that dreams sometimes record events occurring in the world of the dead. U Khin Nyut had dreamt of his dying mother in the very clothes that she had died in, and his wife had dreamt that his mother was coming to live with them. The vast changes in character with rebirth, and the phenomena of a dead person supposedly re-entering a partially (early) developed foetus are the peculiar features in this case. The boy who was born to the Nyut's subsequently lived for five years and died of a sudden illness, the boy while dying had vowed to return. Nyut's wife had dreamt that his mother was departing from the house looking rather grim. Three years later Nyut's wife became pregnant again and a girl child was born, the girl just after she was able to speak claimed to have been the dead boy and Nyut's mother in former lives, and could recall several characteristics and incidents from these former lives. The newly born daughter had several tell tale birth marks which signified events in her former life as a boy. Of course markings could be suggestions coming from the mother, but in this case the boy had some adhesive stuck to his skin for a blood transfusion which reappeared in the new born daughter as a square mark of paler skin colour, not a significant incident from the parent's viewpoint. The three year gap between death and rebirth can once again be accounted for by a subconscious 'existence', as sequenced in the *paṭiccasamuppāda* (Samarasinghe, 1988).

These cases raise the question of personality, from one birth to the next. It appears certain that a continuity of one individual to another occurs, and with the Buddhist concept of *anātma* (non-self) even in this very life, rebirth and continuity of personality, does not pose a problem. However, what traits, characteristics, desires and resulting actions (*kamma*/karma) are continued, needs to be investigated. I feel that both Vedic and Buddhist conceptions and beliefs on re-birth can form a healthy alternative to the 'Abyss of Nothingness' at death belief of a modern secular society, and a starting point for in-depth investigations. At least the great terror of dying could be done away with, without the deep romanticism of a permanent state of bliss or despair, as is the case between the secular/religious pendulum swings.

In conclusion, the Buddhist doctrine of rebirth is similar to that of its Vedic origins (Bodhi, 1978), but denies all attempts to build an essence (soul, *ātman*) to such a process. A person's unique history suffices to distinguish being 'A' from 'B'. The causal chain from moment to moment is unbroken at death and re-becoming occurs. No point of beginning is observed to this causal chain, only an end for an enlightened being *(nibbāṇa)*. There is also recognition of shared personal histories in Buddhism, emphasized in particular in the Sanskrit *sūtras* (Reat, 1993). These shared histories in particular give rise to a fine emotion, known in English Buddhist terminology as compassion *(metta)*, which is the cornerstone of the *Boddhisattva* ideal. This could form a fine social motif as an alternate to individualism.

REFERENCES

Bodhi Bikkhu (Tr. from Pâli). (1978). *Brahmajāla Sūtra.* Kandy, Sri Lanka: Buddhist Publication Society.

— (1995). *Mahānidāna Sutra: The Great Discourse on Causation.* Kandy, Sri Lanka: Buddhist Publication Society.

De Zoysa A. (2001). Cross-cultural influences on Einstein's early theory of relativity. *Open University Review.* V6:1 Sri Lanka.

Mendis, N. K. G., Bodhi & Horner, I. B. (1993). *The Questions of King Milinda: An Abridgement of the MilindapanÞha.* Kandy, Sri Lanka: Buddhist Publication Society.

Rahula, W. Bh. (1996). *What the Buddha Taught.* Kandy, Sri Lanka: Buddhist Publication Society.

Reat, N. R. (1993). *The Śālistambha Sūtra,* Tibetan Original, Sanskrit Reconstruction, English Translation, Critical Notes (Including Pāli Parallels, Chinese version, and Ancient Tibetan Fragments). Delhi: Motilal Banarsidass.

Samarasinghe, A. (1988). *Case of Win Win Nyunt.* Kandy, Sri Lanka: Buddhist Publication Society.

Stevenson, I. (2000). *Cases of Reincarnation Type: Ten Cases from Sri Lanka*. Ratmalana, Sri Lanka: Sarvodaya Vishva Lekha

Story, F. (1975). *Rebirth as Doctrine and Experience Essays and Case Studies*. Kandy: Buddhist Publication Society.

— & Vajira. (1988). *Last Days of the Buddha the Maha Parinibbana Sutta*. Kandy, Ceylon: Buddhist Publication Society.

The *Pañca Kośa*s and Yoga

H.R. NAGENDRA

Contemporary science has been greatly influenced by the matter-based paradigm in its understanding and methodologies of exploring the physical world. Classical Indian thought, however, has emphasized the role of a consciousness-based approach towards understanding the world. The two are not mutually exclusive, as both are interdependent and play an equal role in understanding different aspects of the world. While the matter-based approach has yielded the technological advances that we are now so dependent on, the consciousness-based approach has the potentiality for understanding aspects of the world and ourselves that have not been adequately answered from a matter-based approach. It is here that classical Indian thought makes its greatest contribution to the understanding of the world, through its consciousness-based approach, which has its roots in ancient Vedic literature.

As old as 4000 years, if not more, the *Vedas* are essentially in two parts – karma *kāṇḍa* (and *upāsanā kāṇḍa*) and *jñāna kāṇḍa*. The karma *kāṇḍa* concentrates on the ritualistic aspects of this knowledge-base, and the *jñāna kāṇḍa* part contains the knowledge part of the *Vedas* called Vedânta contained in *Upaniṣads*.

The *Upaniṣads* are a culmination of Vedic knowledge. The knowledge and approaches mentioned therein are akin to scientific principles and methodologies, experimental in nature, and verifiable by first-person methodologies, which is the essence of a consciousness-based approach. The style of the *Upaniṣads* is in the form of questions and answers between students and teachers. The teacher is open-minded to learn more, and thereby become better prepared to impart the wisdom he has acquired through study, first-person experience and revelations. The student, called *śiṣya,* is sincere, committed and interested in unravelling the mysteries of the deeper world. With utmost humility, he is prepared to change and transform himself under the guidance of his guru. The *Taittiriya Upaniṣad* delineates the process by which a student is directed to unravel the reality and mystery of this universe by himself, through systematic guidance by his teacher, called the guru.

For instance, in the *Taittiriya Upaniṣad,* the teacher Varuṇa directs his student Bhṛgu to investigate and find out for himself *Brahman* by a process of *tapas*. He provides a hint as to how to do *tapas*: "that from which you are created, sustained and into which you go back (when you die) is *Brahman*. That process of search is *tapas*. Hence, find out *Brahman* by *tapas* – "*tapasā Brahma vijijñāsasva*"). The Sanskrit term *tapas* refers to a personal endeavour of discipline, undertaken to achieve a goal, accompanying hardships. Earliest reference of this word is to be found in the *Ṛg Veda* where it is used in the sense of 'pain, suffering'. It is usually applied in religious and spiritual terms, but can be applied to any field or context. In essence, it is an intense seeking of answers through an introspective, first-person methodology.

The Five Layers of Our Existence (*Pañca Kośas*)

In the tradition of Yoga and the *Upaniṣads* there are five levels of existence in human condition. The person is encaged, as it were, in five sheaths (*koṣas*). The grossest and the outermost, the physical frame, is called the *annamaya kośa*, followed by the *prāṇamaya*, *manomaya*, *vijñānmaya* and the subtlest, the *ānandamaya kośa* (Figure 1).

The *annamaya kośa*—the gross physical body, which is the sheath of food (*anna*) — the physical or gross body, nurtured by food. It is related to anatomy and physiology. The second subtler sheath is the *prāṇamaya kośa*—the sheath of bodily functions, featured by the predominance of *prāṇa*, the life principle, which flows through it through invisible channels called *nāḍīs*. The next sheath in order of subtlety is the *manomaya kośa*—the sheath of sensory capacities, the *vijñānamaya kośa*—the sheath of cognitive functions, and finally the *ānandamaya kośa*—the sheath of blissfulness. The *prāṇamaya, manomaya*, and *vijñānamaya kośas* are the regions of paranormal phenomena (Figure 1).

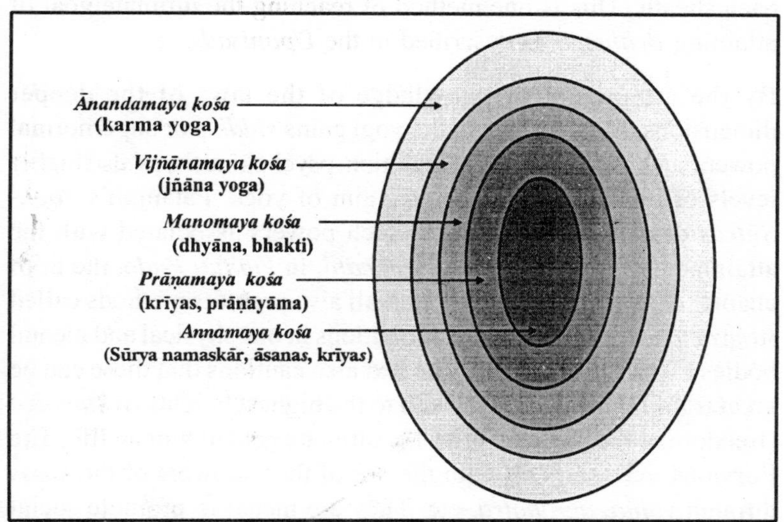

Figure 1: Five Sheaths (*Pañca Kośas*) and IAYT for Common Ailments

As the sheaths become subtler, there is progressive influence of consciousness in one's being, the freedom of operation in the living being increases, the bondage with the body decreases and the bliss associated with it also increases. While in *manomaya kośa* the creative power predominates, in *vijñānamaya kośa* the power of discernment and discrimination predominates; bliss is embodied in the *ānandamaya kośa*, the highest state of evolution in the manifested existence, and is the subtlest among the five sheaths of existence. Beyond all these five layers is pure consciousness called *Brahman*, which is beyond space, time and causation. It is the real self, the Unchanging Reality, transcending mind, intellect, memory and ego. It is what illuminates through the five layers and is the reality from where all creation emerges and into which they go back.

In his journey towards the ultimate, man crosses these sheaths of existence one by one. Through analysis, called *panca kośa viveka* (knowing through experiencing the five levels of existence) and the associated practices called *tapas*, man transforms himself by gradually getting relieved from the bondages and constrictions of each sheath. This is one method of reaching the ultimate goal of attaining *Brahman* as described in the *Upaniṣads*.

By the attainment of knowledge of the laws of the deeper dimensions of our universe, the yogi gains *siddhis* or supernormal powers such as telepathy, precognition, psychokinesis, as also higher levels of bliss, which is the true aim of yoga. Patañjali's *Yoga-Sūtras* describe in vivid detail such powers associated with the attainment of higher levels of *samādhi*. In *Vibhuti Pada*, the third chapter of the *Yoga-Sūtras*, Patañjali also presents methods called *saṃyama* to bring about transformations in our physical and mental bodies to get these powers. The text also cautions that these can be great traps on the path of growth to the highest heights of *kaivalya* (freedom of the human spirit), the ultimate goal of human life. The Pūrva-Mīmāṁsā deals with the use of these powers of the *kośas* through *yajña*, *agnīhotra,* etc. They are meant to promote social harmony and create ideal social orders by bringing benefits to the individuals performing the same as also the atmosphere around. *Mantras* (Vedic hymns) and *yantras* (apparatus) were used profusely in these *yajñas* (sacrifice) and rituals as the key instruments for the flow of higher powers of *prāṇa* into the grosser levels, like a lens focusing the light energy to burn a paper.

Health and Illness

According to the World Health Organization (WHO), "Health is not only the absence of infirmity and disease but also a state of physical, mental and social well-being." Health and ill-health are not two discrete entities as commonly understood, but health should be conceived as a continuous function indicating the state of wellbeing. In Figure 2, Quadrant I represents illness; below this man acts instinctively and is akin to an animal man.[1] Quadrant I is the region of normal health. As one moves along the line further up, he becomes healthier featured by the dormant faculties expressing more vividly in man. This is shown as the region of super man, the next region after the human spectrum. In this state, the limitations of normal man, namely the strong urges of thirst, hunger, fear and sex are reduced greatly and are fully under control. In the concept of Sri Aurobindo, the new faculties of deeper perceptions of the world beyond the five senses emerge in this phase of superhuman existence. Further growth leads man to unfold even deeper layers of consciousness and widen the spectrum of his knowledge to move towards divinity or perfection. In this march towards perfection, yoga is a systematic conscious process for accelerating the growth of a human being from his animal level to normalcy, then to superhuman level and to ultimately to divinity. It is a systematic methodology for an all round personality development—physical, mental, intellectual, emotional, and spiritual components of man. Thus yoga in its general methodology for the growth of man to divine heights includes techniques useful for therapeutic applications in making man healthier.

---

[1] Food, sleep, fear and procreation (instinctive actions) are common to man and animals. It is the conscious thinking faculty, the power of discrimination that characterizes man.

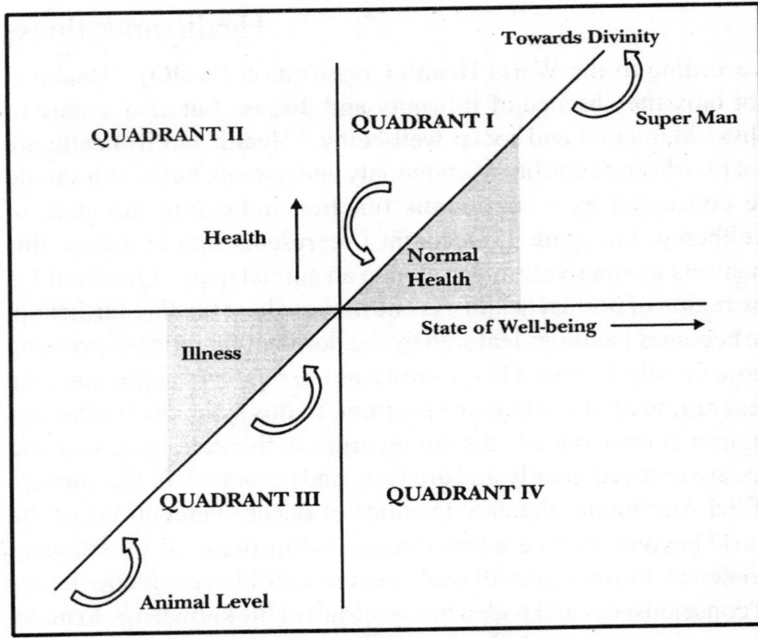

Figure 2: Concept of Health

To meet the challenge of contemporary ailments, a multidimensional approach is required, which incorporates the physical, mental and spiritual needs of the person. Yoga provides this holistic approach. The Integrated Approach of Yoga Therapy (IAYT) offers this total solution, using the hidden powers of the *kośas* for healing.

Yoga

Derived from the verbal root *yuj*, the term "*yoga*" means joining – joining our small individual personality with the all pervasive cosmic personality, raising ourselves from the animalistic level to normal human beings, great human beings, super beings, divine beings and to reach highest levels of perfect health featured by total freedom, knowledge and bliss (Figure 3). As defined by Patañjali in the *Yoga-Sūtra*s, yoga is to gain mastery over the modifications of the mind. This mastery involves two dimensions: i) to get better powers of concentration and ii) to get the power to silence all modifications of the mind. Patañjali prescribed the eight-limbed *Aṣṭāṅga* yoga for this purpose. *Haṭha* yoga texts offer to us the *mudrās*, *bandhas* and *kṛyās*. The other methods of yoga include *jñāna* yoga, *bhakti yoga* and *karma yoga*.

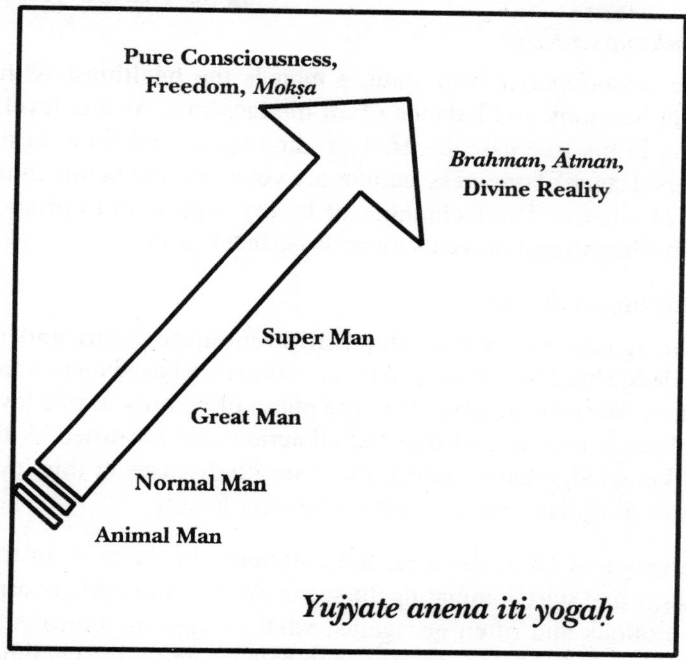

Figure 3: Concept of Yoga

The Integrated Approach of Yoga Therapy (IAYT) uses all the four main streams of yoga—*karma yoga, jñāna yoga, rāja yoga and bhakti yoga*. The path of action, karma yoga, in blissful awareness forms the key strategy to work at the *ānandamaya kośa* state. The path of intellect, *jñāna* yoga at the *vijñānamaya kośa* level; Meditation of *Rāja* yoga for gaining mastery over the mind; and the science of emotional culture (*bhakti* yoga) is used at the *manomaya kośa.* The breathing practices and *prāṇāyāma* of Rāja and Haṭha yogas are adopted for *prāṇamaya kośa.* Yoga postures, yoga diet and cleansing techniques, *kṛyās*, are used at the *annamaya kośa* level. Thus, the IAYT works at all levels offering effective solutions to solve the challenges of the disorders of the present times to ward off illnesses (*vyādhis*). Alongside the advantages of the modern medical advances, the IAYT works as an effective adjunct to the modern medicinal practices.

The *Pañca Kośas*

Ānandamaya Kośa

In the *ānandamaya kośa* state, a man is the healthiest with a perfect harmony and balance of all his faculties. At this level, a man is in his true essence, transcending space and time. In this universal stage of one-ness, actions are yet to emerge in this causal state of silence. The techniques of karma yoga help to promote positive health and move us towards perfect health.

Vijñānmaya Kośa

At the *vijñānamaya kośa* state, differentiations start and the knowledge base is complete. All our actions are based on this total wisdom. We can see persons in the phase of activity at this level. But there is total knowledge and all actions are governed by this total knowledge-base. Hence, there are no diseases at this level. We can designate this as a state of perfect health.

Emergence of likes, dislikes, and emotions slowly grow in their intensity and start dominating the scene. Actions now get governed by emotions and often go against what is right as indicated by *vijñānamaya kośa*. This creates an imbalance and is the beginning of all ailments and is called as *ādhi*.

In the IAYT process, when a person is at this level, cognitive transformations take place through lectures and individual counselling sessions so that the healing process is augmented and stabilized on a long-term basis.

Manomaya Kośa

At the *manomaya kośa* state emotions dominate and start governing our actions. It is at this state that imbalances start developing. Likes and dislikes come into play, and imbalances amplify resulting in mental illnesses called *ādhis*. At this stage there are no symptoms at the physical level. Prompted by the perceptual growth of desires, these mental disorders congeal and begin to manifest externally. Gradually they percolate to the physical frame. Preponderance of *ajñāna* (ignorance about the nature of the real self and its true state of bliss) leads man to perform wrong actions, such as the eating of unwholesome food, living in unhealthy dwellings, doing things at untimely hours, injuries inflicted, association with impure thoughts etc. These varieties of physical diseases are called *vyādhis* or secondary diseases.

The *ādhi* (primary diseases) are twofold – *sāmānya* (ordinary) and *sāra* (the essential) (Figure 4). The former includes diseases incidental to the body while the latter to the rebirth to which men are subject. The *sāmānya ādhi* are normally produced during interactions with the world. These may be termed as psychosomatic ailments. When suitably dealt with, *ādhi* of this ordinary type will cease to affect the individual. Along with it are destroyed the physical ailments, *vyādhi*, caused by these *ādhi*. The subtler *ādhi* of the essential type, *sāra ādhi*, which causes the birth of the physical body can be destroyed only by the realisation of the causal states of mind and a corresponding ability to live in the *vijñānamaya* and *ānandmaya kośas*. In that case, then, man transcends the cycles of birth and death.

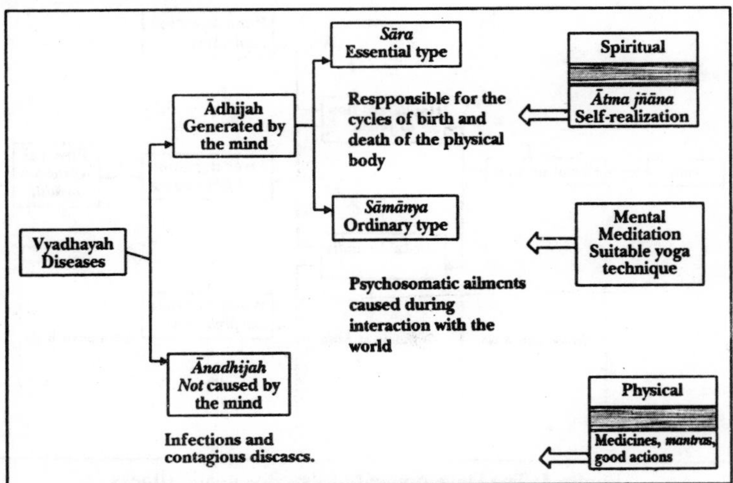

Figure 4: A Schematic Diagram of Illnesses

This concept of *vyādhi* caused by *ādhi* is summarised in figure 5. The figure also depicts the second class of ailments – *anadhijah vyādhayah*, those not originating in the mind, including infectious and contagious diseases. Through conventional medicine, *mantras* (with their natural vibrational characteristics), and good actions (bringing about purity of mind, allowing the *prāṇa* to flow freely in the body) diseases can be cured.

Psychosomatic illnesses are caused when the mind is agitated during our interaction with the world at large; the physical body also follows in its wake. These agitations cause fluctuations in the *prāṇa* in the *nāḍīs*. The *prāṇa* flows in the wrong path without rhythm and harmony, and the *nāḍīs* can no longer maintain stability and steadiness.

At *manomaya kośa* level the speed of the mind is reduced by the practice of *dhyāna* and by *bhakti* yoga, which is a means of channelling emotions in a positive direction. The emotional imbalances are brought down by the art of sublimation of emotions. They eradicate the root cause of the diseases—*ādhi*. Advanced techniques mentioned above harness the energy at this level to bring about powerful healing of even the dreaded diseases as cancer.

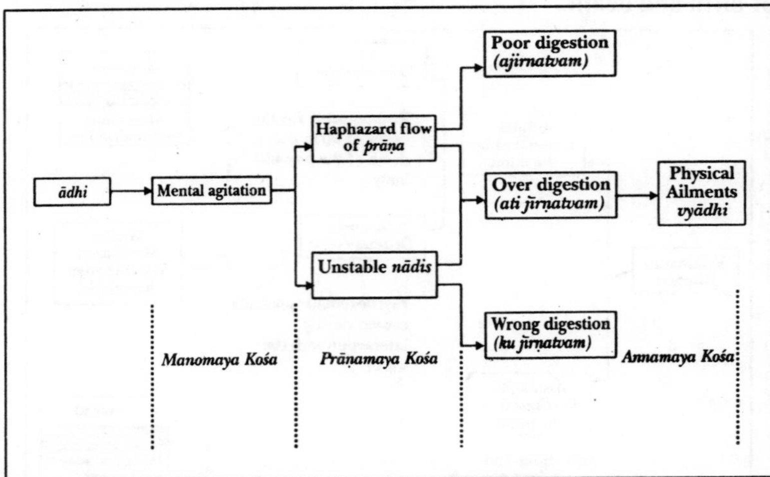

Figure 5: The Development of Psychosomatic Illness

The concept of *prāṇa* is commonly misunderstood as air entering in and going out of the body, as that which governs breath, or as nothing but nerve impulses. However, *prāṇa* is the basic life principle. In its dormant form, it exists in the mineral world. The primary facets of *prāṇa* start manifesting in the vegetable kingdom. As it attains full form in the animal and human spectrum, newer and more complex faculties emerge. The structure of the body is also suitably transformed giving scope for the fuller manifestations of the emerging higher capacities, the mobile limbs and the senses. In different parts of the body, different aspects of *prāṇa* work with proper coordination and organisation between them. In the human system, the ancient seers have identified five major facets of *prāṇa*, carrying out five major functions.

The five different manifestations of the *mukhya prāṇa* (the principal *prāṇa*) are: *prāṇa*, *apāna*, *samāna*, *vyāna*, and *udāna*. As the *Praśna Upaniṣad* describes, the *apāna* is in the organs of excretion and procreation; in the eye, ear, nose, and mouth dwells the *prāṇa* itself; in the middle is the *samana,* upward the *udana* and all over the body is *vyāna*.

The manifestation of the principal *prāṇa* (*mukhya prāṇa*) in the lower regions of the abdomen is termed as *apāna*. *Prāṇa* acts in the upper regions—face, nose etc., which *essentially* correspond to the force that activates breathing. That which keeps the balance between the upper and lower forces (*prāṇa* and *apāna*) is called *samana*. *Vyāna* is that aspect of the principal *prāṇa* that flows through each and every *nāḍī*, coordinating the functions of the different aspects of the *prāṇa*.

Through the practice of proper breathing, *kriyā* and *prāṇāyāma*, we start affecting the *prāṇamaya kośa*. Suitable types of *prāṇāyāma* and breathing help to remove agitations in *prāṇic* flow in the *prāṇamaya kośa*. Thus, ailments are dealt with at the *prāṇamaya kośa* level.

Prāṇāyāma is the process of gaining control over the *prāṇa*. Normally there are three components of breathing: inhalation, exhalation and cessation of breathing. They are termed, *pūraka*, *recaka*, and *kumbhaka*. In *kumbhaka* the cessation of breathe can occur in three ways: after inhalation (*pūraka* or *antarya kumbhaka*), after exhalation (*reçaka* or *śūnya* or *bāhya kumbhaka*) and an automatic suspension of breath not due to a preceding process of breathing (*kevala kumbhaka*). A glimpse of this may be experienced for a short time by a preceding *kṛiyā* like *kapālabhāti* due to hyper oxygenation. Authentic *kevala kumbhāka* is that which occurs without a preceding *kriyā*, and is the goal of almost all *prāṇāyāma*. The various effects of *keval kumbhaka* include deep relaxation, lowered metabolic rate, serene blissfulness, expansiveness, and single thought, which are essentially the effects of meditation (*dhyāna*) and super-consciousness (*samādhi*).

Samādhi's at the *manomaya kośa* level create imbalances and percolate to the gross physical frame through the *prāṇamaya kośa*, in which disturbances in the flow of *prāṇa* and instability of the *nāḍīs* are caused, manifesting as irregularities in the form of haphazard, jerky and fast breathing. These imbalances of *prāṇamaya kośa* percolate into the gross body becoming *vyādhis* (illness) such as psychotic and neurological disorders, asthma, cardiac disorders and such.

A direct effect on this level is made possible by the last three limbs of the *aṣṭāṅga* yoga of Patañjali—*dhāraṇā*, *dhyāna* and *samādhi*. The culturing of the mind is accomplished by initially focussing the mind (*dhāraṇā*), followed by relaxed dwelling of the mind in a single thought (*dhyāna*) for increasing durations leading ultimately to super consciousness (*samādhi*). A progressive habituation allows the mind to remain relaxed during the period of meditation (*dhyāna*). The benefits of a simple standardised technique, such as Transcendental Meditation (TM), are numerous, particularly its application to any psychosomatic illnesses.

The imbalances of the *prāṇamaya kośa* are brought to a balance by practices shown in Fig 5. The fast (*kriyās*) and slow (*prāṇāyāma*) breathing practices bring the most fascinating results. Breath is a bridge between the body and mind.

Annamaya Kośa

At the physical body level yogic practices mentioned above improve the stamina, bringing balance in the autonomic nervous system.

The special techniques for each of the ailments provide reduction of symptoms of the diseases at the physical level. In case of severity of illness which prevents the performance of yoga, medication is used as an adjunct to enable the patient to perform the practices with ease. Relaxation at the body level provides deep rest to the physical system, so that the healing powers can manifest to solve the problems. Yoga diet featured by *sattva* adds dimensions to healing.

Summary

Indian psychology postulates that the consciousness shines forth in five *kośas* (sheaths). In the *ānandamaya kośa* state, we are in our causal state of highest bliss and wellbeing. In the *vijñānamaya kośa* state, differentiations start and the knowledge base is established. All our actions are based on this total wisdom. Hence, there are no diseases and is a state of perfect health. At the *manomaya kośa* state emotions dominate and start governing our actions. Disorders start at this level as *ādhis* and percolate down through *prāṇamaya kośa* to the physical body, *annamaya kośa*, becoming the *vyādhis*. The IAYT developed and pursued at our centre uses the four main streams of yoga — *karma yoga, jñāna yoga, rāja yoga and bhakti yoga*. The path of action, karma yoga, in blissful awareness forms the key strategy to work at the *ānandamaya kośa* state. The path of intellect, *jñāna* yoga at the *vijñānamaya kośa* level; meditation of *rāja* yoga for gaining mastery over the mind and the science of emotional culture (*bhakti* yoga) to eradicate the *ādhis* are used at the *manomaya kośa.* The breathing practices and *prāṇāyāma* of rāja and haṭha yogas are adopted for *prāṇamaya kośa.* Yoga postures, yoga diet and cleansing techniques, *kriyās*, are used at the *annamaya kośa* level. Thus, the IAYT Integrated Approach of Yoga Therapy works at all levels offering effective solutions to address the challenges of the disorders of the present times to ward off illnesses (*vyādhis*). Alongside the advantages of the modern medical advances, the IAYT works as an effective adjunct to the modern medical practices.

BIBLIOGRAPHY

Bharati, J. (1986). *The Essence of Yogavāsiṣṭha.* Madras: Samata Books.

Nagendra, H.R. (1985). *Yoga: Its Basis and Applications.* Bangalore: Swami Vivekananda Yoga Prakashana.

— (2005). *Raja Yoga.* Bangalore: Swami Vivekananda Yoga Prakashana.

Nagarathna, R. & Nagendra, H.R. (1986). *New Horizons in Modern Medicine.* Bangalore: Swami Vivekananda Yoga Prakashana.

— (2002). *Yoga for Promotion of Positive Health.* Bangalore: Swami Vivekananda Yoga Prakashana.

Paramahamsa, Y. (1970). *Autobiography of a Yogi.* Bombay: Jaico.

Pratinidhi, B.P. (1966). *The Ten Point Way to Health.* Bombay: Taraporevala.

Ranganathananda, Sw. (1993). *The Message of Upaniṣads.* Bombay: Bharatiya Vidya Bhavan.

Satprem, Sri (1973). *Sri Aurobindo: The Adventure of Consciousness.* Pondicherry: Sri Aurobindo Ashram.

SVYASA (2004). *Research Contributions of VYASA, Vol. 1: Therapeutic Applications of Yoga.* Bangalore: Swami Vivekananda Yoga Prakashana.

Taimini, I.K. (2001). *The Science of Yoga.* Chennai: The Theosophical Publishing House.

Vivekananda, Sw. (1995). *Rāja-yoga.* Pithoragarh: Advaita Ashram

Cognitive Processing as Depicted in the *Yoga-Sūtras*

K.M. Tripathi

From the very beginning, Indian psychology has focused its interests on the study of mind and consciousness. Consciousness has been assumed as the primal state of psychic entity, whereas the mind has been normally seen as a modification of consciousness, coloured with the impressions of the external sensorial materialistic world. Traditional Indian scholars have assumed that colours or impressions of the sensorial materialistic world corrupt the quality of consciousness. On the other hand, psychology as pursued in the West looks upon external materialistic world as a positive modifier of mind or consciousness. A review of the multifarious contributions made by traditional Indian seekers leads to an observation that Indian psyche has assumed three levels of the being and the becoming of consciousness. They are: 1) physical being and becomingness, 2) mental being and becomingness, and 3) spiritual being and becomingness.

1. **CONSCIOUSNESS OF PHYSICAL BEING AND BECOMINGNESS:** This is the lower level of consciousness, possessed by normal men and women, and very much based on materialistic awareness. In classical Indian perspective, one's physical being is assumed to be made of *vāta*, *pitta* and *kapha*. Persons having this level of consciousness are satisfied with material gains. The aim of life is 'eat, drink, and be merry' and to strive for collecting things of material abundance.

2. **CONSCIOUSNESS OF MENTAL BEING AND BECOMINGNESS:** This is somewhat upper human level of consciousness. This level of consciousness is assumed to be formed by the *sattva*, *rajas* and *tamas*, the three fundamental psychical modes, underlying *prakṛti* (the primal nature) and contributing to the activation of all psychical elements. This level is characterized by curiosity, quest and pursuit of knowledge, as well as success, failure and stress in life.

3. **CONSCIOUSNESS OF SPIRITUAL BEING AND BECOMINGNESS:** This is the upper human level of consciousness. It is the integration of *sat*, *cit* and *ānanda*, the primordial entities latent in the supreme being. Because of being as inseparable part of the supreme being, it is universal being represented in all the human spirits. Therefore, despite the materialistic affluence, the deep-seated underlying want of human psyche is the pursuit of bliss and spiritual fulfilment in life

According to Indian mythological traditions, it is said that Patañjali concentrated his interest on the management of all the above said levels of the being and the becoming of consciousness. Believing that Patañjali and Caraka were the two roles, adopted by the same person, it is said that through the *Yoga-Sūtra*, he suggested the strategy to deal with the mental and spiritual levels of being and becomingness of consciousness, while through the *Caraka-Samhitā* he evolved the system of complete life science to manage the factors of physical as well as mental levels of being and becomingness of consciousness. In his eminent composition *Yoga-Sūtra*, Patañjali has propounded the system of *Aṣṭāṅga-Yoga*, which deals with the refinement of cognitive process. The *Yoga-Sūtra* starts with the description of different kinds of mental states with special reference to the sensory involvement and cognitive stages. Further, it concentrates on the classification of the sources of knowledge and the progressive levels of higher states of consciousness attained through the practice of *antaraṅga yoga* or *saṃyama*, escorting the state of transcendence (*samādhi*). Different limbs of *bahiraṅga yoga* indirectly bring about the deservingness for attaining true cognizance and knowledge of real 'self' in the yoga aspirant.

Mental Planes, Dispositions and Psychic States

Patañjali defines Yoga as the state of restraint of psychic modifications (YS: 1.2-3). From *Upanisdic* point of view (*Māndukya Upaniṣad,* 2-5), psychic activity has two kinds of involvement, i.e., active and passive; moreover the psyche can be in two states: aware state and slumbering state. On the whole, the psyche forms four states: wakefulness (*jāgṛti*), profound sleep (*suṣupti*), dreaming, i.e., paradoxical sleep (*swapna*), and transcendental state (*turīya*). Out of these four states, wakefulness is the aware and active state whereas the transcendental state is attentive but passive state of consciousness (psyche). The dreaming state appears as slumbering passive state but in reality, during the dreaming state, the human psyche is in an active role and undergoes different moods and feelings. During the state of profound sleep, one's psyche, of course, adopts a passive slumbering state. While defining yoga as the restraint state of psychic modifications, Patañjali admits *turīyāvasthā* or transcendental state as the ultimate state of human psyche (YS: 1.2-3). *Turīyāvasthā* is the state fit for unlimited modification in the human psyche.

	Involement of Psychic Activity ↓ ↓	
States of Psyche ↓ ↓ ↓	Active ↓	Passive ↓
Aware →	*jāgrat*	*turīya*
Slumbering →	*swapana*	*suṣupti*

Figure -1

However, in case of common incidence (YS: 1.4), Patañjali identified five kinds of modifications commonly occurring in the psyche as below:

(1) *pramāṇa* (right cognizing), (2) *viparyāya* (erroneous perception), (3) *vikalpa* (erroneous conception), (4) *nidrā* (absence of *pramāṇa, viparyāya* and *vikalpa*) and (5) *smṛti* (revival of mindfulness). (See Fig. 2).

Patañjali starts the *Yoga-Sūtra* with an explanation of these modifications. He reserves the first and foremost place for the *pramāṇa* (right cognizing) as the principal modification of psyche, taking place during the wakeful state. Standard means of cognizing are of two kinds: direct and indirect. Direct means of cognizing is the sense evidence (*pratyakṣa*) escorting the perception whereas the indirect sources of cognizing may be divided into two categories: cognizing through own mental faculties (*anumāna*) and cognizing

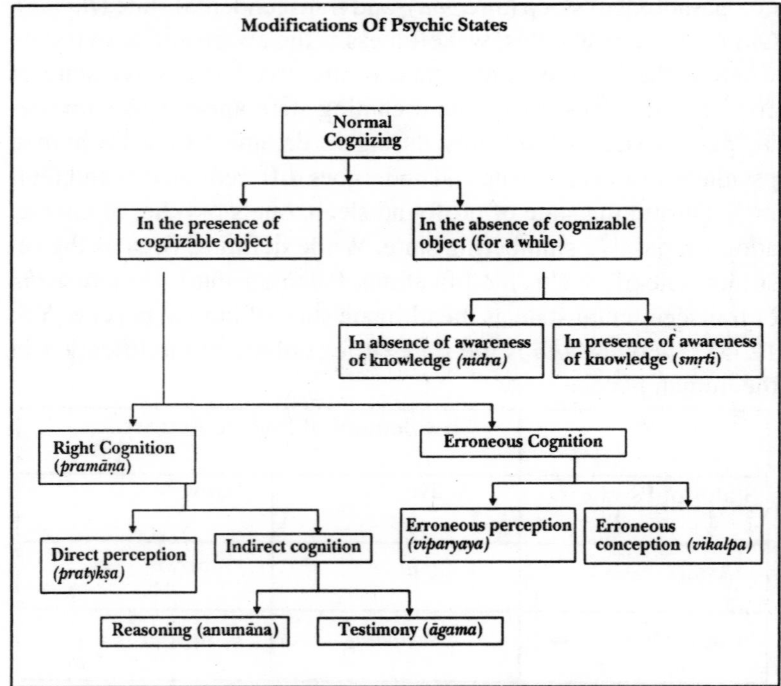

Figure 2: Modification of Psychic States

with the help of authentic persons (*āgama*). Thus, these three principal sources of knowledge are possible. They are described by Patañjali as follows: (1) sense evidence or perception (through senses); (2) logical inference or reasoning (through the mind); and (3) testimony or verbal cognition (through spoken or written evidences).

Many a time, due to certain limitations of sensory system, sense evidence leads to erroneous perception. Thus, erroneous perception is our destiny in general. Being termed as *viparyāya* (illusion), it has been identified as the second essential modification of psyche by Patañjali. As far as inference is concerned, it is rigorously regulated by the different principles and rules of thinking by the system of logic or Nyāya. Otherwise the comprehension by inference is essentially assumed to be fallacious. However, after being passed through proper processing and regulations, there are less possibilities of wrong inference. The testimony is frequently corrupted by the aspirations and fancies of the human mind. Many a time our wrong perceptions *(viparyāya)*, get mixed with corrupt cognitions and bring about wrong cognitions. Thus identified, it is a very common human psychic modification, termed as *vikalpa*. It is included as third principle modification of the human psyche by Patañjali. Through proper sense evidence, reasoning and verbal cognitions, one progresses from erroneous perceptions *(viparyāya)* and conceptions *(vikalpa)* towards right cognitions. Thus erroneous perception is human misfortune and right cognition *(pramāṇa)* is due to our diligence. *Pramāṇa, viparyāya and vikalpa* are the means of interaction between our consciousness and the outer world. However, while interacting with the world, *pramāṇa* facilitates the integration of psychic energy, *viparyāya and vikalpa* bring about diffusion of psychic energy, and exhaustion that finally causes want of rest leading to the sleep. Therefore, in the absence of *viparyāya and vikalpa,* there will be less possibility of sleep and it will promote the emergence of meditative state (*turīyāvasthā*). Sleep is a temporary stage, which aims at relieving of psychic exhaustion.

As discussed earlier, during the state of sleep, the psyche assumes a passive state. Therefore all through the sleep all the above said psychic modifications are not existent. Good sleep is not only essential for physical wholesomeness but also for the quality of mental well being, that's why profound sleep state offers a good support to the mindfulness, and assumed to be near to the psychic state of transcendence. The mindfulness appearing after sleep or a gap of uninvolvement is called *smṛti*, which is the fifth principal modification of psyche. Whereas *smṛti* denotes the same or the decreased state of pre-acquired cognition, the transcendental state is supposed to be the promoter of cognition. Notwithstanding that *smṛti* is complete or partial retrieval of the first three psychic modifications i.e. *pramāṇa, viparyāya* and *vikalpa*, it is positively influenced by the quality of sleep also. Thus, it is related as well as supported by the other four modifications of psyche.

Components of Cognition

Sensory aspect of any part or single entity of the world (*saṃsāra*), having potentialities of causing somewhat sensory-motor or affective excitation of either low or a high intensity, is called *viśaya* (sensual object); whereas the sensory aspects, initiating a cognitive process in mind are called *avabodha* (percept). *Saṃsāra* (world) is the whole and *viśaya*s are parts of the *saṃsāra*. Since *saṃsāra* may not be the subject of mere sensory activity, therefore, despite appearing tangible and physical, it is relatively subtler than the *viśaya*. *Viśaya*s are direct objects of the senses. *Saṃsāra* is the subject or object of mind, not of the senses. *Saṃsāra* may be experienced but cannot be sensually attained. Integration of different sensory and perceptual aspects of any entity or object forms a *pratyāya* (concept) of the object of focus, in the mind. A *pratyāya* may be concerned with any kind of the mental faculty, viz., imagination, thinking, learning, memory and experiencing (sensing or feeling). Thus, the *viśayas* are the subject of sensation, whereas *pratyāya*s are formed through the integration of perceptions.

Pratyāyas may be categorized into two kinds: *vyasti pratyāya* (concept of particular object or entity) and *samasṭi pratyāya* (general concept). *Samaṣṭi pratyāya* is also called *sampratyāya* (conception). *Sampratyāya*s escort the thinking process. The flow of *pratyāya* s (concepts) and *sampratyāyas* which form the process of thinking, might lead to any conclusion or cognition. When the thinking process is relative but abstract, it leads to the comprehension of *saṃsāra;* but when it is comparatively absolute, it leads to the *vijñāna* (super knowledge). The thoughts related to the tangible aspects form the experience whereas absolute (not related to the particular) thinking about tangible aspects leads to the *vitarka* (deliberation).

The fundamental aim and final objective of the Yoga system of Patañjali is to attain *prajñā* by the physical, psychological and astral yogic practices, ultimately leading to the transcendental state of psyche (YS: 1.18, 1.20). According to *Yoga-Sūtra*: 'Uninterrupted attention on the chosen bit of cognition is meditation'.

Thus, Patañjali presents meditation as a cognitive yogic practice (YS: 3.2). Normally meditation is a process, which begins with a vision, reflection or query and it might further lead to a momentary or prolonged state of transcendence which may finally result into attainment of any wisdom, intuition or ultimate realization (YS: 3.5).

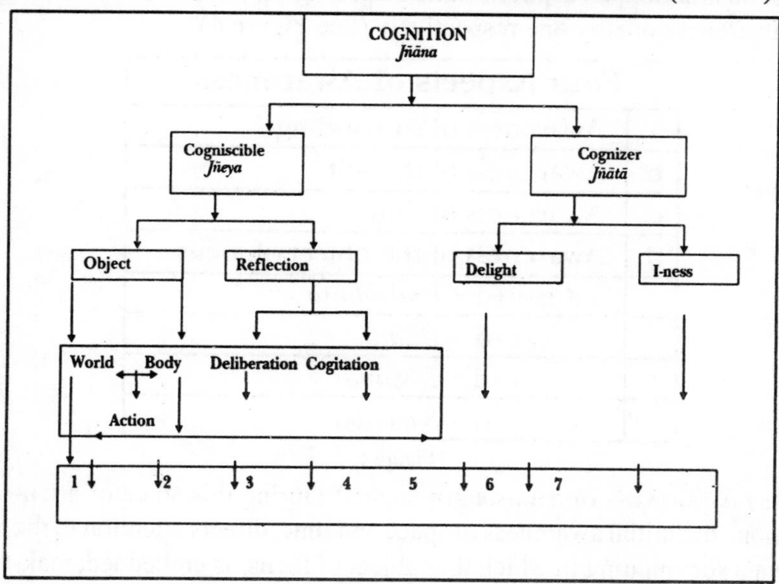

Figure 3

Cognitive Progression during *Antaraṅga-Yoga*

In *Aṣṭāṅga Yoga* of Patañjali, the eight limbs of yoga have been divided into two categories or steps of yoga, i.e., *bahiranga* yoga (exterior yoga) and *antaraṅga* yoga (interior yoga). In the *aṣṭāṅga* yoga, *antaraṅga* yoga (interior yoga) occupies the focal place because it leads to meditation and transcendence as well as to the higher spiritual levels. Normally the process of *antaraṅga yoga* begins with a particular/peculiar perception, reflection, or any query that might finally lead to a momentary or prolonged state of transcendence. *Pratyāhāra* starts when the activities of the sensory organs go to passiveness and the role of mental function becomes prominent. Initially an aspirant has to make his reflections in order. The disciplining of the mental reflections gradually leads to composure of the mind. After attaining mental calmness, the process of attention at mental level gets lucidity. While attending to any object, the process of perception of the object involves four aspects: (1) awareness of the surrounding, (2) awareness of the self, (3) awareness of time and (4) awareness of the object of focus. In the course of abstraction, an aspirant starts disposing the above said levels of awareness one by one respectively (See Figure 4).

Four Aspects of Awareness	
a.	Awareness of surrouding
b.	Awareness of the self
c.	Awareness of time
d.	Awareness of the object of focus.
	a + b+c+d = *Pratyāhāra*
	b+c+d = *Dhārā*
	c+d = *Dhyāna*
	d = *Samādhi*

Figure 4

(a) AWARENESS OF THE SURROUNDINGS: During this stage of attention, the initial awareness of space and time, directs attention to the vast surrounding in which the 'object of focus' is embedded, making this initial stage of attention somewhat effortful.

(b)Awareness of the self: Gradually, in subsequent stages, the above said space-awareness starts altering from massiveness to subtleness resulting in a gradual cutback of the concreteness of time-awareness and further leads to the increased disappearance of space-awareness. As Pillai (1997) says, the total absorption in any external object may enable a person to move away from the limitations of the surrounding and the awareness of the self-existence.

(c) Awareness of time: In the next stage, as time awareness shifts from concreteness to subtleness, the lucidity of the sense of the 'object of focus' attains extra profoundness. Time is an essential dimension of perception of the matter or physical world. However, time awareness represents the psychological aspects of being.

(d) Awareness of the object of focus: The process of gaining profoundness of the meaning of 'object of focus', is followed by and associated with the decrease of awareness of one's physical and psychological counterparts of being. This adds a qualitative excellence in the sense of the object leading to the emergence of transcendence escorting the wisdom based on 'object of focus' (*Yoga-Sūtra,* 3–1-3).

Further Refinement of Cognition through the Transcendental States

As the meditative state deepens, initially the person relinquishes the awareness of his/her physical being; thereby the tangibility of the object of focus is also gradually attenuated. At this stage, only the reflections associated with the object of focus persist in their possible psychic subtlety. The reflections associated with the object of focus may be represented in the ecstatic psyche either as a post experiential deliberation (*vitarka*) or (at times followed by it) as thoughtfulness (*vicāra*). In case the reflections, (associated with the post experiential deliberation of the object of focus), are led to the ecstatic state, it is known as experiential deliberative ecstasy (*vitarkāṇugata samādhi*).

In this ecstatic state, in addition to the 'I consciousness', the experiential reflections are also implicitly accompanied by the cogitation and blissful state associated with it. At times this ecstatic state may be followed by the ultra-experiential or ultra-deliberative transcendence (*nirvitarka samādhi*). Most of the great scientific inventions, literary, artistic or musical compositions are supposed to be the outcome of either the ecstatic or transcendental states. These post-experiential deliberative ecstatic states may be later on sublimated by the thoughtful transcendental state (*vicārāṇugata samādhi*). At this stage of transcendence, the thought associated with the object of focus is also inherently accompanied by the bliss of gnosis and 'I consciousness'. The 'I consciousness' is the bearer of gnosis as well as bliss; otherwise the process will be purposeless. This state of thoughtful transcendence is the source of all wisdom and intuitions. This transcendental state may be sublimated by the ultra-reflective or super gnostic ecstatic state bringing about the super-truthful wisdom (*ṛtambhara prajñā*). In this state, consciousness attains its maximally clean and wholesome form.

As the cogitative modifications of consciousness are extinguished to make consciousness increasingly lucid, the blissful property of consciousness is proportionately increased and later on the transcendental state is advanced into sheer blissful ecstatic state of consciousness (*asmitānugata samādhi*). At this stage of transcendence, the 'blissfulness' is essentially accompanied by the bearer being (of bliss), i.e., 'I consciousness'. And finally, in the Supra-cognitive transcendental states (*samprajñāta samādhi*), transcendence with sheer 'I consciousness' comes into being. It is the preceding state of *mahat* (universal undivided consciousness of Sāṃkhya philosophy). The states of supra-cognitive transcendence are completed at the level of attaining super gnostic ecstatic state (*ṛtambhara prajñā*) causing super-truthful wisdom, however mostly the super gnostic ecstatic state terminates with the attainment of blissful ecstatic state, and finally, as the 'transcendence coinciding with the I consciousness'.

Vitarka (Sensation)	+	*Vicāra* (Thought)	+	*Ānanda* (Bliss)	+	*Asmitā* (I-ness)	=	*Vitarkānugata Samādhi* (Transcendence succeeded by experience)
	+	*Vicāra* (Thought)	+	*Ānanda* (Bliss)	+	*Asmitā* (I-ness)	=	*Vitarkānugata Samādhi* (Transcendence succeeded by thoughts)
			+	*Ānanda* (Bliss)	+	*Asmitā* (I-ness)	=	*Ānandānugata Samadhi* (Transcendence succeeded by blissfulness)
					+	*Asmitā* (I-ness)	=	*Āsmitānugata Samadhi* (Transcendence succeeded by I-consciousness)

Figure 5

As explained earlier, pure consciousness is one and indivisible. In the Sāṃkhya school of Indian philosophy, this fundamental level of consciousness has been termed as *mahat* and in the early Upaniṣadic tradition of thought it has been identified as *vijñānamaya kośa* (the gnostic sheath). Aurobindo termed this entity as the 'Universal Mind'. Due to a number of factors, this pure consciousness is apparently realized as divisible in different kinds of modifiable levels. For an easy understanding, let us call all these modifiable levels as paradoxical levels of consciousness. The factors, causing positive or negative impacts on the transformation of paradoxical consciousness into the pure consciousness (the emergence of pure consciousness) may be categorized or listed as follows: (a) body and senses, (b) space, time and surrounding (c) intellect, ego and conscience, (d) subconscious and unconscious psychic activators, (e) extrasensory experiences, (f) imprints of prior birth/ generations, (g) transcendental realizations and (h) cosmic realizations.

Of these, factors belonging to categories (a), (b) and (c), occupy a lions share in our general awareness. Let us term these categories as premier categories of consciousness. Until one is partially or completely alleviated from the premier categories of consciousness, one may not access the further deeper levels of (d) or (e), which may be characterized as the deeper categories of consciousness. Moreover, without being devoid of these premier and deeper categories of the paradoxical consciousness, one cannot get entry in the consciousness–categories of (f) or (g), which may be designated as the super–consciousness category. However, to attain the super consciousness level of realizations, an aspirant should cut him/herself off from the lower levels of premier and deeper categories of consciousness, ranging from (a) to (e). It may be formulated as below:

If paradoxical consciousness (divisible levels of conscious) is Pc, then

$Pc - \{a + b + c\} = Dc;$

Dc = Deeper categories of consciousness (subconscious and unconscious impressions and extra sensory experiences).

If general awareness is Gc, then

$Gc - (Dc + Pc) = Sc$

Sc = super–consciousness level (transcendental and cosmic realizations)

For the realization of ultimate level of pure (indivisible) consciousness, one has to cut himself off from all the relatively lower levels of consciousness, ranging from (a) to (g). Actually the decrease in diversions of psychic (*prāṇic*) energy, promotes the concentration of energy to make the consciousness more lucid.

During any interaction between mind and the object of focus, these factors influence one's cognition. Among them, factors related to the body and senses on the one hand and the awareness of time and external surrounding on the other, have primary intense impact on consciousness, whereas the factors of intellect, ego, conscience, subconscious and unconscious impressions of mind may have relatively secondary effect. Sometimes the imprints of prior birth (as per the traditional Indian view) modulate the nature of cognition.

Besides, a number of extrasensory experiences in the form of transcendental and cosmic realizations regarding the object of focus may also have positive influence on the quality of cognition. To attain this super-consciousness category, the dominating effects of body, senses and external surroundings, should be moderated and the underlying influence of the ego, subconscious and unconscious impressions should be optimized, so that while interacting with intellect, the imprints of prior birth and conscience may bring about their distinct manifestations in the form of super-knowledge. However, to obtain extrasensory cognition, transcendental knowledge and cosmic realizations regarding the object of focus, an aspirant has to lessen not only the pronounced impact of the premier categories of consciousness but also the impressions of deeper categories of consciousness. Sometimes, though not always, this state may also be the precursor of realizing the imprints of prior births. In the traditional Indian system of psychics or *manas-śāstra*, these factors are found to be responsible for the apparent fractionisation of consciousness which is in reality one and indivisible.

Approaching Super-Cognitive Levels

The approach for attainment of super cognitive levels requires simple, natural, moral, and peaceful life-style. Furthermore, it needs sincere, regular, constant, and progressive practice of eight limbic system of Yoga as propounded by Patañjali, starting with the practice of yogic abstinence and observance (*yama and niyama*), proceeding with the practices of yogic breathing and abstraction and finally leading to the different stages of meditation. After being deeply absorbed in meditation, one may realize any reasonableness or cognizance or a realization of the ultimate self.

Occasionally it happens that in any peaceful solitude environment:

- whenever one's mind is free from violence, lust, temptation, fear and worries,
- and one's physical system is wholesome, contented and relaxed,

- accidentally, with the help of any sensefull verse, melodious tune, sylvan scene or blissful feeling,
- one's body, bioenergy and mind are in relaxation.

All at once it may make one oblivious of his apparent self and at any moment several components of yoga are spontaneously combined together, which lead one's consciousness to the state of *samādhi. Samādhi* (transcendental state) further leads to the attainment of wisdom. The trial of making this rare but spontaneous natural creative stage into an attainable one is the subject-matter of *aṣṭaṇga yoga* system (Tripathi and Singh, 1984).

Samādhi initially gives way to approach the gnostic sheath of the self. At this level of gnostic sheath of self, one is able to understand that which is normally unseen and is the source of wisdom and creative intelligence. This level of self is helpful in creating excellent art of artists, composing sublime poetry for the poets, great inventions for scientists, as well as it renders pious divine bliss to devotees and saints, and genuine solution to the seekers.

REFERENCES

Anantharaman, T. R. (1983). Yoga-Vidya and Yoga-Vidhi. *The Yoga Review*, Summer & Autumn, III (2 & 3), 119-137.

Feuerstein, G. (2002). *The Philosophy and Practice of Patañjala Yoga Tradition: Its History, Literature, Philosophy and Practice*. Delhi: Motilal Banarasidass.

Pillai, C. (1997). Towards the inner world. *Yoga and Total Health*, Vol. XL II, June, II, 3-4.

Sadhakas. (1995). *A New Approach to Success* (pp. 9-21) Bombay: The Yoga Institute.

Tripathi, K.M. & Singh, R.H. (1984). Astangic Yoga: Its symmetrical wholeness and mutual interrelations with special reference to Yama, Niyama and Samādhi. *The Yoga Review*, Spring & Summer, IV (1 & 2), 27-40.

Patañjali *Yoga-Sūtras* and Parapsychological Research: Exploring Matches and Mismatches

William Braud

This presentation addresses interrelationships between concepts and practices described in the Patañjali *Yoga-Sūtras* and certain conceptualizations, research methods, and empirical findings within the discipline of parapsychological research. My aim is to describe ways in which Indian psychophysical practices and principles, as illustrated in the Patañjali *Yoga-Sūtras*, both inform and are supported by psi research and theory, and to indicate instances in which aspects of yogic practice and parapsychological research match or mismatch each other. In this presentation, *psi* is used as a theoretically neutral term for psychic functioning.

The Patañjali *Yoga Sūtras* and the Aims and Practices of Yoga

The Patañjali *Yoga-Sūtras* is a collection of 196 interrelated sutras or aphorisms, organized into four chapters or books (*pada*). The first chapter (*samādhi pada*) consists of 51 *sūtras* that deal in a general way with special forms of attention and consciousness that are the goals of yoga. The second chapter (*sādhanā pāda*) consists of 55 *sūtra*s that describe the most important practices of this spiritual discipline. The 56 *sūtras* of the third chapter (*vibhūti pāda*) describe the extraordinary powers or attainments (*siddhis*) that can result from intense yogic practice. The fourth and final chapter (*kaivalya pada*), which some believe to be a later addition to the earlier three chapters, consists of 34 *sūtra*s and describes the independence and emancipation that can be the fruit of diligent yogic practice.

The filling out and interpretation of the *sūtra*s took the form of *commentaries*. In the case of the *Yoga-Sūtra*s, important early commentaries were the *Yogabhāṣya* of Vyāsa (sixth and seventh centuries), the *Tattvavaiśāradī* of Vācaspati Miśra (ninth century), the *Rājamārtaṇḍa* of King Bhoja (eleventh century), the *Yogavārttika* of Vijñāna Bhikṣu (sixteenth century), and the *Maṇiprabhā* of Sarasvati Rāmānanda (sixteenth century) (see Eliade, 1975). Modern English translations of the *Yoga-Sūtra*s, along with selected commentaries, can be found in Rama Prasada (1910/2003), Woods (1927), Mishra (1963), Prabhavananda and Isherwood (1969), Taimni (1975), Vivekananda (1982), Brown (1999), and Govindan (2001).

Yoga builds upon the metaphysical foundation of the ancient Sāṃkhya system, but whereas Sāṃkhya is intellectual and theoretical, Yoga is experiential and practical. The goal of Yoga is bivalent – to achieve emancipation from conditioned matter and mind (*prakṛti*) and to achieve oneness or union with unconditioned, pure consciousness (*puruṣa*). This bivalent aspect also is operative, more mundanely, in the practice of ordering and unifying the usually dispersed and undisciplined activities of the mind in order to eventually transcend even this more organized and controlled mental condition.

The *Yoga-Sūtra*s provide step-by-step instructions for ceasing to identify with the fluctuations or modifications (thought waves, whirlpools) of the mind (*citta-vṛtti*) and for ultimately achieving complete independence and isolation from matter/mind and liberation as pure consciousness. In the course of this spiritual discipline of constant practice (*tapas*) and detachment (*vairāgya*), one encounters various obstacles or hindrances (*kleśa*s, afflictions) that disturb the equilibrium of the mind: ignorance (*avidyā*), egoism (*asmitā*), attachment (*rāga*), aversion (*dveṣa*), and clinging to life (*abhiniveśa*). These five hindrances are the chief causes of confusion and suffering in life. Patañjali identified eight practices that help one overcome the hindrances, increase discriminative discernment, and move forward in one's psychospiritual development. These are the eight limbs (*aṣṭāṅga*) of yoga praxis: abstentions or restraints (*yama*), observances or disciplines (*niyama*), posture (*āsana*), control of breath/*prāṇa* (*prāṇāyāma*), withdrawing sensory activity from control by external objects (*pratyāhāra*), concentration (*dhāraṇā*), meditation (*dhyāna*), and absorption (*samādhi*). By engaging in these practices diligently and intensively, the yogin can acquire progressively greater control of body, senses, emotions, and thoughts; recognize and discriminate these limited and limiting disturbances (the seen) from one's true Self (the Seer); become capable of direct supersensory knowing; and ultimately become fully Self-realized in attaining liberation (*kaivalya*). At certain stages of the yogin's progressive development, various attainments or accomplishments (*siddhi*s, powers) emerge. It is with these *siddhi*s, the practices with which they are associated, and their relevance to parapsychology, that this presentation is chiefly concerned.

The Aims, Methods, and Findings of Psi Research

Parapsychology, or what might appropriately be called *psi inquiry*, addresses three major types of paranormal experiences and phenomena. The first type is *receptive psi* or *direct knowing*, in which one acquires accurate knowledge or information about events or experiences beyond the reach of the conventional senses. This form of psi has been described as *extrasensory perception* (*ESP*), *psi cognition*, or *anomalous cognition*. Receptive psi can manifest itself as *telepathy* (paranormal knowledge of the mental content or experiences of others, often at a distance; a kind of direct mind-to-mind communication), *clairvoyance* (paranormal knowledge of some objective events, objects, or occurrences, often at a distance; a kind of mind-to-object interaction), *precognition* (paranormal knowledge of future events; a kind of foreknowledge or future-telling beyond what is possible through rational inference), and *retrocognition* (direct, paranormal knowledge of events in the past, especially of events that one might not have personally encountered, and which, therefore, are beyond the range of personal memory). Recently, the terms *remote viewing* and *remote perception* have been used to describe cases of clairvoyance, and *premonition* and *presentiment* sometimes are used to describe cases of precognition.

The second form of psi can be described as *active psi* or *direct mental influence*, but the most commonly-used terms are *telekinesis* (movement at a distance) and *psychokinesis* (*PK*; mind-induced movement or mind-over-matter). Recently, the term *anomalous perturbation* has been used to describe these instances in which physical events apparently are influenced – directly and often at a distance – without the use of conventional muscular or motor systems or by their extensions or tools. Psychokinetic influences may manifest as gross movements or any other changes in remotely or distantly situated objects or living systems or as more subtle changes (especially in large numbers of randomly varying events) that may not be immediately obvious to the naked eye but can be revealed through statistical analysis.

The third form of psi can be described as *survival* (of bodily death) or *afterlife evidence*. This refers to various kinds of experiences or occurrences that suggest that some form of personality, individuality, or consciousness might survive the death of the physical body. Phenomena and experiences suggestive of postmortem survival include apparitions, hauntings, poltergeist occurrences, mediumistic communications, physical mediumship phenomena, some out-of-body experiences, near-death experiences, and past-life recall and reincarnation memories.

Scientific and scholarly inquiries into psi experiences and phenomena have been carried out using four major approaches: case studies, field investigations, experimental/laboratory studies, and experiential explorations. These four approaches, in their own distinctive ways, have yielded two major types of findings: (a) proof-related findings that simply demonstrate the existence of certain forms of psi, and (b) process-related findings that indicate the modulating influence of particular physiological or psychological variables on the strength or likelihood of psi. A description of these many findings is beyond the scope of this presentation. I will address here only certain process-related studies and findings that involve variables directly or indirectly related to the principles and practices of the Patañjali *Yoga-Sūtra*s. Additional comprehensive and detailed information about psi functioning may be found in the following resources: Braud (2003); Edge, Morris, Palmer, and Rush (1986); Griffin (1997); Krippner (1977, 1978, 1982, 1984, 1987, 1990, 1994); Kurtz (1985); Parker and Brusewitz (2003); Radin (1997); Rammohan (2002); Rao (2001, 2002); Targ, Schlitz, and Irwin (2000); Thalbourne and Storm (2005); and Wolman (1977).

Interrelationships of *Yoga-Sūtra*s, *Siddhi*s, and Psi Research

Various exercises described in the *Yoga-Sūtra*s, especially in the second and third chapters, are quite relevant to research in parapsychology. These practices, which have variously been described as forms of royal (*rāja*), eight-limbed (*aṣṭāṅga*), or action (*kriyā yoga*, are designed to systematically and progressively free the practitioner from disturbances or distractions at various levels — social, environmental, somatic, emotional, and cognitive. Their chief applicability to psi inquiry is that these practices might help practitioners become generally less distracted and calmer in body and mind, and this increased quietude, accompanied by a more inwardly-directed focus of attention, might facilitate access to more subtle, internal carriers of psychically-sourced information. Honorton (1974, 1977, 1981) likened the Patañjali yogic practices to a systematic program of psychophysiological noise- or distraction-reduction that might help reduce factors that ordinarily interfere with or mask psi "signals". Braud (1975, 1978) identified several sources of psi-interfering "noise" or distractions and described methods for reducing interferences at these various levels. Many of these noise-reducing, psi-conducive procedures closely resemble the yogic self-regulation practices described by Patañjali. In addition, some of the attainments (*siddhi*s) themselves, described in the third chapter (*vibhūti pāda*) of the *Yoga-Sūtra*s, closely resemble forms of psi that are of great interest to parapsychologists.

The first five limbs (*aṅga*s) are preparatory and set the stage for the successful practice of limbs six, seven, and eight—the three inner limbs (*antar-aṅgam*) that constitute yoga proper. Their practice reduces internal, cognitive distractions. When *dhāraṇā*, *dhyāna*, and *samādhi* (concentration, meditation, and profound absorption) are practiced together, the composite process is called *saṃyama*. *Saṃyama* might be translated as *constraint*; *thorough, complete, or perfect restraint*; or *full control*; it might also be translated as *communion* or *mind-poise*. *Saṃyama* conveys a sense of knowing through being or awareness through becoming what is to be known. Through mastery of *saṃyama* comes insight (*prajñā*), and through its progressive application, in stages, come knowledge of the Self and of the various principles of reality (*tattvas*). With increasing yogic practice come a variety of mystical, unitive experiences, states, conditions, or fulfilments, the various *samādhi*s.

The *Siddhi*s

The third chapter (*vibhūtī pāda*) of the *Yoga-Sūtra*s describes the various attainments or accomplishments (*siddhi*s, powers) that arise when *saṃyama* is applied in various ways and to particular objects. Patañjali provides a selective listing of these attainments. Some (e.g., Taimni, 1975) have suggested that Patañjali may deliberately have introduced incomplete and even misleading information into the *siddhi* listings, in order to minimize their misuse by inappropriately prepared or ill-motivated practitioners. It might also be argued that some of these *siddhi*s might best be understood not literally but metaphorically or anagogically, instead.

Some of the *siddhis* are relatively mundane, some physiological, some psychological, some paranormal, some spiritual and mystical. Some of these might be understood as the fruits of ordinary deep thinking or pondering, whereas others might be resultants of other forms of knowing — direct knowing, insight, intuition, or revelation. Some of the *siddhis* (e.g., knowing the thoughts of others; clairaudience, knowledge of the subtle, concealed, and remote) are identical, or similar, to forms of receptive psi previously mentioned.

The relevance of the *siddhis* to psi inquiry becomes clear. Study of the *siddhis* could help in elaborating the nature of some psi manifestations already familiar to psi researchers and also could help reveal other forms that have not yet been explored in parapsychology. Of greater interest, in the context of process-related psi studies, examination of the eight-membered (limbed) path of yogic practice, in the course of which the *siddhis* are believed to spontaneously or deliberately manifest, could reveal methods through which psi functioning might be fostered or enhanced. A greater production of psi experiences could, in turn, facilitate both the study and understanding of psi.

Yogic Practices and Psi Research

In certain areas of process-related psi research, researchers have explored the possible psi influences of factors directly or indirectly related to the eight major forms of yogic praxis. Representative examples of these areas, and their correspondences with the eight practices, are presented in Table 1.

TABLE 1

Psi Research Areas	Yogic Practices
	Yama (restraints) *Niyama* (observances)
Relaxation research Hypnosis research Physiological research	*Āsana* (postures) *Prāṇāyāma* (vital energy/breath control)
Dream telepathy research Ganzfeld research	*Pratyāhāra* (sensory withdrawal)
Concentration/visualization in receptive psi Concentration/visulization in active psi Meditation research Absorption research	*Dhāraṇā* (concentration) *Dhyāna* (meditation) *Samādhi* (absorption)

Table 1 is organized simply to indicate concentrations and patterns of research, rather than precise one-to-one correspondences; it is recognized that the various yogic practices are interrelated, as are the processes at work in the various psi research areas.

SOMATIC QUIETUDE. The cluster of relaxation, hypnosis, and psychophysiological psi studies are related to the cluster of *āsana* and *prāṇāyāma* practices in that all of these involve a reduction in somatic distractions. The muscular, autonomic, and emotional quietude that accompany *āsana* and *prāṇāyāma* praxis have been produced, in psi research, not by those particular techniques but have been mimicked by related methods of progressive muscular relaxation, autogenic training, hypnosis, biofeedback, and self-regulation procedures. In receptive psi studies, research participants have been asked to describe hidden pictorial targets under conditions of induced relaxation, and relaxation results were compared with those obtained under suitable control or contrast (nonrelaxed or tension-induced) conditions. In some cases, degree of relaxation was monitored via electromyographic recording. Analyses of bodies of research using relaxation techniques have yielded strong evidence for accurate psi functioning under conditions of relaxation, and some studies indicated significant positive correlations between degree of relaxation and degree of psi accuracy (see Braud, 2002; Honorton, 1977; Storm and Thalbourne, 2001).

Hypnosis studies are relevant, here, because of the strong relaxation component present in most hypnotic conditions. Reviews and meta-analyses of research findings indicated that hypnosis was conducive to receptive psi functioning (see Braud, 2002; Honorton, 1977; Schechter, 1984; Stanford and Stein, 1993).

Somatic quietude also is reflected in reduced physiological arousal, as indicated by reduced sympathetic nervous system activity. A review of relevant laboratory studies indicated enhancement of receptive psi under conditions of reduced sympathetic nervous system activity (Braud, 1981b, 2002).

SENSORY RESTRICTION. In the yogic practice of *pratyāhāra*, attention is withdrawn from external objects that usually provide stimulation of the senses. Two conditions that duplicate this sensory restriction process have been studied extensively in the laboratory, and both have been found to be psi-favourable. These two conditions are the nocturnal dream and the *Ganzfeld* procedure. In both of these, there is a reduction in the processing of external sensory information, an inward-turning of attention, and an increase in imaginal activity and (internal) visual imagery. Receptive psi has been studied in the laboratory under both of these conditions. In dream-telepathy studies, persons were monitored in a sleep laboratory and awakened and asked to describe dream content when electrophysiological monitoring equipment indicated the presence of dreaming (rapid eye movements, an activated electroencephalographic pattern, and reduced muscular tension). In *ganzfeld* studies, uniform visual and auditory fields were produced by means of unpatterned light and sound stimulation; such sensory restriction or privation can produce an altered state of consciousness that resembles the twilight (hypnagogic/hypnopompic) state between waking and sleeping. In both sets of experiments, the research participant's task was to become psychically aware of the content of a visual target picture hidden from normal sensory access — i.e., placed at a distance or viewed by another person at a distance. Reviews and meta-analyses of the results of many dream telepathy and *ganzfeld* telepathy experiments indicated that both of these conditions of sensory restriction/sensory withdrawal were favourable to receptive psi functioning (see Braud, 2002; Child, 1985; Rao, 2002).

COGNITIVE QUIETUDE. Like bodily, emotional, and sensory quietude, cognitive quietude — a stilling of the thought ripples that can disturb a quiet, tranquil mind, such as the condition that can accompany meditation — also might be psi-favourable. This inference that meditation might be psi-conducive is supported by findings that meditation tends to be accompanied by reduced muscular tension and reduced autonomic (sympathetic) arousal, and also by traditional Indian beliefs and anecdotal observations that paranormal events (*siddhi*s) may occur spontaneously at certain stages of meditative practice (see, e.g., Kanthamani, 1971; Rao, Dukhan, and Rao, 1978; Smith, 1966). With these possibilities in mind, Honorton (1977) reviewed 16 experimental studies of psi performance during or immediately following meditation and found that 9 of the 16 studies yielded significant evidence for psi (in both receptive [ESP] and active [PK] forms). Some of this research was further reviewed by Rao (2002), who warned that some of these studies—like studies of meditation and other processes—suffered from a lack of appropriate control or contrast conditions. Another review, focusing on the possible role of meditation in psychokinesis performance, found that results of all but one of eight studies were consistent with the expectation that the practice of meditation would be favourable to the occurrence of psychokinetic effects (Braud, 1989). It should be pointed out that in many of the meditation-psi studies, the "meditation" process studied has been of a rather "mild" form, rather than the much more intensive forms of *dhāraṇā*, *dhyāna*, and *samādhi* (and their conjoint practice, as *saṃyama)* treated in the *Yoga-Sūtra*s.

Related to meditative conditions is the construct of *absorption*, as used in psychological research. In the latter, absorption typically is defined as "a 'total' attention, involving a full commitment of available perceptual, motoric, imaginative, and ideational resources to a unified representation of the attentional object" (Tellegen and Atkinson, 1974, p. 274). Note that this form of absorption is not necessarily identical to the form of absorption that may occur in the yogic practice of *samādhi*. A standardized measure of (the psychological form of) absorption has been used in some psi studies.

Only some of these studies (e.g., Stanford and Angelini, 1984) have found significant positive correlations between psi performance and absorption. However, Stanford (1987) has suggested several aspects of the psi-absorption studies that might have obscured the predicted relationship between these two variables.

In an early study, Lesh (1970) reported findings that suggested that a group of persons who practiced a form of meditation (Zen sitting meditation, *zazen*) daily for 4 weeks improved significantly in their empathic/affective sensitivity ability. These findings are relevant in that empathy is closely related to psychic sensitivity — especially to telepathy, the original meaning of which was feeling (literally, suffering) at a distance. In the Lesh study, interesting qualitative experiences suggestive of psi (i.e., shared imagery) also were reported.

Concentration has not been formally studied in psi research. More informal observations have suggested that concentration on target events, and then the release of such concentration, often has been used by successful participants as they prepare for their psi "testing" (e.g., White, 1964); and concentration on target events in ESP tests and on desired outcomes in PK tests invariably is present to some degree in nearly all experimental studies. The degree and quality of concentration, in a sense that more closely resembles *dhāraṇā*, would seem to be a useful topic for future psi research.

In summary, the roles of the last three limbs of yogic praxis have, thus far, not been tested adequately in contemporary psi research. Work with research participants who have practiced meditation more extensively and intensively is recommended.

Yoga *Siddhis* and Psi Research Findings: Additional Matches and Mismatches

Findings from experimental psi research studies are relevant to the *Yoga-Sūtra*s comments on *siddhi*s in two ways:

1. Certain "attainments" mentioned in the *Yoga-Sūtra*s' third chapter have, indeed, been found to occur in carefully designed labo-

ratory studies (viz., studies of telepathy, clairvoyance, precognition, psychokinesis).

2. Some of the yogic practices mentioned in the *Yoga-Sūtra*s have, indeed, been found to be associated with enhanced psychic functioning. As indicated above, significant evidence for psi functioning has been found in association with at least rudimentary forms of practices (such as sensory withdrawal and meditational or protomeditational techniques) that reduce sensory, somatic, and cognitive distractions or disturbances. Because significant results have been observed in connection with limited forms of these practices, it is possible that more extensive and intensive practice of the same or similar techniques might yield even stronger or more consistent psi results.

There has been a curious absence of systematic psi research on the possible roles of the first two, foundational limbs of yogic practice – *yama* and *niyama*. Additionally, the possible effects of *āsana* and *prāṇāyāma* have not been directly assessed in formal psi research, although very preliminary and partial forms of such exercises are included in at least some of the psi-conducive procedures employed in psi research laboratories. Finally, the progressive and intensive conjoint presence – as *saṃyama* – of *dhāraṇā*, *dhyāna*, and *samādhi,* has not been adequately explored. Investigations of these neglected areas can be ways in which future psi inquiry might be usefully informed by the *Yoga-Sūtra*s.

Still other psi findings are relevant to the Patañjali *Yoga-Sūtra*s and *siddhi*s. There is a nonlocal aspect to psi functioning. Both receptive (ESP) and active (PK) forms of psi can operate at a distance – through space (when distant targets are involved and in findings derived from group or global consciousness studies; see Nelson, 2001; Radin, 1997) and through time (in instances of precognition and retroactive intentional influences; see Braud, 2000). These findings are congruent with *Yoga-Sūtra*s claims of processes that are not bound by the usual constraints of space, time, and agency. In addition, some psychical researchers accept that a case may be made for the possibility of past lives (see Mills and Lynn, 2000), which is consistent with certain reincarnation claims found in the *Yoga-Sūtra*s and elsewhere in Indian philosophy and psychology. Also consistent with some *Yoga-Sūtra*s claims are findings regarding out-of-body experiences (see Alvarado, 2000) and other psi-related experiences and events (see Cohen and Phipps, 1992).

The foregoing findings indicate that psi functioning may be especially likely and effective under special conditions induced by practices similar to those described in the *Yoga-Sūtra*s. However, psi functioning also occurs spontaneously in lived experience and also under more "ordinary" conditions in the laboratory. For example, it has been claimed that no special conditions or psychological preparations are needed for successful "remote viewing". One of the *Yoga-Sūtra*s (IV: 1) suggests that *siddhi*s might be the result of birth, herbs, *mantra*s, intense practice, and cognitive absorption. Thus, certain individuals might have greater predispositions for psi functioning than others due to genetics (and, in Indian worldviews, "birth" would include possible *kārmic* influences from past lives in which yogic or yogic-like practices had indeed occurred) and environmental influences and practices (other than yogic praxis). Forms of "preparation" such as those just mentioned could be responsible for some instances of facile psi functioning seemingly unconnected with formal yogic or yogic-like practice and their resultant conditions. According to Yogic views, although psi might occur spontaneously and sporadically in anyone's experience, strong, consistent, and controllable forms of psi may require the support of the processes and practices described in the *Yoga-Sūtra*s.

Yogic techniques reduce sensory, somatic, and cognitive distractions and foster an inward deployment of attention. The reduction of usual sources of interfering or masking "noise" can allow the more facile detection and description of already-present, subtle carriers or vehicles of psi information – i.e., thoughts, images, and feelings that otherwise might be ignored. In addition to reducing noise, the various techniques also reduce various internal and external *constraints* on the brain-mind, de-structuring the brain-mind and allowing changes (of the types we call "psychic") to occur more readily in the first place (Braud, 1981a). That is, yogic techniques may help the brain-mind become less inert and more labile (freely variable).

With respect to the three *guṇa*-s (fundamental characteristics, qualities, or ways of being of matter/mind [*prakṛti*]) that are prominently described in the *Yoga-Sūtra*s, and the Yoga and Sāṃkhya systems in general, the more labile/freely variable brain-mind that can be fostered by yogic practices would have less of the characteristics of extreme *rajas* (the principle of energy, excitement, force, restlessness, activity, projection), and of extreme *tamas* (the principle of mass, inertia, sluggishness, resistance, passivity, obscurity), and more of the characteristics of *sattva* (the principle of balance, orderliness, information, intelligence, essence, calmness, clarity, expressiveness; a harmonizing of *tamas* and *rajas*). What are viewed, in the *Yoga-Sūtra*s, as optimal conditions for human psychospiritual development may also correspond to optimal conditions of psi functioning.

Functions and Limitations of *Siddhi* Experiences

Traditionally, aspirants have been warned of the dangers inherent in the *siddhi*s. Although the *siddhi*s are said to develop spontaneously during the course of one's intensive yoga practices, the recommendation is that one should not seek these out, pay special attention to them, or cling to them, but rather, one should treat them as natural by-products of one's psychospiritual work and move forward in that work.

The *siddhi*s might become obstacles because they could shift one's attentional focus to outward things and because they might call attention to egocentric concerns. Both of these emphases could tempt and sidetrack the aspirant from the major aim of yogic practice — to reduce and ultimately eliminate the thought waves of one's mind so that one no longer falsely identifies *puruṣa* with the manifestations of *prakṛti* and achieves Self-realization.

However, the *siddhi*s also can serve several useful functions. Because these are considered by-products of proper practice (especially of *saṃyama*), their appearances can serve as signposts, as indicators of one's psychospiritual progress. They can provide useful assurances and confidence in what one is doing and in the validity of the principles that inform one's practices. Some *siddhis* can help dispel some illusions – e.g., the illusion that one is always and forever bound by space, time, and agency. Further, acquaintance with certain *siddhis* might help an aspirant's understanding of the more subtle realms explored through yogic practice, and may even serve as useful tools in these explorations.

When yogic principles and practices were codified in the Patañjali *Yoga-Sūtras*, there was widespread acceptance of other ways of knowing, being, and doing, and of spiritual realities; and remarkable feats and powers were not as necessary to convince one of the reality of these other possibilities. In today's more sceptical age, the existence of "signs" such as the *siddhis* can serve as intimations and reminders of alternative, less familiar aspects of reality. The *siddhis* may serve very different purposes for different times, cultures, persons, and phases of life.

A serious student begins exploring Yoga not to acquire curious powers, but to attain a greater understanding of oneself and of reality at large. The *siddhis* might be encountered in the process, but quickly transcended. So, too, parapsychologists can, in time, pass beyond an exclusive interest in the well-recognized psi phenomena and advance to a consideration of larger and more spiritual matters. The *Yoga-Sūtras* can provide guidance in such a quest. Prior uses of yoga-related processes in psi research might be likened to stealing jewels from temples. A deeper appreciation of these processes might foster a realization of the purposes for which the temples were constructed in the first place.

There has been considerable interest in the possible role of the investigator in psi research — i.e., in psychologically mediated or psi-mediated experimenter effects (Palmer, 2002). The relevance of the *Yoga-Sūtras* to this issue is that by engaging in yogic practices, themselves, investigators might more thoroughly acquire the preparation and adequacy (*adaequatio*; see Schumacher, 1978) that might allow them to plan and conduct their psi research projects more creatively and interpret their findings more accurately and effectively.

REFERENCES

Alvarado, C.S. (2000). Out-of-body experiences. In E. Cardena, S.J. Lynn, & S. Krippner (Eds.), *Varieties of Anomalous Experience: Examining the Scientific Evidence* (pp. 183-218). Washington, DC: American Psychological Association.

Braud, W.G. (1975). Psi-conducive states. *Journal of Communication,* 25, 142-152.

— (1978). Psi conducive conditions: Explorations and interpretations. In B. Shapin & L. Coly (Eds.), *Psi and States of Awareness* (pp. 1-41). New York: Parapsychology Foundation.

— (1981a). Lability and inertia in psychic functioning. In B. Shapin & L. Coly (Eds.), *Concepts and Theories of Parapsychology* (pp. 1-36). New York: Parapsychology Foundation.

— (1981b). Psi performance and autonomic nervous system activity. *Journal of the American Society for Psychical Research,* 75, 1-35.

— (1989). Meditation and psychokinesis. *Parapsychology Review,* 20, 9-11.

— (2000) Wellness implications of retroactive intentional influence: Exploring an outrageous hypothesis. *Alternative Therapies in Health and Medicine,* 6 (1), 37-48.

— (2002). Psi favourable conditions. In V. W. Rammohan (Ed), *New Frontiers of Human Science* (pp. 95-118). Jefferson, NC: McFarland.

— (2003). *Distant Mental Influence: Its Contributions to Science, Healing, and Human Interactions*. Charlottesville, VA: Hampton Roads Publishing Company.

Brown, D. (1999). *The Upanishads: Seven Upanishads and the Aphorisms of Patañjali of Ancient India*. Los Angeles: Philosophical Research Society.

Child, I.L. (1985). Psychology and anomalous observations: The question of ESP in dreams. *American Psychologist*, 40, 1219-1230.

Cohen, J.M. & Phipps, J.F. (1992). *The Common Experience*. Wheaton, IL: Quest.

Edge, H., Morris, R., Palmer, J., & Rush, J. (1986). *Foundations of Parapsychology: Exploring the Boundaries of Human Capability*. Boston: Routledge & Kegan Paul.

Eliade, M. (1975). *Patañjali and Yoga*. New York: Schocken Books.

Govindan, M. (2001). *Kriya Yoga Sutras of Patañjali and the Siddhas*. Bangalore : Babaji's Kriya Yoga Order of Acharyas Trust.

Griffin, R.R. (1997). *Parapsychology, Philosophy, and Spirituality: A Postmodern Exploration*. Albany: State University of New York Press.

Honorton, C. (1974). Psi-conducive states. In J. White (Ed.), *Psychic Exploration* (pp. 616-638). New York: Putnam's.

— (1977). Psi and internal attention states. In B. Wolman (Ed.), *Handbook of Parapsychology* (pp. 435-472). New York: Van Nostrand Reinhold.

— C. (1981). Psi, internal attention states, and the Yoga Sutras of Patañjali. In B. Shapin & L. Coly (Eds.), *Concepts and Theories of Parapsychology* (pp. 55-68). New York: Parapsychology Foundation.

Kanthamani, B.K. (1971). Psychical study in India—past and present. In A. Angoff & B. Shapin (Eds.). *A Century of Psychical Research: The Continuing Doubts and Affirmations* (pp. 131-138). New York: Parapsychology Foundation.

Krippner, S. (Ed.). (1977, 1978, 1982). *Advances in Parapsychological Research* (Vols. 13). New York: Plenum.

— (Ed.). (1984, 1987, 1990, 1994). *Advances of Parapsychological Research* (Vols. 4 - 7). Jefferson, NC: McFarland.

Kurtz, P. (Ed.). (1985). *A Skeptic's Handbook of Parapsychology*. Buffalo, NY: Prometheus.

Lesh, T.V. (1970). Zen meditation and the development of empathy in counselors. *Journal of Humanistic Psychology, 10*(1), 39-74.

Mills, A. & Lynn, S.J. (2000). Past-life experiences. In E. Cardena, S.J. Lynn, & S. Krippner (Eds.), *Varieties of Anomalous Experience: Examining the Scientific Evidence* (pp. 293-314). Washington, DC: American Psychological Association.

Mishra, R.S. (1963). *The Textbook of Yoga Psychology*. New York: Julian Press.

Nelson, R. (2001). Correlation of global events with REG data: An Internet-based nonlocal anomalies experiment. *Journal of Parapsychology, 65*, 247-271.

Palmer, J. (2002). The challenge of experimenter psi. In V. W. Rammohan (Ed). *New Frontiers of Human Science* (pp. 142-157). Jefferson, NC: McFarland.

Parker, A. & Brusewitz, G. (2003). A compendium of the evidence for psi. *European Journal of Parapsychology, 18*, 29-48.

Prabhavananda, S. & Isherwood, C. (1969). *How to Know God: The Yoga Aphorisms of Patañjali.* New York: Mentor.

Prasada, R. (1910/2003). *Patañjali's Yoga Sutras, with the Commentary of Vyasa and the Gloss of Vachaspati Misra*. New Delhi: Munshiram Manoharlal.

Radin, D.I. (1997). *The Conscious Universe: Truth of Psychic Phenomena.* San Francisco: Harper Collins.

Rammohan, V.G. (Ed.) (2002). *New Frontiers of Human Science.* Jefferson, NC: McFarland.

Rao, K.R. (Ed.). (2001). *Basic Research in Parapsychology* (2nd edn.). Jefferson, NC: McFarland.

— (2002). *Consciousness Studies: Cross-cultural Perspectives.* Jefferson, NC: McFarland.

— Dukhan, H. & Rao, P.V.K. (1978). Yogic meditation and psi scoring in forced-choice and free-response tests. *Journal of Indian Psychology,* 1, 160-175.

Schechter, E.I. (1984). Hypnotic induction vs. control conditions: Illustrating an approach to the evaluation of replicability in parapsychological data. *Journal of the American Society for Psychical Research,* 78, 1-27.

Schumacher, E.F. (1978). *A Guide for the Perplexed.* New York: Harper & Row.

Smith, H. (1966). Parapsychology in the Indian tradition. *International Journal of Parapsychology,* 8, 248-263.

Stanford, R.G. (1987). Ganzfeld and hypnotic-induction procedures in ESP research: Toward understanding their success. In S. Krippner (Ed.), *Advances in Parapsychological Research,* Vol. 5 (pp. 39-76). Jefferson, NC: McFarland.

— & Angelini, R.R. (1984). Effects of noise and the trait of absorption on ganzfeld ESP performance. *Journal of Parapsychology,* 48, 85-99.

— & Stein, A. (1993). A meta-analysis of ESP studies contrasting hypnosis and a comparison condition. *Proceedings of the 36th Annual Parapsychological Association Convention,* 105-125.

Storm, L. & Thalbourne, M.A. (2001). Paranormal effects using sighted and vision-impaired participants in a quasi-ganzfeld task. *Australian Journal of Parapsychology,* 1, 133-170.

Taimni, I.K. (1975). *The Science of Yoga*. Madras, India: Theosophical Publishing House.

Targ, E., Schlitz, M. & Irwin, H.J. (2000). Psi-related experiences. In E. Cardena, S. J. Lynn, & S. Krippner (Eds.), *Varieties of Anomalous Experience: Examining the Scientific Evidence* (pp. 219-252). Washington, DC: American Psychological Association.

Tellegen, A. & Atkinson, G. (1974). Openness to absorbing and self-altering experiences ("absorption"), a trait related to hypnotic susceptibility. *Journal of Abnormal Psychology*, 83, 268-277.

Thalbourne, M. & Storm, L. (Eds.). (2005). *Parapsychology in the Twenty-first Century: Essays on the Future of Psychical Research.* Jefferson, NC: McFarland.

Vivekananda, S. (1982). *Raja-yoga*. New York: Ramakrishna-Vivekananda Center.

White, R.A. (1964). A comparison of old and new methods of response to targets in ESP experiments. *Journal of the American Society for Psychical Research,* 58, 21-56.

Wolman, B.B. (Ed.). (1977). *Handbook of Parapsychology*. New York: Van Nostrand Reinhold.

Woods, J.H. (1927). *The Yoga System of Patañjali.* Cambridge, MA: Harvard University Press.

The Question of Post-Mortem Survival: Empirical Evidence and Theoretical Issues

K. Ramakrishna Rao

One of the perplexing problems that has agitated the thinkers around the world during their quest to understand the nature of humans and their destiny is the question of survival, life after death. What does *death* mean? Does it annihilate the whole of the person, or is there anything left which persists after death?

No one can reasonably argue that nothing survives one's death. Obviously, a man's memories survive in the minds of those who knew him. His records, legacy, the progeny, and possessions survive, from which the historians may reconstruct the past of this person. However, these are not the things we refer to when we speak of survival. Obviously the person is more than her possessions; but then what is it that makes a person *that* person. What is it that defines the person? Where does the uniqueness of a person consist? The grown up person is not, for all appearances, the same as the infant who has grown to be that person. Yet there is continuity and identity. What is it that gives the identity? Some think that there is something unique about the person that gives her own identity. Perhaps it is her soul/spirit; or it is her unique physical manifestation as a system. For some others, it is the continuity itself that constitutes the identity of the person. We find various versions of this in Buddhist thought. Orthodox Hindu systems subscribe to the notion that there is a nonphysical, unchanging aspect to one's being that does not cease to exist with the disintegration of the body after death. However, it is arguable if by survival we refer to this nonphysical/spiritual aspect of being because it is ex-hypothesis eternal, unchanging and independent of the person. Moreover, we need independent evidence to believe that indeed such spiritual existence is real before we attribute survival to it. In a significant sense, when we speak of survival we mean something we know and experience as belonging to or part of the person who exists no more and is believed to be deceased.

It is difficult to say what life is and when and how it begins. It is equally difficult to precisely pin point death even though we all seem to know and identify life and death almost intuitively.

The person, as observed, is a living physical system with a set of orchestrated functions that operate in a rhythm, playing a tune as it were. Living consists in playing that tune. The interruption of the system's rhythm by the nonfunction of one or more of the vital subsystems such as the heart or the lever is considered death. Advances in medical science and technology have made it possible at least in principle that the weak and malfunctioning subsystems of the body (the organs) may be repaired or replaced without interrupting the rhythm of the system. However, if the rhythm itself is broken for any length of time the body is considered dead and cannot be revived. A body that can be revived and resurrected is not dead. By survival therefore we refer to something other than the deceased body.

Is there anything, other than the body that perishes at death or the eternal spirit that has no death, to which the question of post-mortem survival refers? This is the big question. I believe the question of survival as an empirically verifiable issue seems to rest squarely on the possibility of the existence of something intermediary between the unchanging, permanent, spiritual substance like soul or *atman* and the body that perishes at death. Does parapsychology have anything to offer that throws light on it?

Parapsychology and the Problem of Survival

The survival problem seems to be the main challenge that led most of the earlier psychical researchers such as those at the Society for Psychical Research in London and their counterparts in the US to study parapsychological phenomena. The culmination of this effort may be seen in F.W.H. Myers' (1915) seminal work *Human Personality and Its Survival of Bodily Death*. In a sense parapsychology is a by-product of survival research.

Subsequently, however, the application of scientific method to study phenomena like telepathy and clairvoyance became an end in itself; and few ventured out into the exploration of the problem of survival of human personality after death. In fact, case studies and qualitative research prominent among early psychical researchers gradually gave away to quantitative research and experimental investigations by parapsychologists. This transition became almost complete with the establishment of the parapsychology laboratory at Duke University and the crowning of J.B. Rhine as the leader. Rhine ruled parapsychology for almost fifty years. Interestingly, Rhine began his work at Duke to study some ostensible cases of survival; but he soon abandoned that project declaring that the problem of survival of human personality after death was not researchable at the time because there were no appropriate scientific methods that could provide unambiguous evidence for it. Therefore, the research on the survival problem was put on the shelf, never to be revived during his life time.

As mentioned, Rhine began with an interest in survival research. What sent Rhine and his wife to Duke University to work with psychologist William McDougall was a grant from John F. Thomas, a retired official in the public school system of Detroit. After the death of his beloved wife, Thomas held sittings with mediums who gave enough information known only to him and his deceased wife to warrant the possibility that the mediums were indeed communicating with his deceased wife. Thomas provided the grant to enable Rhine to study with McDougall the material he obtained with mediums in the US and England. As his wife Louisa E. Rhine, who worked with her husband in parapsychology all along, tells us, the Rhines not only had an open mind to consider the possibility of survival of human personality after death, but they also entertained the belief that "there is some evidence that under certain conditions actual communication with the living by the dead can occur" (L.E. Rhine, 1983, p.116).

What is it then that changed Rhine's direction from engaging in survival research to carrying out experimental psi research almost exclusively? One reason of course is the success of his experimental program which made him instantly famous. He was doubly fortunate first to find some extraordinarily gifted subjects like Pearce and second to have very able colleagues to assist him.

There was another good reason. As Rhine began his experimental studies of extrasensory perception (ESP) at Duke University, he had an opportunity to work with Eileen J. Garrett, one of the most famous mediums of the time. In studies carried out by Rhine and his associates at Duke, Mrs. Garrett was able to give in a state of trance significant information relating to people that she had no normal way of knowing. However, these people were not deceased persons, but living individuals seated as experimental subjects in an adjoining room. The results suggested that the information obtained in a trance state by the medium may not be necessarily from the dead, but could be from the living sources as well. Again, during the same period, Mrs. Garrett was administered the ESP tests developed by Rhine to investigate ESP among college students. The results of the tests with Mrs. Garrett as a subject were highly significant suggesting that she possessed a high level of ESP ability (Birge and Rhine, 1942). If Mrs. Garrett had a high level of ESP, her earlier readings presumed to have come from the deceased could have been received from the living who had access to that information. Therefore, any evidence for survival hypothesis should control for and rule out the possibility of ESP on the part of a living person as a source for the information bearing on survival. Rhine felt that he really did not have reliable methods to exclude ESP on the part of the living as an alternative to the hypothesis that the ostensible information originated from the deceased person.

I worked with the Rhines for a number of years. In fact, I was chosen by them to succeed J.B. Rhine as the Director of the Institute for Parapsychology. Even though I was more challenged by the theoretical aspects of survival than Rhine did, I pretty much agreed with him that we simply did not have appropriate methods to reliably investigate the question of life after death. Survival meant the existence of some kind of a noncorporeal spiritual entity. How can we ever establish empirically the existence of a spiritual substance? Therefore my research in parapsychology was largely confined to laboratory type of research. With this bias stated at the outset, let me review in a summary form some of the empirical evidence that is offered as possible evidence in favour of the survival hypothesis, viz., that an aspect of the person survives the bodily death.

Any empirical considerations of survival raise the following questions: First, what is the evidence for survival? Second, how good is the evidence? Third, if the evidence is good, is survival the only possible or the most probable explanation? The following sources of evidence are usually cited in favour of the survival hypothesis: (1) spontaneous nonrecurrent paranormal experiences of people that have a bearing on the question of survival; (2) recurrent spontaneous occurrences such as hauntings and poltergeist phenomena; (3) the alleged controls of mediums claimed to be deceased persons; (4) alleged cases of cross-correspondence; (5) apparitions; (6) out-of-body experiences; (7) near-death experiences; and finally (8) claimed memories of a former incarnation.

Spontaneous Experiences Bearing on Survival

These are the cases in which a deceased personality is alleged to have communicated a piece of information to a living agent. There are indeed a large number of cases which fall into this category.

For example, L.E. Rhine had 258 cases in her collection of spontaneous cases bearing on survival. The following is a typical case. A woman reported that her mother was dead for years. One day she left her little boy in the bedroom and went into the kitchen. While in the kitchen she suddenly heard the voice of her mother calling her by name and asking her to go quickly to the bedroom, which she did to find that the boy had climbed on a chair and was leaning over a red hot stove trying to get something off the mantel (L.E. Rhine, 1960). The woman obviously believed that her deceased mother's intervention saved the boy from a serious fire hazard. The main difficulty in placing too much confidence in these spontaneously occurring cases is our understandable inability to assert or deny the factuality of the reported experiences. These experiences could, of course, be evaluated in the same manner as any verbal testimony is evaluated. However, parapsychologists have not found that the time and effort spent on validating personal experiences is worth the trouble. The more profitable course of action, it is suggested, is to collect numerous cases and study their apparent similarity with the expectation that the common characteristics running through a great many cases are less likely to be due to human frailties and biases of various sorts.

Apart from the lack of conclusiveness, the main difficulty with spontaneous experiences bearing on survival is the fact that most, if not all, of these experiences can be explained on the basis of known ESP abilities of the living without assuming the survival of a deceased personality, unless one is willing to defend a spiritualistic hypothesis of ESP. For example, it is possible that the woman in the case mentioned might have known by ESP that her son was in danger and that her mother's voice was only an unconscious projection of her ESP awareness of the impending danger. Of course one could argue that telepathy itself is mediated by a spirit. But, the spirit hypothesis of telepathy has been proved to be farfetched. According to this hypothesis, when A gets a telepathic message, a spirit S apprehends the information first and then communicates it to A. But how does the spirit obtain the information in the first place? Also, by what processes does the spirit communicate with the human beings, unless we assume that the latter are capable of receiving such communications? We have to assume ESP or some such ability on the pant of the spirit. It is more parsimonions then to assume ESP on the part of the living rather than postulate the existence of spirits. So Ockham's razor shaves the "spirits" of the spirit hypothesis!

Louisa E. Rhine (1961) whose study of spontaneous cases is perhaps the most respected of its kind, analyzed the cases bearing on survival in her huge collection. She found that survival related experiences occur like other ESP experiences in the form of dreams, intuitions and hallucinations as well as physical effects. She tried to find out whether the initiative for these experiences rested primarily with the living agent or with the deceased person, assuming that if the latter was the case it is more likely that the communication came from the deceased. She found several spontaneous experiences which seemed to suggest on the surface that the deceased personality had induced the experience. But, on further analysis, it appeared that in most of the cases bearing on survival, the initiative of a living agent could not be completely eliminated. She recognized, however, that there were a few cases in which the initiative of the deceased person seemed the only possible explanation. Thus, while Mrs. Rhine's collection does not provide any compelling evidence for survival, it keeps the question of survival still alive.

Recurrent Spontaneous Occurrences

Recurrent cases of survival often occur as hauntings or the poltergeist type of phenomena (see Owen, 1964; Roll, 1968) involving physical disturbances associated with a particular house or place. They occur over an extended period of time and are sometimes regarded as the mischief of discarnate spirits. One of the poltergeist type cases, closely observed and investigated by two parapsychologists J.G. Pratt and W.G. Roll (1958), relates to disturbances at Seaford, Long Island in USA. Poltergeist is a German word which means "noisy spirit". Pratt and Roll provide a detailed description of the disturbing occurrences that took place over a period of several days in the home in which the Herrmann's with their two children aged 13 and 12 lived. It was observed that objects in the house were disturbed in unexplained manner. These included objects moving without any contact and when no one was near the object. Some of these occurred when Pratt and Roll were in the house. Is this a case in which unseen "spirits" were moving the objects?

After careful study of the case, Pratt and Roll considered the following alternative hypotheses – (1) fraud on the part of some one involved in the case; (2) psychological maladjustment of someone in the household who is causing these without being noticed; (3) these occurrences had natural physical causes; and (4) some kind of psychokinetic (parapsychological) effect that was moving the objects. Pratt and Roll considered the first three alternatives as unlikely and the PK hypothesis "worthy of consideration" even though the evidence was not compelling. The general consensus among psi researchers is that what appear to be genuine poltergeist cases are more likely to be cases of recurrent spontaneous psychokinesis (RSPK) rather than the work of disembodied spirits. What one needs to know is the true source of these occurrences in order to ascertain their bearing on the survival hypothesis. But unfortunately, most of the poltergeist reports are inconclusive as to the agency responsible for these affects. In some instances, it is reasonable to assume that some maladjusted person in the family or in the neighbourhood is responsible for the disturbances. In some others, natural causes, such as underground water, may have caused them. And in those few cases in which the effects are more likely psi-mediated, it is not possible to eliminate the hypothesis that these occurrences are due to the exercise of psi abilities by living persons rather than the dead.

The Alleged Controls of Mediums

The essential feature of a medium who enters into a trance-like state is a kind of dissociation. In the majority of cases, the normal personality of the medium seems to be obliterated and a secondary personality takes it place. Many mediums claim that during the entranced state they are possessed by some discarnate agency in the form of one or more controls, claimed to be the "spirits" of deceased persons, who are alleged to give the ostensible paranormal information. One cannot really take these claims too seriously because, first, there were mediums like Madame Morel (studied by Osty) who never claimed to have had any controls. Second, there is much evidence to show that the alleged spirit controls are only psychological constructs of the medium. Finally, most of the mediumistic material can be explained, if we assume that the medium has ESP abilities, as we have noted in the case of Mrs. Garrett.

Consider, for example, the following case which, on the surface, looks like pretty convincing evidence in favour of the survival hypothesis. It is reported that S.G. Soal obtained through Mrs. Cooper, a medium, a communication purported to have come from his friend Gordon Davis, who was believed to be dead. The voice and the mannerisms of the medium when this communication was received were strikingly similar to those of Gordon Davis. Soal was indeed led to believe that the communication was really from his friend. The information obtained through Mrs. Cooper also tallied significantly with Soal's knowledge of Davis. The astonishing feature of this case is that it was found later that Davis had not really died but was still living. We have referred earlier to the study of Mrs. Garrett by Rhine, which shows that mediums in their trance states could obtain information from the living as well.

There are, however, cases like the "Lethe" case, in which the deceased spirit of Myers was alleged to have communicated through Mrs. Piper. The case is indeed impressive as to the detail and richness of the material received in the form of allusions that did not certainly seem intelligible to the medium or the sitters at the time of receiving them. Considerable research had to be done in the "Lethe" case to discover the bearing of these allusions on the message in point. These cases are indeed intriguing, if true, and deserve careful study.

Cross-Correspondences

The cases of cross-correspondence are occasionally cited as evidence of survival. The cross-correspondence cases are those in which the same message purported to come from a single discarnate agency may be obtained through the automatic writings of several sensitives. What one sensitive has written may be a continuation, repetition, or illustration of what some other sensitive has produced in her automatic writing. One main difficulty with the cross-correspondence cases is that it is difficult to evaluate the significance of the correspondences, since a certain number of them can always be expected by chance alone.

Two scripts written at random may contain many similarities if the interpreter takes the trouble to find them. The reported studies of cross-correspondence cases seldom had any controls to eliminate this possibility. It is also very difficult to eliminate the hypothesis of telepathy from some living agent. The fact that these messages were often communicated in a disguised, symbolic fashion does not give them any special status different from ESP, since ESP is reported to manifest in a number of disguised forms.

Apparitions

The most dramatic kind of spontaneous psi experiences is the apparitional type. Oxford philosopher H.H. Price (1960) defines apparition "as a visible but non-physical phenomenon closely resembling a particular human being" (p.110). The human being referred to may be living or dead. Those apparitions resembling the dead are sometimes offered as evidence of survival after death.

Most genuine apparitions may be explained as telepathically induced hallucinations. British psychical researcher G.N.M. Tyrrell (1947) proposed such a hypothesis. According to this theory, a thought in the mind of a person especially in a crisis situation may have a telepathic effect on another person. This telepathic impression may manifest itself to the person in the form of a visual hallucination as in the case of the experience of an apparition. There are, however, some that seem to be so realistic and impressive that they are taken as some sort of transported spirit images involving true exteriorization. Here again it is not theoretically necessary to assume another type of objective existence indicating a personality that can survive outside one's body, unless the observed effects cannot be explained by assuming parapsychical abilities on the part of the living.

Out-of-Body Experiences (OBEs)

OBEs are fairly widespread among the normal population (Monroe, 1971; Rogo, 1978). The following is an example of a case mentioned by H.H. Price (1960) taken from R.C. Johnson (1953). "I was conscious of being two persons – one lying on the ground.... My clothes on fire and waving my limbs about wildly.... The other 'me' was floating up in the air about 20 feet from the ground, from which position I could see not only my other self, but also the hedge and the car.... I remember quite distinctly telling myself, 'It's no use gibbering like that – roll over and over to put the flames out.' This my ground-body eventually did.... The flames went out, and at this stage I suddenly became one person again."

Some who have studied such experiences take them as evidence for survival. Believing that the person is a composite of spirit and body, any experience of feeling out-of-body for them is an attestation of the existence of a spirit that does not need the body to survive. But then others who do not subscribe to such a belief may reasonably demand public manifestation of these experiences, because there is the need to rule out the possibility that the OBEs are simply due to one's active imagination. There is indeed a limited amount of evidence that the OB experience could not have been born out of sheer imagination (Tart, 1968; Osis, 1978). Even when such evidence exists, however, it is difficult to rule out a parapsychological explanation such as ESP, which appears to be more parsimonious than the spirit hypothesis.

Near-Death Experiences (NDEs)

There is a lot of folklore in many cultures testifying that people at the hour of death have remarkable and unusual experiences that give them visions of dead relatives, religious figures, and glimpses of what is believed to be the after-world. Osis (1961) and Osis and Haraldsson (1977) surveyed deathbed observations of physicians and nurses. Their findings show that (a) the duration of the experiences was short; (b) the apparitions were seen coming from another world and were usually of relatives; (c) most patients appeared to "go" to the other world, and (d) the most frequent emotional response after the experience was one of peace and serenity, and religious ecstasy.

With the advances in the practice of medicine, it is no longer very rare to revive a person who has been found to be clinically dead for a while. Such near-death cases have been a subject of study (Kübler-Ross, 1969; Moody, 1975; Ring, 1980). Many near-death cases do not reveal any unusual experiences. However, what is interesting is that when they do, they appear similar. For example, it is common for persons having NDEs to report that they travelled through a dark passage, emerging into a brilliant light. Meeting a luminous person of tremendous personal significance is also not uncommon. What is even more remarkable is that some of them report significant transformations in their lifestyles after they have had the experience.

V. Krishnan (1985; 1988) made some important theoretical observations on near-death experiences. First, he critically examined near-death experiences as evidence for survival of consciousness beyond physical death. Second, he made empirically verifiable suggestions for understanding out-of-body visions. Pointing out that out-of-body experiences tend to occur under conditions of sensory deprivation, Krishnan (1993) suggests that out-of-body vision may be a way of satisfying the need for information or stimulation and it may be "useful therefore to investigate whether sensory deprivation, or the stress that it causes, has biochemical or other concomitants that can alter receptor sensitivity" (p. 259).

Reincarnation Studies

Reincarnation is an active belief among many in various parts of the world. The doctrine of karma and rebirth is one of the pervasive themes of Indian thought. Numerous reports of ostensible cases of reincarnation have appeared in the popular media. However, the credit for pioneering systematic research of reincarnation-type cases goes to Ian Stevenson of the University of Virginia, who earned his reputation first as a psychiatrist with a special expertise in clinical interviewing. His initial step in researching reincarnation was to examine the published reports of several hundred cases of claimed memories of past lives. He found among them 44 cases in which there were apparent recollections of specific people, places, or events relating to a person who was deceased before the birth of the subject. As may be expected because of the widespread belief in reincarnation in that part of the world, a majority of these cases were from India and Burma. After examining possible alternative hypothesis to reincarnation, including fraud, cryptomnesia, racial memory, ESP and possession, Stevenson (1960) concluded that reincarnation is "the most plausible hypothesis for understanding the cases of this series" (p.108). He was cautious, however, in pointing out that he did not consider them to "prove reincarnation either singly or jointly."

The second phase of Stevenson's research was to personally investigate the alleged cases of reincarnation himself instead of depending on the reports of others. This took him to various parts of the world. His research results were first published in his book *Twenty Cases Suggestive of Reincarnation.*

Stevenson (1974) concludes his review of the first cases he himself investigated "without opting firmly for any one theory" as an explanation for all cases. He believes, however, that the evidence in support of the reincarnation hypothesis has increased since his first review. "This increase," he points out, "has come from several different kinds of observations and cases, but chiefly from the observations of the behaviour of the children corresponding to past life memories and the study of cases with specific or idiosyncratic skills, and with congenital birthmarks and deformities" (p. 384).

The behavioural features associated with these children believed to be reincarnations of previously deceased persons include:

> (a) Repeated verbal expressions by the subject of the identification; (b) repeated presentation of information about the previous personality as coming to the subject in the

> form of memories of events experienced or of people already known; (c) requests to go to the previous home either for a visit or permanently; (d) familiar address and behaviour toward adults and children related to the previous personality according to the relationships and social customs which would be proper if the child really had the relationships he claims to have had with these persons; (e) emotional responses, e.g., of tears, joy, affection, fear, or resentment appropriate for the relationships and attitudes shown by the previous personality toward other persons and objects; and (f) mannerisms, habits, and skills which would be appropriate for the previous personality, or which he was known to possess. (p. 360)

C.T.K. Chari (1967) published a critical review of Stevenson's *Twenty Cases*. He argued that Stevenson's inability to understand the local languages and his dependence on interpreters was a major weakness in his studies. Chari pointed out the disparity in the frequency of cases reported in North and South India and the time trends in the occurrence of these cases, which, according to him, are due to social and cultural factors. "The South Indian cases that I have been able to investigate personally," he wrote, "have been very, very few and far too unconvincing" (p. 218). Chari also called attention to some discrepancies between the earlier reports of these cases and Stevenson's report, thus raising the question of the reliability of the sources of information. Chari also expressed scepticism about birthmarks as evidence of reincarnation. He wondered further how reincarnation could be a viable explanation in cases where the alleged reincarnated person was still living after the individual carrying the "memories" was born. Finally, he concluded that the reincarnationist interpretation of these cases fails to appreciate the possibility of the operation of what he called general psychometric ESP, which could in principle account for the alleged paranormal events in these cases.

The third step in Stevenson's reincarnation studies was to involve others, not merely as interpreters and translators, but as independent investigators so as to enhance the reliability and authenticity of the reports. One of Stevenson's Indian collaborators, Satwant Pasricha of the National Institute for Mental Health and Neuro-Sciences, Bangalore, points out that her data are similar to Stevenson's in numerous and important respects. She argues that such cross-cultural regularities in the data indicate that the reincarnation experience may be genuine and not due to cultural expectation or fraud (Pasricha, 1990).

An important case investigated by Stevenson and others independently is the case of Sharada, which in many respects is very unusual. Uttara was born on March 14, 1941 in Nagpur. She had a normal childhood, attended college, and obtained postgraduate degrees in English and Public Administration. When she was about 32 years old, she began behaving strangely and spoke in a language other than Marathi (her mother tongue), which was later identified as Bengali. Beginning in March of 1974 there were periodic alterations in Uttara's personality. These episodes occurred more than fifty times, each episode varying in duration from over forty days to just a couple of hours. In the altered state she called herself Sharada, the daughter of a Sanskrit scholar who lived at Burdwan in Bengal. She claimed that she was the wife of a physician by the name of Viswanath Mukhopadhyaya of Shivapur in Bengal and that she died of snakebite at the age of 24, when she was in the seventh month of her pregnancy.

According to the investigators, Uttara, in Sharada phase, wrote, spoke, and conversed in Bengali, a language she did not understand or speak as Uttara. As Sharada, Uttara manifested behavioural characteristics appropriate to a Bengali woman of 19th century and gave information about people and events that she could not have normally known.

The case of Sharada is different in some important ways from typical reincarnation-type cases, which normally appear during the childhood years of the subject. When Sharada emerged, Uttara was already 32 years old. In some cases of xenoglossy (the apparent ability to recite or converse in an unlearned language), the alleged paranormal linguistic ability has manifested under hypnosis.

In the case of Uttara, it manifested naturally, even though there is some reason to believe that the early Sharada episodes occurred when Uttara was in an altered state of consciousness following meditation.

Prof. V.V. Akolkar, a social psychologist, investigated the Sharada case completely independent of Stevenson, using his own method. Akolkar interviewed a large number of people associated with the case, including Uttara, and observed the Sharada phase several times. Apparently he had an excellent rapport with Uttara. She spent two days in Akolkar's house in Poona; and the Sharada phase appeared there as well. Apart from the usual interviewing associated with cases such as these, Akolkar (1992) was able to obtain considerable psychological information that seemed to suggest that there was some overlapping between the two personalities. Akolkar, like Stevenson, appears to favour reincarnation as more appropriate explanation of the Sharada case than alternative hypotheses.

Stephen Braude (1992) has criticized Stevenson and associates for not adequately going beyond the surface characteristics into the psychodynamic factors influencing the behaviour of Uttara and important persons associated with her. As he puts it, "the reader gets no feel whatever for Uttara and other relevant individuals as persons. We have no idea of what moved them or what their needs and desires were.... In fact, it is quite remarkable how little effort Stevenson apparently made to dig beneath the surface of their concerns, either in the actual course of investigation or in his subsequent evaluation of the case material" (pp.135-136).

The involvement of several independent, well-qualified investigators, like Akolkar and Pasricha, who clearly have the necessary understanding of the cultural factors, greatly enhances the credibility, authenticity, and reliability of the Sharada case. There is no doubt that Uttara in her Sharada phase was able to read, write, and speak Bengali, a skill that she was not known to possess as Uttara. Also, there is little doubt that some of the information that Sharada gave corresponded in significant measure to persons who lived in Bengal during the early nineteenth century. Beyond this, the interpretation of the case at this stage remains very much a matter of one's preference based on prior inclination.

Stevenson's preference for a survivalist explanation of past life memory cases, especially those involving the manifestation of skills such as speaking in unlearned languages, is based on his assumption that skills require practice and that therefore they may not be acquired paranormally without practice. This position is contested by S.E. Braude (1992) on the grounds that (a) "cases of multiple personality suggest that dissociation facilitates the development or acquisition of personality traits and skills which might never be developed or displayed under normal conditions" (p.139); and (b) "suddenly emerging skills of child prodigies often far exceed anything displayed by the subjects investigated in xenoglossy cases or other cases suggesting survival" (p.141). Stevenson (1992) counters by arguing that he knows of no evidence that child prodigies "manifested the skills without practicing them. If they did, perhaps they brought the skills from a previous life" (p.149).

There may be those who reject altogether any paranormal explanation of this or similar cases. Stevenson (1984) himself refers in his book to the newspaper reports containing allegations that Uttara learned Bengali in a normal way. He also acknowledges that a "vociferous critic," who was "sure that Uttara had taken extensive lessons in Bengali," (p.141) and who gave him the names of persons who could provide the necessary information. The search led Stevenson and Pasricha to T.K. Waghmare, who said that "he had seen Uttara taking a test in Bengali" (p.141) Stevenson believes, however, that Waghmare may have mistaken Shailaja, Uttara's sister, for Uttara. Both Stevenson and Akolkar discuss other possibilities of Uttara learning Bengali in a normal way. For example, a friend of Uttara claimed that he and Uttara studied Bengali during their final year in high school and "progressed enough to read a Bengali primer" (Akolkar, 1992, p. 215) and that Uttara's older brother told Akolkar "Uttara had learned Bengali" (p. 215). Stevenson mentions that two of Uttara's relatives have some knowledge of Bengali, including her younger brother, Satish. He also mentions that Uttara in a Sharada phase was reading a Bengali book when Bhattacharya and Sinha visited her. Both Stevenson and Akolkar remain unconvinced, however, that Sharada's skills in responsive xenoglossy could be explained even if we grant that Uttara had learned normally how to read Bengali.

What Can We Make of the Reincarnation Evidence?

Some peculiar characteristics that are reported to have been manifest in some alleged reincarnation cases are worth pursuing further. The ability to speak in languages not known to the agent is one of those. While it is possible to cross the barriers of language by means of extrasensory perception (Rao, 1963), we still have no evidence that the ability to speak an unknown language can also be acquired by means of ESP. There are some cases in which it is claimed that the subjects performed skills which they had never learned before, ostensibly by the invasion of a spirit or because these skills were learned in a previous birth. Since, as far as our present knowledge goes, at least some of our skills cannot be acquired by a mere knowledge of them without the necessary practice, if one can exhibit mastery of a skill which he could not conceivably have learned before, it is argued, then there is a reasonable case for the surviving personality. This is the line of argument pursued by C.J. Ducasse (1961).

Raising the question "what would constitute conclusive evidence of survival," Ducasse (1961) argues that ingenious feats of invention and creative activity reported in such cases as the "Lethe" case cannot be explained on the hypothesis of ESP, for something different from ESP in kind seems to be involved. As far as our knowledge of ESP goes, we have access only to items of information. In those cases in which the knowledge possessed consists of mental skills, as in the case of responsive xenoglossy, something more than ESP appears to be involved, since, apart from these cases, there is no evidence that ESP can accomplish these feats.

Undoubtedly, cases of responsive xenoglossy and those involving the exhibition of unlearned skills are indeed impressive, if their authenticity can be taken for granted. It seems, however, that a survivalistic interpretation of such cases involves a basic contradiction. In order that the display of an unlearned skill may be construed as evidence of the intervention of a surviving agency, one would have to assume that these skills cannot be acquired except by practice. In the acquisition of skills, the practice necessarily refers to the coordination of muscular and other bodily activity and not exclusively to the mind of the person acquiring the skill. How, then, can we say that possession by another mind can help one acquire a skill? Also, if it is assumed that the skill is actually learned by the mind and not the body (an assumption which it is difficult to substantiate), why then do most of us need to learn again all the skills which our minds must have learned in their previous incarnations? At least in those alleged cases of reincarnation, we should find that all those skills acquired in the previous incarnation are present. The logical difficulties thus make us wonder whether these impressive cases may in fact suggest, instead of a surviving agency, a more pronounced or marked psi ability which can accomplish these impressive skills without practice. Alternatively, the authenticity of the cases themselves or reporting of them may be disputed, as in the case of Uttara speaking in Bengali.

At the present stage, therefore, it would seem that the only type of observational evidence bearing on survival that we can collect is the collection of spontaneous cases in which the motive and the initiative seem to come from a deceased person. If there are a sufficiently large number of such cases, a study of them may give us clues that may be observationally verifiable. The fact that there are a few in the existing collections is sufficient reason to look for more. For the present, then, the prospect of obtaining any conclusive evidence for survival is by no means good. On the one hand, there is a need for determining the limits of psi – what it can achieve and what it cannot achieve. On the other hand, a breakthrough in methodology is required to quantify survival evidence and also unambiguously determine the source of psi.

From the presently available anecdotal evidence, which is somewhat strengthened by systematic studies by a few serious scientists, the most we can say in favour of survival research in general and of the reincarnation hypothesis in particular is that the empirical evidence at best is suggestive and in no case conclusive. There are several plausible alternative explanations that should be addressed in future research before taking the evidence as compelling. (For a more detailed review of reincarnation studies see J.M. Matlock [1990]). There are two problems that need to be addressed to make further progress in survival research. One is methodological and the other is conceptual. The methodological problem as mentioned relates to the question who is the one responsible for an alleged ESP communication or PK effect, i.e., the source of psi. The conceptual problem concerns what it is that is purported to survive the disintegration of body after physical death.

Source of Psi

In a given experimental situation, the experimenter administers an ESP test to a subject, collects the data, analyzes the data and concludes whether the hypothesis under consideration is supported or not. In such an experimental paradigm, it is assumed of course that the real source of psi is the subject; it is she who gives evidence or otherwise. For someone who is unfamiliar with psi research, all this is as simple as that; and the source of psi is obviously the subject. Regrettably, however, the ESP results suggest that the matter is far more complicated than that. A review of the literature suggests that the experimenter is an important variable in ESP research. Typically, some experimenters are admittedly more successful in eliciting positive results than some others. Worse, the success of the experimenter appears to involve more than her psychological ability to relate to the subject, motivate her and so on. Rather the experimenter's effect itself appears to be paranormal. Reviewing the relevant literature I concluded: "However inconvenient they may be for interpreting experimental results, and whatever may be the difficulties they may pose for designing psi experiments, experimenter effects have come to stay in parapsychology, and future researchers must attempt to address the range, magnitude and the process of these effects" (Rao, 2001, p.19).

Experimenter psi effects appear as strong as the evidence for psi itself. Further, we hardly have any clues as to how the experimenter influences the outcome of a psi experiment. There is need to reconsider the traditional assumption that the subject is the source of psi. The Western experimental paradigm of testing for psi is best suited to reject the null hypothesis and provide evidence for the existence of a cognitive anomaly. Parapsychological research needs to go beyond collecting evidence for the existence of an anomaly. There is need for methodological innovations, not merely improvements in this area, to ascertain the source of psi. Unable to identify unambiguously the source of psi, the person from whom a communication is received, parapsychologists are in no position to meaningfully investigate the problem of post-mortem survival.

What Is It That Survives?

The conceptual issue is one of defining clearly what it is that is believed to survive physical death. Clearly it should be something that relates to the person and does not disintegrate with the cessation of life in the body, as we know it. Though Rhine's Laboratory at Duke shelved the survival question and did not pursue any empirical investigations of it, Rhine himself was not unconcerned with the implications of parapsychological findings to post-mortem existence. In an editorial for the *Journal of Parapsychology* Rhine (1943) acknowledged that the ESP ability for which he and his coworkers collected compelling evidence is a "strong alternative" to survival hypothesis. However, he noted: "We have had to know that man possesses ESP and PK capacities in order to make any tentative conception of an existence beyond the transitions of bodily death a reasonable one. Without them, such survival could not occur and be discovered." In a lecture in 1947 in Washington, D.C. and again in his Frederic W.H. Myers Memorial Lecture in London during 1950 he appealed for a new approach "to find out, on the basis of incontestable evidence, just what the post-mortem destiny of personality really is." Rhine (1956) published later a review article "Research on Spirit Survival Re-examined." He concluded the review with this note: "In spite of the difficulties, there is now in the present review more cause for optimism of a kind than has been warranted for many decades.... Having established that there is in personality something more than its physical basis, parapsychology now has before it the further program of investigating this larger personal domain to see, among other things, what degree of independence there may be between that which is physical about personality and that which is extraphysical."

During June of 1959 Rhine organized at his Laboratory a symposium on "Incorporeal Personal Agency (IPA)" with, among others, the distinguished philosopher from Oxford University H. H. Price as a principal participant. From these events we can readily see that on the one hand Rhine had a continuing interest in survival research and on the other hand what he was looking for as a surviving entity is the incorporeal personal agency, a spirit with a personality. It is the inability to come up with appropriate methods that would adequately address the question of the existence of such spirits that held him and his colleagues back from launching any major research program in his fifty years of involvement in parapsychology.

While Rhine's notion of survival of a discarnate soul/spirit is perhaps consistent with Christian belief in the existence of spirits and their leaving the body at the time of death, it does not fit so well with, for example, the belief in reincarnation. Christians believe in resurrection but not reincarnation. Resurrection, like reincarnation, involves embodied form; but the resurrected body is, however, the dead body that comes alive. In reincarnation, there is a completely new body, which is unrelated in most respects to the body in a previous incarnation. Contrary to Christian belief, reincarnation does not appear to be any more mysterious or paradoxical than "resurrection of the flesh" after the decomposition or dispersion of the body by burial, cremation or otherwise (Ducasse, 1961).

Now, the question, what is it that is supposed to survive, has not been addressed with any degree of clarity either by Rhine or other parapsychologists including those working with the reincarnation hypothesis, leaving it to the imagination of the researcher. Without the required clarity as to what it is that survives death, it is difficult to collect appropriate evidence and adequately evaluate it. If the surviving entity is incorporeal personality, what is it that is conveyed by the term "personality?" Personality, as a psychological concept, is a construct and does not convey the sense of a unique individual. Personality in the sense of personal identity, the self-sameness, connotes something altogether different. Buddhists have argued plausibly that there is no need to postulate an enduring entity that survives and reincarnates. Rather the person in their view is no more than a continuing conglomeration of a series of psychic events. Again, in philosophical systems like Yoga, there is an eternal *puruṣa* that does not disintegrate with the demise of the body. However, the question of survival is completely irrelevant to *puruṣa* and for that matter even to the Christian spirit inasmuch as that both of them are assumed to be eternal. In the case of *puruṣa*, it is considered unchanging and unaffected by the body with which it is associated. What changes, survives and reincarnates appears to be the mind of the person rather than the spirit, a position not too different from the one advocated by Buddhists. Again, what appears to be of greater relevance is the concept of karma, which is linked in Indian thought with the theory of rebirth and reincarnation. Therefore, a brief discussion of post-mortem survival in Indian psychology may be relevant; and hopefully it may shed some light on the research constraints that have held parapsychologists back from studying the problem in any depth. I will confine my discussions largely to the Yoga system and Buddhism.

KARMA AND REINCARNATION IN INDIAN PSYCHOLOGY

Karma, *dharma* (right conduct) and *mokṣa* (liberation) are the core concepts in Indian philosophical systems. Different systems may use different words but the connotations are not far apart. For example, in Sāṃkhya-Yoga we find *kaivalya*, referring to liberation whereas it is *nirvāṇa* in Buddhism and *mokṣa* in Vedānta. It is generally agreed that one is born with karma and accumulates karma during his lifetime by his thoughts and actions. We are conditioned beings because of our karma. It makes us creatures of habits, biases and predispositions. It detains us, as it were, in a deterministic universe. By our true nature we are, however, unconditioned beings. Therefore, the goal of human endeavour is to find one's freedom (*mokṣa*). The way to achieve this is the path of *dharma*. Understanding *dharma* and acting following its precepts one may overcome karma and its effects.

We find the rudiments of the law of karma in the *Vedas*. The faith and devotion to gods contained in the Vedic hymns was followed by the growth of a complex system of sacrificial rites. Though in each sacrifice certain gods were invoked, the gods themselves become less significant than the rituals of the sacrifice. Sacrifice was regarded as possessing a mystical potency. It was also called karma, an unalterable law capable of producing distinct effect, good or bad, moral or immoral. Thus it appeared that the objects of sacrifices were fulfilled not by the grace of gods, but as a natural result of the sacrifice itself. Vedic people also believed in the recompense of good and bad actions in worlds other than our own.

In the *Upaniṣads* we find the doctrine of transmigration, sometimes combined with the Vedic idea of recompense in other worlds. Reference is made to two different paths the soul takes after leaving the body at the time of death. In the *pitṛyāna* (the way of fathers), the soul reaches the moon and stays there until the effects of its good deeds last and returns to be born again. In *devayāna* (the way of gods), those who cultivate faith and asceticism enter the *Brahman*, never to reborn again. In other words, the soul stays temporarily disembodied or becomes permanently liberated.

Another line of Upaniṣadic thought refers directly to the doctrine of transmigration without mixing with the idea of reaping fruits for one's actions (karma). We find Yājnavalkya saying in the *Bṛhadāraṇyaka Upaniṣad*, the self at the time of death leaves the body with the knowledge, skills and experience it has collected during the life time. Armed with these, the self finds an abode in a newer body. The self that undergoes rebirth is thus a unity not only of moral and psychological tendencies, but also of all the elements which compose the physical world. The whole process of one's changes follows from this nature of his; for whatever he desires, he wills, and whatever he wills he acts, and in accordance with his acts, the fruits happen. The emphasis here is on the desire of the self and the consequent fruition of it through will and action. The most distinctive feature of this doctrine is *that it refers to desires as the cause of rebirth and not karma.* Karma is merely a connecting link between desire and rebirth. When the self ceases to desire, it suffers no rebirth and becomes immortal.

Karma in Yoga

The doctrine of karma becomes more complex in later Hindu thought. The Yoga system, for example, incorporates it into its theory of mind. The mind, *citta*, contains *saṃskāras* and *vāsanās* that predispose people to act in certain ways, to desire certain things and to believe in some ideas. *Vāsanās* are the subliminal latencies acquired in this or previous births but recarried into the present. In other words *vāsanās* and *saṃskāras* are the carriers of karma, the effects of past actions. They are the vehicles through which karmic consequences may manifest. *Saṃskāras* may be eradicated by forming habits of contrary tendency. Also, the *citta* has latent power that can be used to restrain itself and give it a new direction. The yoga method of practice is recommended for achieving such volitional control.

In *Yoga-Sūtras*, Patañjali refers to karma in the second (YS: 2.12-14) and the fourth chapters (YS: 4.7-9). In the second chapter, karma is discussed in the context of *kleśas*, the hindrances that one must overcome to practice yoga effectively and attain *kaivalya*, a state of perfection and freedom from all bondages. Patañjali deals in *sūtras* 12, 13 and 14 with the question why is it so necessary to destroy the *kleśas*. Pointing out that *kleśas* are a continuous source of pain, Patañjali provides a theory of behavioural causation and postulates the existence of *karmāśaya* a permanent depository of accumulated karma. *Karmāśaya* is the receptacle of one's past actions as well as the womb of dispositions to act in future. In a sense, it is the pervasive unconscious that has profound and dynamic impact on the life and living of the person now and later.

As Patañjali states: "*Karmāśaya* (the receptacle of karma), which is source of all that happens in this or future lives, is rooted in *kleśas*" (YS: 2.12). *Karmāśaya* is the depository of all the effects of one's thoughts, passions and actions and it is the womb of all the dispositions to act. As Taimni (2005) writes, "the important point to note here is that though this 'causal' vehicle [*karmāśaya*] is the immediate or effective cause of the present and future lives and from it, to a great extent, flow the experiences which constitute those lives, still, the real or ultimate cause of these experiences are the *kleśas*. Because, it is the *kleśas* which are responsible for the continuous generation of *karmas* and the causal vehicle merely serves as a mechanism for adjusting the effects of these *karmas*" (pp.158-159).

In Yoga psychology, one's thoughts, passions and actions generate *karma* and the *karma* is coloured and even driven by the *kleśas*. A person's present behaviour is on the one hand prompted by the past karma and on the other hand it generates new karma which in turn affects future behaviour. In a sense, therefore, one's current behaviour is determined and controlled by past experiences and future behaviour is conditioned by the present and past experiences. *Karmāśaya* is the storehouse that contains karma and dispositions to act and thus controls the process of behaviour causation and is of crucial importance in understanding the behaviour of beings.

Yoga subscribes to the doctrine of reincarnation and the continuity of the mind after the dissolution of the body. Along with the mind, the *karmāśaya*, its unconscious surround, survives and influences/causes the future births. Consequently the person may not reap the consequences of his/her actions now or later in this life. Certain karma is typically meant for future lives. Yoga classifies *karma* into several categories and identifies those karmic actions that bear results in the present life and those that are likely to frutify in future lives. What is interesting here is the recognition that one's behaviour is not random and unpredictable. If we know one's past fully we can pretty much predict what is likely to happen in future, as long as one is afflicted with *kleśas*. The only way karma once deposited can be emptied from the *karmāśaya* is by bringing it to "fruition".

Once registered in "life's ledger", karma debit may be erased only by paying it.

However, as the next *sutra* states, there is a way out to deal with kārmic deposits by learning about how the *karmāśaya* leads to the continuance of the cycle of birth and death. "As long as there is the root [*kleśa*s], it [*karmāśaya*] functions generating birth, determining the duration of life and the nature of experience" (YS: 2.13).

*Kleśa*s are the roots that help nurture the *karmāśaya* and make it functional, frutifying karma and yielding its fruits. When these roots are cut, the kārmic deposits become like seeds that are husked or burnt, which are completely incapable of sprouting. As Vyāsa comments, "the latent deposits of karma, when encased within hindrances, are propogative of fruition, but neither the winnowed hindrances nor seed in the condition of having been burned by the Elevation (*prasamkhyāna*) [is propogative] (Woods, 1914/2007, p.123).

It follows that the *kleśa*s not only cause and sustain the *karmāśaya,* they also control the results flowing from it. This has twin implications. First, *kleśa*s are primary determinants in programming life in its various facets and determining one's behaviour in predictable ways. Second by dealing with them, such as eradicating them, the programme can be altered. Here then is the escape from the otherwise pervasive determinism that characterizes behaviour.

Patañjali tells us how the past karma determines what goes on in the present life causing pain and pleasure. "They [birth, longevity and experiences in life] have as their fruit pain or pleasure depending on whether their cause is meritorious (*puṇya*) or of demerit (*pāpa*)" (II.14). What one experiences as pain or pleasure is a matter of the antecedent actions whether they are virtuous or violative of right conduct. While pain is experienced as anguish to be avoided and pleasure is pursued as a joyous act, Yoga suggests that both kinds of experiences are to be avoided because what appears as pleasure turns out at the end as a source of pain. As Vācaspati Misra explains, "neither joy nor extreme anguish can exist without the other" (Woods, 1914/2007, p.132). Pain is that which is "inherently adverse" to the progress of the person in pursuit of self-realization. Therefore, the yogin sees only pain even when he encounters pleasure because it is also adverse to his goal.

In the fourth chapter (*Kaivalya Pāda*), the context of discussion of karma is not one of overcoming *kleśa*s (hindrances) but attaining *kaivalya*. Patañjali says that in the case of yogis karmas are neither white nor black; for others it is of three kinds (YS: 4.7). The three kinds mentioned are (i) white, which are virtuous, and causing joy and happiness (ii) black, which are vicious and painful, and (iii) mixed, i.e., virtuous in some respects and not so in other respects. In order to achieve *kaivalya*, the accumulated karma has to be exhausted and no more further karma accumulated. The past karma comes to fruition when the appropriate conditions are present (YS: 4.8). *Saṃskāra*s and *vāsanā*s are carriers of karma and they manifest in experience under favourable conditions. *Vāsanā*s are nonlocal and beyond space and time and yet the cause-effect relation holds for them as well (YS: 4.9). How is this possible? Because *vāsanā*s lay dormant in the mind and they manifest themselves when conditions are conducive and ripe. Memory is the key. Every act causes an impression, which produces a memory trace, which in turn leads to action at an appropriate time, resulting again in new *saṃskāra*s and *vāsanā*s. This is the kārmic cycle.

The kārmic cycle is the cause of multiple incarnations. It is carried by the *karmāśaya* and *buddhi*, the most significant functional aspect of the mind, which survives bodily death. *Buddhi*, however, is not incorporeal like *puruṣa*. It is material, albeit subtle. In virtue of the continuation of *buddhi* with the accumulated karmas, it is possible to have access to the memories of past lives. Perhaps this is what happens in some cases suggestive of reincarnation. So, if we follow the Yoga theory, then, what we look for in the quest to understand the problem of survival is the *buddhi* associated with the deceased person and not the incorporeal personal agency, which being incorporeal by assumption is closed to empirical observation and study.

The concept of karma is not limited to the Hindu tradition. In fact it is the unorthodox systems of Indian philosophy like Buddhism and

Jainism, excluding of course the Cārvāka school, that regarded karma as the centre piece of their systems.

Karma and Rebirth in Buddhism

The doctrine of karma and rebirth is accepted by the Buddha; and it is central to various schools of Buddhism. In *Milinda Pañha* we find Nāgasena saying "it is through a difference in their karma that men are not all alike." Actions devoid of craving, desire and infatuation do not produce effects in this life or later lives. In fact the potency for rebirth is latent in the act of craving without which actions would have no fruits good or bad. It is through desire that karma finds its scope for giving fruit. With the cessation of desire there is nothing which can determine rebirth.

Karma (*kamma* in Pali) is the predisposing factor that is assumed to be responsible, not only for a continuing cycle of birth and death, but also for one's state of being at any given time. Karmas are considered to be of four kinds, which are based on the effects they produce. First are those which produce impure effects and cause bad results. Second are those which produce pure effects and cause good results. Again there are those that produce partly good and partly bad results. Finally, there are karmas that produce neither good nor bad effects but contribute to the destruction of past karmas. The root cause of karma is binding volition and the states associated with it. Where such volition is not present, actions cannot produce any karma.

Although the mental states that are fixed and determined are the resultants of karma, karma itself is produced by apperceptual acts that are free. Man's behaviour is conditioned by all sorts of circumstances, but he is still free to adapt himself to his environment through his volition. It is this exercise of volition, which is involved in reflective thinking and in representative apperception that gives rise to karma. The Buddhist manuals describe the nature and the strength of volitions, and how karma affects behaviour in this birth and the births to follow. The volition of such developed persons as the Buddha and his *arahants* does not, however, carry any karma with it because it is free from evil tendencies and binding attachments. It should be understood that all apperceptive acts that are of the character of inoperative thoughts do not transform themselves into karma.

In Buddhaghosa's *Visuddhimagga,* we find twelve kinds of karmas, distinguished from three different viewpoints. First, there are: (1) karmas which bring about results in this birth; (2) karmas that will be effective in the next life; (3) those that will become operational in some life thereafter; and (4) karmas "that have been." The last mentioned is, in effect, inoperative karma. Karma "that has been" is so-called because "there was no fruit of *karma,* there will be no fruit or *karma,* there is no fruit of karma" (Buddhaghosa, 1923, p.724).

Second, there are (5) weighty karma, (6) abundant karma (7) proximate karma and (8) outstanding karma. The weighty (such as killing one's mother) and abundant karmas – as opposed to light and slender deeds – are the first to yield fruit. The proximate karma is the recollection at the time of death by which, according to Buddhists, one is reborn. "That karma which is not of the first three kinds, and which has had many opportunities of repetition, is *outstanding karma*. In the absence of the other three kinds, it brings on rebirth" (Buddhaghosa, 1923, p.725).

Third, there are four other kinds of *karma*. They are in Buddhaghosa's words:

> "reproductive karma, maintaining karma, unfavourable karma, destructive karma. Of them *reproductive* karma is both moral and immoral, and reproduces the resultant aggregates of the mind and matter at rebirth. The *maintaining* karma is unable to reproduce a result. It maintains and prolongs the happiness or ill, which arises when rebirth has been granted, and a result yielded by another karma. The *unfavourable* karma oppresses, afflicts and gives no opportunity of long life to the happiness or ill, which arises when rebirth has been granted, and a result yielded by another karma. The *destructive* karma, though itself moral and immoral, kills some other karma

which is weak, inhibits its result and makes room for its own results. That result, which is due to the opportunity thus given by the karma, is called *uprisen* result."

(Buddhaghosa, 1923, p.725).

In Buddhistic psychology, the concept "karma" approximates what we may call "programming". Karma determines both the hardware as well as the software, inasmuch as Buddhists believe that even the physical form is a fruit of past karma. The Buddhistic conception of karma is not a fatalist postulate indicating some kind of pervasive determinism. Rather, it explains how modifications in the programming process can be brought about. Volition (*cetanā*) is the key concept here.

Volition is both a source of accumulated karma and also an instrument to bring about changes in the programmed psyche. Volition is the mental function that coordinates and closely binds other functions of the mind. It gives direction to our activity as well as provides necessary energy for action. In its karma-producing aspect, it creates in us the illusion of "I-ness," and all actions and experiences thus gain ego-reference. Whenever there is such ego-reference, all related actions produce karma, which, in turn, conditions subsequent behaviour. Ego, then, is an epiphenomenon; it results from the way the volition functions to bind the various psychic structures. This means that the ego itself is not an intrinsic structure necessary for all our mental processes. Therefore, we do not find ego included among the five *skandhas* of the mind. It is not to be found even among the seven universal elements (*cetasikas*) of consciousness. Ego is merely a creation of our volition.

At the same time, Buddhism recognizes that volition can – by being directed in meditation (*jhāna*) and other means of psychic development–function in such a way that the resultant experiences do not have ego-reference. Such actions are those that are necessarily not motivated and determined by previous karma. All karma-motivated experiences have ego-reference as their basic characteristic, that is, the experiences are regarded as belonging to the experiencer. The very process of experiencing is itself processed through a program that is determined by karma. In such a situation, the cognitions experienced or the knowledge derived from them are personal in the sense that they are dependent on the nature and condition of the experiencing person. To transcend this personal character of cognition and knowledge, it is necessary that the knowledge process be free from the influences of *karma* and its associated habits and reflex like responses. In other words, the person in the existential context is conditioned. Freedom consists in making oneself unconditioned.

How can this be done? This brings us to a critically important point in Buddhistic psychology. In cognitive processes, the normal flow of *bhāvāṅga* is halted, but the *bhāvāṅga* itself gets perturbed and goes into a state of convulsion. *Bhāvāṅga*, it appears, is the medium through which karma influences one's being and behaviour. Buddhists believe that it is possible to eliminate karma influence, so that the resulting knowledge escapes the limitations of the human condition. The human condition, which is characterized as a continuous cycle of birth and death, is a preprogrammed cognitive style and behaviour disposition, which sets boundaries and limits to what one can experience and the sense that can be made of the experience. Transcendence is thus a release of the "imprisoned splendour", to use R.C. Johnson's phrase, made possible by the breaking of ego shackles and karma influences. We are told, for example, that a meditator in attempting to reach the *appana* state seeks to reflect the image of an object without stimulating *bhāvāṅga*. If she is successful, he enters the *jhāna* state, which leads her progressively to transcendence. Cognitively, a state of transcendence is one where the person is able to image and reflect on an object without stimulating *bhāvāṅga*. The resultant knowledge is perfect in the sense that it is unbiased, objective, and impersonal.

We may note here the interesting difference between Sāṃkhya-Yoga and Advaita Vedānta on the one hand and Buddhism on the other. *Bhāvāṅga* is a concept specific to Buddhism. In some respects it is similar to *buddhi* and *karmāśaya* but also quite different from them. *Bhāvāṅga* is the unconscious stream of awareness and the carrier of karma like the *saṃskāras* and *vāsanās*. The *saṃskāras*, however, are part of the *buddhi* and do not constitute a separate stream of subterranean flow of consciousness. In Yoga, we presuppose the existence of *puruṣa*, a centre of consciousness, without which no conscious awareness is possible. The light of consciousness shines on the *vṛtti* of the *buddhi* to render the mental states subjectively experienced. In Buddhism no such separate source of consciousness is assumed. Consciousness is considered an intrinsic aspect of mental states themselves. In *bhāvāṅga* it is subterranean; and in phenomenal states it is overt and associated with subjective experience. In transcendental states, it is nonrepresentational and devoid of sensory content. This notion is somewhat similar to the subconscious/subliminal self of F.W.H. Myers (1915) and his analogy of the light spectrum. At one end of the spectrum is the *bhāvāṅga* mentation, at the other end are the transcendental states of *jhāna*. Buddhists, however, will not accept the notion of subliminal self.

The differences between the Hindu systems we discussed and Buddhist schools are at the metaphysical level. For example, Yoga subscribes to the notion of substantive *puruṣa*. Similarly, in Advaita, *Brahman*/*Ātman* is the ground condition of consciousness. Buddhism rejects the notion of any such substantive ground reality, whether mind or matter. However, by accepting the reality of transcendental states of consciousness in the non-empirical realm (*lokottara*), which are essentially devoid of content and therefore nonintentional, Buddhism does not reject the notion of pure consciousness. In fact, pure consciousness is implied in the higher states of *jhāna*. This point is mute in early Buddhism, but becomes more explicit in the later writings of Mādhyamika and Yogācāra thinkers.

The concept of pure consciousness is somewhat alien to Western psychology, which by and large considers consciousness as essentially intentional, meaning that consciousness is always of or about something. Therefore, the survival of consciousness may make some sense from the Western perspective, but when one considers consciousness-as-such as non-intentional and devoid of content, the question of survival becomes irrelevant to pure consciousness. Therefore, whereas parapsychology as it has developed in the West is looking for consciousness with its content to survive, from the Indian perspective, the survival issue relates to something other than consciousness-as-such, variously called *puruṣa* or *ātman*. It is the karma deposits in the mind whether called *karmāśaya*, *buddhi* or *bhāvāṅga* that are believed to survive and reincarnate. Again, the Western perspective makes it difficult to extend survival to include reincarnation and eventual liberation as the Indian theories emphasize.

To sum up, then, there is from the perspective of Indian psychology the stream of consciousness which, functioning at the subliminal level, is the basis of the subjective feeling of continuity and identity and which is the binding influence on our perceptions, thoughts, actions, and feelings. It is this stream that is believed to survive; it is the basis of reincarnated personality. From this we could generate a number of hypotheses to study if the above reviewed thoughts behind the process of reincarnation are indeed sustainable by empirical data. A deep study of yogic and Buddhist literature on this subject could throw significant light on the empirical issues related to the problem of post-mortem survival in general and the issue of reincarnation in particular.

It is tempting to think that it is the karma that survives. But, then, how does karma survive. As we have noted, in much of Indian thought karma is not some kind of principle behind pervasive fatalism, as often misunderstood in the West (Farquhar, 1971). Rather it is an impulse or disposition generated by one's actions and experience that lies dormant and influences one's cognition and conduct. This is something that will not be contested to a large extent by current common sense and even main stream science because depth psychology since Freud made us aware how the unconscious influences our beliefs and behaviour. However, this possibility is pretty much limited to the present life. To extend its existence beyond to previous or future lives, in which there is no manifest continuity, is an assumption that at once meets with not only general resistance but also outright rejection. How can karma accumulated by an individual affect another individual? What is it that carries karma between two distinct physical systems situated at two different points in time? We know little about the carriers of karma that can accomplish this and fit into current scientific notions. *Saṃskārās* are hypothetical psychical structures. What is their physiogenic base? Can it be the genes? Can genes carry dispositions? Is information a component of the dispositions? If dispositions are rooted in cortical traces, these traces are lost with the decay and dissolution of the brain. How then are the contents of information transmitted as suggestive in some of the reincarnation cases? Is there anything in psychology that comes close to explaining such a possibility without assuming the existence of incorporeal agencies like spirits?

Jung and Karma

C. G. Jung's notion of archetypes is possibly the closest among western psychological constructs relevant to survival issues. There is no secret that Jung was significantly influenced by Indian thought, Hindu as well as Buddhist, even though he was somewhat ambivalent in acknowledging it. Harold Coward (1975/2001) suggests that "the Eastern concept of karma and rebirth continued to reappear in Jung's thinking. In fact, careful analysis demonstrates that his attitude to karma and rebirth changed dramatically over the years. During the last years his thinking came very close to the Indian perspective" (p.116). It would seem that it was the *Yoga-Sūtra*s of Patañjali and Vyāsa's commentary on it that had a profound influence on Jung's thinking about the archetypes.

For Jung, karma first seemed to be some kind of "psychic heredity". Psychic heredity, according to Jung, consists in the "inheritance of psychic characteristics, such as predisposition to disease, traits of character, special gifts and so forth." Archetypes are the carriers of psychic heredity. Jung (1959) concedes in a footnote, while discussing specific archetypes that his notion of archetype "does not suggest as much as *karma* does to the Indian" (p.140n). The archetype relates to the collective unconscious, which implies collective karma as distinguished from a person's individual karma. Reincarnation presupposes the continuation of the personal karma; and Jung was not first disposed to accept such a possibility. Therefore, he wrote, "it is by no means certain whether continuity of personality is guaranteed or not: there may only be a continuity of karma" (Jung, 1969, p.113).

Chapter III of *The Archetypes and the Collective Unconscious* (Jung, 1969) deals with the question of rebirth. At the outset, Jung distinguishes between five forms of rebirth. First is what he calls "metempsychosis", which refers to transmigration of souls. It may indicate soul passing through "different bodily existences" or a mere "life sequence interrupted by different reincarnations" as the Buddha has conceived. The second form is reincarnation, which entails not only the life sequence but also continuation of personality with accessibility to memories of previous lives. Also, "reincarnation means rebirth in a human body" (Jung, 1969, p.113). The other forms of rebirth include in Jung's view (3) resurrection, (4) rebirth proper and (5) transformation.

Resurrection is of course the popular Christian version of survival. Rebirth in the strict sense, according to Jung, is "rebirth within the span of individual life" (p.114). In this sense rebirth is renewal without any change of being. The fifth is indicated by the transformation of the person, which is a form of "indirect rebirth". It is not indicated by death and rebirth but involves "participation in the process of transformation", such as participation in a ceremony after which one finds herself totally transformed.

As Coward points out, Jung appeared to be more open to the possibility of rebirth in his later years, even though he did not consider the empirical evidence compelling. Jung seems to consider rebirth as a "psychic projection", a "projected personification" as Coward puts it. It would seem that his own personal experiences in dreams led Jung to a more favourable view of reincarnation. "Later in life," writes Coward (1975/2001), "Jung's dreams, which for him were empirical reality, gave him evidence pointing to his own reincarnation. It was the evidence of his own dreams, plus those of a close acquaintance, which led to a very positive assessment of Indian karma and rebirth theory in the last years before his death" (p.124).

There is a chapter "On Life After Death" in Jung's autobiography, *Memories, Dreams, Reflections*. This chapter clearly suggests that

Jung did consider the psychological function of karma in rebirth. Therefore, from a Jungian perspective, the study of the possibility of post-mortem survival should focus on the psychological manifestation of karma in the thoughts, actions and attitudes of the person. In other words, what we may look for are not memories in reincarnation cases or physical appearances as in birthmarks but the unconscious springs of dispositions, *saṃskārās* and *vāsanās* that could not have been due to present life experiences. The behaviour unlearned in this life and the impressions that could not have been in the present life could be important variables for researching reincarnation. Also, Jung's notion of psychic projection can be developed to study survival materials as in the case of "possessions" and mediumistic material.

REFERENCES

Akolkar, V.V. (1992). Search for Sharada: Report of a case and its investigation. *Journal of the American Society for Psychical Research*, 86, 209-247.

Birge, W.R. & Rhine, J.B. (1942). Unusual types of persons tested for ESP: I. A professional medium. *Journal of Parapsychology*, 6:85-94.

Braude, S.E. (1992). Survival or super-psi? *Journal of Scientific Exploration*, 6, 127-144.

Buddhaghosha (1923). *Visuddhimagga* (The Path of Purity). 3 Vols. M.T. (Trans.) London: Oxford University Press.

Chari, C.T.K. (1967). New light on an old doctrine. *International Journal of Parapsychology*, 9, 217-222.

Coward, H. (1975/2001). Karma, Jung, and transpersonal psychology. In V. Hanson and R. Stewart and S. Nicholson (Eds.). *Karma: Rhythmic Return to Harmony*. Delhi: Motilal Banarsidass (pp.115-135).

Ducasse, C.J. (1961). *A Critical Examination of the Belief in a Life After Death*. Springfgield, IL: C. C. Thomas.

Farquhar, J.N. (1913/1971). *The Crown of Hinduism*. Delhi: Oriental Publishers.

Johnson, R.C. (1953). *The Imprisoned Splendour*. London: Hodder & Stoughton.

Jung, C.G. (1959). *Alon: Researches into the Phenomenology of the Self*. (R.F.C. Hall, Trs.). New York: Pantheon Books.

— (1969). *The Archetypes and the Collective Unconscious*. (R.F.C. Hall, Trs.). Princeton, N.J: Princeton University Press.

Krishnan, V. (1985). Near-death experience: Evidence for survival? *Anabiosis*: *The Journal of Near-Death Studies*, 5 (1), 21-38.

— (1988). OBEs in the blind. Letter to the editor. *The Journal of Near-Death Studies*, 7, 139.

— (1993). The physical basis of out-of-body vision. Letter to the editor. *The Journal of Near-Death Studies*, 11, 257-260.

Kübler-Ross, E. (1969). *On Death and Dying*. New York: Macmillan.

Matlock, J.M. (1990). Past life memory case studies. In S. Krippner (Ed.), *Advances in Parapsychological Research*, Vol. 6 (pp.184-267). Jefferson, NC: McFarland.

Monroe, R.A. (1971). *Journeys out of the Body*. New York: Doubleday.

Moody, R.A. (1975). *Life after Life*. Covington, GA: Mocking Bird Books.

Myers, F.W.H. (1915). *Human Personality and Its Survival of Bodily Death*. (Two Vols.). New York: Longmans, Green & Co. (Original work published in 1903).

Osis, K. & Haraldsson, E. (1977). *At the Hour of Death*. New York: Avon Books.

Osis K. (1961). *Deathbed Observations by Physicians and Nurses*. New York: Parapsychology Foundation.

— (1978). Out-of-the-body research at the American Society for Psychical Research. In D.S. Rogo (Ed.), *Mind Beyond Body* (pp.162-169). New York: Penguin Books.

Owen, A.R.G. (1964). *Can We Explain the Poltergeist.* New York: Garrett Publications

Pasricha, S.K. (1990). *Claims of Reincarnation: An Empirical Study of Cases in India.* New Delhi: Harman Publishing House.

Pratt, J.G. & Roll, W.G. (1958). The Seaford disturbances. *Journal of Parapsychology*, 22, 79-124.

Price, H.H. (1960). Apparitions: Two theories. *Journal of Parapsychology*. 24, 110-128.

Rao, K.R. (1963). Studies in the preferential effect II: A language ESP test involving precognition and "intervention." *Journal of Parapsychology*, 27, 23-32.

— (2001). *Basic Research in Parapsychology*. Jefferson, NC: McFarland.

Rhine, J.B. (1943). ESP, PK, and the survival hypothesis. (Editorial). *Journal of Parapsychology*, 7, 223-227.

— (1956). Research on spirit survival re-examined. *Journal of Parapsychology*, 20, 121-131.

Rhine, L.E. (1960). Symposium on incorporeal personal agency (IPA). The evaluation of non-recurrent psi experiences bearing on postmortem survival. *Journal of Parapsychology*, 24, 8-25.

— (1961). *Hidden Channels of the Mind.* New York: William Sloane Associates.

— (1983). *Something Hidden.* Jefferson, North Carolina: McFarland & Company.

Ring, K. (1980). *Life at Death: A Scientific Investigation of Near-death Experience.* New York: McCann & Geoghegan.

Rogo, D.S. (1978). *Mind Beyond the Body: The Mystery of ESP Projection*. New York: Penguin Books.

Roll, W.G. (1968). Some physical and psychological aspects of a series of poltergeist phenomena. *Journal of the American Society for Psychical Research*, 62, 263-308.

Stevenson, I. (1960). Criteria for the ideal case bearing on reincarnation. *Indian Journal of Parapsychology*, 2, 149-155.

— (1974). *Twenty Cases Suggestive of Reincarnation* (2nd edn.). Charlottesville, VA: University of Virginia Press.

— (1984). *Unlearned Language: New Studies in Xenoglossy*. Charlottesville, VA: University Press of Virginia.

— (1992). Survival or super-psi: A reply. *Journal of Scientific Exploration*, 6, 145-150.

Taimni, I.K. (2005). *The Science of Yoga: The Yoga-Sutra of Patanjali in Sanskrit with Transliteration in Roman, Translation and Commentary in English*: Adyar, Chennai : The Theosophical Publishing House.

Tart, C.T. (1968). A psychophysiological study of out-of-body experiences in a selected subject. *Journal of the American Society for Psychical Research*, 62, 3-27.

Tyrrell, G.N.M. (1947). The modus operandi of paranormal cognition. *Proceedings of the Society for Psychical Research*, 48, 65-120.

Woods, J.H. (1914/2007). *The Yoga System of Patanjali*. Delhi: Motilal Banarsidass.

Approaches to the Study of Reincarnation

S.N. Arseculeratne

Reincarnation is probably the most popular term used to denote the reappearance of a permanent entity, the soul, in a new physical incarnation. However, as Buddhism denies the existence of a soul, alternative terms such as *re-birth* or *re-becoming* are suggested as more appropriate. The Buddhists claim that there is no permanent entity that could be reincarnated; to them a new birth occurs but one that expresses the karmic determinants of 'a' former existence, but without the replication of 'the' former person.

I think it is premature to apply the term, *theory,* to reincarnation because in a strict scientific sense, a theory is one that has a base in established fact that has been subjected repeatedly to investigation for validation or falsification, such as the theories in the physics of heat, light and sound. Further, a theory must have predictive value and must apply to a wide range of phenomena. Karl Popper (1986) suggests that a scientific theory should be accessible to falsifiability rather than merely to verification. The alleged phenomenon of reincarnation has not yet been subjected to these processes of scientific investigation, although recent trends appear to be, hopefully, moving in that direction. I would meanwhile, therefore use the term, the *idea* of reincarnation.

There have been many anecdotal reports on instances of supposed reincarnation, such as the well-known Bridey Murphy case (Stevenson, 1974), and the writings of Edgar Cayce. However, it is essential to investigate these claims using novel scientific methodologies; then, *if* these claims are validated, to attempt to derive nomothetic bases or hypotheses, to establish them as scientifically validated phenomena, for after all, one of the hall-marks of scientific progress is the search for explanations for the phenomena that are validated.

The Investigation of Possible Instances of Reincarnation

As has been pointed out earlier (Arseculeratne, 2001a), the processes of scientific investigation and routes to scientific discovery as applied in the hard sciences, cannot be rigidly applied to the question of reincarnation and other paranormal phenomena. For instance, control of variables is a standard technique in conventional scientific investigations. However, as in the social sciences, it is difficult or near impossible to do so with the phenomena of reincarnation. In conventional science, the investigator is outside the experimental system but in some events as in the investigation of psychological interactions and parapsychology, the effect of the investigator, even as a non-participant observer is very well established. The approach that several important investigators of reincarnation have used is, what I would call, the legal or circumstantial approach, that is, the use of corroborative or circumstantial evidence and the exclusion of fraud; this approach is well illustrated in the works of the pioneer in reincarnation studies, Ian Stevenson (for example, see Stevenson, 1974; Stevenson, 1987).

Beloff (1993) has made some important observations on research on reincarnation. He notes that while the validation of childhood recollections of previous lives is an important route, there are some disadvantages that are faced: (1) investigators from the West have found these cases to occur in "remote parts of the world"; (2) there are methodological problems for such investigators, regarding access and the establishment of confidence among the subjects, language, interpretations; (3) the lapse of time between the receipt of information and access to the scene in remote areas. On the other hand Beloff notes that most of these cases occur in countries such as India and Sri Lanka that have entrenched religious and culturally acquired beliefs in reincarnation. It thus follows that researchers from South Asia are favourably disposed and are possible at a comparative advantage for such research. The works of Satwant Pasricha in India and of the late Godwin Samararatne in Sri Lanka are noteworthy in this respect. However, this is a disadvantage too, as the researcher may be striving to "prove" a long held cherished belief, thereby introducing the factor of subjective bias in analyzing the data, rather than being completely objective in data gathering and analysis.

Let me briefly comment on some approaches and on evidence that has been gathered so far, beyond mere anecdotal evidence. Ian Stevenson stands out as the pioneer, or as Beloff refers to him as "one exceptional individual", in the systematic exploration of the validity of the idea of reincarnation. Erlandur Haraldsson in Iceland has also contributed to the literature on investigations on reincarnation. While spontaneous recollections of adults and, more commonly, young children about previous lives initiated exploration of the validity of their claims, experimental hypnotic regression to childhood and to previous lives have also been used. However, Beloff (1993) comments "...hypnotically-induced regression to childhood is now regarded more as a case of simulation than of actual reliving of past episodes" (p. 206) Ellison (2002) was of a similar view: "The first thing to say is that age regression under hypnosis seems to lead usually to fiction and fantasy and not to what looks like genuine memories of earlier lives." He further noted: "The best evidence for 'genuine' reincarnation appears to be that produced in such quantity and high quality by Stevenson in his work all over the world with children having appropriate memories." More remarkable are the cases described by Stevenson in his presentation on

"The contribution of certain congenital abnormalities to the mind-brain problem" at the 112th annual sessions of the Sri Lanka Medical Association in 1999 that had *The Decade of the Mind* as its theme; these constitute, as Beloff (1993), stated ".... an important component of the general evidence for reincarnation" (p. 213).

Mechanisms of Reincarnation with Special Reference to Congenital Deformities

The next step is to offer, though perhaps prematurely, some hypotheses as to possible mechanisms of reincarnation, especially of those instances of congenital defects and their possible links to previous lives. Some ideas were explored (Arseculeratne, 2001b) in attempting to explain the remarkable cases of birth defects in cases of reincarnation described by Stevenson, in relation to the mechanism of "... the transference of the characteristics of the deformity from the prior event and its accompanying psychological trauma to a similar physical defect and a mental state of mind, in a subsequent life." I referred to three ideas in biology – Lamarckism, sociobiology and the functioning of DNA. The reason for my speculations, indeed they can be no more than speculations at present, is that it is now opportune to attempt to formulate hypotheses derived from psi phenomena which themselves do not fit into the conventional paradigms in science.

(1) The first idea that I address is Lamarckism. In popular terms, this refers to the inheritance of acquired characters; the prolonged use or disuse of an organ is impressed in some way in the mechanisms that perpetuate such characteristics in the offspring in a modified organ. The parallel I draw is between 'disuse or use' in biology and the damaging events in Stevenson's cases; with both, they have some imprint on the genes that ultimately express themselves in the altered organ. In both Lamarckism and the contrary view of evolution through genetic change and natural selection, "*... information from the environment must be transmitted to the organisms. In Lamarckism the transfer is direct*" (Gould, 1982). In extrapolating the Lamarckian mechanism to Stevenson's cases I have to assume that the events, in the previous lives, lay in some obscure

form before they made their physical imprint on the genes and then in the bodies in a subsequent birth. There is one critical difference between the Lamarckian process and that I extrapolate to Stevenson's cases; and that lies in the *need* perceived by the organism for the modified characteristic (such as the long neck of a giraffe for its access to leaves on tree-top) as an attribute of survival advantage. In the prior events in Stevenson's cases, there does not seem to be survival advantage and the need of the transmitted characteristic. Indeed it may be disadvantageous as in the case of the Balangoda boy with the deformed arm in one of Stevenson's cases.

The difficulty however, of accepting Lamarck's view is that it has never had experimental demonstration of a mechanism for its operation; "But, so far, we have found nothing in the workings of Mendelism or in the biochemistry of DNA to encourage a belief that environments or acquired adaptation can direct sex cells to mutate in specific directions" (Gould, 1983). Beloff however cites the work of William McDougall, later continued by J. B. Rhine, that the inheritance of an induced behavioural phenomenon in the offspring of untaught rats was demonstrated. However, Stevenson, having read my commentary on his congenital defects report, wrote: "I noted with pleasure your reference to Lamarckism. It seems to me that Lamarckism might be a word to use in considering how abilities—both physical and mental—may increase from one life to another" (Stevenson 2001, personal communication).

(2) The second idea I would deal with is the postulate of genetic transmission of behavioural patterns, popularized by Edward O. Wilson, as socio-biology that claims that "*...behavioural and, in man, cultural attributes will affect the course of organic evolution through their modification of the selective processes operating on the gene pool" (Encyclopaedia Britannica* 18, 807). As with Lamarckism, the obstacle to the acceptance of this view is the lack of evidence that DNA, the seat of genetic determinism of inborn characteristics, can be affected by culture or behaviour.

(3) It then remains to invoke another view that includes a demonstrable cause-effect relationship that involves congenital deformi-

ties. That is of Rubella (German measles). The infective process by the virus of rubella in the mother that also spreads to the foetus, results in physical damage including malformations in the foetus through, possibly, immunological mechanisms. There is no evidence in Stevenson's cases that the mother had such an infection; even if she did, it would be very difficult to explain why the defects in the newborn were so remarkably like that suffered by the subject in the former birth; a leg that was severed in a train accident is paralleled by a short deformed leg in the newborn. If the Rubella parallel applies, then one has to explain how the events or forces they resulted from, imprinted themselves on the genes without the intervention of DNA or mutated genes, an explanation that has no seeming demonstrable biological basis.

(4) Finally, I seek recourse to the ideas in Buddhism that have what appears to be a cogent explanation, though it must lie outside the ambit of conventional science.

Francis Story (1973) wrote: "In Buddhist philosophy it is axiomatic that more than one cause is necessary to produce a given result, so that while character may be partly drawn from heredity, and partly modified by environment, these two factors do not in any way rule out the third factor, that of the individual Sankhāra (sic) or karma-formation-tendency developed in previous lives, which may prove itself stronger than either of them.... (Curiously Ian Stevenson had a similar view about "a third factor of influence in addition to our genetic make-up and environmental experiences'(North 1997)." Story (1973) continued, "That the mind, or rather the mental impressions and volitional activities, produce changes in the living structure, is a fact that science is beginning to recognize."

I think the crucial relevance of Story's comments to Stevenson's cases lies in his statements that: "When full control of the subject's mind is gained, the required suggestions can be made with every confidence that the mind of the subject will carry them out, and the astonishing thing is that not only does the mind obey, but the body also responds. If, for instance, the idea of a burn is conveyed through the mind, the mark of a burn duly appears on the flesh on the spot indicated, without the use of any physical means to produce it..... All this has a distinct bearing on the manner in which the mental impulses generated in past lives, particularly the last mental impressions at the time of the preceding death, influence the physical make-up and often predetermine the very structure of the body in the new birth." What closer parallel can one get to Stevenson's congenital defects? In quoting the Buddhist view, Story added; "In accordance with the principles of Abhidhamma psychology, this last thought-moment would determine the character of the *patisandhiviñāna*, (connecting consciousness or re-birth consciousness), and would thus become the chief factor in determining the conditions of the new birth."

An Alternative Approach to the Investigation of Reincarnation

An alternative approach to the investigation of reincarnation is by means of correlating the present life circumstances with the Indian ola leaf horoscopes, which give remarkably accurate statements on the lives of the subjects up to the time of reading. For example in a case reported earlier (Arseculeratne, 1998/1999, 2001c) accurate predictions were made for a family of five for up to 32 years, two of whom had their leaf horoscopes read 24 years apart, by a reader who was unaware of the relationship between these two persons. The events in their current lives closely paralleled the events relating to all five persons as deduced from the two leaf readings, and the events, some of them unfortunate, were related to their actions in their previous lives, as read from the ola leafs, thus providing circumstantial evidence not only for reincarnation but also for the operation of *karma.* This provided preliminary evidence of their authenticity of the ola leaf readings. A confirmatory test of authenticity, recommended by Stevenson, gave a positive result (Arseculeratne and Sambandan 2001/2002). Indeed the occurrence of putative reincarnation is necessarily dependent on the existence of a karmic account that has to work itself out in a future birth. According to Buddhist ideas, once the karmic account is closed, no further birth occurs.

Conclusion

In conclusion, I refer again to the Buddhist concept of *anatta*, (absence of a soul). If there is no soul, the question can be asked, what then is it that is reborn? The neurophysiological findings of Newberg, D'Aquili, and Rause (2001) are relevant to this quandary as they demonstrated that the concept of "I" is an artefact created through the sensory input, by the circuitry of the normal brain. It is my speculation, as stated earlier, that karmic forces or energies created in a previous existence express themselves when the opportunity presents itself in a new physical being, without a necessary link to or reproduction of the personality that originally created them.

Finally there appear to be some loose ends that need to be identified. Firstly, Fontana (2002) in his Foreword to Ellison's book wrote that "… out-of-body experiences indicated to him that consciousness can exist outside the brain and the physical body..." Secondly, Fuller (1979) documented the meticulous records of communications through mediums with the spirits of dead air pilots, whose remarks seem to reproduce exactly, their knowledge including technical knowledge, feelings and attitudes that were remarkably congruous with technical data known before the crash or revealed after it. Thirdly, Sir Oliver Lodge (1916) documented, with cogent evidence, the communications through a medium with the 'spirit' of his son Raymond who died in World War I. These are case histories that, as Fuller (1979) wrote, "… brought many discerning, and even sceptical, people to the unalterable conclusion that there is life after death." One can then asks, what comparison could these 'personalized' spirits, that is, a spirit with all the psychological attributes of the previous owner but without his body, have with the presumably anonymous or de-personalized, karmic forces, that express themselves in another birth? These questions are perhaps relevant to the Buddhist ideas of *atta patilābha* (attainment of self-hood) (P.D. Premasiri, 2005; personal communication), that again I am not competent to discuss.

In the last analysis, Stevenson's comment on reincarnation needs attention; "We can never show that it does not occur; nor are we ever likely to obtain conclusive evidence that it does" (North 1997). That lesson in caution and conservativeness in the investigation of so complex a phenomenon as reincarnation that is strewn with pitfalls for the unwary is a good lesson for us all. Another point I would make is that the exploration of this phenomenon goes back to the nature of scientific inquiry and the investigation of the paranormal, a debate that impinges on the fundamental question of doubt and certainty, even in science. Kitcher (1988) at the end of his essay *Believing where we cannot prove* wrote in defence of Darwin's 'theory of evolution', despite the absence of proof for it; perhaps the idea of reincarnation might merit similar treatment.

There are two topics in the paranormal literature that need to be considered with reincarnation—*Cryptomnesia* and *Multiple Personality* (North, 1997). However, I would think that the approaches made by Stevenson and others in the investigation of their cases would exclude these as alternative explanations. Stevenson (1988) has also illustrated the pitfalls of deception and self-deception in alleged instances of reincarnation.

REFERENCES

Arseculeratne, S.N. & Sambandan, S. (2001/2002). Studies on the paranormal - 2: Further investigations on the authenticity of the ancient Indian ola (palm) leaf ('Nadi') horoscopes and the question of 'Free-will' and 'Determinism'. *Sri Lanka Journal of the Humanities*, XXVII & XXVIII, (1&2), 185-196.

— (1998/1999). Studies on the paranormal. 1 - The Indian ola leaf horoscopes and the ideas of karma and reincarnation. *Sri Lanka Journal of the Humanities*, XXIV & XXV, 231-246.

— (2001a). The scientific approach to research on the paranormal. In N. Senanayake (Ed.), *Trends in Rebirth Research*. Ratmalana, Sri Lanka: Visva Lekha Press

— (2001b). A commentary on Professor Ian Stevenson's case studies: The contribution of certain congenital abnormalities to the mind-brain problem. In N. Senanayake (Ed.), *Trends in Rebirth Research.* Ratmalana, Sri Lanka: Visva Lekha Press.

— 2001c. An alternative approach to the study of rebirth through the Indian ola leaf horoscopes. In N. Senanayake (Ed.), *Trends in Rebirth Research.* Ratmalana, Sri Lanka: Visva Lekha Press.

Beloff, J. (1993). *Parapsychology A Concise History.* London: The Athlone Press.

Ellisson, A.J. (2002). *Science and the Paranormal: Altered States of Reality.* Edinburgh: Floris Books.

Fontana, D. (2002). Foreword to Arthur J. Ellison's *Science and the Paranormal: Altered States of Reality.* Bristol: Floris Books.

Fuller, J.G. (1979). *The Airmen Who Would Not Die*. London: Book Club Associates.

Gould, S.J. (1982). *The Panda's Thumb: More Reflections in Natural History.* New York: Norton.

Kitcher, P. (1988). Believing where we cannot prove. In E.D. Klemke, R. Hollinger & A. David Kline (Eds.). *Introductory Readings in the Philosophy of Science*. Buffalo, NY: Prometheus Books.

Lodge, O. & Lodge, R. (1916). *Raymond, or Life and Death: with Examples of the Evidence for Survival of Memory and Affection after Death.* New York: G.H. Doran.

Newberg, A.D'Aquili, E. & Rause, V. (2001). *Why God Won't Go Away; Brain Science and the Biology of Belief.* New York: Ballantine.

North, A. (1997). *The Paranormal. A Guide to the Unexplained.* London: Cassell PLC.

Popper, K.R. (1986). *Objective Knowledge: An Evolutionary Approach.* (rev. edn.). Oxford: Clarendon Press.

Premasiri, P.D. (2005). *Personal Communication.*

Stevenson, I. (1974). *Twenty Cases Suggestive of Reincarnation.* Charlottesville: University Press of Virginia.

— (1987). *Children Who Remember Previous Lives: A Question of Reincarnation.* Charlottesville: University of Virginia Press.

— (1988). Deception and self-deception in cases of the reincarnation type: seven illustrative cases in Asia. *Journal of American Society for Psychical Research,* 82, 1-31.

— (2001). *Personal Communication.*

Story, F. (1973). *The Case for Rebirth.* Kandy, Sri Lanka: The Buddhist Publication Society.

Evolving Indications of Global Consciousness

Someday after mastering winds, waves, tides and gravity, we shall harness the energies of love, and then, for the second time in the history of the world, man will discover fire.

—Teilhard de Chardin

ROGER D. NELSON

Overview

The Global Consciousness Project (GCP) is an international collaboration of researchers interested in the developing frontiers of consciousness research. We record a continuing time series of parallel data sequences from physical random sources located in a wide geographic distribution. The resulting well-calibrated database can be used for various purposes, with a primary focus on correlations with physical and social variables. One of the most intriguing applications is an effort to determine whether we can detect faint glimmerings of a coalescing layer of intelligence for the earth, what Teilhard de Chardin called the Noosphere. More mundane possibilities range from correlations with geophysical and cosmic measures to correlations with social indices such as stock market fluctuations or gauges of news intensity.

We maintain a network of detectors located around the world in 65 host sites, from Alaska to New Zealand. These devices generate random data continuously and send it for archiving to a dedicated server in Princeton, New Jersey. The data are analyzed to determine whether the sequences of unpredictable random values contain periods of structure that may be correlated with major events in the world. According to standard physical theory, there should be no structure at all in these random data. Yet, we find that many of the global events we look at are associated with striking patterns in the data. Special times like the celebrations of New Years, and tragic events like the attacks on September 11, 2001, show changes that are correlated with shared periods of deep engagement or widespread emotional reactions. In addition, we find long-term structure in the data, which, again, should not be there, and it is apparently correlated with social measures.

The data are vetted and subjected to rigorous standard procedures to ensure they are free from defects (for example, from mechanical or electrical failures). Our analyses establish that the non-random behaviour cannot be attributed to mundane sources such as electrical grid stresses, mobile phone activity, or ordinary electromagnetic fields. The evidence suggests instead that the anomalous structure we see is somehow related to periods of coherent focus of human attention generated by extraordinary events. It is tempting to interpret the findings as evidence for an emergent global consciousness. (For more detailed information, see the GCP website at http://noosphere.princeton.edu).

The Background

Laboratory experiments (Dunne, Nelson, Dobyns, and Bradish, 1997) demonstrate that intentions can affect random processes, and field trials with groups (Nelson, Bradish, Dobyns, Dunne, and Jahn, 1996, 1998) show that strong and resonant engagement seems to affect physical random event generators (REGs). We have evidence from controlled experiments for an interaction of mind and the environment. But, the next step is a big one. How do we make the leap from local experiments to a world-spanning network testing for signs of a "global consciousness"? Why should there be any effect of a world-wide New Year's celebration, or the beginning of a war, or a billion people watching a funeral ceremony, on REG devices placed in far corners of the world?

Invoking a metaphor, it may be helpful to envision a "consciousness field". Picture a faint radiance of information extending out indefinitely from each mind, with a wavelike interpenetration creating tenuous interference patterns that differ depending on our intentions and our degree of engagement. Such patterns might reinforce each other, as resonant sound waves meld into a chord. Remember that this is a metaphor; there is no physical energy that we can directly measure generating such an interaction. Yet, there appears to be something like a nonlocal field carrying information that may be responsible for the anomalous effects in studies with REGs. Our network is designed to capture or absorb the subtle effects of such a field, which we think may be a manifestation of interacting fields of thought and emotion all over the world. We apparently are able to detect something of this when large numbers of people become attuned to a common interest and feeling.

Friends and colleagues around the world form a network of people with interest in the Global Consciousness Project who are willing to set up a computer to host an egg – one of our REG based detectors. A map of the world, below, shows the network of opportunistically located host sites.

We collect data continuously, day and night, month after month, generating a parallel history of synchronized readings from all over the globe. We thus have random data corresponding to every moment, and naturally covering every momentous occurrence on the world stage. These data are the same kind as those in laboratory experiments showing what appear to be non-local correlations with human intentions and emotions. Our central archive is thus a database of responses that might be registered when a major event stimulates an unusual coherence of thought and emotion anywhere in the world.

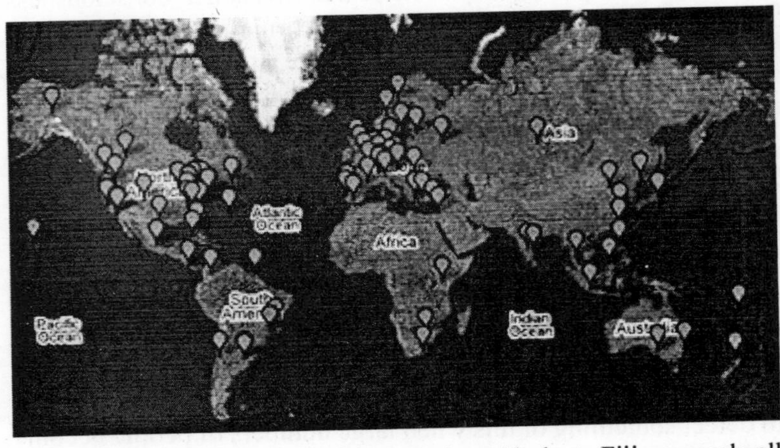

GCP eggs are located around the world, from Alaska to Fiji, on nearly all continents and in most time zones. There are approximately 65 operational nodes in mid 2007.

Picturing Outcomes

With the data in hand, we ask what happens during a global event. The measures we use are designed to identify small signals in what is typically a very noisy background of random numbers. Even tiny changes from what's expected, if they are consistent, can become "statistically significant" indicators of a real effect. We interpret departures from the expected behaviour in our data as a measure of something related to consciousness, following principles developed over decades of laboratory research (Radin and Nelson, 1989) indicating that human intentions and special states of consciousness can affect the randomness of such devices. To show how the analysis we use can reveal structure, we will look at some special cases that illustrate how graphs of the data represent the correlations we are interested in, and help to impart meaning to the dry statistics.

The database contains many cases where the data show a departure from expectation that might be interpreted as evidence for a burgeoning global consciousness. It is important to acknowledge there may be other causes or explanations, such as an effect of the experimenters' strong interest, but we are sure at this point there is no mistake – the data show real anomalies. The scale and nature of the effects is evident in a six-hour period centred on the beginning of NATO bombing in Kosovo, March 24 1999. This was judged by the Western nations and the US in particular to be the only choice available to stop the ethnic war in Yugoslavia. It was a shock to the world, even though it was not unexpected. The GCP data appear to be markedly different before and after the beginning of the bombing. For the three-hour period leading up to the first explosion, the trace is a classic random walk, with no noticeable trend. Then, beginning abruptly at that time, the trace changes; the next three hours no longer look random. This is, of course, a picture of statistical quantities, and as a single instance, does not answer the question. But it is not a lone example. It turns out that about two thirds of our formal tests have a positive trend supporting the hypothesis, and almost 20% are statistically significant at the level where we expect 5% by chance. Such results begin to add up to a persuasive case, even though the effects we seek to capture are subtle.

Three hours preceding and three hours following the beginning of bombing in Yugoslavia. Adapted from a figure by George deBeaumont.

Terror and Tragedy

Several other cases of violent disruptions of the social fabric have been assessed, and most, though not all of them show substantial effects. The clearest of these cases was the terrorist attack of September 11 2001, during which we see extraordinary departures of the data from expectation. The deviations match the intensity of this event, which, without question, affected our global consciousness deeply. Because this was an extreme instance of what we call a global event, we looked at it from every angle, with results detailed in several publications (Nelson, 2002; Nelson, Radin, Shoup, and Bancel, 2002; Radin, 2002). The graph below gives an idea of the kind of departures found in the data on that terrible day. The figure traces the variability among the 37 REG devices reporting on September 10, 11, and 12. Early in the morning of the 11th, the eggs began showing consistently large variance, and that tendency continued until about 11:00 or a bit later. After the second tower fell, the variance became compressed, and remained smaller than usual until early evening. This is a remarkable figure in many ways. The peak departure on September 11 has odds of less than one in a thousand, and is essentially unique; no other day in the four years of data to that time shows such a large deviation. There is also a startling but clear indication that the EGG network began to react well before the first plane hit the World Trade Centre. There may be a more mundane explanation (chance fluctuation is possible, though extremely unlikely) but this looks as if our global consciousness somehow registered a precognition or a presentiment (Bierman and Radin, 1997) of the terrible events to come.

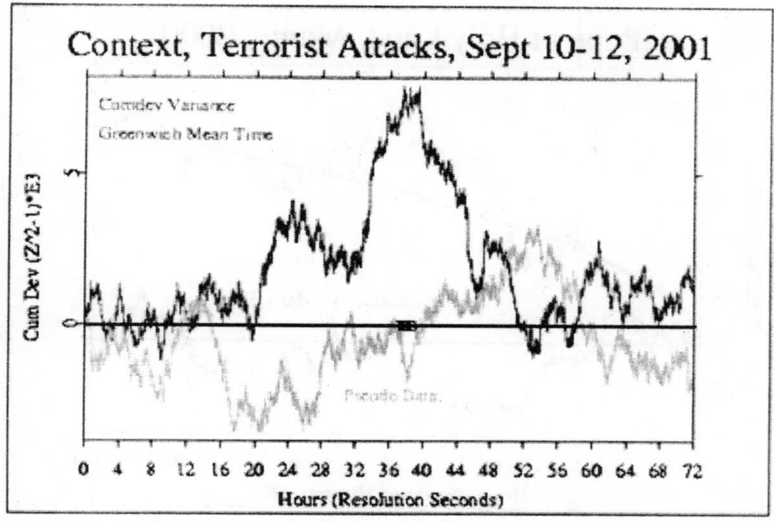

On Sept 11 2001, the EGG data show highly significant aberrations in the variance. It shows a large spike on the 11th compared with surrounding days. In contrast, a pseudorandom dataset shows a random walk.

Religion and Ritual

The intuition that there is a deep sharing of emotion during big events on the world stage leads to asking what states of consciousness might have manifestations in our data and under what range of circumstances. An event that attracted a great deal of media attention and was followed with positive regard by people everywhere was the week-long pilgrimage of Pope John to the Middle East to sites that are regarded as the sacred locus of origin for three of the world's major religions. The data have a persistent trend over the six-day period that certainly does not look random. The sustained departure was so striking that I felt compelled to extract and process a special "control" dataset to be sure there was no mistake. The control data are a splendid example of a random walk, wandering up and down, but showing no trend at all.

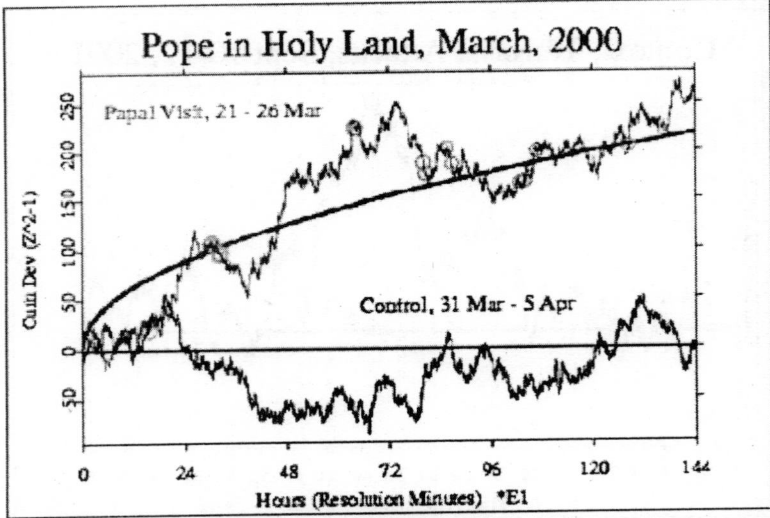

The Pope's pilgrimage to the Middle East was the focus of news because it was a sign of hope for resolution of the unending strife. The lower trace shows the same analysis on control data taken 10 days later.

Concern and Compassion

In early 2003, concern about a possible war in Iraq was at the forefront of world news, and a focal issue for our hypothetical global consciousness. On the 15th of February, enormous numbers of people in the great cities of the world came together in demonstrations aimed to show worldwide support for peaceful resolutions of the conflicts in Iraq and elsewhere in the Middle East. The GCP network seemed to respond. The data are clearly random for the first few hours of the GMT day, but around 11:00, when people were assembling for major demonstrations in Berlin, Rome, and London, the composite measure departed from expectation with a steep trend that continued for the rest of the day. Taking a careful scientific stance, we recognize that the deviation could be just a chance variation, but the timing and the strength of the trend are striking. In the growing context of similar outcomes for other major events with global social impact, it seems justifiable to tentatively interpret the correlation as an effect of many millions of people expressly sharing their concern and compassion.

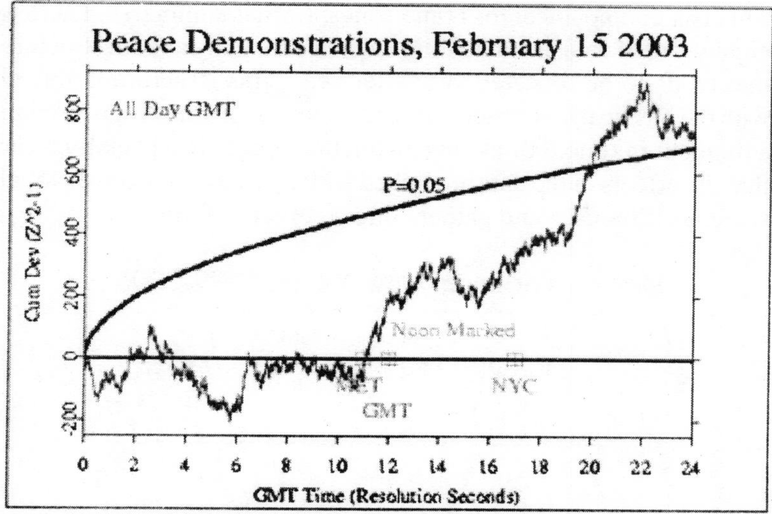

Gathering great numbers to show opposition to the Iraq war, and support for peaceful solutions to political crises in the Middle East. A strong trend begins at midday, corresponding to the demonstrations.

Celebrations

Perhaps the most obvious global event for which widespread engagement can be predicted ahead of time is the celebration at New Years, in which there always is great interest and participation practically everywhere in the world, albeit with special intensity in the west. One of the first items entered in the GCP Hypothesis Registry was a prediction of non-random patterns in the data collected during a period of 10 minutes surrounding the midnight transition from 1998 to 1999. New Year celebrations are a time of shared thought and feeling. People feel relaxed and easy in groups whose focus is on friends and on an optimistic vision of the future. We proposed to look for changes around midnight in each time zone, especially where there are widespread celebrations, using epoch averaging to compute statistics. Each year since then, we have made similar predictions, and while there are some years with unimpressive results, the composite outcome is persuasive. The data aren't random; instead, they show a pattern centred on midnight that is not only visually compelling, but is also statistically significant.

This is a composite across time zones, further summarized across eight years of data, and it is solid evidence for non-random structure that tends to be repeated year after year. This structure is linked with the physically abstract, but socially immanent transition through a moment in time. I think this distinction makes it especially clear that the effects in the data are linked with consciousness on a global scale, as it focuses and gathers into a coherent form.

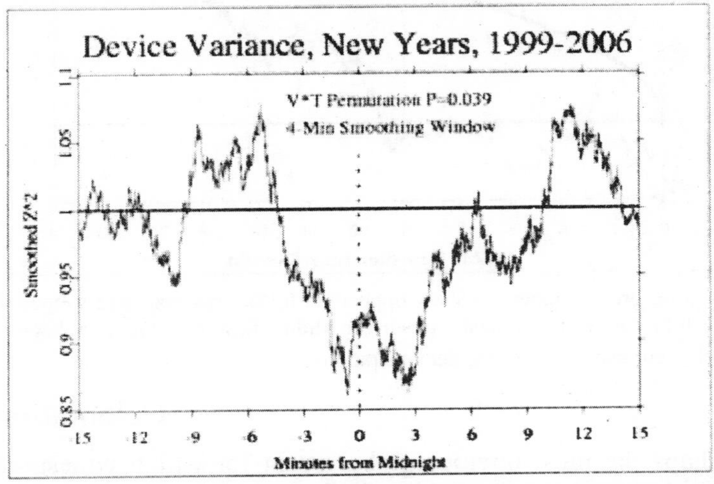

Changes in the variance across eggs during the New Year transition. The midnight epoch for all time zones are signal averaged for each year. The figure shows the average over 8 New Years from 1998-1999 to 2005-2006.

Multiple Perspectives

The search for explanations and for causal relationships remains ahead of us, but work toward that end already yields interesting results. Over the past three years, the GCP database has been subjected to a re-analysis based on a rigorous normalization. Given the normalized data, it is possible to create new and very informative pictures, visualizing long-term changes and structure. In addition to the event-based analysis, we can look at overall trends, and at correlations of the data with external variables representing social issues and conditions. For example, we find that correlations among the eggs are stronger when an independent measure of "news intensity" is high.

When we look at the database as a whole, as in the next figure, it is visually evident that the data are not a random walk. There appear to be long trends, and if it can be established that these are real, the next question is to determine what might cause them. Recent work, based on splitting the data into independent subsets, provides solid evidence that the long trends are not chance fluctuations. When we take data from alternate seconds, and draw the same picture with each of the two datasets, the resulting traces are strongly parallel. Modelling these curves provides a set of coefficients that can be subjected to statistical analysis, and the outcome shows that the apparent correlation is statistically significant. This is a strong indication that our long running database of physical random numbers is affected in subtle but objective ways, by external factors that we can seek to identify.

The upper figure shows that after the end of 2001, the data have a striking negative slope (it is statistically significant). What is more interesting, the overall shape of the long-term GCP data trace is correlated with a sociological measure, presidential approval rating registered in repeated polls (lower figure). Our ongoing work seeks to establish similar linkages with other indicators of widespread sharing of perceptions and emotional states.

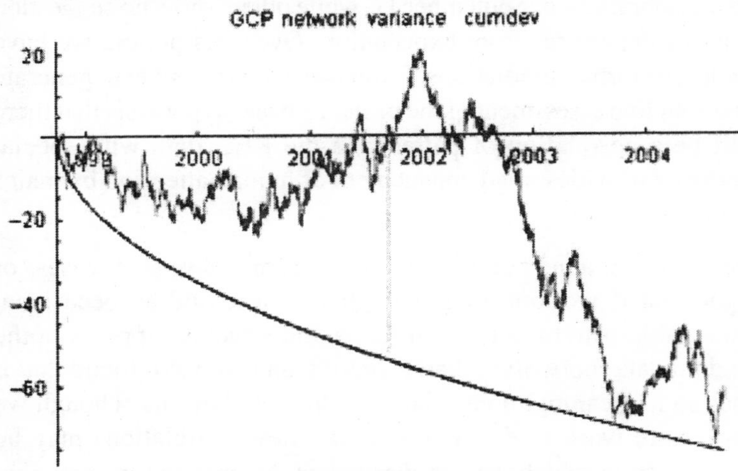

Percent approval   Presidential Approval Rating (red) vs GCP network variance cumulative deviation

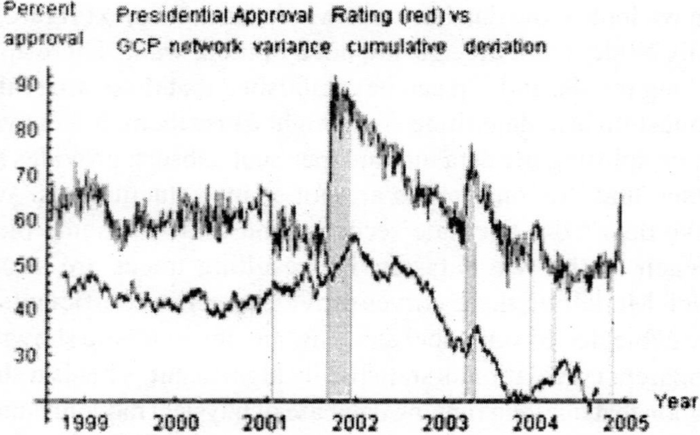

The full database over 6 years shows distinct trends (top) that are not random fluctuations. The trends are correlated with social measures such as Presidential polling data (bottom).

The Bottom Line

In the first eight years of the GCP, we have identified two or three major events every month, well suited for testing the notion that we may be able to detect the presence of a shared field of consciousness. Some results are as striking as the pictures of New Year celebrations or September 11, while others show no suggestion at all of departures from expectation. Over this period, we have made 226 formal predictions. From these, it is possibie to generate a bottom line assessment of the project's basic hypothesis that there will be a correlation of patterns in the REG data with special moments of widespread engagement of human attention by major events.

We might be able to ignore the data from a few such cases, or argue that if we look long enough we must find an occasional remarkable pattern in random fields, but structure appears in the random data more often than it should, and we have found that it does so in meaningful correlation with global events. Though we have more work to do, it seems that these correlations may be material from which we can derive insights into the far-reaching capabilities of consciousness. The grand, composite result, shown graphically in the next figure, represents the repeated confirmation of our simple hypothesis, and it clearly isn't just a chance fluctuation. The graph shows the cumulative departure from chance of over 200 tests of the hypothesis that major global events will correlate with structure in data that should be truly random. It summarizes eight years of experience with the GCP network responding slightly but reliably to events of importance to people around the world. The odds that such a large accumulated deviation from a random relationship would occur by chance are on the order of a million to one.

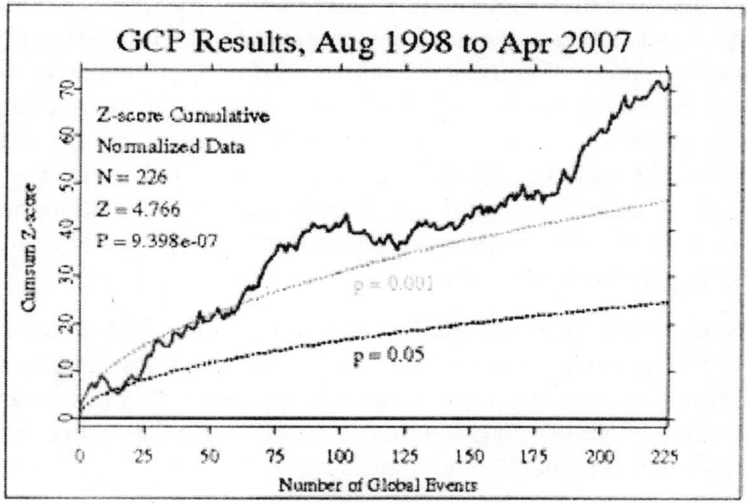

Cumulative total deviation of results for 226 formal hypothesis tests. The dotted smooth curves show the 5%, and 0.01% significance criteria. A truly random trace would fluctuate around a level trend at zero on the ordinate.

Measure and Meaning

Defining global events is necessarily somewhat arbitrary, though there are cases that most people readily agree upon. Moreover, there are general ways of assessing the data to see if there is any unexpected structure. The news intensity and long trend examples show that although our original analysis was focused on data corresponding to major events, we don't need to identify the events specifically, or even to know about them; a correlation exists in any case.

Our primary results are based on correlating specially chosen moments, usually drawn from world news headlines, with data taken at the same time by the EGG network. When we assess the correlations carefully, we find a tendency for the data to be different from what is expected of random data, leaving only a few possibilities to consider. It may be that the interest and desires of the people in the EGG project produce what is called an "experimenter effect" which is registered by the detectors. It may also be that the nature of the question we ask somehow shapes the outcome, and there may be subtle contributions from other sources. The results are remarkable in any case, but I think it is fair to say that the pattern of correlations shows a primary influence linked with the events themselves. While we cannot at this point claim that "global consciousness" is the responsible agent, my detailed experience with the complete database leads me to believe it is a good candidate for a major role. That is, I think the deviations are most clearly and most strongly related to the important world events and human reactions to them as the main source of the effect.

Overall, it is arguably simplest to interpret the anomalous trends in the data as evidence that something like our hypothesized global consciousness exists in a faint but detectable form. But there are a number of challenging issues to address before drawing that conclusion as a final interpretive model.

We can be quite sure these results represent a genuine anomaly, but at this point, it is not possible to offer a definitive explanation. There are suggestions that might begin to explain these effects, although these remain speculative. One of the most promising physical models is drawn from David Bohm's theory of active information Bohm, 1980). In his terms, information (and concomitant meaning) can be nonlocal, extending indefinitely throughout space and time. Active information can be envisioned as a potential field interacting in the development of manifestations in the physical world. Thus, active information is virtual, but when a "need" for it exists, the need actualizes the information by creating (or being) a repository for it. In such a model, the question we ask in the Global Consciousness Project plays the role of the need for information, making it possible for the inchoate meaning of a major event resonating in global consciousness to manifest as subtle changes in the behaviour of our detectors.

Suggestions of a universal mind, made in many intellectual and cultural traditions, appear to have a modicum of support in the GCP results. The idea of a large-scale group consciousness, potentially engaging whole populations, gains some credence. At the very least, these results are consistent with the idea that a subtle linkage can exist between widely separated people, and that we may be interconnected on a grand scale by consciousness fields. It is interesting to consider that the GCP is the product of a sequence of unlikely "chance" meetings and connections. There is a reflexive irony in this, for the database produced by the collaboration allows us to examine distortions of chance itself, apparently wrought by consciousness reaching out to generate interconnections in the material world.

What should we take away from this scientific evidence of interconnection? If we are persuaded that the subtle structuring of random data does indicate an effect of human attention and emotion in the physical world, it points to a creative quality of consciousness. The implication is that what we envision has a small but real increase in its likelihood of coming to exist in the world. This confers both a possibility and a responsibility on us for shaping our future as participants in a conscious evolution. A global consciousness will surely strive for spiritual growth, and personal and planetary wellness.

Acknowledgements

The Global Consciousness Project would not exist except for the immense contributions of Greg Nelson and John Walker, who created the architecture and the sophisticated software. Paul Bethke ported the egg software to Windows, thus broadening the network. Dean Radin, Dick Bierman, and others in the planning group contributed ideas and experience. Rick Berger helped to create a comprehensive Web site to make the project available to the public. Peter Bancel has been a major contributor to the analytical program. The project also would not exist but for the commitment of time, resources, and good will from all the egg hosts. Our financial support comes from individuals including Charles Overby, Tony Cohen, Reinhilde

Nelson, Michael Heany, Alexander Imich, Richard Adams, Richard Wallace, Anna Capasso, Michael Breland, Joseph Giove, J. Z. Knight, Hans Wendt, Jim Warren, and major donations from an anonymous contributor. The Institute of Noetic Sciences provides logistical support as a non-profit home for the project, and the Lifebridge Foundation has provided generous support for documentation of the GCP. Finally, there are very many friends of the EGG project whose good will, interest, and empathy open a necessary niche in consciousness space.

REFERENCES

Bierman, D.J. & Radin, D.I. (1997). Anomalous anticipatory response on randomized future conditions. *Perceptual and Motor Skills*, 84, 689-690.

Bohm, D. (1980). *Wholeness and the Implicate Order*. Boston: Routledge & Kegan Paul.

Jahn, R.G., Dunne, B.J., Nelson, R.D., Dobyns, Y.H., Bradish, G.J. (1997). Correlations of random binary sequences with pre-stated operator intention: A review of a 12-year program. *Journal of Scientific Exploration*, 11 (3), 345-368.

Nelson, R.D. (2002). Coherent consciousness and reduced randomness: Correlations on September 11, 2001. *Journal of Scientific Exploration*, 16 (4), 549-570.

—, Bradish, G.J., Dobyns, Y.H., Dunne, B.J. & Jahn, R.G. (1996). Field REG anomalies in group situations. *Journal of Scientific Exploration*, 10 (1), 111-141.

— (1998). Field REG II: Consciousness Field Effects: Replications and Explorations. *Journal of Scientific Exploration*, 12 (3), 425-454.

— Radin, D.I., Shoup, R. & Bancel, P.A. (2002). Correlations of Continuous Random Data with Major World Events. *Foundations of Physics Letters*, 15 (6), 537-550.

Radin, D.I. (2002). Exploring relationships between random physical events and mass human attention: Asking for whom the bell tolls. *Journal of Scientific Exploration*, 16 (4), 533-548.

— & Nelson, R.D. (1989). Evidence for consciousness-related anomalies in random physical systems. *Foundations of Physics*, 19 (12), 1499-1514.

Teilhard de Chardin, P. (1959). *The Phenomenon of Man*. New York: Harper & Row, Publishers.

On Individual Differences in Extrasensory Perception

SUITBERT ERTEL

Introduction

It is widely believed that everybody has a "sixth sense" (ability of extrasensory perception, telepathy, precognition etc.). My own view on this issue is ambiguous. On the one hand, I found that ESP abilities as tested by the ball drawing procedure that I routinely apply – to be explained below – are sparsely distributed. But why should a sixth sense be restricted to particular individuals, while the other five senses are shared by all people? Supposing extrasensory perception is nature's gift, then it must have been developed by evolution, which is based on an unrestricted transmission of genes among members of populations.

On the other hand, some even ordinary skills exist which are not shared by all members of populations. Mulacz (2004, p.135) drew attention to the fact that "… [some] abilities are definitely not equally distributed". For example:

- Absolute pitch: Only .05% of the general population possess this skill.
- Synaesthesia: Between .05% and .001% possess this skill
- Mathematical wizards: A mere handful of individuals exist worldwide.

Thus, ESP too might be another skill of limited distribution.

Every year since 1997, I conduct experiments on extrasensory perception using psychology freshmen at the Georg-Elias-Müller-Institut University Göttingen, Germany, as participants (Ertel, 2005 a, b). In this paper, I present the experimental method, followed by the results, which indicate substantial individual differences in ESP. However, as the results indicate, some participants who do not exhibit ESP under the standard test conditions, may do so under special circumstances.

The Ball Drawing Test

Procedure

Participants are handed an opaque plastic bag containing 50 ping pong balls on which the numbers 1 to 5 are written, each number on ten balls. The subjects are asked to shake the bag and to pull a ball out of the bag. But first he must guess which number the drawn ball will carry. The guessed number (a "call") is recorded, the number subsequently drawn is also recorded and the ball is put back into the bag. This constitutes one trial. Each trial is repeated 60 times in exactly the same manner to complete a "run". After being instructed, participants take the material home and perform six runs at self-selected times. They are told in advance that should their hit scores deviate from chance they may be invited to complete additional experiments under controlled conditions in the laboratory.

This test requires not much of a researcher's time. Participants need roughly 1 ½ hours for six test runs, a total of 360 trials, which is the minimum number needed for reliable scores. Four runs and eight runs have occasionally been done to explore the test's reliability.

Modifications of Conditions

The standard ball test procedure, as described, may be easily modified: The experimenter may write number words on the balls instead of digits; or meaningful words of varying content or affective tone, names of liked or disliked persons; or colours, symbols etc. One may instruct participants to avoid drawing certain targets instead of hitting them, they may conduct this experiment in cooperation with some test partner or in small competing groups. The procedure may be varied in many ways so as to test hypotheses that might shed light on the processes on which ESP is dependent. This test might be used as tool for various purposes.

Results

Results obtained in the tests carried out so far the hit distribution may be summarized as follows:

For unselected psychology student classes (N = 238 participants, female 84%):

- 22.8% is the average observed hit rate, expected hit rate being 20% ($Z = 20.6 \;\; p < 10^{-20}$).
- 25% or more hits on average were obtained by n = 50 (= 21%) participants ofthe sample. With 25% hits of 360 trials an individual participant's score is very significant (p = .01, one-tailed).
- 28% or more hits on average were obtained by N = 29 (= 12%) participants. With 25% hits an individual participant's score reaches p = .0001(one-tailed).
- 31% or more hits on average were obtained by N = 10 (= 4%). With 31% hits an individual participant's score reaches p = .000,001 (one-tailed).

Safeguards

Sensory leakage: One might suspect that participants, while touching and grasping the balls in the bag, are more or less able to obtain sensory cues even though the numbers are written with ordinary ink, the traces of which cannot be discriminated by tactile perception. Or participants might discriminate temperature differences if the balls should warm up in the participant's hand before they are put back into the bag. Not shaking the bag sufficiently might support ball recognition in addition. Yet if participants would really benefit from sensory and mnestic information, then hit scores should gradually increase across trials (learning effect). In order to test this hypothesis, hits were summed separately for each trial #1 through #60 across runs and participants. Figure 1 shows that no learning pattern (gradual increase of hits from trials #1 through #60) is visible, neither for low hitters nor for high hitters. For high hitters, the learning hypothesis should apply in the first place. Hit scores are also shown separately for the first and last (= fourth) run of the participants' test series. Hit levels of fourth runs are not higher than hit levels of first runs which they should, above all for high hitters, if learning had played a role.

The safeguard just described may be called *post-cautionary* because it has been applied *after* data collection. Its results suggest: Learning effects *did not* occur. Post-cautionary safeguards, as shown here, may be regarded as equally safe as *precautionary* safeguards whose aim is to make sure, *before* collecting the data, that learning effects *cannot* occur. In my view, *parapsychologists* are mistaken to regard ESP research without precautionary safeguards as downright unacceptable. For the ball test, precautionary safeguards are also conceivable, experimenters might ask participants to use gloves, to select balls, for each trial, from alternating bags, they might use a lotto ball machine and might exclude immediate feedback of drawn numbers etc. The advantage of post-cautionary controls is, aside from more naturalness of conditions and more technical parsimony that researchers will come to actually know whether suspected artefacts really exist. If the ball test results would show that the participants' scores gradually increase across trials, then and only then would particular precautionary safeguards have to be regarded as indispensable.

Bias: One might also suspect that participants may be able to put a ball back involuntarily to certain corners of the bag so that, on a next trial, they can grasp it more easily once again. Did they really make use of this advantage? If they did, then high-scorers in the ball drawing test would obtain larger hit scores for numbers that they called right after having just drawn them compared with

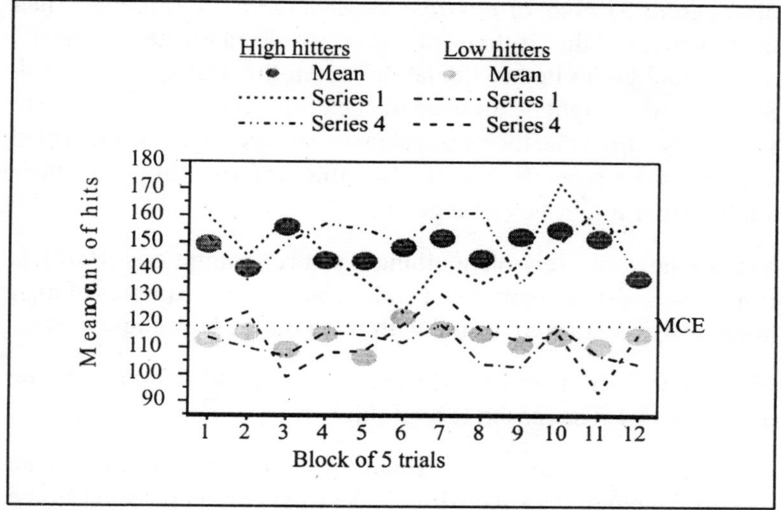

Figure 1: Mean hit count for 119 high hitters (hit average per run >=12.7) and 119 low hitters (hit average <12.7) across 12 blocks of trials. Each block represents summed hits for 5 successive trials. Each run comprises 12 blocks of 5 trials. Hit counts are also given separately for the 1st and 4th of four successive runs.

numbers that they called after having drawn them two or more trials earlier. The difference between hit scores for calling just-drawn numbers (JDNs) minus hit scores for other numbers was therefore calculated for each participant (N = 238). This difference variable should correlate with the participants' overall hit scores. But the correlation is negligible (r = .05, n.s.). So this suspicion is again not substantiated.

Fraud: One might suspect that some participants completing this test at home might have tampered with their records. This is not likely, a priori, for three reasons: 1) *Conflicting motivation:* Students generally want to know whether they have psi ability or not. They could not find that out if they tampered with their record; 2) *Economy of effort expenditure:* It takes less time and energy to record one's called and drawn numbers as instructed than to tamper with one's record because cheating would have to be done with time-consuming caution and attention. Excess hits would have to be kept within realistic limits, otherwise their fraud might be discovered; 3) *Fear of possible disadvantages:* Participants had been instructed that if their hit record would range above chance they would be invited to the lab to repeat this test under control. Students who might be inclined to cheat, for whatever reasons, are likely to be afraid that their fraudulent behaviour might be uncovered and that their reputation at the Institute and possibly even their study career might be endangered.

Yet one need not rely on soothing a priori assumptions. Ball test runs have also been completed under control. Two samples of high home test scorers were tested with two guiding hypotheses:

Hypothesis 1: Hit rates of participants scoring high at home decline under control. The reason is twofold:

- *Unfavourable conditions:* Being observed continuously by an experimenter is expected to be less psi-conducive than home test freedom. Tension and fear of failure are generally regarded as detrimental to ESP.
- *Regression towards the mean:* Large deviations from the mean of any distribution are generally succeeded by less large deviations from the mean. This is an ordinary statistical effect which is superimposed upon psi-based deviations.

Hypothesis 2: Under control, hit rates of high home test scorers still lie significantly above chance. The supposed reason is that if genuine psi was effective under home test conditions, then it can hardly disappear entirely under lab conditions.

Results

Both hypotheses were confirmed with sample #1 (N = 16) and replicated with sample #2 (N = 13), see Table 1. Participants completed six test series each (= 360 trials) at home and under control. A procedural difference exists between the samples: Participants of sample #1 completed the standard procedure using digits 1 to 5 as targets, while sample #2 participants completed ball selections using the five digits plus two colours as targets, i.e., on each ball either red or green dots had been sprinkled among the numbers. The probability of hitting both, numbers and colours on which the final score was based, was p =.10. Figure 2 shows results for the first sample. Surprisingly, three participants obtained significantly *higher* hit rates under control compared with their home performance. It is unreasonable to assume that they used some fraudulent technique at home in order to *diminish* their hit rates.

		Condition				Difference between home and lab	
		Home		Lab			
Sample	N	ES	sd	ES	sd	t	df
1	16	0.37	0.13	0.12	0.21	-3.02	15
	Significance			Chi^2 = 721.7, df = 16 $p < 10^{-15}$		P = 0.004	
Sample 2	13	0.28	0.16	0.10	0.15	-3.00	13
	Significance			Chi^2 = 223.9, df = 13. $p = < 10^{-15}$		P = 0.006	

Table 1: Home test and lab test (control) results (effect size ES and standard deviation) for sample 1 (5 digits, expectancy .20) and sample 2 (5 digits plus 2 colours, expectancy .10). Significance of difference between the two conditions.

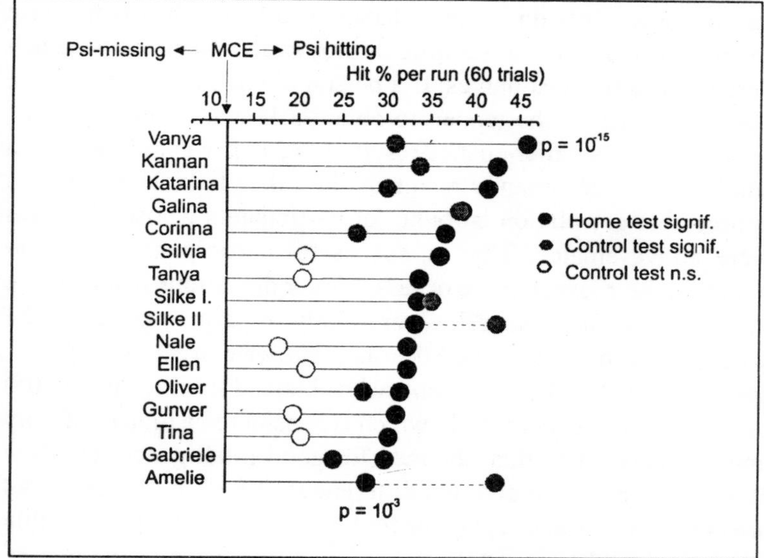

Figure 2: Hit rate (mean for 60 trials) for sample 1 (N = 16), ball drawing test, under home test (black) and lab conditions (*gray,* if significant, *white* if not significant). Participants are rank ordered by their home test result, Vanya ranks first, Amelie last.

Individual Differences

Accident-prone car drivers are likely to cause accidents repeatedly, some unfortunate disposition contributing to such unlucky events is involved. Do lucky events, due to more *fortunate* personal dispositions, occur repeatedly, such as high scores in the ball test? Are hit scores obtained from the ball drawing test "reliable", to use the technical term?

The tests had been completed at home. Hit scores for runs #1, #3 and #5 were summed (see the X scale) as were hit scores for runs #2, #4, and #6 (see the Y scale). The total (N = 143)[1] has thus been split into two halves and the scores for each half of the test were correlated with each other. The split-half correlation was r = .61, a Spearman-Brown correction of this correlation indicating the reliability of the two halves combined, yields r' = .75.

Figure 3 shows the hit percent deviations from chance (expected 0%). It can be seen that participants whose scores fall between the lower and upper bound of confidence (see the dashed verticals), i.e., those who obtained mere chance results which was the case for the majority of the sample, do not show much consistency between the two test halves. If a person obtained a larger chance results at t_1 he or she tended to obtain a larger or lower chance results at t_2, a smaller chance result in one half went along with a smaller or larger chance result of the other half. However, an appreciable correlation is found for participants whose hit levels were above chance. That is, successful participants tended to maintain their levels, more or less. Larger deviations from chance in one half of the test series were likely to be maintained in the other half of the series. The Spearman-Brown corrected split-half-correlation of N = 34 participants who obtained significant (p = .05) or larger hit rates was r' = .85 which is considered a high reliability and compares with that obtained for good intelligence tests like WAIS-III. In sum, individual differences of ESP ability exist and are fairly reliable and replicable for high-hitting participants within test sessions.

[1] For the split-half reliability calculation 96 participants completing only four runs were not used.

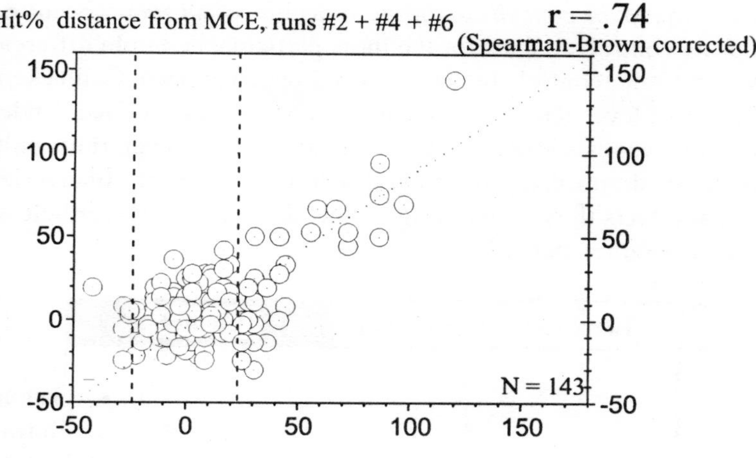

Figure 3: Hit % deviation for runs #1 + #3 + #5 (X-axis) and runs #2 + #4 +#6 (Y-axis).

Is ESP ability replicable across test sessions? It is, as may be demonstrated by an example of time series of individual ball test participants who completed extensive test series. Figure 4 shows hit scores of three family members, grandmother (Galina), mother (Tanya) and son (Vanya, 9 yrs) across 28 runs, 16 runs by each were done at home. Mother Tanya acted as the experimenter for Galina and Vanya, Tanya was also her own subject. Additional 12 runs were done under my control and with presence of an assisting student. It can be seen that the three participants differ considerably regarding (1) mean hit level, (2) run score variance, and (3) reaction to the control condition.

Mean hit level: Galina's and Vanya's hit count, whose average levels do not differ much, exceed Tanya's level almost all the way through.

Run score variance: Galina shows a remarkably stable hit level. Tanya's scores are less stable, Vanya's scores are comparatively unstable.

Reaction to the control condition: A decline of hit scores occurred during control sessions for the three participants, but in different ways: Under control, Tanya's scores dropped at once, Galina kept her home level across seven runs, then her scores declined. Under control, Vanya's scores first rose rapidly across seven runs, only then they dropped, again rapidly. The three participants' time series of psi effects thus display fingerprint-like features. Nevertheless, they are rather stable.[2]

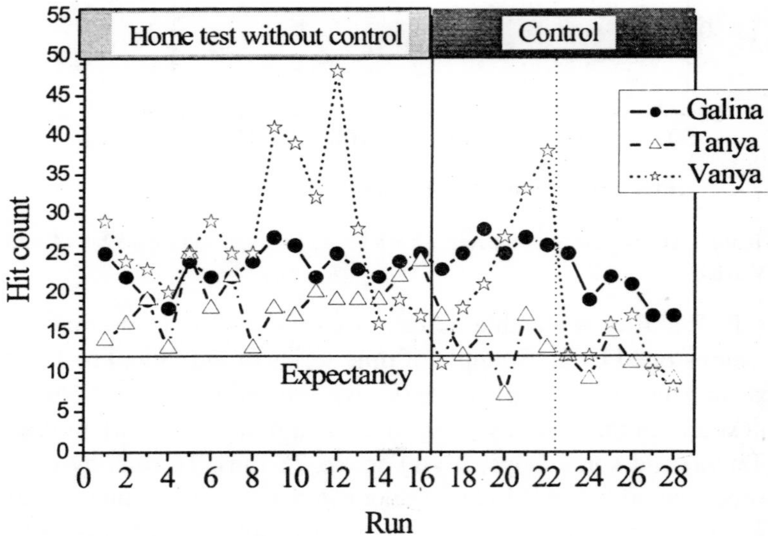

Figure 4: Time series of Galina's, Tanya's and Vanya's hit counts for home test and succeeding lab test period.

[2] Vanya's and Galina's decline for runs # 22-28 occurred after an inserted period, between #22 and #23, of three runs which were completed under control of a skeptical experimenter at IGPP, Freiburg (Ertel, in print). The decline of their hit rates across runs # 22-28 at Göttingen University might be an after effect of more stressful Freiburg conditions. After completing run #28 at Göttingen, under my control, a large number of ball test runs succeeded at the family's home in Kiev, under various procedural variations and under Tanya's control as before (runs #1 to 16), with hit rates similar to their earlier levels. With Vanya and Galina, no persisting decline of ESP test results has not been observed across 2001-2007).

Hidden Psi Ability of Random Scorers?

Do ball test participants with scores persisting at chance levels lack any psi ability? As indicated earlier, some observations are inconsistent with this supposition. Particular procedural changes may be necessary to elicit ESP with participants whose scores are random under standard home test conditions. Two case studies may illustrate how procedural modifications might become effective.

Oliver: Cooperation with a psi-gifted friend: Oliver, a psychology student, was enthusiastic about astrology and other esoteric ideas, he believed in UFOs and ESP and wanted to obtain proof that he possessed psi power. But as Figure 5A shows, Oliver's hit scores did not deviate, across 32 runs (i.e., 1,860 trials), from the horizontal line of chance expectancy.

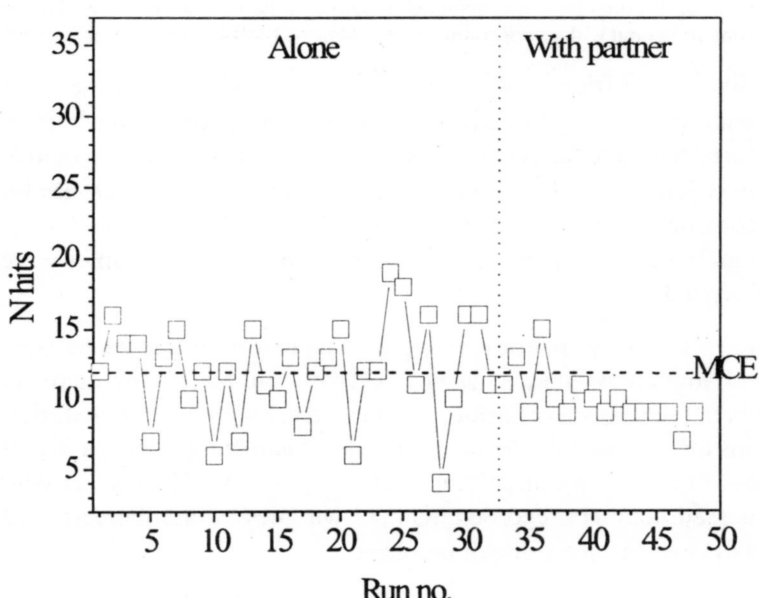

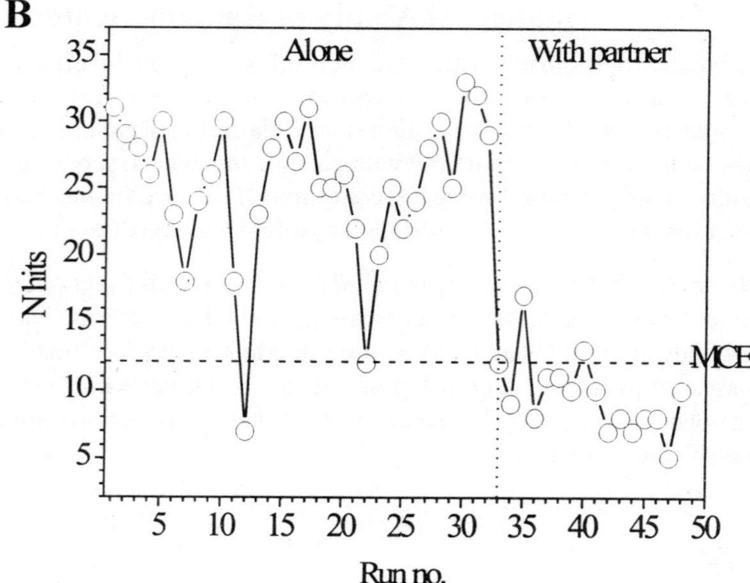

Figure 5: A. Number of hits obtained by Oliver in home tests, completed alone (Runs 1 -32) and with a cooperating partner (Runs 33 – 48). 5B. Same for Barbara.

Oliver's girl friend and student companion Barbara, on the other hand, was an exceptionally good ball test participant with whom he shared the same flat (later they married). She obtained large positive deviations from chance across 32 runs. For only one run her hit score dropped below the expectancy line. Barbara and Oliver completed 32 runs alone, in separate rooms, the testing times were independent.

When 32 runs were done, I suggested them to continue the ball test with mutual assistance. One of the two should guess the numbers which the respective partner would then draw on his/her next trial. This they did across 16 runs. The tasks of number guessing and ball drawing were switched from one run to the next. The partner who guessed numbers recorded his/her own guessed numbers as well as his/her partner's drawn numbers.

I thought that Oliver's scores would increase when Barbara guessed the numbers that he would draw subsequently. This, however, did not happen, as Figure 5 A shows. Oliver's scores did gradually deviate from the chance level, however, the direction was negative (psi missing). His overall negative deviation from chance across 16 runs with Barbara as partner was even highly significant. Apparently, psi must have been effective when he selected the balls. The fact that the deviation was negative is merely another issue, a problem of bi-directionality (Rao, 1965), it does not weaken the conclusion.

Barabara's scores (Figure 5B) that she obtained when Oliver guessed the numbers of her next draws also changed remarkably, they dropped immensely, apparently due to her friend's involvement. The deviations from chance were still significant, however, like Oliver's scores, with psi-missing direction. In the present context, only Oliver's results are of prime interest since this participant, without any ESP-deviation when completing the ball test alone, can nevertheless not be called psi-insensitive. He manifested psi sensitivity, with missing direction, while being joined at this task by his psi-gifted girl friend.

Ania: Using colours in addition to numbers, and lagged effects: Ania, a student of religion, compares with Oliver, regarding belief in psi. She was even keener at finding proof that she was able to guess the numbers that she would draw subsequently. Before beginning her university studies, while still at school, she had already tested herself, with the help of her friend, using Zener symbol cards. According to her account their tests had been fairly successful. But my analysis of the data that she had saved yielded mere chance results and her ball drawing test results obtained under home conditions were as well inconspicuous across 32 runs (= 1,920 trials). Expected were 384 hits (= 20%), she obtained 383 hits (= 19.9%).

Ania was not on good terms with numbers, she said. She would prefer guessing Zener symbols using the ball drawing procedure. A new set of balls was therefore put up, five Zener symbols appeared on 50 balls, each symbol on 10 balls. Thus the chance probability for hits was again 20% as it had been with numbers. Ania completed 16 runs (= 960 trials), but the results were again random. Expected were 192 hits, Ania obtained 205 hits (= 21.4%).

Ania said she would also prefer colours to numbers. So we tried colours in two ways. For a colour test version #1 all digits 1 were written green, all digits 2 were written red, 3 yellow, 4 blue, and digit 5 was written black. Visual differences among digits had thus been increased. For the first time, Ania succeeded in surpassing the expected mean hit score of 20% significantly. A preferential response (Rao, 1965, p. 242) had occurred. Across two series of 16 runs each (1,920 trials), she obtained 425 hits (22.1%), expected are 384. But her overall score was due to successes only in the first of the two series where she succeeded with 246 = 25.6% hits (p = .00,001, one-tailed). Her success did not replicate at all in the second series where she obtained only 179 =18.6% hits, even less than the expected 192 =20%. Anyway, her successful ball drawing result in series #1 (25.6%) seems to indicate an occasional breakthrough of psi power. The decline of Ania's hit rate from 25.6% to 18.6% was highly significant (Chi^2= 13.6, df= 1, p= .0002). This looks as if her flashing psi manifestation was followed by heightened subconscious control. Rao (1964, p. 245) conjectured that psi-missing might generally be due to a "built-in defence mechanism which may have led to the progressive disuse of psi."

Does more evidence exist for assuming that subconscious psi suppression occurred in Ania's ball test performance? Ania also completed the colour version #2 of this test. For version #2, the balls carry the five numbers, all written with black ink as in the standard procedure. But, in addition, either red or green dots are sprinkled among the numbers. A participant guesses one of five numbers (hit probability 20%) as well as one of two colours (probability 50%), e.g., "five green" or "three red". For colour plus number hits the probability is 10%. At completing this ball test version, Ania's subconscious psi power had an opportunity to 'reject' numbers as inappropriate and to 'choose' instead colour for increasing hit rates above chance. This, however, did not happen. The difference between observed and expected hits is not significant, as shown in Table 2.

TABLE 2: ANIA'S NUMBER-PLUS-COLOUR TEST (8 RUNS, 480 TRIALS).

	Hits				
	Expected		Observed		
	N	%	n	%	Difference
Colour	240	50	230	47.9	n.s.
Number	96	20	100	20.8	n.s.
Both	48	10	46	9.6	n.s.

However, I found another indication of possible psi inhibition. Quite a few of Ania's ball selections seem to have been delayed by one trial. This may be called a 'lagged hits effect' which had already become apparent sporadically with other participants, e.g., with Galina, Vanya and Tanya under stressful Freiburg control conditions (Ertel, in print). The effect resembles the well-known *displacement effect* which has been extensively studied with symbol card data (Milton, 1988). A person's drawn numbers, even though at the chance level for numbers that they just called, might exceed expectancies for numbers called one trial earlier – too late to be taken as hits and actually not considered as hits by participants (they may occasionally remark: "too late", "I needed that number before").

Ania's total data (96 runs), generated under the standard and various other conditions, was therefore analysed with particular interest in 'delayed hits'. The result is shown in Figure 6. The X-scale represents successive delays of trials, starting with undelayed ball selection for which Ania actually made her calls (delay = 0). The graph shows that Ania obtained the highest "hit" rate with one trial delay which was very significant (1,225 hits with 5,760 trials = 21.27%, Binomial p = .009, one-tailed). Her immediate hit rate (delay = 0), the one she was actually interested in, was insignificant

(19.99%). The main point here is that, apparently, Ania produced above chance frequencies, however 'hidden' or 'misplaced' by one trial delay.

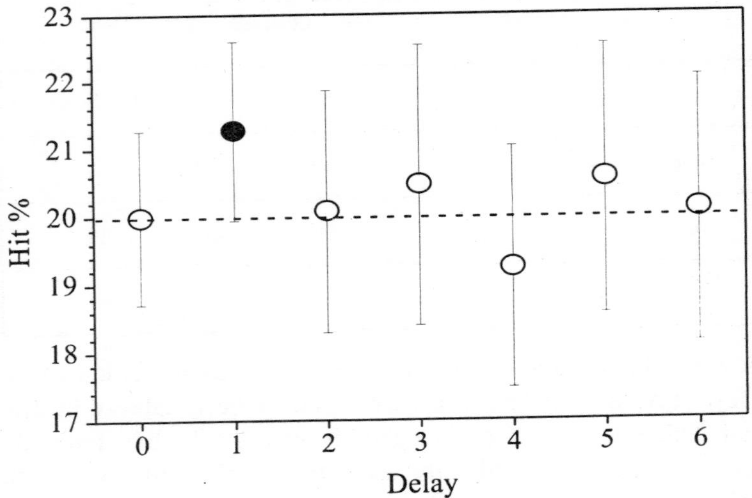

Figure 6: Ania's hit rates for proper trials (delay = 0) and with delays of 1 to 6 trials. The analysis is based on 12 series of 8 runs each (total 96 runs), the error bars represent standard deviations across 8 series.

Summary, Discussion and Conclusion

The results may be summarized and commented as follows:

1. *The test device:* The ball drawing test appears to be an appropriate device for testing ESP ability. Home test conditions without control are parsimonious as well as permissible because 'post-cautionary' controls may replace, without loss of confidence, common precautionary controls. Lab control of successful home test participants may be applied by experimenters as a final step of an investigation. Ball test-selected participants may also be used, instead of unselected samples, for any further psi experiment consistent with the conviction of Barrington, Stevenson, and Weaver (2005, pp. 3-4): "Experiments with groups of ordinary people rest on the false assumption that the capacity for paranormal communication is evenly distributed among humans. We do not think this of other abilities."

2. *Individual differences:* As a result of individual differences, significant ESP effects on ball hit rates are rare. Among those who show psi sensitivity the effect sizes vary widely. The reliability of varying hit rate levels is appreciable. Regarding the distribution of psi in the population, this result is consistent with a 'psi-star hypothesis' rather than with a 'democratic hypothesis' (see Millar, 1979; Keil, 1980).

One should keep in mind that reliabilities of individual ESP test scores, as obtained in the present study, are generally based on 360 trials per person. Reliabilities are lower with smaller numbers of trials and may drop to insignificance with, e.g., 40 trials as in one of Haraldson's (1983) studies where retest correlations were as low as .13, .08, and .04. With 40 trials, an obtained hit rate of .25 (expected .20) is insignificant, but very significant with 360 trials (p = .01). Apparently for the same reason, Watt and Ravenscroft (1999), whose ESP test scores were also based on only 40 trials, did not find a correlation between ESP and another perceptual defensiveness criterion. A similar criticism of insufficiently reliable psi scores in correlational psi studies can be found in Boller and Bösch (2000).

3. *Low scorers:* Participants without surplus hits under ordinary conditions at home might nevertheless show psi effects by using alternative targets (e.g., preferred colours instead of disliked numbers) or under test partner conditions. It is not permitted to deny individuals, scoring at chance levels under ordinary test conditions, any psi ability. However, it is inadvisable to recruit individuals with possible psi inhibition for experiments for which an easy and uninhibited manifestation of such ability is required.

4. *Defensiveness and inhibition:* Psi effects might appear 'disguised' and inhibited, e.g., they may come one trial late. A negative relationship between defensiveness (perceptual) and extrasensory perception as found repeatedly by Haraldson and Houtkooper (1992) might have been effective in Ania's test taking. Lack of inhibition has also been regarded as a necessary psi-conducive condition by Stanford (1964).

The observation of individual differences in psi test research with high split-half and retest reliability might be apt, in principle, to challenge personality psychologists of the mainstream. Personality may be described by a multitude of constructs such as introversion-extraversion, neuroticism, openness, dogmatism, authoritarianism, dominance, sensation seeking, field dependence-independence etc. The results presented above suggest that ESP-proneness or psychic ability might become another candidate for personality description. However, new personality constructs would be accepted by the mainstream only if they are operationalized by some standardized measuring device guided by the rules of psychometric test construction. Unfortunately, parapsychologists have not yet realized that proper test construction in their field is a crucial demand. Without developing standardized measuring tools for assessing ESP proneness, mainstream scientists will hardly be inclined to deal with the paranormal.

REFERENCES

Barrington, M.R., Stevenson, I. & Weaver, Z. (2005). *A World in a Grain of Sand: The Clairvoyance of Stefan Ossowiecki.* Jefferson, N.C.: McFarland

Boller, E. & Bösch, H. (2000). Reliability and correlations of PK performance in a multivariate experiment. In *The Parapsychological Association 43rd Annual Convention: Proceedings of Presented Papers* (pp. 380-382). Durham, NC: Parapsychological Association.

Ertel, S. (2005a). The ball drawing test: Psi from untrodden ground. In M.A. Thalbourne and L. Storm (Eds.). *Parapsychology in the Twentieth Century* (pp. 90-123). Jefferson NC: McFarland.

Ertel, S. (2005 b). Psi test feats achieved alone at home: Do they disappear under lab control? *Australian Journal of Psychology,* 10 (2), 149-164.

Haraldsson, E. & Houtkooper, J.M. (1992). Effects of perceptual defensiveness, personality and belief on extrasensory perception tasks. *Personality and Individual Differences,* 13, 1085-1096.

Haraldsson, E. (1983). Retest reliability of ESP and sheep-goat scores. In *Research in Parapsychology* (pp. 197-198). Metuchen, N.J.: Scarecrow Press.

Keil, J. (1980). The distribution of psi ability and psi performance. *European Journal of Parapsychology,* 3, 177-183.

Millar, B. (1979). The distribution of psi. *European Journal of Parapsychology,* 3, 78-110.

Milton, J. (1988). Critical review of the displacement effect: I. The relationship between displacement and scoring on the intended target. *Journal of Parapsychology,* 52, 29-55.

Mulacz, P. (2004). Physical mediumship: Open questions from the past – a challenge for the future. In *The Parapsychological Association 47th Annual Convention: Proceedings of Presented Papers* (pp. 315-316). Vienna, Austria: Parapsychological Association.

Rao, K.R. (1965). The bidirectionality of psi. *Journal of Parapsychology,* 29, 230-250.

Stanford, R.G. (1964). Attitude and personality variables in ESP scoring. *Journal of Parapsychology,* 28, 166-175.

Watt, C. & Ravenscroft, J. (1999). Defensiveness, neuroticism, and extrasensory perception. *The Journal of the American Society of Psychical Research,* 93, 341-354.

A Re-Analysis and Summary of Data from a Study of Experienced Versus Novice Yoga Practitioners

JERRY SOLFVIN
SERENA RONEY-DOUGAL

Introduction

This paper describes a re-analysis and summarization of data collected over a two year period which examines the yoga-psi relationship in a yoga ashram cultural setting. This series tests, the possible association between yogic attainment and psychic awareness. Yogic attainment is conceived for the purposes of this series to be a composite measure including: number of years of yoga practice, which includes *āsanas, prāṇāyāma* and meditation; official title or ranking within the yogic tradition; regularity of yoga practice. Psi awareness is defined as performance on a computer-based, free-response, psi task involving identification of precognitive video targets.

This series began in 2002 with an initial series of experiments conducted at a university in an ashram in Bihar, India. The findings were reported at the SPR international conference (Roney-Dougal, 2002). The first year was a preliminary exploration for the type of study that might be appropriate for an ashram setting. A variety of different studies were run by the students and this project was considered the most suitable for development. No formal statistical analyses were done as none of the studies warranted this level of analysis.

Further experiments were conducted in India under the hypothesis that yogic attainment is related to psi awareness in 2003 and 2004. It was decided to conduct a review and re-analysis of the combined data from these two years using meta-analytic methods (Rosenthal, Rosnow and Rubin, 2000) in order to plan the design of a similar series of studies to be conducted in 2006. The post-hoc and exploratory nature of the analysis allows for considerable freedom to discover potentially interesting underlying patterns which were hitherto unseen.

Part I: Data From 2003

In 2003, testing was conducted at the Satyananda Ashram in Bihar, India. There were 34 voluntary participants including three ashram visitors (V), nine students (ST) with less than two years formal training and experience; ten *sannyāsins* (SN) who have taken some degree of yogic initiation and have two through ten years experience (*jijñāsu* and karma *sannyāsins*), and twelve swamis (SW) who are also known as *pūrṇa sannyāsins* as they have taken full yogic initiation. The gender and age breakdowns are presented in Table 1, below, along with the *Yogic Attainment Questionnaire* (YAQ) averages, numbers of psi sessions completed, and test results for each subgroup. This is followed by Figure 1 which graphically displays psi scoring by group and sex (excluding visitors).

TABLE 1 – SUMMARY DATE FROM 2003 FOR ALL PARTICIPANTS

Group	N	Age Mn(sd)	Min/Max	YAQ	N Sess.	Psi (MnRnk)	t-test	2-tail P
SW	12	44.6(9.6)	25/59	1074/897)	35	2.49(1.17)	-0.07	0.943
F	9	45.3(10.9)	25/59	1212/(986)	25	2.48(1.26)	-0.08	0.938
M	3	42.3(4.5)	38/47	659/445)	10	2.50(0.97)	0.00	0.999
SN	10	31.4(7.9)	22/50	380(285)	35	2.74(1.12)	1.12	0.208
F	5	31.4(4.5)	24/36	372(305)	15	2.80(1.26)	0.92	0.374
M	5	31.4(11.0)	22/50	388(299)	20	2.70(1.03)	0.87	0.397
ST	9	38.2(8.4)	26/50	129(84)	24	2.71(1.08)	0.94	0.356
F	3	42.3(8.0)	34/50	182(100)	12	2.92(1.16)	1.24	0.241
M	6	36.2(8.5)	26/49	103(69)	12	2.50(1.00)	0.00	0.999
V	3	28.3(0.6)	28/29	34(25)	8	2.63(1.06)	0.33	0.749
F	2	28.5(0.7)	28/29	47(16)	7	2.57(1.13)	0.17	0.873
M	1	28.0(--)	28/28	59(--)	1	3.00 (--)	--	--

Note: Psi Mn Rank is the unweighted average of all trials by anyone in the group.
Group: Swamis (SW); Sanyasins (SN); Students (ST); Visitors(V)

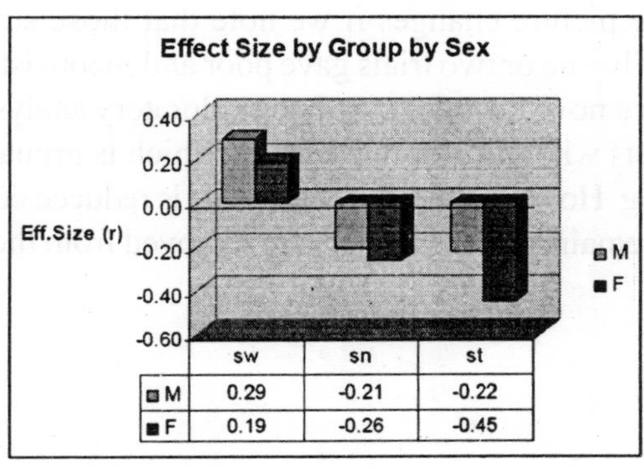

Figure 1: 2003 Mean Psi Score (Rank) by Sex, by Group (excluding visitors)

The psi testing consisted of a computerized precognitive free response task. Participants were instructed to take a brief meditation of their own choosing, followed by a "mentation" period during which they attempted to tune into the target stimulus. Then the target set was viewed and rated for correspondence with the mentation period.

The psi score for each trial was a rating from 1 - 100 assigned to the actual target, with 100 being best and one worst. This was converted into a rank score of 1 – 4, with one being best and four being the worst. The final score is the mean of the ranks assigned to the actual targets dependent on the number of sessions the participant undertook.

The data in the Table 1 and Figure 1 above shows the predominant tendency towards psi-missing in the 2003 data. With the chance level being Mean Rank of 2.5, and with *lower rank* scores indicating psi-hitting, it can be seen that three of the subgroups are very close to chance expectation on psi scoring (male & female SW, male ST), and the remaining three groups are psi-missing, but not significantly so. Thus, there's no suggestion of any subgroup scoring significantly different from chance expectation, nor is there any indication of between group differences. Even the deceptively large visual difference in Figure 1 between male and female students does not approach statistical significance.

However, the picture changes if we note that those subjects who completed only one or two trials gave poor and inconsistent results. Thus we can remove them for post-hoc exploratory analyses, leaving the 17 subjects who did 3 or more trials, which is arguably a more valid sampling. However, the student sample is reduced considerably – only three remain, and the visitors are removed from the sampling.

TABLE 2 – SUMMARY DATE FROM 2003 FOR PARTICIPANTS COMPLETING 3 OR MORE PSI SESSIONS

Group	N	Age Mn(sd)	Min/Max	YAQ	N Sess.	Psi (MnRnk)	t-test	2-tail P
SW	7	46.9(4.6)	41/59	1165(705)	27	2.26(1.16)	-1.08	0.292
F	5	47.8(5.5)	41/59	1265/(838)	19	2.26(1.28)	-0.80	0.432
M	2	44.5(3.5)	42/47	916(3.1))	8	2.25(0.89)	-0.80	0.451
SN	7	30.7(9.4)	22/50	287(164)	30	2.77(1.14)	1.29	0.208
F	3	29.7(4.9)	24/33	304(173)	12	2.83(1.27)	0.91	0.382
M	4	31.5(12.7)	22/50	257(182)	18	2.72(1.07)	0.88	0.392
ST	3	37.7(11.0)	34/50	122(79)	16	2.88(0.96)	1.57	0.138
F	2	42.3(11.3)	34/50	141(100)	10	3.00(1.05)	1.50	0.168
M	1	29.0(--)	29/29	83(--)	6	2.67(0.82)	0.50	0.638

Note: Psi Mn Rank is the unweighted average of all trials by anyone in the group.
Group: Swamis (SW); Sanyasins (SN); Students (ST); Visitors(V)

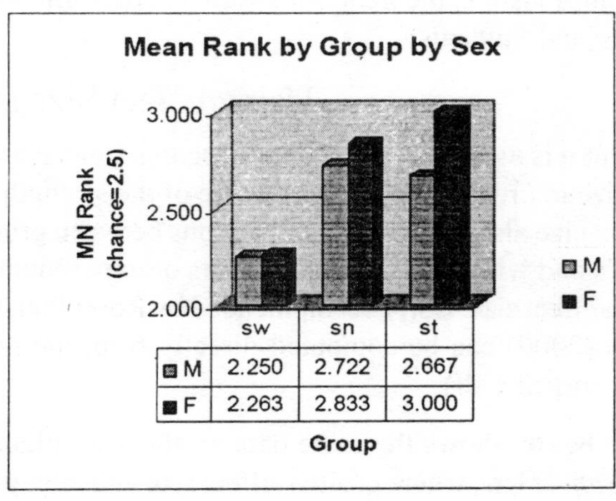

Figure 2: 2003 Mean Psi Score (Rank) by Sex, by Group (Participants Completing 3 or More Sessions)

Figure 2 shows a different picture than Figure 1. Eliminating the subjects with too few trials (less than 3) has little effect upon the psi scoring for the male and female *sannyāsin* and student groups, as can be seen by comparing the graphs, but both male and female swamis can be seen to have performed much better (lower mean ranks) than previously revealed. With this new refined dataset, swamis mean rank score of 2.26 (sd = 1.16) is not significantly better than chance expectation of 2.5 (t (26) = -1.08, p = .392, two-tailed). However, when compared to *sannyāsin*s and students in this same study, we find swamis performed significantly better than both groups (vs. SN: df = 55, p = .05, one-tailed; and vs. ST: df=41, p = .04, one-tailed).

It seems reasonable to assume that excluding those who aborted (for whatever reason) before completing at least 3 sessions/trials gives us a more valid indicator of psi-scoring for the groups which they represent. This view is bolstered by reiterating that those participants with only one or two trials, regardless of group assignment, performed highly variably on the psi task. Thus, to eliminate them is to reduce extraneous variance in the psi data. As an added bonus to this "cleaning" of the dataset, a hitherto unseen trend becomes visible, the trend for swamis to perform better than *sannyāsin*s and students.

Using Effect Size Display

At this point it is useful to convert the psi scores from average rank to effect size in order to get a truer picture of the strength of these data. Effect size also facilitates comparisons between groups with unequal n's and with data from other years or experimenters. The correlation effect size, ES(r), recommended by Rosenthal, Rosnow, and Rubin (2000) can be computed directly from the t-statistic: ES(r) = t / sqrt(t2 + df)

The figure below shows the same data as above in Figure 2, but displaying *effect size*, where positive effect size indicates psi hitting while negative effect size indicates psi missing.

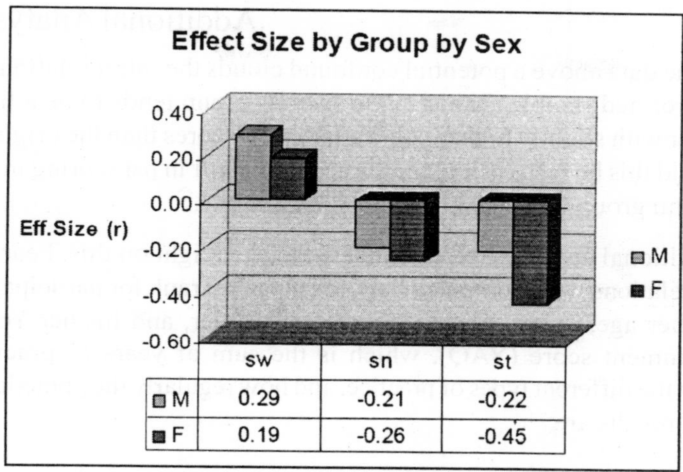

Figure 3: 2003 Effect Size by Sex, by Group (Participants Completing 3 or More Sessions)

In this effect size display, it can be seen that the 2003 data show some interesting (absolute value) effect sizes. Psi scoring in parapsychology studies ranges widely but generally a psi effect size of .25 to .35 would be considered "successful". (The power analysis for the current study was based on that level of expectation.) Thus, we can see in the effect sizes that both male and female swami groups show a *small* but respectable positive effect, while the *sannyāsin*s and particularly students were actually scoring rather strongly in the psi-missing direction. In parapsychological research, psi-missing such as this is often associated with negative psychological factors (e.g., conscious or unconscious resistance to the task or outcome). Thus, using effect size suggests that there may have been more going on in the 2003 data results than at first met the eye. To summarize, speculatively, the 2003 results showed effects of interest albeit with uninterpretable directionality.

We must keep in mind that these results are post-hoc, there have been multiple analyses, and the p-values above are only presented as a rough indicator of the magnitude of the relationships under discussion.

Additional Analyses

In the data above a potential confound clouds the interpretation. In the refined sample (Table 2) the swamis group tends to be a little older with slightly higher yogic attainment scores than the original. Could this be responsible for the apparent shift in psi scoring in the swami group?

Additional analyses were conducted to shed light on this. Pearson correlations were computed between mean psi rank for participants, his/her age, years of practicing yoga, gender, and his/her Yogic attainment score (YAQ), which is the sum of years of practice with the different types of practice, and how regularly they practiced. The results are:

TABLE 3: 2003 DATE: CORRELATIONS AMONG SELECTED VARIABLES

	Psi	Age	Gender	Yrs. Practice
Age	-.15	–	–	
Gender	.03	.30	–	
Yrs Prac.	-.11	.67*	.43	
YAQ	-.57*	.33	.25	.65*

In this correlation matrix, Psi Score (av. rank) is not significantly related to age, gender, or years of practice, but is significantly related to YAQ (r = -.57, t(15) = 2.69, p = .017, two-tailed). Higher YAQ corresponds to better psi scoring (lower mean rank) as was predicted. In the original sample of 31 swamis, *sanyāsins*, and students, this correlation was non-significant (r = .13).

As might be expected, YAQ shows a small positive relationship with age (r = .33, p = .19, two-tailed), and Years of Practice is significantly related to age and YAQ. (r = .67 and r = .65, respectively, both p < .01, two-tailed).

Finally, using multiple regression to predict psi score based upon both these predictors, we find that the YAQ score accounts for virtually all of the explained variance and age does not contribute significantly. Thus, age of participants is not a confound in this data. Yogic attainment, as defined by the YAQ used in this study, may be. We can't be certain whether it accounts for the different psi scoring of swamis, *sannyāsins*, and students, with these small sample sizes.

Part II: Data from 2004

In 2004, the study continued with some changes. In 2004, there were 18 participants, including 6 each of swamis, *sannyāsins*, and students. Each participant completed exactly six (6) sessions of the psi task. The Yogic Attainment Questionnaire (YAQ) was revised for 2004. (see Appendix A). In 2004, the participants were all instructed to use the same meditation (known as "*ajapa japa.*") during the meditation session prior to the free-response mentation period. Table 4 below summarizes the results for 2004:

TABLE 4 – SUMMARY DATE FROM 2004

Group	N	Age Mn(sd)	Min/Max	YAQ	N Sess.	Psi (MnRnk)	t-test	2-tail P
SW	6	41.5(8.5)	26/50	10047(6002)	36	2.42(1.25)	-0.40	0.70
F	5	41.2(9.4)	26/50	9993(6738)	30	2.33(1.21)	-0.75	0.46
M	1	43.0(--)	43/43	10320(----)	6	2.83(1.47)	0.55	0.60
SN	6	29.5(3.8)	23/34	2565(1182)	36	2.44(1.03)	-0.32	0.74
F	3	32.3(1.5)	31/34	2994(765)	18	2.11(1.02)	-1.61	0.13
M	3	26.7(3.2)	23/29	2136(1535)	18	2.78(0.94)	1.25	0.23
ST	6	32.2(1.9)	30/35	1440(834)	36	2.36(1.10)	-0.76	0.46
F	3	33.7(1.5)	32/35	2020(803)	18	2.39(1.09)	-0.43	0.67
M	3	31.0(1.0)	30/32	860(286)	18	2.33(1.14)	-0.62	0.54

Note: Psi Mn Rank is the unweighted average of all trials by anyone in the group.
Group: Swamis (SW); Sannyasins (SN); Students (ST); Visitors(V)

The three groups, as expected, differ (significantly) from one another on the YAQ. However, there was also considerable variability on the YAQ measure, owing to the considerable refinement from the previous year. On the psi measure, overall, the 18 participants (108 sessions) tended toward psi-hitting but not significantly (mean rank = 2.41, sd = 1.12). This reversed the psi-missing tendency of the previous year (2003) when all participants who completed at least 3 sessions averaged 2.60 (sd=1.13) on the psi task for the 73 sessions.

Year	SW	SN	ST	ALL
2003	2.26(1.16)	2.77(1.14)	2.88(0.96)	2.60(1.13)
(Selected data)	27	30	16	73
2004	2.42(1.25)	2.44(1.03)	2.36(1.10)	2.41(1.12)
	36	36	36	108

Effect Size Analyses

The comparison of the groups for 2003 and 2004 can best be viewed by effect size ES(r). As before, the signs (positive, negative) of the effect sizes are adjusted for convenience – positive indicating psi-hitting and negative indicating psi-missing. Figure 3 shows this comparison.

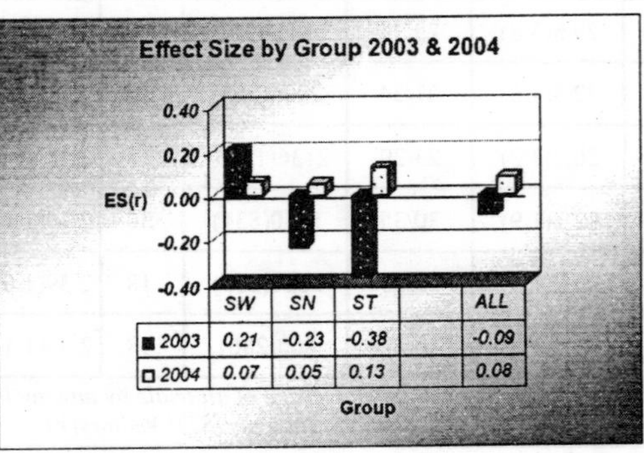

Figure 3

In Figure 3, the negative psi scoring (psi-missing) in the 2003 data shows up quite clearly. But Figure 3 also shows the strong effects – positive and negative – observed in 2003 relative to 2004.

However, as we explore the 2004 data more closely, we find that there may be interesting effects there as well. We next compare the gender effects for '03 and '04 in the following effect size displays. Recall that the 2003 data did not have any appreciable gender effects.

Figures 4 and 5 (below) show the gender breakdown of effect sizes for 2003 and 2004 data, respectively. While males and females scored about the same levels in their respective groups (SW, SN, ST) in 2003, that was not the case in 2004. Overall, the females in '04 score rather well, though non-significantly, on the psi task, mean rank of 2.29 (ES(r) = 0.19, t(65) = -1.54, p = .12, 2-tailed). The males in '04 score slightly negatively, mean rank = 2.60 (ES(r). = -.09). The overall difference between males and females in 2004 is not statistically significant (p = .17, 2-tailed).

The females in all three groups scored positively on the psi task, with the three female *sannyāsins* (SN group) showing the strongest, though still non-significant, psi result (mean rank = 2.11, sd = 1.02, t(17) = -1.61, p = .12, 2-tailed). This is an effect size of ES(r) = .36, in the small-medium range often associated with "good" psi performance. With male *sannyāsins* scoring nonsignificantly negatively (mean rank = 2.78, sd = 0.94), there is a significant difference between the male and female psi scoring, t(34) = 2.03, p = .05, 2-tailed. This gender effect does not hold for the other groups (SW, ST) and may be an artefact of fortuitous sampling.

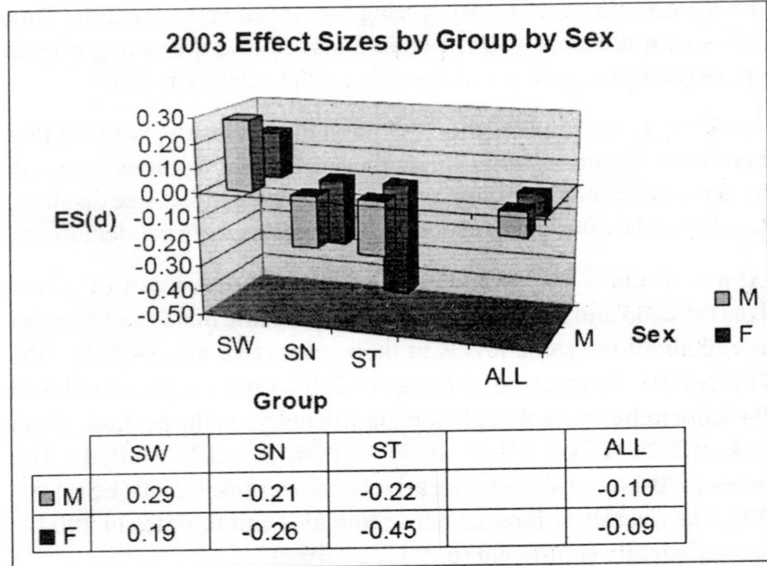

	SW	SN	ST		ALL
M	0.29	-0.21	-0.22		-0.10
F	0.19	-0.26	-0.45		-0.09

Figure 4

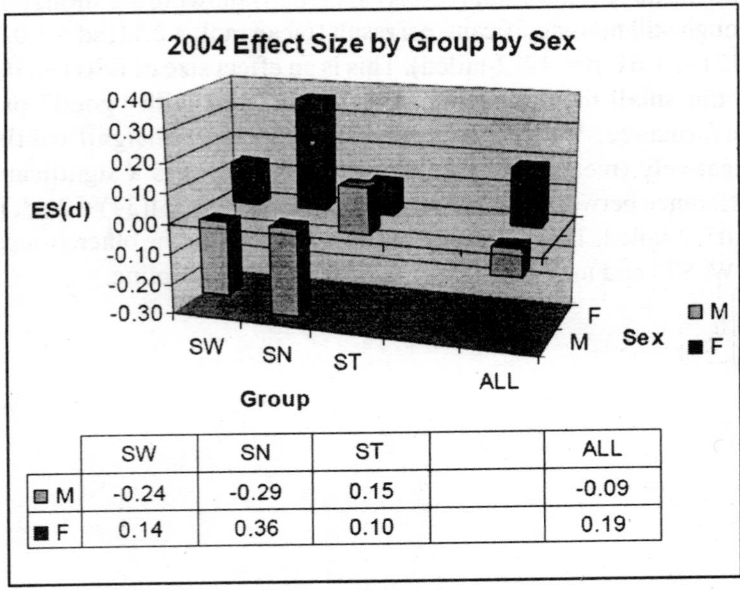

	SW	SN	ST		ALL
M	-0.24	-0.29	0.15		-0.09
F	0.14	0.36	0.10		0.19

Figure 5

Another question for the '04 data is whether the correlation between psi score (rank) and Yogic Attainment Questionnaire score observed in 2003 was continued. The simple (Pearson) correlations among the key variables in '04 are shown below:

TABLE 5: 2004 DATA: CORRELATIONS AMONG SELECTED VARIABLES

	Psi	Age	Gender
Age	.10	–	-.40
Gender	-.34	-.40	–
YAQ	.15	.71	-.31

In 2004, psi scoring is slightly correlated with gender (as discussed above), but near-zero with YAQ, and age, although both are in the predicted direction. Participants who were older and had higher YAQ scores tended to give more positive psi results. However, YAQ and age are correlated even more strongly in '04 than in '03. Thus, this is a complicated situation for which we have too little data and too many variables. The most we can hope for here is to shed some light on this issue for planning our future studies. We already know that gender is a factor in this study from our earlier considerations. Now we can see that this is not entirely clear either. Gender correlates in '04 with age (which was a potential confound in '03) and with YAQ – females participants tend to be younger and have lower YAQ scores. (Note: we could throw "years of practice" into this porridge and almost certainly find further correlations, but we hope that age and YAQ cover that other variable sufficiently.)

Thus, the question regarding possible correlation of psi with yogic attainment (YAQ) in the 2004 data must be answered, "We don't know!" The small observed simple correlation (r = .15) may be confounded by other factors and therefore might actually be considerably more or less than .15. There is insufficient data to unravel it.

Summary and Conclusion

This study is about the use of exploratory analysis in search of otherwise hidden patterns in data. While one must keep in mind that whatever is discovered in this search cannot be treated the same as the results of a pre-planned experiment, what is gained is the flexibility to examine possible trends and patterns for future investigation.

The first major intervention done here is the post-hoc screening of the 2003 participant pool to include only those who have completed at least three psi trials. In a small sample study such as this, it is usual to include every possible participant in order to preserve as much statistical power as one can. However, we must not lose sight of the fact that a representative sample is more urgent for generalization of results than sample size. That is, a representative sample is necessary and sufficient for generalizability while a large sample size is neither. In this particular instance, we argue that the participants in 2003 who completed at least three psi sessions are more likely to be representative of the population of concern. Three trials may be the minimum needed to overcome (or at least dilute) the effects of task novelty on the average scores. Stated another way, the 2003 data is now readdressed to a different population, the population of meditators who complete at least three psi sessions.

By reducing the participants in this way from 31 to 17 some relevant patterns in the 2003 data are revealed. While the scoring of the *sannyāsin*s and students remains about the same as in the full original sample, the 7 swamis who completed three or more psi sessions are seen to perform much better on the psi task, significantly better than the *sannyāsin*s and students who completed at least three sessions. However, the swamis psi performance is not statistically significantly better than chance. Could that be due to the small n of the reduced group?

By converting the data from mean rank into effect size we gain the ability to examine it from a different angle. The effect sizes for the swamis psi-scoring, particularly male swamis, is in the range of successful psi studies generally, and certainly in the range of what we expected for successful psi performance when we were planning this study.

But the more interesting revelation from the effect size display is the unexpected psi performance of the *sannyāsin* and student groups, albeit in the negative (psi-missing) direction. Thus, we can see anew the 2003 data suggesting psi effects in all groups - psi-hitting for swamis, and psi-missing for *sannyāsin*s and students.

When the 2004 data is examined using effect sizes, it appears at first to be totally devoid of psi effects. When broken down by gender a different picture emerges, showing a clear gender effect for the 2004 data which was not present in the 2003 data. In 2004, there were more female participants (especially swamis) and the females' psi scoring accounted for virtually all of the positive scoring. When we re-examine 2003 data in light of this, we see that males in all three groups scored slightly more positively than females- more psi-hitting for swamis and less psi-missing for *sannyāsin*s and students – but the 2003 gender difference was too small to consider anything more than chance fluctuation. Thus, we need to reappraise the question of gender effects in the context of this study. There are good reasons to raise this question since all data was collected by a female experimenter (SRD). Further, all of the psi sessions were conducted in her private room at the ashram.

The correlational analyses for 2003 shows support for the main hypothesis of this study–the Yogic Attainment Questionnaire correlates positively with psi-scoring, significantly so in the reduced sample of participants completing at least three sessions. The 2004 data shows a small, (non-significant) positive correlation between psi-score, and the reworked Yogic Attainment Questionnaire. Arguably, this correlational statistic showed the hypothesized relationship more clearly than the group comparison approach (SW vs. SN vs. ST).

The group comparisons are, after all, quasi-experimental because we cannot randomly assign participants to the SW, SN, ST groups. Therefore, the test of the yoga-psi hypothesis is *necessarily* correlational rather than causal in any case. A true experimental independent variable with randomly assigned treatment and control groups is not applicable here. This suggests that in the future this study be more clearly positioned as a straight correlational study of the predictability of psi-scoring via the separate and collective aspects of yogic attainment. Specifically, this means de-emphasis of the SW, SN, ST classifications, which may be influenced by socio-political considerations unlikely to be relevant to psi performance. Rather, emphasis should be placed on the assessment of the individual and collective dimensions of yogic attainment as this relates to psi-scoring.

As for methodological suggestions for continued research along these lines, there are many that can be put forth as a result of this analysis.

First, it is important that participants complete more psi sessions. The three session minimum used for 2003 data should be increased to at least 4, but preferably 6 or even 8 sessions, in order to improve internal and external validity of the psi measure.

Second, the study should be clearly positioned as correlational. This conceptual decision has a number of design implications, such as:

- de-emphasizing or even eliminating the SW, SN. ST classifications;
- focus upon accurate assessment of separate and summary aspects of yogic attainment;
- refining YAQ using item analysis techniques and factor analysis;
- focus on prediction of psi-scoring;
- emphasis on predictors which could lead to a true experimental design;

- adding potential moderating variables (covariates) to the design (such as Stroop test).

Third, gender effect must be reduced or excluded. The gender effect noted in this study could be socio-psychological, biological, possibly related to the yogic attainment predictor variable, or something else. In any case, it confounds our attempts to determine whether or not there is a relationship between yogic attainment and psi-scoring. Attempts should be made to neutralize this potentially confounding variable, in the protocol – by screening for gender – or in the analysis, by covering gender.

Fourth, the cross-cultural aspects of this study need be carefully considered (Rao, 2002). At a minimum, this means assuring that all assessments and procedures are culturally appropriate. It also means that the cultural meanings implicit in the tasks and instructions be continually reviewed and questioned. Moreover, the procedures which appear to have worked well with one cultural group cannot be assumed appropriate for another – even closely related - cultural group.

Fifth, the psi-missing in this study is problematic and every possible means to eliminate it should be employed. It is, of course, important to recognize psi-missing as psi. Based upon previous parapsychological studies, every attempt should be made for experimenters to hold positive attitudes during the collection and analysis of the data. It is important to recognize that the psi-missing may emerge from cross-cultural issues and to continually examine these.

Overall, the data which is presented here for 2003 and 2004 provide a good basis for the continued pursuit of the possible relationship of yogic attainment and psi scoring. Further research is needed and warranted, and the exploratory analyses presented here provide some guidance as to where the efforts of that research should be directed.

YOGIC ATTAINMENT QUESTIONNAIRE (2004)

Name:				Date:
1.	For how many years have you been practicing yoga:			
2.	During this time -			
a)	For how many years have you practiced: asana	as a daily practise	as a weekly practise	irregularly
		estimate hours/day	estimate hours/week	estimate hours/year
	Please circle the level of practise you are doing at the moment.			
b)	For how many year have you practised: pranayama	as a daily practise	as a weekly practise	irregularly
		estimate hours/day	estimate hours/week	estimate hours/year
	Please circle the level of practise you are doing at the moment.			
c)	For how many years have you practised: meditation	as a daily practise	as a weekly practise	irregularly
		estimate hours/day	estimate hours/week	estimate hours/year
	Please circle the level of practise you are doing at the moment.			

d)	For how many years have you practiced: yoga nidra	as a daily practise	as a weekly practise	irregularly
		estimate hours/day	estimate hours/week	estimate hours/year
	Please circle the level of practise you are doing at the moment.			
e)	For how many years have you practised: shatkarmas (plese specify the one/s you do)	as a daily practise	as a weekly practise	irregularly
		estimate hours/day	estimate hours/week	estimate hours/year
	Please circle the level of practise you are doing at the moment.			
3)	The following question are to get some idea of your level of attainment in antar mouna meditation. Please rate on 1 - 7 scale your present level of achievement at the different stages, where 1 means not at all thought to 7 meaning complete attainment of that stage.			

Stage 0						
1	2	3	4	5	6	7
Body discomfort brothers me				Full kaya sthairyam		
Stage 1						

<table>
<tr><td>1</td><td>2</td><td>3</td><td>4</td><td>5</td><td>6</td><td>7</td></tr>
<tr><td colspan="4">thoughts distract senses/breath awareness</td><td colspan="3">full concentration</td></tr>
<tr><td colspan="7">Stage 2</td></tr>
<tr><td>1</td><td>2</td><td>3</td><td>4</td><td>5</td><td>6</td><td>7</td></tr>
<tr><td colspan="4">senses distract spontaneous thought/chiddakash awareness</td><td colspan="3">full concentration</td></tr>
<tr><td colspan="7">Stage 3</td></tr>
<tr><td>1</td><td>2</td><td>3</td><td>4</td><td>5</td><td>6</td><td>7</td></tr>
<tr><td colspan="4">difficulty in creating, maintaining and disposing chosen thought/chiddakash</td><td colspan="3">full concentration</td></tr>
<tr><td colspan="7">Stage 4</td></tr>
<tr><td>1</td><td>2</td><td>3</td><td>4</td><td>5</td><td>6</td><td>7</td></tr>
<tr><td colspan="4">difficulty in maintaining focus and disposing of spontaneous thought</td><td colspan="3">full concentration</td></tr>
<tr><td colspan="7">Stage 5</td></tr>
<tr><td>1</td><td>2</td><td>3</td><td>4</td><td>5</td><td>6</td><td>7</td></tr>
<tr><td colspan="4">difficulty in maintaining thoughtlessness</td><td colspan="3">full concentration</td></tr>
<tr><td colspan="7">Stage 6</td></tr>
<tr><td>1</td><td>2</td><td>3</td><td>4</td><td>5</td><td>6</td><td>7</td></tr>
<tr><td colspan="4">difficulty in maintaining focus on psychic symbol</td><td colspan="3">full concentration</td></tr>
</table>

Acknowledgements

Grateful thanks to Paul Young for his financial assistance; also to the Perrott-Warwick fund and Bial Foundation grant no. 64/04, whose financial assistance is gratefully acknowledged; to Paul Stevens for his ESP programme, to Jezz Fox for his Precog programme, to David Luke for help with the questionnaire, and to all the participants who gave so much and without whom it could not have happened. An earlier version of this paper was presented at the 25th Society for Psychical Research Conference, Manchester, England, Sept. 2003.

REFERENCES

Rao, K.R. (2002). *Consciousness Studies: Cross Cultural Perspectives*. Jefferson, NC and London: McFarland.

Roney-Dougal, S.M. (2002). Psi experiments in an ashram. Paper presented at the 26th International Conference of the Society for Psychical Research, Manchester, Britain, September 2002.

— (2003). Free-response psi experiments in a yoga ashram: Preliminary studies (Part 2). Paper presented at the 27th International Conference of the Society for Psychical Research, Manchester, Britain, September 2002.

— & Solfvin, J. (In preparation). Yogic attainment in relation to awareness of precognitive targets. Submitted for publication.

Rosenthal, R., Rosnow, R.L. & Rubin, D.B. (2000). *Contrasts and Effect Sizes in Behavioral Research: A Correlational Approach.* Cambridge, UK: Cambridge University Press.

Solfvin, G., Kelly, E. & Burdick, D. (1978). Some new methods of analysis for preferential-ranking data. *Journal of the American Society for Psychical Research*, 72, 93-110.

Anomalous Anticipatory Skin Conductance Response to Acoustic Stimuli: Experimental Results and Speculation upon a Mechanism[1]

EDWIN. C. MAY[2]
TAMÁS PAULINYI[3]
ZOLTÁN VASSY[4]

Introduction

Vassy conducted what he conceived of as a classical, but remote, conditioning experiment in the 1960's which was reported much later (Vassy, 1978). In that experiment, a sender, who was sensorially isolated from a receiver, was shown a randomly determined light flash as a signal to "transmit" a telepathic warning message (i.e., a putative conditioned stimulus) to the receiver that he/she was about to experience a mild electric shock (i.e., unconditioned stimulus) in

[1] Reprinted with permission from *The Journal of Alternative and Complementary Medicine*, 2005, 11(4), 695-702

[2] Laboratories for Fundamental Research, Palo Alto, CA, US

[3] Szintézis Szabadegyetem, Budapest, HU

[4] AION Foundation, Budapest, HU

their left hand, while their skin conductance was monitored continuously in their right hand. The stimuli timing was such that if there were to be a conditioned response to the telepathic conditioning stimulus, it would appear before the unconditioned stimulus and a few seconds before the well-known unconditioned response (Woodworth and Schlosberg, 1961). Using manual and graphical methods of analysis, Vassy analyzed 10 sender-receiver sessions and found that six pairs were individually significant at the $p < 0.01$ level. While impressive, these results were obtained with visual meter readings and not with state of the art equipment and techniques. However, the experiment was repeated in 2002 with 50 sender/receiver pairs and showed significant evidence ($p < 0.01$) in the first of three series of what appears to be a telepathically conditioned response (Vassy, 2003). Subsequent series, however, with some changes of equipment and protocol did not produce significant effects. Another interpretation of such significant effects might be that receivers may have been responding in advance (i.e., anticipation) to future electroshock stimuli (Vassy, 2003).

Radin and Bierman began investigating, and observing significant anticipatory differential orienting effects in skin conductance responses prior to emotional and neutral photographic stimuli (Bierman and Radin, 1997; Radin, 1997a, 1997b). Radin coined the term *presentiment* to describe this type of orienting effect.

More recently, significant anticipatory effects were observed not only with skin conductance measures but also with electroencephalogram and electrocardiogram measures (R. McCraty, 2004a, 2004b).

We believe there may be a complication that might confound the interpretation of all of the presentiment results—photographic, cognitive stimuli can elicit idiosyncratic responses. For instance, a photographic stimulus that has been previously rated as having a low average affectivity may have, for some individual participants, a large affectivity, and vice versa. This reduces the contrast between arousing and calming presentations and constitutes an unwanted source of variance in these designs.

May and Spottiswoode adopted a different approach to remedy this possible confound. They replaced the emotional visual stimuli with acoustic startle stimuli and vastly simplified the analysis. Their dependent variable was the difference of proportions of prestimulus intervals that contained fully-formed non-specific skin conductance responses (ns-SCR) prior to acoustic stimuli compared to prior to silent controls. The null hypothesis was that these proportions should be equal. The first 105 participants of 125 reported later (Spottiswoode and May, 2003) were considered a pilot study. After trying a number of different approaches and parameters, they found mean proportions of 0.099 and 0.064 before acoustic stimuli and silent controls, respectively. Instead of an expected ratio of 1.0, they found a ratio of 1.53 ($Z = 2.84$, effect size = 0.086 ± 0.030, $p(1t) = 0.002$).[5]

In a 100-participant formal follow-on study (May and Spottiswoode, 2007) they reported proportions of 0.162 and 0.087 prior to acoustic and control stimuli, respectively, for a ratio of 1.87 ($Z = 5.08$, effect size = 0.162 ± 0.032, $p(1t) = 1.79 ' 10^{-7}$).

The results of these anticipatory studies imply a particular mechanism; individuals somehow appear to be able to respond psychophysiologically in advance of cognitive arousing or acoustic startle stimuli. However, we suggest an alternative interpretation that involves an anomalous anticipatory effect in such a way to mimic physiological responses.

Method

Our approach was a modification of standard skin conductance methods that were used in the previous acoustic prestimulus response studies.

Skin Conductance and Other Hardware

We used an SC5-SA skin conductance monitor, manufactured by Contact Precision Instruments. This unit is specified to have an

---

[5] The effect size is defined here as the proportion Z-score divided by the square root of the number of acoustic stimuli.

absolute accuracy of ± 0.1 ìSiemens, a DC excitation voltage of 0.5 V, a constant sample rate of 40 samples per second, a 24-bit precision, and a relative accuracy of 5.96 ´ 10^{-6} ìSiemens. The unit contains a hardware low-pass filter with an upper cutoff frequency of 10 Hz to prevent aliasing.

The electrodes used were 12 mm Ag/AgCl (Med Associates TDE-022SN) and were applied with an electrode paste of 0.5% saline in a neutral base (Med Associates TD-246). The electrode surface, which was surrounded by a 2 mm high Teflon rim, was covered with a film of electrode paste even with the rim and the electrodes were fastened to the distal phalanges of the first and second fingers of the non-dominant hand by a loop of adhesive skin tape. The electrode cables were secured to the palm by a third piece of tape to minimize any mechanical motion being transmitted to the electrodes.

We used high-quality, and active noise-canceling headphones.[6]

Stimuli

Unlike earlier studies, no acoustic stimulus was repeated throughout the run. A few examples included: air raid signal, ambulance, machinegun, and white noise.[7]

The acoustic startle stimuli were examined with an audio editing program and adjusted to provide about 97-dB intensity with 1-second duration. Controls (i.e., null stimuli) were markers placed into the skin conductance data stream and did not have an associated audio file. To eliminate possible extraneous sources of stimuli, the participant wore sound isolating headphones during the trial ensuring a low background sound level during the experiment sessions.

At the start of the data collection code, a list of 20 possible stimuli was randomly ordered and each successive acoustic stimulus was taken in turn from the randomized list. In this way, we assured that no acoustic stimulus would be repeated, and that each participant would receive a personalized order of stimuli.

---

[6] Sony Model MDR-NC5.

[7] Full stimuli details are available from the authors.

In this study, the inter-stimulus interval (ISI) was uniformly and randomly distributed between 30 and 50 seconds for a mean ISI = 40 seconds, using the Marsaglia pseudo random number generator (Marsaglia and Zaman, 1987). The total number of stimuli for each participant was 30 and no attempt was made to counterbalance the types.

At the end of a particular ISI, the stimulus type was determined by electron shot noise within a non-algorithmic, non-deterministic random number generator that was developed in the physics department at Ulm University in Germany.[8] This device and its associated driver software passed the "Gold Standard" for random number generators—The DieHard tests.[9] If this generator returned a binary one, an acoustic stimulus was presented; if it returned a binary zero, a silent marker into the skin conductance data stream was generated.

Software

The data collection code, which ran on a Sony VAIO laptop, was coded in Microsoft's Visual Basic language. Skin conductance data were transferred from the serial port buffer into the computer memory at each stimulus opportunity. After the data were stored in memory, the hardware generator described above determined the stimulus type of the next stimulus. The analysis software was coded in Research Systems, Incorporated 4th generation, vector processing computation language, IDL.[10] The next acoustic stimulus file was loaded in memory during the post stimulus period of the previous acoustic stimulus.

Analysis

The dependent variable was the difference of proportions between the number of 3.5-second prestimulus regions prior to future acoustic

---

[8] Details of this generator may be found at http://hlhp1.physik.uni-ulm de/~freitag/spinoffs.html.

[9] See http://stat.fsu.edu/~geo/diehard.html for information and source code of these tests.

[10] Details of Interactive Data Language can be found at www.rsinc.com.

and control stimuli (i.e., p_a and p_c, respectively) that contained a single ns-SCR.

The standard relation for the Z-score for the difference between two proportions is given by (Utts & Heckard, 2004)

$$Z = \frac{p_a - p_c}{SD},$$

where the standard deviation, SD, is given by :

$$SD = \sqrt{p(1-p) \times \left[\frac{1}{N_a} + \frac{1}{N_c}\right]},$$

and p is given by :

$$p = \frac{(p_a N_a + p_c N_c)}{N_a + N_c}.$$

For this type of analysis to be valid, the proportions, p_a and p_c, must be random variables; that is, they must be statistically independent. Even though ns-SCR's within a given participant arguably might not be independent, the necessary random element is provided by the stimuli timing and stimulus type. So regardless of any putative lack of statistical independences due to the ns-SCR's, the proportions are independent and the proportion difference is not artifactually different from zero under the null hypothesis.

ns-SCR Definition and Detection

Figure 1 shows a ns-SCR from an acoustic prestimulus sample from one of the participants in our study.

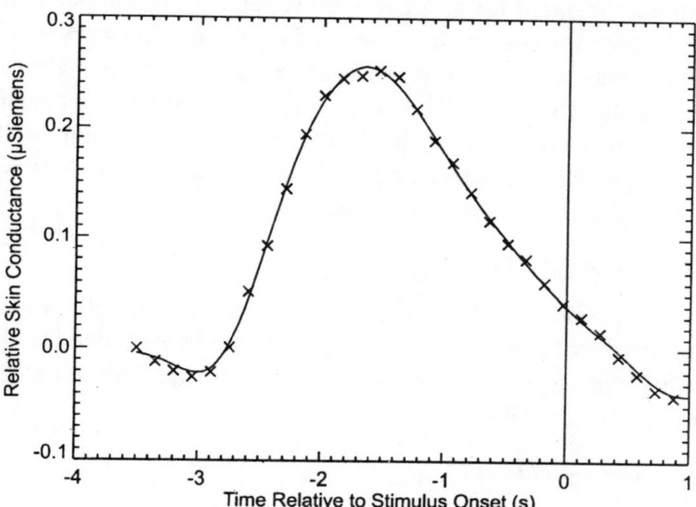

Figure 1. Example of data smoothing and cubic spline fit. The ''s represent every fifth data point and the solid curve is the spline approximation

Using the cubic spline routine from Research Systems Incorporated IDL library, we down-sampled the data by a factor of five and constructed a spline approximation to that data. Then using the same routine, we up-sampled the resulting spline and created a final spline approximation shown as the solid line in Figure 1. One property of a cubic spline is that the first derivative is well behaved. Therefore, we used standard calculus techniques to determine minima and maxima within a given prestimulus region.

Conservatively, we specified that the following conditions must be met before we would declare a ns-SCR had been detected.

- A single minimum must be followed by a definitive maximum. That is, the first derivative of the skin conductance data must be zero at the maximum.

- The amplitude of the ns-SCR must meet or exceed a given participant-dependent threshold.

To determine the threshold, a participant's total skin conductance record was scanned for ns-SCR's; however, an interval between -7 to +10 seconds was excluded around each stimulus marker. The threshold was set at 10% of the average of all ns-SCR's above a floor of 0.005 ìSiemens. The 10% value was arbitrary, but earlier studies demonstrated that the results were independent of the threshold, and as we will show below, the results of this study was also independent of the threshold choice.

Data Inclusion Criterion

Because the stimulus types were random but not counterbalanced, we required that a participant's data would not be included if either stimulus type exceed 20 (i.e., 20 of one stimulus type out of 30 is significant at p = 0.049).

Participant Selection

All participants were recruited as volunteers from the student body of the Szintézis Szabadegyetem ("Synthesis" Free University) in Budapest. This school specializes in the study of various parapsychological and more esoteric phenomena.

Trial Protocol

All trials were conducted in the school's laboratory facility. The laboratory is acoustically isolated from the control room and is often used in sensory isolation experiments.

A participant entered the facility and was offered refreshments and pleasant conversation. Then one of the two experimenters (i.e., Vassy or Paulinyi) invited the participant to rinse their hands in water (no soap), dry them thoroughly, and enter the laboratory. While the skin conductance electrodes were being applied to the subdominant hand (see above), the experimenter described the up-coming session in detail. The participant was shown their skin conductance changes resulting from rapid deep breaths and a surprise hand clap. In addition, they were given a sample sound (not from the set of experimental stimuli) through the headphones and given the opportunity to quit if the sound was too uncomfortable. They were advised on the use of a "panic" button to exit the run if necessary. The experimenter emphasized in this way that they were in charge of the session and could quit at any time.

All of this activity was designed to last approximately 10 minutes to allow the electrode and electrode cream to normalize with the participant's skin. The participant was advised to keep his/her eyes closed during the session; that they would hear a voice message informing them when the session was complete; and that the run would automatically begin two minutes after the session was initiated by the experimenter. The experimenter left and secured the door to the laboratory.

At the end of the session, the participant was immediately shown the statistical results, individual stimuli examples, and their post stimulus responses. These data were discussed in the best possible terms.

Results

We conducted the experiment with 50 self-selected participants of which 33 were female. Ages ranged from 17 to 74 with a mean and median of 38.4 and 37.0, respectively. We excluded no individuals from this study. Table 1 shows the results of the primary analysis.

TABLE 1

Interval Type	**# of Intervals Containing a ns-SCR Response**	**# of Prestimulus Intervals**	**Proportion with a ns_SCR Response**
Before a Control	63	775	0.081
Before a Stimulus	82	725	0.113

The null hypothesis was that the proportions should be equal (i.e., a ratio of 1.0), but as Table 1 shows we observed a ratio of 1.39

(Proportion Difference Z = 2.08, n = 725, effect size = 0.077 ± 0.037, p(1t) = 0.019). The effect size was defined as the proportion difference z-score divided by the square root of the number of acoustic stimuli. In this experiment, Vassy was the experimenter for 21 people with a total of 302 acoustic stimuli (Proportion z-score = 1.33, effect size = 0.0766 ± 0.0575), while Paulinyi was the experimenter 29 people with a total of 475 acoustic stimuli (proportion z-score = 1.59, effect size = 0.0775 ± 0.0486). Thus, the overall result was equally contributed by the two experimenters, Paulinyi and Vassy (difference t-score = 0.0122, df = 773, p = 0.495).

At the participant level, the Stouffer's Z for the 50 sessions was 2.017 leading to a session effect size of 0.285±0.141.

Discussion

We compared this result to the original 105-pilot dataset because those participants were unselected and the experimenters were new to this type of study. This parallels the results reported in this study, as one of us (May) was not an experimenter, and Paulinyi and Vassy were also new to this type of study. Table 2 shows the results for the two datasets.

TABLE 2

Item	105-Pilot	50-Budapest
# of Stimuli	1106	725
Intervals with ns-SCR's	109	82
Proportion with ns-SCR's	0.0986	0.1131
# of Controls	994	775
Intervals with ns-SCR's	64	63
Proportion with ns-SCR's	0.0644	0.0813
Ratio (MCE = 1)	1.53	1.391
Proportion Z-Score	2.84	2.08
Effect Size	0.086±0.030	0.077±0.037
P-Value	0.002	0.019

The difference between the two study effect sizes is not significant ($t = -0.188$, $df = 1829$, $p = 0.575$). The study reported here is a conceptual confirmation of the results from the pilot study. Table 3 outlines the protocol differences between the two studies.

TABLE 3

Item	Pilot	Budapest
Number of	105	50
Inter-Stimulus	60±20 Seconds	40±10 Seconds
Stimuli	White Noise	Non-Repeating
Experimenters	May/Spottiswoode	Vassy / Paulinyi
Culture/Participants	American	Hungarian
Study Duration	79 Days	10 Days

Possible Alternatives to the Primary Hypothesis

In this section we examine a number of possible artifacts that might account for the observed deviation from chance expectation.

Expectation

Possibly the most obvious artifact might be that of a participant's expectations. The acoustic stimuli could be experienced as unpleasant aversive stimuli. That is, as the session may evolve with long periods of silence, a participant might produce more ns-SCR's from anxiety over time and somehow skew the counting statistic. Given an acoustic stimulus, if the distribution of times to the next acoustic stimulus were statistically identical to the distribution of times to the next silent control, no expectation artifact, regardless of type or magnitude, could contribute to the differential outcome measure. Figure 2 shows the distribution of times to the next acoustic stimulus and the next control stimulus.

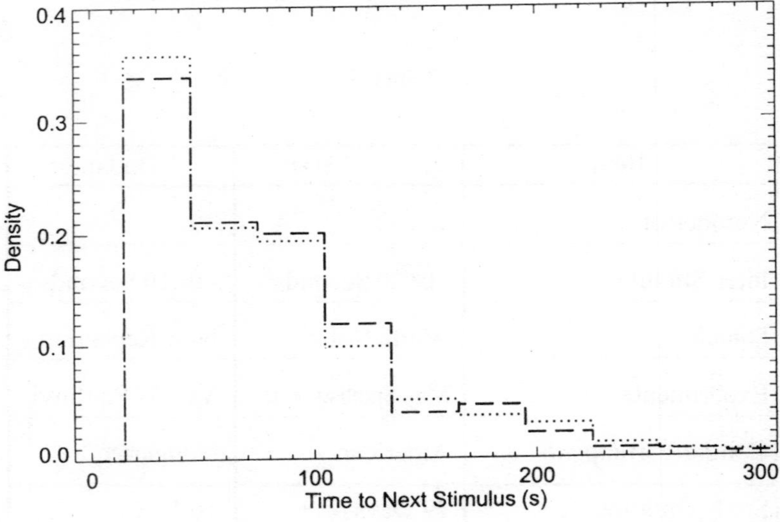

Figure 2. Distribution of times to the next stimulus. The dotted curve is the distribution of times to the next acoustic stimulus and the dashed curve to the next control.

Given an acoustic stimulus, the mean of the distribution of times to the next acoustic stimulus was 80.89 s and to the next control was 82.04 s (Mann-Whitney Uz = 1.045, p = 0.148). The distributions of these times were statistically equivalent (Kolmogorov-Smirnov, *p(1t)* = 0.398). Thus an expectation artifact could not have produced the observed results.

However this argument does not consider whether there was an expectation bias. To address this question we computed the probability of a ns-SCR as a function of time to the next acoustic stimulus and separately to the next control. Figure 3 shows a graphical result for the probability of a ns-SCR prior to an acoustic stimulus as a function of time since the last acoustic stimulus.

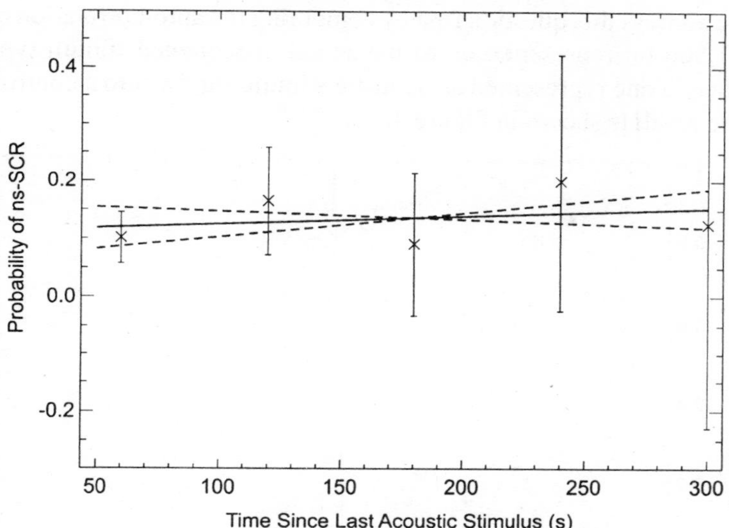

Figure 3. Probability of a ns-SCR as a function of time since last acoustic stimulus. The solid line is the weighted best fit to the data and the dashed lines are the one standard error in the slope. The one standard error the each of the data points are shown as error bars.

The slope of the weighted best fit line was (1.38 ± 2.78) ′ 10^{-4}. Similarly, the slope of the weighted best fine line for the probability of a ns-SCR prior to a control as a function of time since last acoustic stimulus was (2.33 ± 3.37) ′ 10^{-4}. We note that a zero slope (i.e., no expectation bias) is well within the standard errors. Therefore since the distribution of times to the next acoustic stimulus and to the next control from the last acoustic stimulus were statistically equivalent and thus rendered an expectation bias moot, the results shown in Figure 3 and their associated analyses show there was no bias present.

Stimulus Type Generator

In the study reported here, there were 725 acoustic stimuli and 775 controls (Binomial Z-score = 1.29, p = 0.098, effect size/stimulus = 0.033 ± 0.0259). A possible artifact might arise if there were sufficient information in the actual stimulus sequence to allow a participant to infer the next stimulus.

We address this question first by computing the auto-correlation of a 1,500 bit representation of the actual in-sequence stimuli type where a one represented an acoustic stimulus and a zero a control. The result is shown in Figure 4.

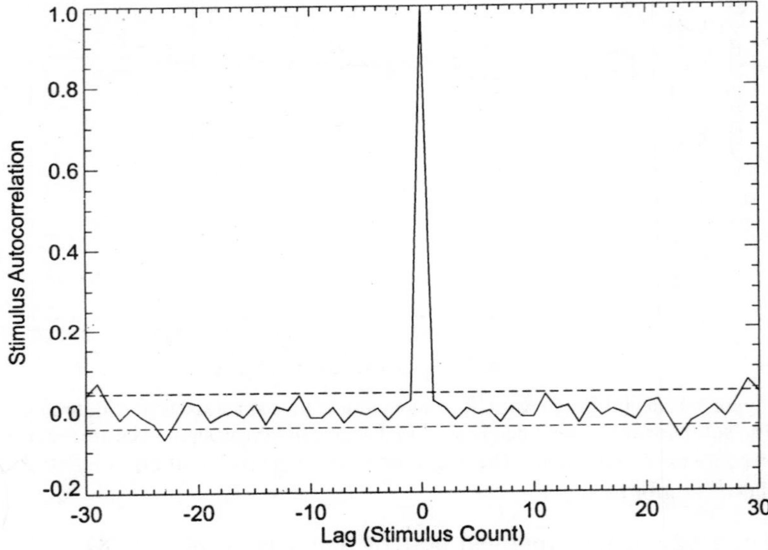

Figure 4. Auto-correlation of stimulus type as a function of stimulus count. The dashed lines are the critical value for a significant correlation (i.e., r = 0.0425, df = 1498).

We computed the auto-correlation for ± 30 lags because that is the only amount of stimuli presented to a single participant. The largest correlation occurred at lag = 30 (r = 0.069, df = 1,498, p(2-t) = 0.0056), and the smallest at lag = 23 (r = -0.0711, df = 1,498, p = 0.0058). Two lags in 30 produced a significant p £ 0.05 correlation (Binomial p = 0,446).

A second approach was to compute the informational entropy in the 1,500 bit sequence. We found that the information was 0.992 bits/bit. That is, it nearly took a single bit to describe each bit in the sequence. This result coupled with the auto-correlation shown in Figure 4 precludes the stimulus generator as a possible source of artifact.

Choice of Threshold for ns-SCR Detection

Based upon previous work (Spottiswoode and May, 2003), we used a threshold of 10% of the mean amplitude of all ns-SCR's above a floor of 0.005 ìSiemens far from all overt stimuli. It is possible that this choice of participant-dependent threshold might have been fortuitous. We examined the proportion difference effect size as a function of the threshold percentage from one to 50%. The results are shown in Figure 5.

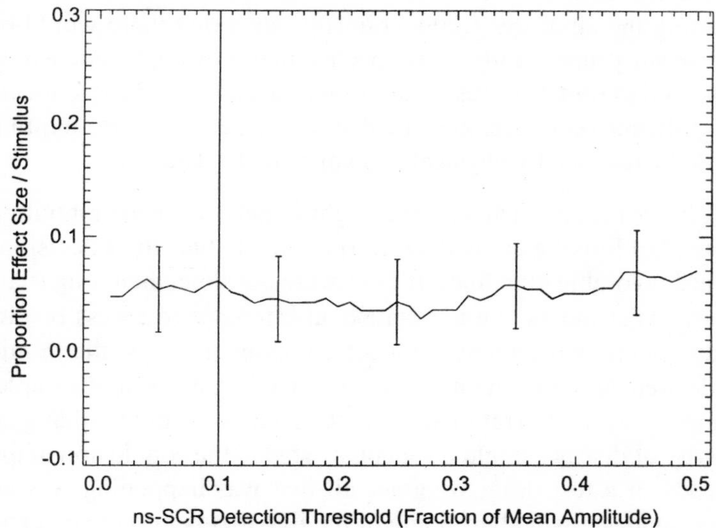

Figure 5. Threshold sensitivity. The error bars are the one standard error of the equivalent effect size.

The vertical solid line shows the value used in this study. By inspection our choice of 10% for the threshold did not induce an artifact.

Two Competing Hypotheses for the Results

The primary hypothesis for this study was that individual's autonomic nervous system responds, in advance, more to future acoustic startle stimuli than to silent controls. However a second hypothesis is more subtle (May, Utts and Spottiswoode, 1995).

To understand Decision Augmentation Theory (DAT), we begin with a hypothetical, yet simple idea. Consider a coin flipper that consecutively flips a fair coin one million times. By definition of a random binary sequence (i.e., heads/tails), there will be subsets of the million flips that appear not to be random. For example a run of 10 heads in a row is half as likely as nine in a row, and so own. Runs of heads of various lengths will be randomly positioned in the million-flip sequence. Suppose now that one is asked to *decide*, by physically looking at the whole coin flip sequence, when to start counting the next, say 1,000, coin flips such that there would be significantly more heads than expected. In this example, one would only need to find 27 excess heads (over the expected 500) to locate a significant sequence, and the decision where to start counting would be reached by physically examining the data.

DAT holds in general that people might somehow use their intuition (instead of looking at the data) to statistically bias their decisions toward favorable outcomes. If DAT were possible, then drug trials or any experiments that use statistical inference to assess results might contain a researcher-induced component that would mimic the desired outcome. In random controlled drug trials, for example, in improper randomization of patients, such as not randomizing on severity of disease, might erroneously lead to the conclusion of the efficacy of a test drug; whereas, all that was happening was an unfortunate statistical grouping of the ill patients into the placebo control group and the healthier patients into the treatment group and that statistic would mimic an efficacious drug that actually was not (Astin, Harkness and Ernst, 2000). In this second example, DAT proposes some form of intuition on the part of an experimenter may induce a weak statistical systematic bias into the patient selection process to mimic drug and/or treatment efficacy (May, 2003).

In the skin conductance experiment reported here, ns-SCR's are quite rare. The overall most likely lability (i.e., probability of observing a single ns-SCR in any 3.5 second period) was 0.031. Additionally, the stimuli were also relatively rare with an ISI = 40 ± 10 seconds. If an experimenter's intuition was subjected to DAT, then it might be "easier" to initiate a run to avoid a ns-SCR in the prestimulus window than to capture one because so much of the skin conductance data was devoid of ns-SCR's. This speculation was confirmed by extensive Monte Carlo simulations. If this form of DAT were present in actual experimental data, it would predict that the significant proportion difference in the anticipatory skin conductance experiment reported above would contain a component that the rate of ns-SCR's in control periods would be *below* that of the rate of the general background ns-SCR rate.

To check this, *post hoc*, we computed an average background ns-SCR rate for each participant as follows. We defined eight 3.5 second intervals near each silent control stimulus. These included four intervals post silent control and four intervals prior to the actual prestimulus interval. The average background rate was computed over 8 × the number of silent controls. Thus for each of the 50 participants we computed: p_1—the ns-SCR rate prior to an acoustic stimulus, p_0—the ns-SCR rate prior to a control, and p_b—the background rate described above.

We computed paired t-tests between p_1 and p_b and between p_0 and p_b.

The pre-acoustic ns-SCR rate was statistically indistinguishable from the background rate (t(49) = 0.163, p(1t) = 0.436); however, the pre-control rate was significantly below the background (t(49) - 2.87, p(1t) = 0.003). This result appears to verify the DAT prediction above.

In contrast, we might expect a physiological model to give the reverse: $p_1 > p_b$ and $p_0 \sim p_b$. That is an individual would be reacting, albeit in advance, to a stimulus and not reacting to a non-stimulus or control.

It seems unlikely that a physiological interpretation could account for a depletion of ns-SCR's prior to null stimuli. This would require not only for an experiment participant to use intuition to know when a randomly determined and un-cued control stimulus was about to occur but at the same time willfully, either consciously or unconsciously, inhibit a ns-SCR for 3.5 seconds in anticipation of the control.

Conclusion

We successfully replicated the earlier work with regard to acoustic stimuli prestimulus response. That is, there is clear evidence for an anomalous preferential anticipatory skin conductance response prior to acoustic stimuli compared to prior to controls. However, the primary hypothesis that individuals are responding in advance to startle stimuli is unlikely to be the case. Rather, there is suggestive experimental and circumstantial evidence that experimenters use their own intuition to sort random ns-SCR's in order to mimic a physiological response—Decision Augmentation on the part of the experimenters. If the significant result from this rather straight forward psychophysiology experiment can be explained by intuition on the part of the experimenter rather than physiological responses on the part of the designated experiment participant, then so also should any statistical inferential results from any study, including those of interest to alternative and complementary medical investigations, be questioned at least with regard to interpretation. A prospective study is needed to settle the question definitively with regard to DAT and prestimulus response.

Acknowledgements

We appreciate and thank the 50 students of Szintézis Szabadegy-etem who graciously volunteered their time and skill to this study. We thank Dr. Richard Broughton for many helpful discussions and for reviewing this manuscript. This study would not have been possible without the support of the Samueli Institute, the BIAL Foundation, and the Laboratories for Fundamental Research.

REFERENCES

Astin, J.A., Harkness, E. & Ernst, E. (2000). The efficacy of "distant healing": A systematic review of randomized trials. *Annals of Internal Medicine,* 132 (11), 903-910.

Bierman, D.J. & Radin, D.I. (1997). Anomalous anticipatory response on randomized future conditions. *Perceptual and Motor Skills,* 84, 689-690.

Marsaglia, G. & Zaman, A. (1987). *Toward a Universal Random Number Generator* (No. FSU-SCRI-87-50): Florida State University.

May, E.C. (2003). Challenges for healing and intentionality research: Causation and information. In W. B. Jonas & C.C. Crawford (Eds.), *Healing Intention and Energy Medicine: Science, Research Methods and Clinical Implications* (pp. 283-291). New York: Churchill Livingstone.

— & Spottiswoode, S.J.P. (2007). Anticipatory Effects in the Human Autonomic Nervous System. *Submitted to The International Journal of Psychophysiology.*

— Utts, J.M., (1995). Decision Augmentation Theory: Toward a model for anomalous mental phenomena. *Journal of Parapsychology,* 59, 195-220.

McCraty, M.A. & Raymond T.B. (2004a). Electrophysiological evidence of Intuition: Part 1. The surprising role of the heart. *Journal of Alternative and Complementary Medicine,* 10 (1), 133-143.

— (2004b). Electrophysiological evidence of intuition: Part 2. A system-wide process? *Journal of Alternative and Complementary Medicine,* 10(2), 325-336.

Radin, D.I. (1997a). *The Conscious Universe*. New York: Harper Collins.

— (1997b). Unconscious perception of future emotions: An experiment in presentiment. *Journal of Scientific Exploration,* 11(2), 163-180.

Spottiswoode, S.J.P. & May, E.C. (2003). Skin conductance prestimulus response: analyses, artifacts and a pilot study. *Journal of Scientific Exploration, 17*(4), 617-641.

Utts, J.M. & Heckard, R.F. (2004). Testing the difference between two population proportions. In *Mind on Statistics* (2nd ed., pp. 459-464). Belmont, CA: Brooks/Cole—Thomson Learning.

Vassy, Z. (1978). Method of measuring the probability of 1-bit extrasensory information transfer between living organisms. *Journal of Parapsychology,* 43(2), 158-160.

— (2003). A study of telepathy by classical conditioning. *Journal of Parapsychology, 68*(2).

Woodworth, R.S. & Schlosberg, H. (1961). *Experimental Psychology*. New York: Rinehart and Winston.

Cognitive Anomalies: Developing Tests for Screening and Selecting Subjects*

K. Ramakrishna Rao

Introduction

The belief in the existence of supernormal abilities among humans and the possibility of developing them through disciplined practices is as old as recorded history. It is widespread across the globe and is prevalent not only in the Indian subcontinent but also in Egypt and Greece to mention a few. There are stories of extraordinary abilities of yogins and *ṛshi*s in our *itihāsa*s and *purāṇa*s. Greece was reputed to have oracles which were able to cognize the events in the past and future and those at a distance that are inaccessible to sensory reach. The *Bible* is full of miraculous events attributed to

* The research reported here is funded by a grant from the Defense Institute of Psychological Research of the Department of Research and Development Organization. The help and assistance of Dr. K. Suneetha, Dr. Sonali Bhatt Marwaha, Dr. N. Sarada, Mr. Jacksan J. Fernandes and Dr. Ch. Srikrishna in collecting the data are acknowledged.

human agencies. We learn from the *Mahābhārata* that Sanjaya had the ability of clairvoyance (*divya-dṛsṭi*) and that he was able to inform king Dhṛitarāṣtra about the events in the battle field as they happened. In Greece, King Croesus of Lydia is said to have successfully tested the psychic powers of the Oracle at Delphi.

In fact, classical Indian thought in its epistemology provides for nonsensory sources of knowing. This is true not only of all the orthodox *darśana*s, with possible exception of Mīmāṃsā, but also of Buddhism and Jainism. What is interesting is that psychic phenomena like clairvoyance are not considered freak and exceptional occurrences. Rather they are regarded as genuine abilities that could be developed. Thus there was in India a science to systematically study psychic phenomena (*siddhi*s) in Hindu as well as in Buddhist traditions. Texts such as *Yogavāśiṣṭha,* Patanjali's *Yoga-Sūtra*s, and Buddhaghosha's *Viśuddhimāgga* have described relevant mental exercises like meditation in great deal, which are often accompanied by acquisition of extraordinary abilities.

There is thus a rich heritage and widespread belief in paranormal phenomena, from antiquity to the present. However, the study of such psychic phenomena received in modern India scant attention. One of the significant reasons for this state of affairs is possibly the fear that these abilities could be destructively used. In fact the tradition itself is opposed to deliberately developing them for their own sake. These abilities are believed to manifest as one practices, for example, meditation. But the goal of the meditator is *kaivalya* or *nirvāṇa*; and psychic abilities may be a distraction and are therefore to be avoided. The practitioners are warned not to be taken in by psychic phenomena because indulgence in them would be antithetical to reaching the ultimate goal of liberation. The Buddha exhorted his disciples; "you are not, O bhikkus, to display before the laity the superhuman power of *iddhi* (*siddhi* in Sanskrit). Whosoever does so shall be guilty of *dukkata*" (*Vinaya Piṭṭaka,* II, 112).

These reservations have justification; but there is also good reason to reconsider them in the present secular context of science. The results of science could be used to promote human well being or to cause destruction. There is no reason why psychic abilities may not be used for good of all. There are many genuine reasons for investigating these unusual phenomena with utmost care and highest standards of scholarship and methodological rigor and using them, if found genuine, to enhance human potentials. First, the implications of the reality of these abilities is truly mind blowing. Second, there is credible evidence for the existence of these phenomena, even though their understanding appears to defy, so far, all attempts in the West. Third, unlike in the West, the existence of psychic phenomena is consistent with the great Indian intellectual tradition. Fourth, if universities and research organizations fail to throw credible light on these phenomena, they will be confined to the nonscientific sector and remain as mysteries and unresolved enigma to be exploited by unscrupulous people. It does not have to be so. Already good beginnings have been made. Concepts, tools, and methods to investigate psychic phenomena are now available. There is great scope for making advances by Indian scientists in this area that would be in our national interest.

PSI RESEARCH IN THE WEST

Reports of controlled observation and study of extraordinary experiences involving premonitions, mind reading, and casting psychic influence on events and objects may be traced back to antiquity. However, scientific attempts to study them are more recent.

Noble Prize winner in physiology, Charles Richet (1923), was one of the earliest to carry out experimental investigations of extraordinary human experiences involving extrasensory communication. He divided the history of field before him into four stages. The first was the mythical stage which lasted up to Mesmer — a period in which miracles and prophecies played a part and were at the root of several religious systems. The second, the magnetic stage, began with Mesmer (1980/1781) and his doctrine of animal magnetism and lasted until the advent of the spiritistic stage in 1848 with the Fox sisters and the widespread interest that followed in the so-called spiritistic manifestations represented by raps and such. Richet credited Sir William Crookes as having ushered in the fourth, the scientific stage in 1872 and expressed the hope that the publication of his own book *Thirty Years of Psychical Research* would "help to inaugurate a fifth, that of recognition as a science" (Richet, 1923, p. 15). Since Richet, massive statistical evidence collected from carefully controlled experiments in support of the existence of psychic phenomena such as extrasensory perception or ESP (awareness of events and objects shielded from the senses) and psychokinesis or PK (direct influence of mind over matter) exists (Rao and Palmer, 1987). Even though the field of parapsychology continues to be controversial and the results of the experimental studies in this area are hotly contested, few among those who are actively involved in it have any doubts about the genuineness of the results and the reality of the phenomena under investigation (Radin, 1997; 2006).

Applications of Psi

Intelligence Gathering and Military Applications

If ESP and PK are genuine phenomena, the scope for their application is limitless. ESP could be used, for example, in intelligence gathering and spying and PK to jam enemy's communication system and effect malfunction of sensitive equipment and so on. These possibilities are not lost sight off by the major military powers. There are reasons to believe that the rival camps during the cold war period toyed with the idea of using psi for military purposes and that they did in fact support some parapsychological research. This area is of course full of rumours, misinformation and fabricated stories; yet the excitement created by them indicates the implied concerns.

The infamous Nautilus story carried by the French press in 1959 is a case in point. Nautilus is an American atomic submarine. It was prominently reported in the French media that the US Navy was using ESP aboard the Nautilus with headlines such as "Has the American military mastered the secret of mind power" and "Will ESP be a deciding factor in future warfare?" The Nautilus story is probably a fiction. However, it had enormous impact on laymen as well as scientists who read those headlines. For example, the Nautilus news provoked the distinguished Russian physiologist L.

L. Vasiliev. He said at a meeting of Soviet scientists in 1960: "We carried out extensive and, until now, completely unreported investigation on ESP under the Stalin regime! ... Today the American Navy is testing telepathy on their atomic submarines. Soviet science conducted a great many successful telepathy tests over a quarter of a century ago: It is urgent that we throw off our prejudices. We must again plunge into the exploration of this vital field" (quoted from Ostrander and Schroder, 1970, p. 6).

There are anecdotal accounts that some in secret British army had psychic family members involved in their military successes (Radin, 1997). General George Patton of US Army is credited with sixth sense (Mishlove, 1993). There are two books on American psychic spying — one by J. Schnabel (1997) and another by J. McMoneagle (1993). The latter in his *Mind Trek* describes the test that was carried out at the instance of the US National Security Council in which correct information relating to secret construction of a submarine in Northern Russia is reported to have been psychically obtained.

Information declassified a few years ago reveals that some agencies of the US government, notably CIA, has supported research in remote viewing, which is another name for ESP, for a number of years. US government sponsored parapsychological research began in early 1970 at the prestigious Stanford Research Institute (SRI), now known as SRI International. This research program was continued until 1989. Again, during the following year the support of the US government was extended to Science Applications International Corporation (SAIC) under the direction of Edwin May who had earlier directed the program at SRI International (See website www.lfr.org for more details). One of the experts commissioned by CIA to evaluate the government program on ESP research, Jessica Utts (2001) of University of California at Davis concluded her assessment thus:

> I believe that it would be wasteful of valuable resources to continue to look for proof. No one who has examined all of the data across laboratories, taken as a collective whole,

> has been able to suggest methodological or statistical problems to explain the ever-increasing and consistent results to date. Resources should be directed to the pertinent questions about how this ability works. I am confident that the questions are no more elusive than any other questions in science dealing with small to medium sized effects, and that if appropriate resources are targeted to appropriate questions, we can have answers within the next decade (p. 133).

Intuition in Business

Many successful business persons are credited with intuitive ability to foresee future and take unexpected decisions. For example, Norma Bowles and Fran Hynds (1978) quote Alexander Poniatoff, founder of Amplex Corporation saying, "In the past I would not admit to any one, especially business people, why my decisions were sometimes were contrary to any logical judgment. But now that I have become aware of others who follow intuition, I don't mind talking about it" (p.114). Similarly, William Keeler, former chairman of Phillips Petroleum, says of intuition: "There are too many incidents that can't be explained merely as coincidences. I had successes in unchartered areas. My strong feelings towards things were accurate when I would let myself go... Oil fields are found on hunches, through precognitive dreams, and by people who didn't know anything about geology" (Bowles and Hynds, 1978, p. 114). Smt. Indira Gandhi told me, while she was the Prime Minister of India, that when she wanted something to happen, she concentrated on it and several times unexpected things happened as she concentrated, wished and hoped for.

Jeffrey Mishlove (1993) in his *Roots of Consciousness* recounts the tests conducted by the *St. Louis Business Journal*. In these tests the performance of a psychic was compared with that of eighteen professional stock brokers over a period of six months. It is reported that the psychic outperformed the stock brokers. Also, the stocks picked by the psychic went up by seventeen percent when the Dow Jones Industrial Average fell eight percent during that period.

The role of "hunches" and intuition in business was the subject of a book entitled *Executive ESP* by Douglas Dean and John Mihalasky of the Newark College of Engineering. Dean and Mihalasky (1974) report significant correlations of business success with the ESP scores of business executives. In one study, they found dynamic (successful) business managers obtained higher precognition scores than nondynamic managers in 16 of the 20 groups they tested. In another study two groups of presidents of business companies were administered precognition tests. A comparison of precognition scores of the presidents with the profit records of their companies showed that the more successful presidents obtained higher scores on precognition tests. These studies and observations are not flawless, but they do suggest the possibility of applying psi for practical use and the need to carry out further research.

Like the hunches of successful business persons, it is said that some of the seminal ideas of great scientists are an outcome of intuitions. Dean Radin (1997) refers to the finding of Buckminister Fuller who examined the diaries of great scientists and inventors. It is reported that "their diaries declared spontaneously that the most important item in connection with their great discovery of a principle that nobody else had been able to discover, was intuition" (quoted from Radin 1997, p. 200). Thus it would seem that intuition might play a useful role not only in decision making but also in engaging in new discoveries.

Psi and Healing Arts

Medical applications of psi are widespread, and they have been in vogue from antiquity. The form of practices may be different in different societies, but the core content appears to be the same, whether we are dealing with shamans, psychic or spiritual healers or witchdoctors. The application of psi in the area of health has two broad lines, paralleling the two basic forms of psi. One involves use of ESP like ability to diagnose disease. The other is the PK like ability to cure disease psychically. There is abundant anecdotal and some scientific evidence to suggest that paranormal abilities may be involved in some of these unorthodox and nonconventional practices of diagnosis and healing.

Edgar Cayce was perhaps the most celebrated "psychic diagnostician" in the US. Cayce (1877-1945) was a professional photographer and had no medical background or training. It is said that he developed his ability when he attempted to treat his own throat problems (Cayce 1969; Bro 1989). During a period extending over forty years, he had seen literally thousands of patients attempting to diagnose and even suggest remedies. In each case, Cayce would enter into a self-induced trance-like state. He would then be given the patient's name and address. Cayce would proceed to give his diagnosis and suggest a course of treatment. A stenographer would record Cayce's statements, which were usually sent to the patient or his/her physician. The suggested treatments are often unorthodox, involving psychological suggestions, herb and food remedies, and sometimes specific chiropractic manipulations. It should be mentioned that the patient was not required to be physically present. All that was needed is patient's name and address. It is believed by his admirers and associates that Cayce would "telepathically tune in on the patient's mind and body" and learn about the affliction.

Inspired by Edgar Cayce's work, Shafica Karagulla, a trained physician, carried out field studies of psychic diagnosis, which she prefers to call "higher sense perception." In her book *Breakthrough to Creativity*, Karagulla (1967) gives a number of examples of psychic diagnosis based on her field studies. The procedure involves asking a reputed psychic diagnostician to diagnose a patient selected by Karagulla at random among patients in a hospital. Neither Karagulla nor the diagnostician would have any knowledge of the patient's condition. Then Karagulla would check the medical records of the patient and compare them with the psychic diagnostician's assessment. Karagulla reported some strikingly accurate diagnoses by the psychic.

It is said that numerous nurses in conventional settings use "therapeutic touch," a psychic healing technique (Quinn 1984). Dolores Krieger (1986), who reported earlier that a healer could influence haemoglobin levels in blood by laying-on-of-hands, had worked with a number of nurses in the US to promote therapeutic touch as a healing technique.

Recent epidemiological research in the area of religiosity and a variety of health conditions suggests significant relationship between religious practices and human health (Koenig, McCullough and Larson, 2001). In a series of studies, Koenig and colleagues looked into various aspects of the relationship between religious activity and health outcomes. They examined the effect of religious involvement on mortality, which showed a significant association between private religious activity such as prayer and longer survival in certain population groups (Helm, Hays, Flint, Koenig, and Blazer, 2000). They also found significantly less anxiety disorders among the people who attended religious services regularly (Koenig, Ford, George, Blazer and Meader, 1993) and an inverse relation between religious coping and scores on depression scales (Koenig, Blazer, Cohen, Pieper, Meador, Shelp, Goli and DiPasquale, 1992). Several studies with different groups ranging from terminally ill (Reed, 1986, 1987) to healthy adults (Mattlin *et al.*, 1990) suggest that a significant majority of people report that they use religion as a coping mechanism to deal with health problems and other stressful situations. As Koenig, McCullough, and Larson (2001) observe, among the 16 studies that have examined possible relationship between religious involvement and blood pressure, 14 report lower blood pressure among the more religious. Steffen, Hinderliter, Blumenthal & Sherwood (2001) reported that among African Americans, religious coping is associated with reduced blood pressure.

Goldbourt *et al*, (1993) reported that in a 23 year follow up study, the risk of death from coronary artery disease (CAD) was 20% lower among the most orthodox Jews than the less orthodox or nonbelievers. In their study of religious struggle as a predictor of mortality among medically ill elderly patients, Pargament, Koenig, Tarakeshwar and Hahn (2001) found that the patients who experience religious struggle in comparison to those who religiously cope with their illness are at a greater risk of death. In a six-year follow-up study of 3968 older adults, they observed, those who attended religious services at least once a week appeared to have a survival advantage over those attended services less frequently. This effect of religious activity on survival, they contend, is equivalent to that of non-smoking vs. smoking on mortality (Koenig *et al.* 1999).

There are several significant studies that explored the relationship between religiosity and a variety of health conditions. In about 150 studies on alcohol and drug abuse and religious involvement, most of the studies "suggest less substance abuse and drug abuse and more successful rehabilitation among the more religious" (Koenig, McCullough and Larson, 2001). Also, numerous studies investigated the effect of religion on mental health, delinquency, depression, heart disease, immune system dysfunction, cancer, and physical disability. (For a comprehensive review of research in these areas, see Koenig, McCullough and Larson, 2001).

Surveys of literature and meta-analysis of published research seem to confirm the claims of individual researchers linking religious practices with better health outcomes. For example, in a systematic and comprehensive review, Townsend, Kladder, Ayele, and Mulligan (2002) assessed the impact of religion on health outcomes. They reviewed all experiments involving randomized controlled trials published between 1996 and 1999 that assessed the relationship between religious practices and measurable health variables. The review revealed that "religious involvement and spirituality are associated with better health outcomes, including greater longevity, coping skills, and health related quality of life and less anxiety." In a meta-analytic review of 29 independent samples McCullough *et al* (2000) reported that religious involvement has a strong positive influence of increased survival ($p < .001$).

If religious involvement does have beneficial health outcomes, as many of the published reports in the West seem to suggest, then we may ask: How does this relationship work? What is its modus operandi, the process that underlies the presumed effect? What is the channel? Who is the source? These important, though often tricky, questions have no easy answers. The favoured explanation is a secular one. Religious beliefs and practices may have psychological effects, which in turn bring about somatic changes. If indeed religious beliefs and activities help to reduce anxiety, stress and depression, they could also help to shield their negative effects on general health and well-being

As Koenig, Larson and Larson (2001) surmise, when people become physically ill, many rely heavily on religious beliefs and practices to relieve stress, retain a sense of control, and maintain hope and sense of meaning and purpose in life. It is suggested that religion (a) acts as a social support system, (b) reduces the sense of loss of control and helplessness, (c) provides a cognitive framework that reduces suffering and enhances self-esteem, (d) gives confidence that one, with the help of God, could influence the health condition, and (e) creates a mindset that enables the patient to relax and allow the body to heal itself. Again, the values engendered by religious involvement such as love, compassion, charity, benevolence, and altruism may help to successfully cope with debilitating anxiety, stress and depression.

All these may be true. Yet, there are issues that go beyond these explanations. For example, if the observed effects of distant intercessory prayer (Mueller, Plevak, and Rummans, 2001) on the health of patients, who did not even know that someone was praying for them, and spiritual healing (Miovic, 2005) are genuine, as they seem to be, the above secular explanations become clearly inadequate. We need more than a healthy mindset on the part of the patient to recover from illness because someone, unknown to him, had prayed for his recovery. There may be more to religion than being a social and psychological support system. However, one may not ignore the fact that research in these areas is controversial and the results hotly contested. Consequently, it is in some ways premature to foreclose the case for or against the reality of psi (the collective name for paranormal ability and its role in the healing process). Instead we may do well to carry out controlled studies with highest standards of research to learn more about psi and how we may select successful subjects who can reliably manifest psi in standard tests.

Scope of the Study

If psi phenomena are genuine, there is enormous scope for their application, as seen from the above. Application requires, however, reliable occurrence of the phenomena. Reliability is greatly enhanced if we can identify people who have this ability to a somewhat higher degree than normal. There is therefore a need for standard tests to screen subjects for their ESP ability. These tests should be culturally relevant and ecologically valid, because cultural and belief factors are known to influence ESP scores. This paper is a partial report of the Phase I of the cognitive anomalies project intended to develop ecologically valid ESP tests for general use to screen subjects and identify those who may more reliably manifest psi. The primary aspect of this phase is focused on testing a large number of unselected subjects on specially designed psi tests with a view to see (a) if overall evidence for psi among unselected subjects can be obtained and (b) whether psi performance among these subjects is related to subject related factors such as personality, attitudes, religious and paranormal beliefs and practices. We report here the results of ESP tests bearing on (a) without relating them to other variables, which would be the subject of other papers to follow.

The main objective of the study is to develop ESP tests that could be routinely used to pre-screen the subjects for selecting "star" performers who could more reliably provide evidence for psi. It is believed that if an ESP test is found to provide significant evidence for psi when used to test a large number of unselected subjects, and if this test is found reliable with replicable effects in confirmatory studies then we may move with confidence to use the items in the test for screening subjects for subsequent testing.

Phase I of the project consisted of three segments. The first segment (S_1) involved (a) developing the necessary questionnaires to measure subjects' attitudes, belief, and personality that may have a bearing on their ESP scores, (b) preparing an ESP screening test procedure for group testing, and (c) learning about the feasibility of administering the questionnaires and ESP tests in a pilot study. In the second segment (S_2) and the third segment (S_3) the questionnaires were suitably revised in the light of the experience gained from the pilot study. The data collected in the second and third segments constituted the main body for analysis of the results of the Phase I.

Subjects

All the subjects in the three segments of Phase I were college students. Their mean age was 20 years. They were students attending colleges in Visakhapatnam area. They included men and women. Some of the colleges are coeducational; a few are exclusively for women. The reason for limiting the study to college going students is that the ultimate goal of the study is to develop and standardize tests for screening recruits to defence services. Therefore, college students are considered to constitute an appropriate and relevant sample.

The data for this project had been collected in three segments during three different periods. Segment 1 (S_1) had a total of 268 subjects with 188 males and 80 females. Data for Segment 2 (S_2) were collected from nine undergraduate colleges. The total sample for this Segment is 873, with 298 males and 575 females. The Segment 3 has a sample of 1031 subjects. Out of these 629 are males and 402 are female subjects. The sample comprised of students belonging to undergraduate and postgraduate colleges. They belonged to the commerce, arts, law, engineering, medical, management, nursing, and hotel management streams. Thus Phase I of the project (including S_1) the pilot segment has a total of 2172 subjects, with 1115 males and 1057 females.

The ESP Test: "How Intuitive Are You?"

How Intuitive Are You? is an ESP test with 12 forced-choice items and one free-response item. The forced-choice items are those for which the subject has to choose one of the alternatives given. The free-response item, on the other hand, has no such alternatives to choose from and the subject can answer in a free descriptive format. The test is designed to measure the psi ability in the mode of precognition. Precognition is the perception of a future event by means of ESP. In this test, the targets (the correct answers to subject's responses) were prepared after the subjects made their responses. Therefore, what is tested is the ESP of the future. All the items of this questionnaire and the relevant pictures are developed by K.R. Rao assisted by the staff of the Institute for Human Science & Service.

The subjects are instructed to mark their answers for the 12 imaginary problem situations, based on their 'gut feeling' and 'intuition' as spontaneously as possible. The first 12 items have a problem situation presented and four alternatives out of which the subject has to select one that he/she feels is the best possible solution. The answer for the 13th item is written by the subject according to the following instructions:

"Now, close your eyes, relax for few minutes, and let your mind wander as if you are dreaming. Then write down the images that come to your mind, the impressions that you get and whatever passes on in your mind during this period."

The targets were generated by using the random algorithm. The random algorithm is a combination of the subtractive algorithm and randomization by shuffling as described in Knuth (1981). The program was written by James Kennedy (JK) and was initially tested by him using frequency tests, run up and down tests, and collision tests as described by Knuth. The program has been used for about 15 years for research randomizations in various situations.

JK generated the targets with a pseudorandom computer algorithm in association with H. Kanthamani (HK) in the US, after the collection of data is completed in India. For each experimental series, three random sequences were generated, one for targets on the forced choice trials, one for assigning the free response target pool, and one for the targets on the free response trials. The random sequences generated by JK were electronically sent to HK in 2 formats. One format was suitable for manual scoring of the data and the other format was compressed for input into a computerized scoring system. HK forwarded the sequences for the forced choice targets and free response target pools to K.R. Rao, Director of the Project. Later, after the free response trials had been judged, the free response targets were forwarded. For each random sequence, the initial seeds were obtained from the computer clock at the time the program was initiated during the phone call between JK and HK. The target lists were given to the appropriate member of the staff after a photo-copied set of subject responses were handed over for safekeeping.

ESP is scored in three different ways because of the intrinsic difference in the nature of the test items. First, two different methods of scoring are employed for scoring the forced-choice items. Six of the 12 items had four graded ratings. These are designated as ESP A items. They are scored giving a score of 4, 3, 2, or 1– 4 for the most appropriate response and 1 for the least appropriate. The other six items have no such graded scoring (ESP B items). They are simply scored as 'hits' or 'misses' and given a score of 4 for hits and a score of 1 for misses. In other words, a score of '4' is assigned when the answer of the subject matched with the target that was generated, which is a 'hit'. A score of '1' is given when the answer marked by the subject did not match with the target, which is a 'miss'.

The Free-response part of the test involved a picture-guessing task. The free-response targets are pictures cut from magazines such as the *National Geographic*, *India Today,* and so on. The target pool consisted of 100 picture sets of four pictures in each set. The sets are so prepared as to have the four pictures significantly different from each other thematically and structurally. The target lists contained a separate target for each ESP response. As mentioned these were generated by JK and HK situated in USA, who had no access to the subjects, after the subjects made their responses. The subjects were responding to targets to be generated later by colleagues about whom the subjects had no knowledge of.

To score the Free-response item, first, a judge with prior training and who is blind to the experimental conditions read each of the responses written by the subjects. Then the judge looked at the target picture set that had been randomly generated for that subject. Looking at the four pictures that belong to each picture set, the judge assigned a score of '4' to the picture that in his/her opinion matched closest to the description given by the subject. Similarly, scores of '3', '2,' and '1' were assigned for pictures with decreasing levels of perceived coincidence. The judge recorded the scores on a standard scoring sheet developed for this purpose. Once the judge finished judging for all the subjects, all the scoring sheets were photocopied and a copy was left with a member of the Institute who had nothing to do with scoring at any stage for safekeeping. The scoring sheets were then scored based on the random target numbers provided by H. Kanthamani, as mentioned, who had no knowledge of the subjects' responses. A total of four target numbers, ranging from 1 to 4 are generated for each subject. These targets were transcribed in the same order below the scores given by the judge. The final score of the subject for the 13th item is the score given by the judge that corresponds to the target picture. The scores were independently checked by two assistants. KRR made random checks to satisfy himself of the accuracy of scoring and recording.

It may be noted that targets were generated after the responses were made so that there is no possibility for anyone involved to influence subjects' responses to bias the results. JK and HK, who generated the targets, did not have access to the responses made by the subjects. All the assistants who collected the data were blind to the targets until they photocopied the response sheets and deposited them for safekeeping before they started scoring the responses in force-choice tests. In free-response tests, the judges did not know what the targets were when they judged subject responses.

Procedure of Testing

The principals of various colleges in the city of Visakhapatnam were sent letters seeking permission to collect data from students studying in the college. The letter gave details about the project and about the testing tools to be administered for collecting data from their students. The researchers visited all the colleges that gave consent and met the teachers and fixed dates suitable for the actual data collection.

On the pre-specified date the research team went to the college and administered the tests, first giving a brief introduction about the project and then necessary instructions to answer the test booklet. Subjects were asked to first fill in their personal details on the booklet. In Segment 1 (S_1) subjects were given instructions to complete all the questionnaires as presented in the test booklet by marking the answers on the separate answer sheet provided for the purpose. The questionnaires included (1) religiosity survey, (2) survey of paranormal experiences, and (3) a personality questionnaire (Myers-Briggs Type Indicator). While administering the test booklet in S_1 it was clear that some questions were not appropriately phrased for the subjects to easily understand. Also, many subjects did not respond to the free-response item in the ESP test. Those few who did, simply described the state of their mind rather than the nature of the target.

After incorporating necessary changes in the *Religiosity Survey* and the *Survey of Paranormal Experiences* questionnaires the data were collected for the next two segments. In Segment 2 and Segment 3 the subjects were asked to first answer the 13th item, that is, the free-response item while taking the "*How Intuitive are you?*" test and then the remaining 12 items of the ESP test. After this, they continued with the other questionnaires.

A faculty member trained in Yoga conducted the relaxation exercise before the testing session began. During this time, all the subjects were instructed to sit straight without intercrossing either their legs or hands, close their eyes and follow the instructions of the yoga expert. The subjects were given ten minutes relaxation exercise. The relaxation procedure involved concentration of 61 points, while imaging a 'blue star' at the place of the specific point of the body being mentioned. After about ten minutes of practice of this procedure, the subjects were asked to slowly open their eyes and were given instructions to continue to be in the state of relaxation. While in this state they were instructed to try to empty the mind of all thoughts. Then they were asked to write in detail, descriptions of any images, impressions, thoughts and feelings that they are perceiving at the given moment.

Collection and Analyses of Data and the Results

By design, we have set our net wide and deep to collect a vast amount of data. Since Phase I is essentially a preliminary exploration to determine the suitability of the projected tests, different measures for dependent and independent variables were included. No attempt was made here to arrive at final conclusions. Rather the intent was one of observing the trends and gazing at a variety of variables that could conceivably affect ESP as it manifests in different modes on various items of the tests. Therefore, ESP itself is measured in different ways in an attempt to relate it to numerous other variables. This complex exercise would be fruitless if our goal was one of netting reliable effects here and now, because the multitude of variables under investigation would result in cancelling each other's effects. However, this phase of the project was undertaken with the explicit purpose of learning about a variety of factors for their possible role in manifesting or inhibiting the occurrence of ESP in routine testing. The assumption is that the elusiveness of ESP is probably due to its sensitivity to a large number of variables, which variously affect the outcome. Once we have the ground data, at least on some of these variables, then, we may be led to relevant and promising hypotheses and more robust methods to test them for their reliability and replicability in the final phase of the project. However, the future success would be predicated on the fact whether or not there is some significant statistical evidence for psi in the data. It is for this reason we introduced yoga practice as an ESP conducive condition before taking the ESP test.

In Phase I testing, the ESP test itself comprised of three categories of items A, B, and C, as will be explained. S_1 comprises data of 265 usable subjects. This segment was meant essentially to prepare the final questionnaires and test measures to be used in the subsequent S_2 and S_3 series. There are 832 subjects in S_2 and 968 subjects in S_3. All the subjects were students enrolled in local colleges.

It should be mentioned at the outset that the ESP tests were administered, as we began Phase I testing, in such a routine and mechanical manner that few parapsychologists would expect ESP to occur in such circumstances. The exception, however, is brief yogic relaxation exercise in S_2 and S_3 segments. Our intention, was to move from Phase I into Phase II progressively to more psi conducive test conditions. In the first segment of Phase I (S_1), for example, no special attention was paid to ESP part of the test. It was administered like any other questionnaire. No information was provided to the subjects about how the targets were/would be generated and who would do what to generate them. Subjects did not even know that it was a precognition test. They did not receive any feedback. The investigators did nothing but read out the instructions contained in the booklet, except for providing occasional clarifications when the subjects raised any question. They acted more like invigilators in an examination hall than experimenters in a psi test. Again, this was by design, because a major goal of the project is to develop standard texts that could be routinely used to screen subjects for ESP.

In the second and third segments, the situation is similar in most respects to S_1; but there is one significant difference as far as the ESP tests are concerned. The difference is that the investigator in S_2 and S_3 attempted to relate himself/herself to the subjects. She asked the subjects to relax themselves before answering the ESP test items and explained to them in some detail about the free-response item. We introduced this change keeping in view the negative ESP scores obtained in S_1. Five differently constituted teams collected data in S_2. In the third segment (S_3), only one team of investigators collected all the data.

In S_1, very few people responded to the free-response item. Even the few who did, merely described the state of mind they were in at that time; and they made no attempt to describe the target. Clearly the instructions were insufficient to elicit subjects' responses to this item. Therefore, it was decided before any scoring was undertaken to delete this item from the data of S_1 segment. Remedial steps were taken in S_2 and S_3 to ensure that the subjects did respond to the free-response item of the test by calling attention to this item during the pre-test introduction.

In responding to items in the ESP test, some subjects failed to answer some of the items. It was decided prior to scoring to insert a randomly selected number to indicate the subject's response in the empty column (the one that the subject failed to respond). However, in cases where a subject left three or more items blank in the forced-choice part of the test, that subject's ESP score was not taken into consideration in computing the ESP results. The same procedure was followed in scoring all the three segments of Phase I ESP data.

The ESP scores themselves are divided into two groups. Items 1 through 12 of the ESP test are forced-choice. Item 13 calls for a free-response. Again, the forced- choice items (1 through 12) are further divided into two groups of six items each. One group includes items which are assigned graded values 1, 2, 3, or 4. This group of items is designated as ESP A. The second group, designated as ESP B consists of six items with no graded values, but are scored either 4 (hit) or 1 (miss). The scores on the free-response item are designated as ESP C. This item was scored as items in A category. The subject received a score between 1 and 4, 4 indicating a hit of ¼ probability.

The following presentation of results begins with macro-global analyses of hits and proceeds to micro-analyses of each and every specific item in the ESP tests for each of the segments and then for pooled data of segments two and three. Thus the analyses of results take place at different levels of complexity, from the most inclusive to the most specific. Any significant results at the macro level are likely to be more robust and replicable than the results in the microanalyses. The micro-analyses, however, are likely the ones to give us a better insight into the variables influencing ESP, if found consistent across the series. As originally planned, the results of S_1 are not combined with S_2 and S_3. They are given separately. However, the data of S_2 and S_3 are added as a measure of their combined effect. These decisions were taken before the results were computed. Even though we decided in advance to use the data of segments 2 and 3 only for all statistical analysis, we are presenting the data of S_1 as well for the sake of sharing all available data.

First Level: Table 1 presents the combined ESP straight hit scores of the three segments of the data. Hits are scored as correct matching of subject's call with the target. The probability of a hit is 0.25. There are 268 subjects in S_1, 873 in S_2 and 1031 in S_3. We rejected the data of 3 subjects in S_1, 41 in S_2 and 63 in S_3 because of their failure to meet the preset criteria for inclusion. They had not responded to three or more ESP items. Thus we have analyzable data for 265 subjects in S_1, 832 in S_2, and 968 in S_3.

In the macro-global analysis of hits, we pooled for each subject the number of hits obtained on all the 12 items in S_1. Since S_1 is the preliminary feasibility study, it was decided in advance to keep it separately from the rest for all the analyses. This is especially relevant to ESP analysis because relaxation instructions/exercises preceded ESP tests in S_2 and S_3. There was no such intervention in S_1. Also, no data are available for item 13 in S_1 segment. Further there are significant differences in the instructions given to the subjects in S_1 and the other two segments. All the 13 items (including the free-response item) in S_2 and S_3 are pooled. The maximum score a subject can obtain is 12 (S_1) or 13 (S_2 and S_3) and the minimum is 0. In S_1, the subjects obtained 762 hits, a deviation of -33 from mean chance expectation. Negative deviation suggests missing, even though the deviation is not statistically significant.

The results for S_2 and S_3 are given in Table 1. In the second segment (S_2) consisting of 832 subjects, the number of hits obtained by the subjects in all the 13 trials is 2781. The deviation is +77. The third segment (S_3) consisted of 968 subjects whose data are available for analysis. The total number of hits obtained by this group in the 13 trials combined is 3234. Again, the deviation (+88) is positive. Together S_2 and S_3 have 1800 subjects. Their pooled ESP hits are 6015 a deviation of +165. The corresponding z is 2.49. The probability that such a deviation is a chance occurrence is almost equal to .01. Therefore, the macro-analysis of the ESP data at the hit level suggests that the results are unlikely due to chance.

TABLE 1: OVERALL ESP (HITS) SCORES

Segment	Subjects (n)	Total ESP Hits	Deviation	z	p
S_2	832	2781	+77	1.70	ns
S_3	968	3234	+88	1.81	ns
S_2+S_3	1600	6015	+165	2.49	0.01

Second Level: At the second level, we have three sorts of analyses. First, we analyzed the data separately for free-response (C) and forced-choice (A and B) items. Second, we analyzed the ESP hits in A and C as one group and in B as the second group. The third analysis compares ESP scoring on A and B items in S_1, S_2, and S_3. The reasons for taking up these analyses as well as the results are given below.

(1) As mentioned, the ESP data in S_2 and S_3 come from two different sorts of test items, free-response and forced-choice. In the former, the universe of targets and consequently the subjects' responses are not limited and preset, whereas in the forced-choice items, the subjects' responses are limited to four predetermined alternatives. The Rhine era of ESP testing was pretty much confined to forced-choice testing. Subsequently, however, the free-response mode gained momentum and is being increasingly used. In fact, there is a general consensus among psi researchers now that free-response testing is more psi conducive. But free-response tests are generally administered individually and are rarely used in group tests. In S_2 and S_3 segments of Phase I, where the free-response item is included, it was group testing. Therefore, the viability of free-response in group tests is something we intended to explore.

Table 2 gives the ESP results of S_2 and S_3 segments, which contain both the forced-choice and free-response items. S_1 segment is not included because there were no scoreable free-response trials in that segment. On the free-response item (C) in S_2, the subjects obtained 233 hits, where MCE is 208. That gives a deviation of +25. In S_3, the subjects obtained 256 hits, a deviation of +14. When

TABLE 2: ESP (HITS) SCORES ON FORCED-CHOICE AND FREE-RESPONSE ITEMS

Segment	Free-Response					Forced-Choice				
	Tri	Hi	Deviation	*z*	*p*	Tri	Hi	Deviation	*z*	*p*
S_2	832	233	+25	2.00	<0.05	9984	2548	+52	1.20	ns
S_3	968	256	+14	1.04	ns	11,616	2978	+74	1.59	ns
S_2+S_3	1800	489	+39	2.12	<0.05	21,600	5526	+126	1.98	0.05

S_2 and S_3 data are combined, we have a deviation of +39 and a z score of 2.12, which is significant ($p < .05$). On forced-choice items, the subjects in S2 obtained 2548 hits (+52). In S_3, they scored 2978 hits (+74). When the data of both the segments are pooled, we find a deviation of +126. The associated z for such a deviation is 1.98, $p = .05$. Thus, there is evidence of ESP in the combined forced-choice data as well.

It should be mentioned that some subjects in S_2 as well as S_3 did not respond to the free-response item. However, we chose a response for them by randomly assigning 1, 2, 3, or 4. This number was scored against the actual target and thus that subject's ESP score was generated. We did this because we did not want to lose the data of these subjects on other variables. There are 89 and 27 such subjects in S_2 and S_3 respectively. We expect that the inclusion of the data of these subjects would only water down the ESP effect, if there is one. If, however, these additional data somehow help to enhance the effect, the results may have to be interpreted differently, either as due to mere chance or as an experimenter effect. Therefore, we evaluated, as a check, the free-response ESP scores of subjects in S_2 and S_3 leaving out the scores obtained on the random responses inserted by the investigators. The total ESP C hits obtained by 743 subjects in S_2 are 212 (+26.25). In S_3 with 941 subjects who completed the free-response trial, there are 246 hits (+10.75). When S_2 and S_3 are combined we have a total of 458

ESP C hits (+37). Such a deviation of 37 has z value of 2.08 ($p<.05$). Thus the deletion of randomly inserted data has no effect on the results. So in all other analyses we have kept the scores of all the subjects, including those whose free-responses were randomly generated.

(2) As mentioned, there are 12 forced-choice items in the ESP test, divided into two groups. All items have four alternative responses. But in one category, the responses have graded value. For example, in item (1), one alternative is the most disastrous. The soldier who takes this route would be killed. The subject who chooses this route gets the lowest score, i.e., 1. On the other hand, there is a route which not only helps to escape but gives useful information for a counter offensive. The subjects who respond by choosing this route get the highest possible score of 4. The subjects who chose the route that would land them as prisoners would get a score of 2, whereas those who chose the route that takes them nowhere would have a score of 3. Items 1, 3, 4, 5, 6, and 8 belong to this category, designated as "A". The other category of 6 items (B) are such that only one of the four alternatives is appropriate. The other three are equally inappropriate. For example, item 2 asks the subject to choose a route that is likely to be taken by the enemy out of the four possible routes. The subjects who chose the correct route to be taken by the enemy would get a score of 4 and all the others get a score of 1.

The free-response item, designated as category C in ESP tests, is of course different from the others. However, in terms of scoring, it is more like items in Group A. the judges who evaluated the free-response item gave the subject a score of 4, 3, 2, or 1, depending on the resemblance of subject's response to the target. They gave a score of 4 for the one with closest resemblance, 3 for the next best, 2 for the one with even lesser resemblance and 1 for the one with least resemblance. The scoring pattern is exactly the same as for items in A (4, 3, 2, 1). Therefore, we combined scores on items in ESP A+C for one analysis in S_2 and S_3 segments. As may be seen from Table 3, the subjects obtained a total of 1525 and 1780 hits on A+C items in S_2 and S_3 respectively. There were no free-response scores for subjects in S_1. The observed hits in S_2 and S_3 combined give a total deviation of +155 which is positive and highly significant ($z = 3.19$; $p < .01$).

In ESP B, there are 1256 hits (+8) in S_2 and 1454 hits (+2) in S_3. Thus items in ESP B give scores too close to MCE to be of any significance. A *t* test of the difference in scoring between A+C on one hand and B hits on the other gives a $t = 2.08$ (1799 df), $p < .05$. Thus we find that subjects did significantly better on items with graded scores than on those which are scored as simply hits and misses. It should be mentioned that the ESP scores themselves are analyzed as hits and not as weighted scores.

(3) Since our interest is one of finding out which type of questions are likely to be more sensitive to ESP, we have compared subjects' scores on group A and group B items.

As mentioned before, in S_1, there are no data for ESP C. Most subjects in this segment did not respond to the free-response item. Therefore, we have only their ESP A and B scores. The 265 subjects in S_1 obtained 358 A hits (-39.5) and 404 B hits (+6.5). The A scores are negative in direction and significantly deviate from chance expectation (z 2.29; $p < .05$, two tail). The B scores, however, are close to chance. A test of the difference between A and B ESP scores in S_1 gives a $t = 1.97$ (p=.05). In S_2 and S_3 also, there is a

TABLE 3: ESP (HITS) SCORES ON A,B,C, AND A+C ITEMS

Segment	n	Analysis	ESP A	ESP B	ESP C	ESP A+C
S_2		Hits	1292	1256	233	1525
	832	Deviation	-44	+8	+25	+69
		z	1.44	0.26	2.00*	2.09*
S_3		Hits	1524	1454	256	1780
	968	Deviation	+72	+2	+14	+86
		z	2.18*	0.06	1.04	2.41*
S_2+S_3		Hits	2816	2710	489	3305
	1800	Deviation	+116	+10	+39	+155
		z	2.58**	0.22	2.12*	3.19**

**p<0.05; **p<0.01*

significant difference in the scoring on A and B items. A t test of the difference gives a t=2.08 ($p<.05$). However in S_1 the scoring on A items is significant missing, whereas in S_2 and S_3 it is significant hitting. On B items, it is close to chance expectation in S_1 as well as in S_2 and S_3. It would seem therefore that A items appear to be sensitive to subject's ESP even though the direction of scoring may depend on other variables, in this case relaxation exercises before taking the ESP tests.

Third Level : The third level is the micro-item analysis with individual items in the ESP test, which contains 12 forced-choice items and 1 free-response item. We had already seen that the scoring on the free-response item is significant in the combined scores of S_2 and S_3. To recall, the 1800 subjects obtained a total of 489 hits where MCE is 450. The observed deviation of 39 hits has a corresponding z score of 2.12 and $p<.05$.

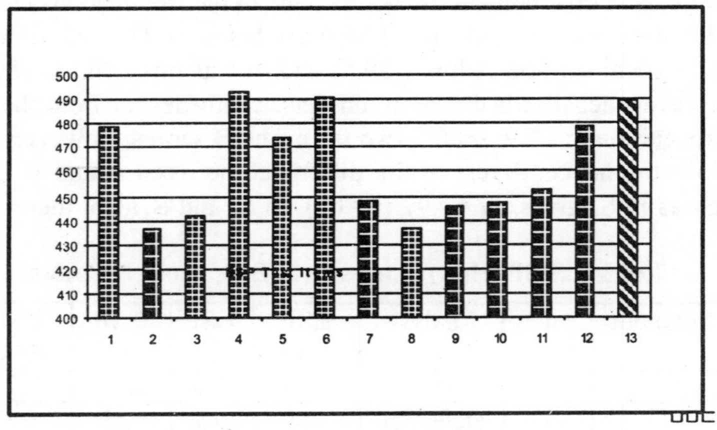

Figure 1: ESP (Hit) Scores on 13 Test items in S_2 and S_3

(Note: The lighter bars of the graph indicates. A group and the darker belong to the B group of items. Item 13 is free response bar.

Figure 1 depicts the scoring on the 13 items in S_2 and S_3. And Table 4 gives the hits obtained on each of the items in all the three segments separately and S_2 and S_3 combined. As may be seen, there is variation in the rate of scoring between the items. Some items appear to register better ESP scoring than others. Question numbers 4 and

Table 4 Overall ESP (Hits) Scores Itemwise

Segment	*n*		Item 1	Item 2	Item 3	Item 4	Item 5	Item 6	Item 7	Item 8	Item 9	Item 10	Item 11	Item 12	Item 13
S_1	265	*Hits*	62	68	62	60	63	67	67	44	70	68	73	58	
		Deviation	-4.25	+1.75	-4.25	-6.25	-3.25	+0.75	+0.75	-22.25	+3.75	+1.75	+6.75	-8.25	
		z	0.60	0.25	0.60	0.89	0.46	0.11	0.11	3.16	0.53	0.25	0.96	1.17	
		p	*ns*	*ns*	*ns*	*ns*	*ns*	*ns*	*ns*	<0.01	*ns*	*ns*	*ns*	*ns*	
S_2	832	*Hits*	228	186	207	227	227	213	225	190	209	203	214	219	233
		Deviation	+20	-22	-1	+19	+19	+5	+17	-18	+1	-5	+6	+11	+25
		z	1.60	1.76	0.08	1.52	1.52	0.40	1.36	1.44	0.08	0.40	0.48	0.88	2.00
		p	*ns*	*ns*	*ns*	*ns*	*ns*	*ns*	*ns*		*ns*	*ns*	*ns*	*ns*	<0.05
S_3	968	*Hits*	251	251	235	266	247	278	223	247	237	244	239	260	256
		Deviation	+9	+9	-7	+24	+5	+36	-19	+5	-5	+2	-3	+18	+14
		z	0.67	0.67	0.52	1.78	0.37	2.70	1.40	0.37	0.37	0.15	0.22	1.34	1.04
		p	*ns*	*ns*	*ns*	*ns*	*ns*	<0.01	*ns*	*ns*	*ns*	*ns*	*ns*	*ns*	*ns*
S_2+S_3	1800	*Hits*	479	437	442	493	474	491	448	437	446	447	453	447	489
		Deviation	+29	-13	-8	+43	+24	+41	-2	-13	-4	-3	+3	+29	+39
		z	1.58	0.70	0.43	2.34	1.30	2.23	0.11	0.71	0.22	0.16	0.16	1.56	2.12
		p	*ns*	*ns*	*ns*	<0.05	*ns*	<0.05	*ns*	*ns*	*ns*	*ns*	*ns*	*ns*	<0.05

6 registered the highest ESP score of 493 (+43) and 491 (+41) respectively. These scores compare favourably with those on item 13, which is a free-response item. The obtained ESP scores on item 4 have an associate z value of 2.34, and for item 6 it is 2.23. Both are significant beyond .05 level.

Items 4 and 6 read as follows:

4. You are flying a bomber aircraft and you are in a position to hit any of the four enemy ships you see below you. You really want to sink only one of them, the mother ship, because it controls the others. The four ships contain separately (1) prisoners taken from your side (2) families of servicemen from the opposite side (3) enemy soldiers or (4) the mother ship that controls the rest. All the ships look alike. You have no clue which one is the mother ship. Circle the ship you will hit first.

Ship to the North

Ship to the South

Ship to the East

Ship to the West

6. There are four vendors in your area who are selling lottery tickets. One of them has the most winning tickets and another has some, but not many. The other two has either one or none of the winning tickets. Circle the vendor from whom, you could want to buy the tickets.

Vendor S

Vendor T

Vendor P

Vendor R

The two items are very different in their import and motivation. One deals with the national security and the other is about winning a lottery.

In S_1 also one item stands out most prominently contributing to psi-missing. On item 8, the total number of hits obtained by 265 subjects is 44, where 66.25 hits are expected by chance. The observed deviation of 22.25 hits gives a *z* score of 3.16, $p<.01$. Item 8 is about the captain of the cricket team.

As may be seen from figure 1 it is the items in A that generally tended to elicit positive scoring. Both items 4 and 6 are A items. However, it should be mentioned that with the exception of item 2, all B items are in the second half of the test. Similarly with the exception of item 8, all the A items are in the first half of the test. Therefore, it is possible that the difference in the rate of scoring between A and B items is no more than a decline effect. The decline of ESP scores from the first half to the second half of the test are not infrequent. A test of difference between the hits in the first and second half of the 12 item forced-choice test gives a *z* of 2.04 ($p<.05$). Thus there is significant evidence for decline from the first half to the second half. Hence, the superiority of items in A over those in B for eliciting psi is yet to be established.

As mentioned, we have a lot more data on the subjects, and the results could be analyzed on the basis of gender, religion, beliefs, attitudes and personality of the subjects. These will be reported later.

CONCLUSION

Since the early work of J.B. Rhine at Duke University seventy-five years ago, there are very few systematic studies of ESP of this magnitude involving so many subjects. This is for a good reason. When a large number of unselected subjects are tested for ESP the results generally tend to favour the null hypothesis because of the bi-directional nature of psi and the inter-subject differences. In an unselected population, some subjects tend to hit and some tend to miss, their scores thus cancelling each other. Therefore, it is unlikely that the combined data of 1800 subjects would provide significant deviation from chance expectation. To our pleasant surprise, however, the results obtained provide significant evidence in support of cognitive anomalies of the ESP type. The test conditions are extremely stringent and it is inconceivable that there are any procedural loopholes permitting leakage of information. Therefore, we are inclined to reject the null hypothesis and consider the ESP results as evidence for the existence of cognitive anomalies in the datas.

We believe also that the relaxation and yoga exercises we have introduced in S_2 and S_3 segments are responsible for overall positive scoring. There is already evidence that meditation is a psi conducive exercise (Rao, Dukhan and Rao, 1978). These results give us added confidence that the test we have attempted to develop has the possibility of being a reliable measure to test ESP. We recognize, however, the effect size involved is very small and that we need to identify other moderating variables for improving scoring rate for possible application of psi in real life situations. It is our hope that further analyses of the results in terms of the subject variables may provide evidence for more robust effects, which could be used for identifying reliable subjects for attempting practical applications of psi. What is even more important is the replication of these results in future studies we hope to undertake in the succeeding phases of this project. At this stage of the project, we can claim no more than that the tests we have used in this study have the promise of providing us a tool to test subjects on a mass scale for screening purposes.

J.B. Rhine of course fell that the ESP cards he had used in his research were also standardized tests that are relatively culture free. There is little reason to think that the present test in any better than the ESP cards test used by Rhine without making appropriate comparative studies. Again, this is something that future research should address.

That there are significant differences in the rate of scoring between A and B items and that the subjects scored quite high on some items (4, 6 and 13) are findings of some interest. However, the observed effect is somewhat contaminated by the fact that all these significant items happen to be in the first half of the ESP test giving raise to the possibility of decline rather than indicate the intrinsic strength of these items. In the follow up studies in the second phase, this needs to be controlled. The fact that the free-response item provides significant evidence in the overall data suggests that we could profitably employ free-response testing in group setting.

REFERENCES

Bowles, N. & Hynds, F. (1978). *Psi Search: The New Investigation of Psychic Phenomena that Separates Fact from Speculation*. New York: Harper & Row.

Bro, H.H. (1989). *A Sear out of Searon.* New York: Penguin, New American Library.

Cayce, D. (1969). *Edgar Cayce on ESP*. NY: Paperback Library.

Dean, D. & Mihalasky, S. (1974). *Executive ESP*. New Jersey: Prentice-Hall.

Goldbourt, U., Yaari, S. & Medalie, J.H. (1993). Factors predictive of long-term coronary heart disease mortality among 10,059 male Israeli civil servants and municipal employees. *Cardiology,* 82, 100-121.

Helm, H., Hays, J.C., Flint, E., Koenig, H.G. & Blazer, D.G. (2000). Does private religious activity prolong survival? A six-year follow-up study of 3,851 older adults. *Journal of Gerontology*, 55A, M400-M405.

Karagulla, S. (1967). *Breakthrough to creativity*. Santa Monica, GA: DeVorss.

Knuth, D.E. (1981) Seminumerical algorithms, In *The art of computer programming*, Vol. 2, 2nd edn. Reading: Addison-Wesley.

Koeing, H.G., Ford, S., George, L.K. Balzer, D.G. & Meador, K.G. (1993). Religion and anxiety disorder: An examination and comparison of association in young, middle ages, and elderly adults. *Journal of Anxiety Disorder,* 7, 321-342.

— Hays, J.C., Larson, D.B., George, L.K., Cohen, H.J., McCullough, M.E., Meador, K.G. & Blazzer, D.G. (1999). Does religious attendance prolong survival? A six-year follow-up study of 3, 968 older adults. *Journal of Gerontology* (Medical Science), 54a(7), M370-M376.

— Balzer, D.G., Cohen, H.J., Pieper, C., Meador, K.G., Shelp, F. Goli, V. & DiPasquale, R. (1992). Religious coping and depression in elderly hospitalized medically ill men. *American Journal of Psychiatry,* 149, 1693-1700.

— Larson, D.B. & Larson, S.S. (2001). Religion and coping with serious medical illness. *Annals of Pharmacotherapy* 2001 Mar; 35 (3): 352-9.

— McCullough, M. & Larson, D.B. (2001). *Handbook of Religion and Health: A Century of Research Reviewed.* New York: Oxford University Press.

Krieger, D. (1986). *The Therapeutic Touch. How to Use Your Hands to Help or to Heal.* NY: Prentice-Hall.

Mattlin J., Wethington, E. & Kessler, R. (1990). Situational determinants of coping and coping effectiveness. *Journal of Health and Social Behavior*, 31 (March), 103-122.

McCullough, M.E., Hoyt, W.T., Larson, D.B., Koenig, H.G. & Thoresen, C.E. (2000). Religious involvement and mortality: A meta-analytic review. *Health Psychology,* 19, 211-222.

McMoneagle, J. (1993). *Mind Trek: Exploring Consciousness, Time and Space through Remote Viewing.* Charlottesville, VA: Hampton Roads Publishing Co.

Mesmer, F.A. (1980/1781). *Mesmerism.* G. Bloch, (Ed. and Trans.). Los Altos, CA: Kaufman.

Miovic, M. (2005). Spirituality, human health and wellness: Overview of the field. In K.R. Rao and S.B. Marwaha (Eds.). *Towards a spiritual Psychology: Essays in Indian Psychology* (pp. 385-386). New Delhi: Samvad India Foundation.

Mishlove, J. (1993). *The Roots of Consciousness.* Tulsa, OK: Council Oak Books.

Mueller, P.S., Plevak, D.J. & Rummans, T.A. (2001). Religious involvement, spirituality and medicine: Implications for clinical practice. *Mayo Clinic Proceedings*, 76, 1189-91.

Ostander, S. & Schroder, L. (1970). *Psychic Discoveries behind the Iron Curtain.* New York: Prentice Hall.

Pargament, K.I., Koenig, H.G., Tarakeshwar, N. & Hahn, J. (2001). Religious struggle as a predictor of mortality among medically ill elderly patients. A 2-year longitudinal study. *Archives of Internal Medicine.* 161, 1881-1885.

Quinn, J.F. (1984). Therapeutic touch as energy exchange: Testing the theory. *Advances in Nursing Science* 6 (2), 42-49.

Radin, D.I. (1997). *The Conscious Universe: Truth of Psychic Phenomena.* San Francisco: Harper Collins

— (2006). *Entangled Mind: Extrasensory Experiences in a Quantum Reality.* New York: Parkview Pocket Books.

Rao, K.R, Dukhan, H. & Rao, P.V.K. (1978). Yogic meditation and psi scoring in forced-choice and free-response tests. *Journal of Parapsychology,* 1, 160-175.

— & Palmer, J. (1987). The anomaly called psi: Recent research and criticism. *Behavioral and Brain Sciences,* 10, 539-555.

Reed, P.G. (1986). Religiousness among terminally ill and healthy adults. *Research in Nursing and Health*, 9, 35-41.

— (1987). Spirituality and well being in terminally ill hospitalized adults. *Research in Nursing and Health,* 10, 335-344.

Richet, C. (1975/1923). *Thirty Years of Psychical Research.* New York: Arno Press.

Schnabel J. (1997). *Remote Viewers: The Secret History of America's Psychic Spies.* NY: Dell.

Steffen, P.R., Hinderliter, A.L., Blumenthal, J.A. & Sherwood, A. (2001). Religious coping, ethnicity, and ambulatory blood pressure. *Psychosomatic Medicine*, 63, 523-530

Townsend, M., Kladder, V., Ayele, H. & Mulligan, T. (2002). Systematic review of clinical trials examining the effects of religion on health. *Southern Medical Journal,* 95, 12.

Utts, J. (2001). An assessment of the evidence of psychic functioning. In K.R. Rao (Ed.). *Basic Research in Parapsychology*. (pp. 110-141). Jefferson, NC: McFarland.

Personality, Religiosity and Paranormal Experiences*

Jacksan Judan Fernandes
Sonali Bhatt Marwaha

Personality

Psychology, from ancient to modern times, has acknowledged individual differences. People are different in many ways; such as, they have different personalities and individual identities. Despite the universality of our species, instincts, emotions and traits, there are marked differences between individuals, due to one's genetic endowment, unique life experiences, and personal perceptions of the world. Our genetic endowment provides us the means by which nurture shows itself, just as surely as they are the means by which nature shows itself. An individual's personality is the complex of mental characteristics that makes them unique from other people. It

* The research reported here is a part of the larger DRDO project directed by Prof. K. Ramakrishna Rao. The authors express their thanks to Prof. Rao and acknowledge the help and assistance of Dr. K. Suneetha, Dr. Ch. Srikrishna, Dr. N. Sarada, Dr Indira Rani, and Mr. Vijaya Raja.

includes all the patterns of thought and emotions that cause us to do and say things in particular ways. At a basic level, personality is expressed through our temperament or emotional tone. However, personality also colours our values, beliefs, and expectations (O'Neil, 2006). Many potential factors are involved in shaping a personality. These factors are usually seen as coming from heredity as well as environment. Research by psychologists over the last several decades has increasingly pointed to hereditary factors being more important, especially for basic personality traits such as emotional tone. However, the acquisition of values, beliefs, and expectations seem to be due more to socialization and unique experiences, especially during childhood. When referring to "personality", we are referring to some intrinsic part of our nature that is beyond the influence of other people (Ridley, 2003).

Many potential environmental influences help to shape personality. Child rearing practices are especially critical. In the Indian cultural context, children are raised to be followers and dependents of the significant elders in their family and the extended community, particularly in the middle and higher income groups. Independence in thought and action is not considered a virtue and a sign of adulthood. In contrast, in the culture of North America, children are usually raised in ways that encourage them to become self-reliant and independent. Children are often allowed to act as potential adults, somewhat like equals to their parents. For instance, they are included in making decisions about what type of food and entertainment the family will have on a night out. Children are given allowances and small jobs around the house to teach them how to be responsible for themselves. Such independence training is believed to promote achievement motivation.

Despite significant differences in child rearing practices around the world, there are some similarities. Boys and girls are socialized differently to some extent in all societies. They receive different messages from their parents and other adults as to what is appropriate for them to do in life. They are encouraged to prepare for their future in jobs fitting their gender. Boys are more often allowed freedom to experiment and to participate in physically risky activities; girls are encouraged to learn how to do domestic tasks and to participate in child rearing by baby-sitting. While earlier views perceived this difference as arising only from differences in socialization, ample multi-disciplinary evidence has been garnered by evolutionary psychologists that these sex differences are inherent and cater to the different biological roles that men and women play (Campbell, 2002).

A few features of human behaviour prove to be less heritable. The sense of humour shows less heritability: adopted siblings seem to have quite similar senses of humour, while separated twins have rather different ones. People's food preferences seem to be barely heritable, as food preferences are developed from early experiences, not genes. Social and political attitudes show a strong influence from the shared environment; liberal or conservative parents seem to be able to pass their preferences to their children. Religious affiliation, too, is passed on culturally, rather than genetically, though not religious fervour (Ridley, 2003, pp. 87-88).

Religion

Religion, as a system of beliefs, is ubiquitous. The role of religion in the personal sphere is evident in every aspect of life from birth to death, marriage, social interaction, politics, health and hygiene, the acceptance or rejection of science, and indeed to our perception of the creation of the world we live in. While personal beliefs and religion are interlinked, as religion is the strongest bond or link between individuals in a group, our beliefs are, in a sense, governed by our religious beliefs, which further influences our worldview. Religion, as one of the major social institutions and belief systems, cannot escape the influence of individual personality, the social structures and strictures that revolve around it. As personality is a composite of both nature and nurture, we find that there is no uniformity in the way a religion is followed. And, as such, individual personality may influence the way a belief is followed.

According to Yinger (1957, p. 9), religion is a "system of beliefs and practices by means of which a group of people struggle with the ultimate problems of human life." Talcott Parsons (1952, p. 367) also sees religious ideas as "answers to the problems of meaning". Reinhold Niebuhr calls religion 'an attempt to explain what cannot otherwise be explained, a citadel of hope built on the edge of despair' (quoted by Yinger, 1957, p.10). Paul Tillich (1957), a liberal theologian, defines religion as "the expression of humanity's ultimate concerns, the articulation of longing for a centre of meaning and value and for connection with the power of being"

Religion is variously defined as: (i) belief in a divine or superhuman power or powers to be obeyed and worshipped as the creator(s) and ruler(s) of the universe, (ii) the expression of such a belief in conduct and ritual, (iii) any specific system of belief, worship, conduct, etc., often involving a code of ethics and a philosophy (e.g., Christianity, Buddhism); (iv) any system of belief, practice, ethical values, etc., resembling, suggestive of, or likened to such system (humanism as a religion) (*Webster's New World Dictionary*).

While religion is the basis of personal, cultural, social and political life, in common dialogue not many ask the question 'what is religion?' It is important to ask this question as it provides a perspective through which to accept the current worldview and the doctrines that we follow. Religion is not a "natural" phenomenon, as say the orbit of the earth around the sun, which is a natural phenomenon. Religion is a creation of man. Aside from the present day major religions, such as Hinduism, Christianity, Islam, Buddhism, Judaism, there have existed in the past, as they do now, many religions that are no longer followed. There were a great many religions followed in ancient and medieval times. Some of the old religions include the tribal religions of India, elements of which have been incorporated into the Hindu religion; aboriginal belief systems of Australia; the Norse Gods of Northern Europe, which find mention only in ancient art and literature; the Greeco-Roman gods such as Apollo and Eros, and the Egyptian gods. These were major religious belief systems with their own dogma, text, followers, and influence over ancient and medieval cultures.

The explanation for religious beliefs and behaviours, and indeed the origin of religions is found in the way all human minds work. Pascal

Boyer in his extensive work on the evolutionary origins of religion has provided an analysis for this basic question about an institution that governs much of our life. There is a great diversity of religions. Ancient religions, with the nature worshippers, Japanese Buddhists, American Southern Baptists, Hinduism, Islam, Zoroastrianism, Sikhism, do not share much in terms of dogma. However, as Boyer (2001, p. 5) points out, "Most accounts of the origins of religion emphasize one of the following suggestions: human minds demand explanations, human hearts seek comfort, human society requires order, human intellect is illusion prone. To express this in more detail, here are some possible scenarios:

Religion provides explanations:

- People created religion to explain puzzling mental phenomena.
- Religions explain the origins of things.
- Religion explains why there is evil and suffering.

Religion provides comfort:

- Religious explanations make mortality less unbearable.
- Religions allay anxiety and makes for a comfortable world.

Religion provides social order:

- Religion holds society together.
- Religion perpetuates a particular social order.
- Religion supports morality.

Religion is a cognitive illusion:

- People are superstitious, they will believe anything.
- Religious concepts are irrefutable.
- Refutation is more difficult than belief.

Though this list is probably not exhaustive, it is fairly representative."

Amongst the intellectual scenarios for the origin of religion, Boyer (2001, p. 11) states that "humans in general have certain general intellectual concerns. People want to understand events and processes—that is, to explain, predict and perhaps control them.

These very general, indeed universal intellectual needs gave rise to religious concepts at some point during human cultural evolution. This was not necessarily a single event, a sudden invention that took place once and for all. It might be a constant re-creation as the need to explain phenomena periodically suggests concepts that could work as good explanations." Boyer presents variations to this theme in his hypotheses that people created religions to explain puzzling natural phenomena; religion was created to explain puzzling mental phenomena; religion explains the origins of things; and religion explains evil and suffering.

However, anthropologists have shown that (i) explaining such general facts is not equally pressing in all cultures and that (ii) the explanations provided by religion are not at all like ordinary explanations. The human mind is not a general purpose explanation system, seeking *and* finding authentic explanations for all the phenomena it finds. There are some phenomena that are beyond the understanding of the human explanation system, which in our primitive years, gave rise to the earth-is-flat, earth-is-centre-of universe perspective, which were disproved as the human mind began to think out of the box and had the advantage of the technology it had developed to decipher the truth.

To be more accurate, it was not humanity as a whole that began to think out of the box during one phase in its evolutionary process; rather, it was a single individual or a group that initiated the process, discovered and invented new things and then shared it with the entire society. The process of gaining acceptance of ideas that were alien to the then current beliefs and thought was by no means easy. Even within the scientific community, ideas that were alien or untenable in the perceptions of the prevalent view were considered heretical. Arrhenius' discovery of ion chemistry, William Harvey's discovery of the circulation of blood, in 1628, Louis Pasteur's germ theory of disease, Chandrshekhar Subrahmanyam's discovery of black holes in 1930 are some early examples. In more recent times, until the 1950's doctors did not believe in child abuse and were mystified by "spontaneous" childhood bruising; psychoneuroimmunology (emotional basis of disease, i.e. the mind-body connection) was ridiculed by the medical profession; when John Baird demonstrated the first T.V. system to British scientists at the Royal Society, his idea was scoffed and ridiculed. Now, these are ideas, principles and technologies that we find difficult to consider that they never existed.

Boyer (2001, pp.18) summarizes that the urge to explain the universe is not the origin of religions. (If this were true, there would be a greater acceptance of the scientifically established explanations on the origins of the universe and life.); the need to explain particular occurrences leads to strangely baroque constructions, such as, there are invisible persons with a great interest in our behaviour, that are widespread all over the world; you cannot explain religious concepts if you do not describe how they are used by individual minds; and religious concepts are probably influenced by the way the brain's inference systems produce explanations without our being aware of it.

Aside from the origin and intellectual scenarios for the development of religion, Boyer posits the emotional scenarios – (i) religion provides comfort, (ii) religious explanations make mortality less unbearable, and (iii) religion allays anxiety and makes for a comfortable world. However, religious concepts do not always provide reassurance or comfort; deliverance from mortality is not quite the universal longing that we often assume; religious concepts are indeed connected to human emotional systems, which are connected to life-threatening circumstances; and our emotional programs are an aspect of our evolutionary heritage, which may explain how they affect religious concepts (Boyer, 2001).

There are social reasoning's on the origins of religions: that religion holds society together; religion was invented to perpetuate a particular social order, and that religion supports morality. However, Boyer states, religion cannot be explained by the need to keep society together or to preserve morality, because these do not create institutions; social interaction and morality are indeed crucial to how we acquire religion and how it influences people's behaviour; and the study of the social mind can show us why people have particular expectations about social life and morality and how these expectations are connected to their supernatural concepts (Boyer, 2001).

Boyer presents his fourth scenario on the origins of religion, that religion is a flaw in mental functioning or that religion is an illusion: people are superstitious and will believe anything; religious concepts are irrefutable, and refutation is more difficult than belief. Boyer dismisses this explanation as unsatisfactory, as he considers that the "sleep of reason" is no explanation for religion as it is. There are many possible unsupported claims and only a few religious themes; and besides, belief is not just passive acceptance of what others say. People relax their standards because some thoughts become plausible, not the other way around (Boyer, 2001).

Considering that religion is a cultural "meme", it incorporates within it all the cognitive and emotional abilities that the human mind is capable of. As intrinsic to a religious person, abilities or concepts such as some people can see the future, are a part of the primitive cognitive repertoire, which, however, is restricted to the shamans and mystics, who are considered to have a personal communiqué with God or the supernatural, which permits them access to the unknown world. Such is the belief.

While religion is a socially acquired system of thought, paranormal abilities are considered to be inherent abilities, very much like creativity, musical skills, and mathematical precocity, to name just a few.

Paranormal Abilities

Since the time of recorded history, there have been accounts of people who are reported to have paranormal abilities. They have either been accorded an exalted position in the priesthood or been persecuted as warlocks and witches, depending on the then existing religious beliefs. However, a great deal of scepticism exists in accepting these experiences as one of human abilities that some individuals may possess.

The general public often confuses parapsychology with spiritualism, ufology, astrological, palm- and tarot-card readings, hypnotic regression to "past lives", and a host of other occult practices. In contradistinction, to these practices, however, parapsychology is concerned with "psychic" abilities that can be studied by observation and experimentation under controlled conditions (Rao, 2001, p. 3).

According to J.B. Rhine, the father of modern parapsychology, parapsychology is "the branch of inquiry which deals with nonphysical personal operations or phenomena" (Rhine and Pratt 1957, p. 7). At the same time, it is assumed, (i) parapsychological events/experiences are natural phenomena; (ii) they are subject to natural laws; and (iii) they may be investigated by methods of observation and experiment as in other natural sciences. The manifest conflict between the two assertions, viz., psychic phenomena are nonphysical and at the same time subject to natural laws, continue to fuel the controversy whether parapsychology is a science.

The term *psi* denotes anomalous processes of information or energy transfer, processes such as telepathy or other forms of extrasensory perception that are currently unexplained in terms of known physical or biological mechanisms. The term is purely descriptive: It neither implies that such anomalous phenomena are paranormal nor connotes anything about their underlying process (Bem and Honorton, 1994).

There are two basic types of functioning that are generally considered under the broad heading of psychic or paranormal abilities. These are classically known as extrasensory perception (ESP)—a term coined by J.B. Rhine in the 1930's—in which one acquires information through unexplainable means, and psychokinesis (PK) in which one physically manipulates the environment through unknown means. The Science Applications International Corporation (SAIC) laboratory, under the direction of Edwin May, developed the more neutral terminology for these abilities; they refer to ESP as anomalous cognition (AC) and to psychokinesis as anomalous perturbation (AP). Anomalous cognition is further divided into categories based on the apparent source of the information. If it appears to come from another person, the ability is called telepathy, if it appears to come in real time but not from another person it is called clairvoyance and if the information could have only been obtained by knowledge of the future, it is called precognition (Utts, 1995). Clairvoyance refers to information received by means other than those of the known senses (taste, touch, smell, sight and hearing); psychokinesis or anomalous perturbation, refers to mental interaction with matter; and precognition refers to the ability to know the future (post-cognition could also be added here, such as the ability to know past lives) (Radin, 1997a).

Charles Richet (1923), a Noble Prize winner in physiology, and one of the earliest to carryout experimental investigations of extraordinary human experiences involving extrasensory communication, divided the field before him into four stages. The first was the mythical stage, which lasted up to Mesmer—a period in which miracles and prophecies played a part and were at the root of several religious systems. The second, the magnetic stage, began with Mesmer (1778) and his doctrine of animal magnetism and lasted until the advent of the third stage, the spiritistic stage, in 1848 and the widespread interest in the so-called spiritistic manifestations represented by raps and such. Richet credited Sir William Crookes as having ushered in the fourth, the scientific stage in 1872 and expressed the hope that the publication of his own book *Thirty Years of Psychical Research* would "help to inaugurate a fifth, that of recognition as a science" (Richet, 1923, p. 15).

The experiments of Charles Richet (Richet, 1884) are methodologically important insofar as they involve the application of the calculus of probabilities. Richet was perhaps the earliest psychical researcher to see the importance of applying statistical techniques to ESP data. He wrote "these methods are not emotional or dramatic like experiments made with powerful mediums, or records on monitions of death, but are precise, and, when the experiment is well designed, undeniable" (1884 pp. 96).

Mackenzie (1977, p. 28), writing on the history of parapsychology, states that the scientific stage of parapsychology began "with the founding of the Parapsychology Laboratory at Duke University in 1927, or perhaps with the first major output of this laboratory, J.B. Rhine's *Extra-Sensory Perception* in 1934." *Extra-Sensory Perception* provided a paradigm for experimental parapsychology. It gave "a shared language, methods and problems" (McVaugh and Mauskopf, 1976). It made a systematic scientific search for psi possible. Rhine sought to establish general laws of psychic phenomena and provided a blueprint for future research activity.

The field of parapsychology utilizes the entire repertoire of scientific methodologies to investigate the phenomena – anecdotal reports, field investigations, surveys, case-study methods, first-person methodologies, and experimental studies under controlled laboratory conditions. Utilization of advanced scientific technologies and statistical methods, and extending the field of inquiry to biological mechanisms by using physiological correlates, EEG and fMRI studies are now a part of the methodological tools for the scientific investigation of anomalous cognitions.

Personality, Religion, and Paranormal Abilities

The interrelation of personality, religion, and paranormal abilities becomes evident at three levels: as inherent abilities, socially influenced, and socially influencing. We all have some type or the other of a personality trait, our religiosity and psi skills are of varying degrees. While basic personality traits are relatively stable across the life span, the question whether religiosity or religious fervour and paranormal abilities are stable across the life span, is a moot point.

Personality and religion have long been associated (James, 1902), and personality may influence whether persons naturally gravitate toward or move away from religious involvement. While religious fervour may be largely dependent on the personality and environment, the manifestation of or personal acceptance and hence manifestation of psi abilities may also be dependent on the cultural and religious beliefs. For instance, the concept of precognition is not alien to the Indian belief system, as it is an accepted part of the larger Indian religio-philosophical thought. This is possible because of the belief in re-birth, which lends itself to such possibilities. An individual who claims to have a paranormal experience is not looked at derisively, rather she may be deified. The same cannot be stated for a person from the Christian affiliation. While the Bible is full of paranormal experiences, in traditional churches we find that church leaders discourage members from believing in anomalous events other than those specified in the Bible (Orenstein, 2002, p. 302). If psi is reported outside of the Biblical text it is often viewed as the work of the Devil or simply fraudulent. However, if psi ability is an innate ability such as musical talent, a personality correlate may be present.

According to the substitution theory, paranormal belief functions as a substitute for religious belief (Hergovich, 2005). In contrast to the substitution theory, there exists the hypothesis that people who believe in angels or wondrous healings also believe in other paranormal phenomena such as ghosts and voodoo (Irwin, 1993; Rice, 2003). Related to the fact that the paranormal is common to religion and parapsychology is the theory of a common worldview (Zusne and Jones, 1989). Religiosity and paranormal belief imply a belief in the existence of phenomena that currently cannot be explained by science.

A number of studies have examined the relationship between paranormal belief and religiosity (Hergovich, 2005). Researchers such as Emmons and Sobal (1981), Persinger and Makarec (1990), and Beck and Miller (2001) have reported a negative relationship between paranormal belief and measures of religious belief. Hergovich (2005) opines that this negative relationship could also be interpreted as a manifestation of rejection of at least some paranormal beliefs (precognition and superstition) by the Catholic Church (Goode, 2000; Sparks, 2001).

Thus, we find that the three components under study here are interlinked in human condition, as inherent abilities and as socially influenced factors. In this paper we take personality as the most well researched inherent component to examine its influence on religion—as a socially acquired component, and psi abilities—as (maybe) an inherent component. We are familiar with different types of personality styles, even though we may not demand scientific evidence to establish this; we are all familiar with religion as one of the defining influences on our lives; some may have personal experiences with psi abilities, while some may be sceptics. Nevertheless, anomalous cognition is a cutting edge science-in-progress with its body of experimental investigations and theories, addressing fundamental issues. Considering the product of these anomalous cognitions are or have been of use, the need to identify those with these abilities becomes imperative (Hergovich, Schott, and Arendasy, 2005).

Further, the acceptance or rejection of paranormal abilities is also influenced by religion. Within the Hindu and Jaina thought they are accepted as an extension of one's abilities that can be enhanced, whereas the Christian tradition discourages belief in psi that is not specific to their religion. To explore this relation, the aim of the present study is to:

- Ascertain if there is any relation between personality factors and religious beliefs – it is hypothesised that a measure of personality, as measured by the MBTI, will not show a correlation with the host of variables associated with religiosity.
- Determine if there is an association between personality and the report of psychic experiences – it is hypothesised that MBTI types will not show a correlation with self-reported psi; and
- Investigate the relationship between religious beliefs and reported psychic experiences – it is hypothesised that the self-report of psi experience will not correlate with variables associated with religiosity.

The Present Study

Demographic Characteristics of Participants

An opportunity sample of 1800 participants was selected. All the participants in this study are students, both male and female, attending colleges in Visakhapatnam area. Their mean age is 20 years. They included men and women, belonging to degree and post graduate colleges, from the faculties of commerce, arts, law, engineering, medicine, management, nursing, and hotel management. Some of the colleges are coeducational; a few are exclusively for women.

	AV. AGE	AV. Education	RELIGION			
			Hindu	Muslim	Christian	Total
Male	20.5 yrs.	Under-Graduate	796 (90%)	24 (3%)	62 (7%)	882 (49%)
Female	19.5 yrs.	Under-Graduate	740 (80.6%)	22 (2.4%)	156 (17%)	918 (51%)
Total			1536 (85%)	46 (3%)	218 (12%)	**1800**

Tools for Investigation

The test booklet included:

1. *The Religiosity Survey* was collated by the Institute for Human Science and Service, from the *Multidimensional Measurement of Religiousness/Spirituality for use in Health Research* (MMR/S), published by the Fetzer Institute (1999) in collaboration with The National Institute on Aging (NIA), part of the National Institutes of Health (NIH), USA;

2. *The Survey of Paranormal Experiences* is based on the *ESP Survey* developed and used in research by John Palmer, at the University of Virginia School of Medicine of the Division of Parapsychology; and

3. *Meyers Brigg Type Indicator* (*MBTI*) is the personality type indicator developed by Isabel Briggs Myers and Katherine Briggs.

All the items were printed in English; in addition, a translation in the regional language, Telugu, was also provided.

Analysis of Data

The data was first analyzed according to the standard procedure and scoring method for each inventory. For further analysis, Pearson's correlation has been used to address the questions raised in the hypothesis.

Results

At the outset, it is essential to reaffirm one of the basic aspects of statistical analysis, as it has a bearing on the interpretation of the results obtained here. As we will see, we find that many of the results obtained are statistically significant. Statistical significance is only one part of assessing the veracity of an observed effect. Traditionally significance counting, that is, determining how many studies or correlations reached the "magic" p-value level of 0.05, was in fashion, but in more modern times, researchers have noticed that two things, at least, determine significance levels. The first and most obvious is the magnitude of the effect under study—is it tiny, medium, or robust. But more importantly, the level of significance is determined by the sample size. As Utts (2003) pointed out, a point-null hypothesis can always significantly be rejected by simply taking more data.

To solve this problem, the trend, primarily in experimental psychology, is to use *effect size*. With the work reported here, Pearson's 'r' correlation coefficient can also be considered as an effect size. To give us the meaning of an actual correlation coefficient, we turn to Cohen (1988), for the interpretation of a correlation coefficient, which depends on the context and purposes. A correlation of 0.9 may be very low if one is verifying a physical law using high-quality instruments, but may be regarded as very high in the social sciences where there may be a greater contribution from complicating factors. Thus, correlation between ±0.1 to ±0.3 is considered small, between ±0.3 to ±0.5 is medium, and between ±0.5 to ±1.0 is considered large.

Correlation between Personality Dimensions and Religiosity

The E/I scales deal with individuals intrinsic interaction with the internal and external world. As such it deals with the orientation towards life. The results of the total participants along these dimensions reveal that extroversion ($r = 0.02$) and introversion are not significantly correlated with religiosity ($r = -0.04$). Even though the relations obtained are not significant, the positive (extroversion)-negative (introversion) direction are indicators of the role of the dimensions in the development of religiosity. The same pattern is observed in the Hindu and Christian sample. However, the opposite is observed for the Muslim sample; a possible reason for this could be the small sample size or differences in the belief system which encourages a more internalised perspective in the following of the faith. However, as the correlations obtained are not significant, it would be inappropriate to draw a conclusion on this aspect, nevertheless, a detailed study focussing on this aspect may be possible.

Whilst sensors rely on that which can be perceived and are considered to be oriented toward that which is real, people with an intuitive preference rely more on their nonobjective and unconscious perceptual processes. These dimensions do not show any influence on religiosity, as observed in this sample. The dichotomous nature of these measures is evidenced in the correlation directions – positive for sensing ($r = 0.04$) and negative for intuitive ($r = -0.03$). No variation in pattern is observed when the sample is classified into religious groups.

The dimensions of making assessment of the environment reveals that the thinking type, i.e., those who primarily use logic and rational processes to make deductions and decide upon action, show a small statistically significant negative relation with religiosity ($r = -0.15$*[1]). On the other hand, respondents scoring high on the feeling type, i.e., those who make decisions that are based on subjective processes

*[1] indicates statistical significance

that include emotional reactions to events – show a small, but statistically significant positive relation with religiosity (r = 0.12*). Analysis of data along the criteria of religion reveals the same pattern in the Hindu sample (T: r = -0.13*; F: r = 0.11*). Whilst the thinking dimension shows a weak negative correlation in the Christian sample (r = -0.20*), no correlation is observed for the feeling dimension (r = 0.10). The same pattern is observed in the Muslim sample.

In the present study, the judgmental person, as defined in the MBTI, (one who uses a combination of thinking and feelings when making decision), shows a small, but statistically significant positive relation with religiosity (r = 0.14*), whereas the perceiving person, (one who uses sensing and intuitive processes), shows a small statistically significant negative relation with religiosity (r = -0.14*). This pattern is observed when data is analyzed on the basis of religious denomination. Although the results are not significant for the Muslim sample, they are in the same direction as for the other groups.

These results indicate that E/I as intrinsic traits are not related to religiosity. On the other hand, the T/F and J/P which are cognitive styles of interacting with the external and internal world appear to be associated with religious attitudes. It is important to point out that the relations observed in all the sets of dichotomous types are in the opposite directions. This is an indication of the validity of the measures and their relations.

Correlation Analysis between Personality, Gender, and Religiosity

Analysis on the basis of gender reveals a difference on the extraversion/introversion scales. Whilst there is no observed effect amongst the male sample on the E/I scales, introverted females display a negative correlation with religiosity (r= -0.08*). However, although statistically significant, the correlation is too weak to be meaningful. Analysis of data along religious lines reveals that extraverted Hindu females show a weak statistically significant relation (r = 0.09*), and a statistically weak negative relation to introversion (r = -0.09*). The data for Hindu males does not reveal any significant relations on the E/I dimensions. Although not significant, it is interesting to note that the results for the Christian and Muslim sample are different in that the direction of relation for extraversion for females is negative, and for introversion positive for Christians and negative for Muslims, as compared to the Hindu sample. For the male Christian and Muslim sample, the direction of relation on the extraversion scale is negative (as compared to the Hindu positive). On the introversion scale, the Christian male is similar to the Hindu male, whereas the Muslim male shows a relation in the positive direction. If extroversion/introversion are considered intrinsic traits, these results bring into focus the influence of culture and religious beliefs in the manifestation of personality traits. Extraversion as a form of behaviour is particularly culturally unacceptable for Christian and Muslim females. Vis-à-vis religiosity, Hindu women have far greater freedom to be expressive about their religious beliefs and behaviours.

For the total sample the S/N scales do not reveal a relation with religiosity for both the genders. Gender difference along religious lines reveals that females show a positive direction on the sensing scale, with Christian females showing a small statistically significant relation (r = 0.19*). As should be expected on the dichotomous scales of the MBTI, the intuitive dimension shows a negative direction, although the results are not statistically significant in relation to religiosity. In contrast to the females, males show a negative direction to sensing, and positive to direction to intuition, although the results are not statistically significant.

Along the cognitive style dimensions, for the females, a small statistically significant positive relation is observed in the feeling dimension (r = 0.14*) and small statistically significant negative correlation in the thinking dimension (r = -0.11*). For males, a small statistically significant negative relation is observed in the thinking (r = -0.12*) dimension; no relation is observed along the feeling dimension for the males (r = 0.03). Analysis along gender and religion lines reveals that females show negative correlation with the thinking dimension (Hindu: r = -0.08*; Christian: r = -0.23*; and Muslim: r = -0.37). A positive relation is observed on the feeling dimension for Hindu, (r = 0.14*), Christian (r = 0.20*) females; for males the relation is in the negative direction, although it is not statistically significant.

Along the dimensions of J/P, females show a small statistically significant positive relation for judging (r = 0.08*) and significant negative relation for perceiving (r = 0.06*), although the relation is too weak to be statistically significant. The same direction of significance is observed for the males; however, compared to the females, the relation observed is statistically small (J: r = 0.17*; P: r = -0.17*). On the judging dimension, Christian females (r = 0.26*) and Hindu males (r = 0.16*) show a statistically significant positive relation and statistically significant negative relation on the perceiving scale Christian, F: -0.23*; Hindu, M: -0.17*). The significance levels obtained are too small to derive any relevant conclusions.

Correlation Analysis between Personality Type and Religiosity

As personality is a compound of a variety of preferences, as depicted in the Myers-Briggs typology, the data were further analyzed after assigning the personality type, based on the standard scoring system of the MBTI, to the total sample. No relation between any specific 16 types and religiosity was observed. Thus evidencing a complex mix of intrapersonal, interpersonal, and social factors as contributing towards religiosity in an individual. Further, as Pittenger (1993) has argued, there is little evidence for the existence of sixteen distinct personality types as measured by the MBTI.

Personality and Paranormal Beliefs

Correlation between Personality and Paranormal Beliefs & Experiences

As with earlier studies, the results of the present study reveal a weak statistically significant correlation between extraversion and paranormal experiences (r = 0.08*), particularly for the Hindu sample (r = 0.06*). Further, a statistically significant positive correlation with the feeling scale is observed (r = 0.04*), which is however too weak to enable adequate interpretation. A statistically significant negative correlation is obtained on the introversion (r = -

0.09*), sensing (r = -0.08*), thinking (r = -0.06*) and perceiving (r = -0.04*) scales with paranormal beliefs. However, once again, these correlations though statistically significant are too weak to be meaningfully in any way. Analysis along religious lines does not reveal any significant relations.

Correlation between Personality, Gender, and Paranormal Beliefs & Experiences

Analysis of data along gender lines shows that females have a small statistically significant positive correlation with extraversion (r = 0.11*); further, a small statistically significant negative correlation is observed on the introversion (r = -0.11*) and sensing (r = -0.11*) scales. The present results do not show a similar pattern for males, in that although introversion shows a weak negative correlation (r = -0.07*), as expected, extraversion does not show a relation (r = 0.04). In addition, males show a weak negative correlation on the thinking scale (r = -0.10*).

Religion based analysis shows that Christians and Muslims do not show any significant correlation with paranormal beliefs on the entire scale. On the other hand, Hindu females show a small statistically significant positive correlation on the extraversion (r = 0.10*) and feeling (r = 0.11*), along with the intuition scale (r = 0.08*) the correlation for which is, however, too weak to be statistically significant. Further, a significant negative correlation is observed on the introversion dimension (r = -0.11*), which is in the expected direction.

Correlation between Personality Type and Paranormal Beliefs & Experiences

Data analyzed according to the 16 MBTI personality types in relation to the paranormal survey, reveals small statistically significant negative correlation only with the INTJ type (r = -0.35*). The rest show no significant relation.

So far we have examined the relation between personality (inherent) and religiosity (acquired) and paranormal experiences (inherent? / acquired?). We find that different aspects of the personality may play a small role in the belief, manifestation, and experience of religiosity and paranormal worldview. However, there does not appear to be any relationship between personality types, religion, and paranormal beliefs. The possible exception is with INTJ type subjects. This needs to be confirmed by future studies.

Correlation between Religiosity and Paranormal Beliefs & Experiences

Particularly in the Indian context, religious experiences are intimately related to mystical experiences. Mystical experiences, by their very nature and manifestation are similar to, if not the same as, paranormal experiences or anomalous cognitions. The Hindu worldview encompasses within it all experiences as manifestations of the ultimate reality, with the tangible material world being just one aspect of the true reality. Alongside this, the concept of the soul as a separate entity occupying the body, and the individual human consciousness being a part of the universal consciousness, makes the existence of extrasensory perceptions just another method of perception aside from the five senses. Thus the "sixth" sense is not considered an anomaly. This continuum of thought, the indivisibility of the sacred and the secular, is reflected in the statistically significant but small positive correlation between self-reported attitude towards and practice of religiosity and self-reported paranormal experiences in Hindu sample, irrespective of gender (r = 0.23*). The differences between the religious groups are significant in that phenomena which are considered out of the ordinary or the paranormal, are considered to be the work of the devil in the Abrahamic religions, but are considered to be well within the range of human experience in Hindu philosophies (Christian: r = 0.01; Muslim: r = 0.11).

Correlation between Personality, Religiosity and Paranormal

Extroversion - Introversion

The EI index is designed to reflect whether the person is an extrovert or an introvert in the sense intended by Jung, who coined the terms. According to Jung's theory, these "type preferences" are inborn and not socially constructed through interaction with parents, family, culture, or other external influences. Even so, the individual is impacted by such influences in the quality and strength of the development in her or his preferences. Nature and nurture are both at play. A supportive environment will facilitate inborn preference development; a contrary environment will impede or retard the natural development of inborn

1. *The Extrovert is oriented primarily to the outer world and thus tends to focus his perception and judgment upon people and things.*

   Extroversion and self-reported psi show a weak positive statistical significance (r = 0.08*); no relation is observed with religiosity.

2. *The Introvert is oriented primarily to the inner world as postulated in Jungian theory and thus tends to focus his perception and judgment upon concepts and ideas.*

   Introversion and self-reported psi show a weak negative statistical significance (r = -0.09*); no relation is observed with religiosity.

To summarize, extroversion-introversion as measured by the MBTI is not related to religiosity, except marginally so for Hindu females. Extroverts show a propensity for psi in experimental studies, but do not reveal the same on a self-report on psi beliefs and experiences.

Sensing - Intuition

Sensing–intuition are the information-gathering (perceiving) functions. They describe how new information is understood and interpreted. These are the nonrational functions, as a person does not necessarily have control over receiving data, but only how to process it once they have it.

3. *Sensors are more likely to trust information that is in the present, tangible and concrete, that is, information that can be understood by the five senses. They tend to distrust hunches that seem to come out of nowhere. They prefer to*

look for details and facts. For them, the meaning is in the data.

Sensing and self-reported psi show a weak negative statistical significance (r = -0.08*); no relation is observed with religiosity.

4. *Intuitives tend to trust information that is more abstract or theoretical, that can be associated with other information (either remembered or discovered by seeking a wider context or pattern). They may be more interested in future possibilities. They tend to trust those flashes of insight that seem to bubble up from the unconscious mind. The meaning is in how the data relates to the pattern or theory.*

   Although in the positive direction, intuition and self-reported psi show no relation; and intuition and religiosity are in the negative direction, however, they show no relation.

To summarize, the relation of sensing-intuition to religiosity and psi beliefs and experiences appears to be rather ambiguous.

Thinking - Feeling

Thinking and feeling are the decision-making functions. They both strive to make rational judgments and decisions using the data received from their information-gathering functions (sensing or intuition).

5. *Those who prefer thinking tend to decide things from a more detached standpoint, measuring the decision by what seems reasonable, logical, causal, consistent, and matching a given set of rules. People who prefer thinking do not necessarily, in the everyday sense, 'think better' than their feeling counterparts; the opposite preference is considered an equally rational way of coming to decisions.*

   Thinking and self-reported psi show a weak negative statistical significance (r = -0.06*); and thinking and religiosity (r = -0.15*) show a small statistical significance.

6. *Those who prefer feeling tend to come to decisions by associating or empathizing with the situation, looking at it 'from the inside' and weighing the situation to achieve, on balance, the greatest harmony, consensus and fit, considering the needs of the people involved. Those who prefer feeling do not necessarily have 'better' emotional reactions than their thinking counterparts.*

   Feeling and self-reported psi show a weak statistical correlation (r = 0.04*); and feeling and religiosity show a small statistical significance (r = 0.12*).

To summarize, the relation of thinking-feeling to self-reported psi and religiosity appears to be weak or too small.

Judging - Perceiving

According to Jung's definition, judging and perceiving reveals the specific attitudes of the functions; it does not imply being "judgmental" or "perceptive". In judging types, the judging function (thinking or feeling) is dominant, and will be directed inward or outward in accordance with the I/E preference.

7. *Judging types tend to prefer a step-by-step approach to life, relying on external rules and procedures, and preferring quick closure. The perceiving function (sensing or intuitive) is the direct opposite of the judging function. According to the MBTI definition, the judging types have their strongest judging function introverted and prefer to "have matters settled."*

   Judging and religiosity show a small statistically significant correlation (r = 0.14*), whereas no such relation is seen between judging and self-reported psi.

8. *The perceiving function (sensing or intuitive) is the direct opposite of the judging function. They tend to prefer relying on subjective judgments, and a desire to leave all options open. According to the MBTI definition, the perceiving types have their strongest perceiving function extroverted and prefer to 'keep decisions open."*

Both self-reported psi (r = -0.04*) and religiosity (r = -0.14*) show a statistically significant negative correlation with perceiving type, which are too weak or too small to permit adequate analysis.

To summarize, the relation between the judging function and religiosity appears to be small, while self-reported psi beliefs and experiences and religiosity do not show a relation with the perceiving function.

Conclusion

The results of this study do not reveal a significant relation between personality types as measured by the MBTI and religiosity. These results are consistent with researches that conclude that personality dimensions are low or unrelated to religiosity. The fact that there are significant correlations, although weak, between cognitive styles as indicated by thinking-feeling and judging-perceiving makes us wonder whether the cognitive styles are socially acquired and not intrinsic for the person. Therefore, we may interpret these results as indicating that personality, an intrinsic aspect, is overridden by socio-cultural learning in developing religiosity, which is learnt or acquired, thereby emphasizing the role of early childhood training and experiences, both in childhood as in adulthood, in the development of a religious attitude.

Thus the role of personality in shaping and committing to a religious process appears not dependent on intrinsic personality traits as such, but may be largely influenced by our interaction with the inner and outer world, and hence is amenable to change, based on changing life influences.

Whilst some earlier studies have explored the relation between religiosity and belief in the paranormal and found a positive relation (Hergovich, Schott, and Arendasy, 2005), other studies (Emmons and Sobal, 1981; Persinger and Makarec, 1990; Beck and Miller, 2001), found a negative relationship that was interpreted as a manifestation of rejection of at least some paranormal beliefs (precognition and superstition) by the Catholic Church (Goode, 2000; Sparks, 2001). Thus, while personality may not be a key factor, the religious affiliation and the worldview propounded by it, appears to play a role in the acceptance, if not experience, of ESP.

Intrinsic personality traits of extroversion and introversion are not related to religiosity, thereby disproving our hypothesis that introversion is correlated with religiosity. Introversion and religiosity are negatively correlated among the female participants of this study. For the male participants, no significant relation is observed on the EI scales.

As reported by experimental studies using free-response and forced-choice methods for investigation anomalous cognitions under various conditions such as the ganzfeld, this self report study of psi experiences and beliefs supports the evidence that extroverts will have a greater propensity of psi experiences

In this largely Hindu sample, religiosity and paranormal experiences show some evidence of a relation. However, Lynne Clarke-Hill (see following chapter), has concluded, that religious people who do not attend church regularly tend to report more paranormal experiences. Some evidence was found to support the hypothesis that religious church attendees tend to report less paranormal experiences. In Hinduism, what is termed as paranormal is within the range of human experiences, and in Christianity, paranormal experiences are perceived as the work of satan. Thus, the role of personal beliefs may be a contributing factor in the experience of or reporting of paranormal experiences. In the West, the rise in new age religions and spiritual beliefs based on Eastern traditions, may be an indicator of the opening of doors to experiences that may be more intrinsic to the human condition.

References

Beck, R. & Miller, J.P. (2001). Erosion of belief and disbelief: effects of religiosity and negative affect on beliefs in the paranormal and supernatural. *Journal of Social Psychology*, 14, 277-287.

Bem, D.J. & Honorton, C. (1994). Does psi exist? Replicable evidence for an anomalous process of information transfer. *Psychological Bulletin*, 115, 4-18.

Boyer, P. (2001). *Religion Explained: The Evolutionary Origins of Religious Thought.* New York: Basic Books.

Campbell, A. (2002). *A Mind of Her Own: The Evolutionary Psychology of Women*. New York: Oxford University Press.

Cohen, J. (1988). *Statistical Power Analysis for the Behavioral Sciences*. Hillsdale, N.J.: L. Erlbaum Associates. cf. http://en.wikipedia.org/wiki/Correlation#cite_note-Cohen88-4. Retrieved on May 19, 2009

Emmons, C.F. & Sobal, J. (1981). Paranormal beliefs: functional alternatives to mainstream religion? *Review of Religious Research*, 22, 310-312.

Goode, E. (2000). Two paranormalisms or two and half? An empirical exploration. *Skeptical Enquirer,* 24 (1), 29-35.

Hergovich, A., Schott, R. & Arendasy, M. (2005). Paranormal belief and religiosity. *Journal of Parapsychology*, Fall, 2005.

Irwin, H.J. (1993). Belief in the paranormal: A review of the empirical literature. *Journal of the American Society for Psychical Research*, 87, 1-39.

James, W. (1902). *The Varieties of Religious Experience*. New York: New American Library.

Mackenzie, B. (1977). *Three Stages in the History of Parapsychology*. Paper Presented at the Quadrennial Congress on History of Science, Edinburgh, Scotland.

Mcvaugh, M.R. & Manskopf, S.H. (1976). J.B. Rhine's extra-sensory perception and its background in psychical research. *ISIS*, 67, 161-189.

Multidimensional Measurement of Religiousness/Spirituality for Use in Health Research: A Report of the Fetzer Institute, National Institute on Aging Working Group. www.fetzer.org.

Myers, I.B., McCaulley, M.H., Quenk, N.L. & Hammer, A.L. (2003). *MBTI Manual: A Guide to the Development and Use of the Myers-Briggs Type Indicator* (3rd edn.). Palo Alto, CA.: Consulting Psychologists Press, Inc.

O'Neil. D. (2006). Personality development. *www.Anthro. Palomar.Edu/Social/Soc3.Htm.*

Orenstein, A. (2002). Religion and paranormal belief. *Journal for the Scientific Study of Religion,* 41, 301-311.

Palmer, J. (1979). A community mail survey of psychic experiences. *Journal of the American Society for Psychical Research*, 73, 221-251.

Parsons, T. (1952). *The Social System*. London: Routledge.

Persinger, M.A. & Makarec, K. (1990). Exotic beliefs may be substitutes for religious beliefs. *Perceptual and Motor Skills,* 71, 16-18.

Pittenger, D. J. (1993). The utility of the Myers-Briggs Type Indicator. *Review of Educational Research*, 63, 467-488.

Radin, D.I. (1997). *The Conscious Universe: Truth of Psychic Phenomena*. San Francisco: Harper Collins.

Rao, K.R. (2001). *Basic Research in Parapsychology* (2nd edn.). Jefferson, NC: McFarland & Company Inc. Publishers.

Rhine, J.B. & Pratt, J.G. (1957). *Parapsychology, Frontier Science of the Mind.* Springfield Ill.: Charles C. Thomas.

Rice, T.W. (2003). Believe it or not: Religious and other paranormal beliefs in the United States. *Journal for the Scientific Study of Religion*, 42, 95-106.

Richet, C. (1884). La Suggestion Mentale Et Le Calcul Des Probability. *Rev. Philos.*, 18, 609–674.

— (1975/1923). *Thirty Years of Psychical Research*. New York: Arno Press.

Ridley, M. (2003). *Nature via Nurture*. New York: Harper Collins.

Sparks, G.G. (2001). The relationship between paranormal beliefs and religious beliefs. *Skeptical Inquirer*, 25, 50-56.

Tillich, P. (1957). *Dynamics of Faith*. New York: Harper & Row.

Utts, J. (1991). Replication and meta-analysis in parapsychology. *Statistical Science*, 6(4), 363-403.

— (1995). An assessment for the evidence of psychic functioning. *AIR Report*.

— (2003). What educated citizens should know about statistics and probability. *The American Statistician*, May 2003, 57(2).

Webster's New World Dictionary of the American Language (1980). New York: Simon & Schuster.

Yinger, M.J. (1957). *Religion, Society and the Individual*. New York: Macmillan.

Zusne, L. & Jones, W.H. (1989). *Anomalistic Psychology: A Study of Magical Thinking*. Hillsdale, NJ: Lawrence Erlbaum.

A Study of the Relationship between Religion, Personality and the Paranormal

LYNNE HILL-CLARK

Introduction

The studies of the paranormal (psi) and religiosity are controversial areas. Operationally defining the terms is one of the major problems faced by researchers when attempting to study religion and the paranormal.

Although religion is a common construct, an operational definition for research is elusive, because of the vast number of ideas, purposes, and their culture specific meanings. It encompasses within it monotheism, polytheism, ritualism, mysticism, spirituality and much more. A variety of definitions are circulating in the literature, but for the purpose of this paper we will refer to religion and spirituality as interchangeable terms. Some scholars in this area prefer to define religiosity as being a part of an organized group who share the same views on a divine or higher being; while spirituality is defined as personal beliefs that one may or may not share with a religious community. Spirituality tends to cover a larger breadth than religiosity, i.e., spirituality is the overall category which may or may not include religion. We do acknowledge that there can be a difference between religiosity and spirituality, e.g., people can be religious (attend religious services) but not be spiritually inclined (striving to be the best they can, and/or striving to find meaning in life) or vice versa. Self report surveys tend to show a large percentage of people who claim to have religious beliefs. Census data indicates that in the West religion is a very important part of many people's lives. The Gallup and Lindsay, (1999) and the Poloma and Gallup (1991) polls reported 97% of residents in the U.S. believe in God and roughly 90% say they pray (cited by Spilka, et al., 2003).

To define paranormal (also known as cognitive anomalies or psi) we include but do not limit psi to such abilities as, 1) clairvoyance—information received by means other than those of the known senses (taste, touch, smell, sight and hearing), 2) psychokinesis—mental interaction with matter, 3) precognition—the ability to know the future (retrocognition could also be added here, such as the ability to know past lives). ESP (extrasensory perception) is yet another popular term coined by J.B. Rhine in the 1930's, which can be used to encompass all these terms mentioned (Radin, 1997). In general, psi is a phenomenon that cannot be explained by the *known* laws of physics.

No matter where one stands on the issue of whether or not paranormal phenomenon exists, one cannot deny that people report having paranormal experiences (Spilka, Hood, et al., 2003). In other words, one may not believe in psi itself but must acknowledge that other people *do* believe in the phenomenon, and quite often report such experiences. To get an idea of how many people report such experiences, Fox (1992) found that 67% of his participants reported having extrasensory experiences (N = 1,439) and 42% claimed to have had contact with the dead (cited by Spilka, Hood, et al., 2003).

Religious beliefs and paranormal beliefs have much in common, as they depend primarily on personal, subjective beliefs and experiences. Religious texts are replete with narrations of paranormal experiences and events, such as, the many different narratives across different religions that tell of prophets who communicate with "God", which is perhaps a form of ESP. Many religions then expect their believers to take these paranormal events literally. Previous research has shown another connection between religion and psi, extroverts have been found to be mentally and physically healthier if they are religious (Koenig, McCullough, and Larson, 2001) and extroverts are also more likely to exhibit psi ability (Rao, 2001).

However, the topic of the paranormal is complicated by the fact that both Western science and some Western religions tend to view the paranormal as taboo. Psi is caught in the middle of what is otherwise a hostile triangle. With Western science claiming that psi cannot exist because it does not follow the *known* laws of physics and in some, perhaps more traditional churches, we find that church leaders discourage members from believing in anomalous events other than those specified in the Bible (Orenstein, 2002, p. 302). To put it another way, the Bible is seen by some religious groups as having a "patent" on the paranormal. The *Bible* is full of narratives of paranormal experiences; however, if psi is reported outside of the Biblical text it is often viewed as the work of the devil or simply fraudulent.

Despite the hundreds of empirical studies that exist, many modern Western scientists remain sceptical of religious and paranormal research. Critics claim that since the phenomena cannot be objectively measured and replicated, their validity as a scientific area of study is suspect. However, there is an abundance of empirical data that lends evidence to the existence of extrasensory abilities in humans. This evidence has been avoided or discarded for many reasons by critics, but a careful review of the vast literature shows that cognitive anomalies do indeed exist. This paper will only cover a couple key studies in the area of psi ability, for further discussion on this topic see Rao (2001), Radin (1997) and for critics of psi see Hansel (1989), Hyman (1996).

Jessica Utts' meta-analyses of research data of the CIA sponsored STAR GATE program, for the American Institutes of Research, is one of the most convincing analyses for the existence of psi phenomena. After a review of the ganzfeld, forced choice and free response data for remote viewing, applying predetermined rigorous criteria, including strong effect sizes and replicability, Utts (2001, p. 132). concluded:

"It is clear to this author that anomalous cognition is possible and has been demonstrated. This conclusion is not based on belief, but rather on commonly accepted scientific criteria. The phenomenon has been replicated in a number of forms across laboratories and cultures. The various experiments in which it has been observed have been different enough that if some subtle methodological problems can explain the results, then there would have to be a different explanation for each type of experiment, yet the impact would have to be similar across experiments and laboratories. If fraud were responsible, similarly, it would require an equivalent amount of fraud on the part of a large number of experimenters or an even larger number of subjects."

Radin and Ferrari's (1991) analyzed 73 relevant articles from 1935 to 1987 resulting in a total of 2,569 participants attempting to mentally influence the outcome of a dice roll. There were 2.6 million dice throws from 148 different experiments and just over 150,000 from 31 control groups where no attempt to influence the outcome was made. The control group's results were at chance 50.02% and the experimental groups score was at 51.2%. This may not seem like much but when we consider that "statistically it results in odds against chance of more than a billion to one" (Radin, 1997, p. 134). We cannot help but regard it as a robust effect. As with all meta-analytic results researchers should consider the "file drawer" problem. Radin reports that 17,974 insignificant and unpublished studies would need to be in existence for the results to be nullified. That is 121 studies for each of the studies analyzed. The chances that there are that many "file drawer" studies out there is very small as there are just not that many experimenters doing this kind of research. To put this into perspective 17,974 studies means that each of the 52 investigators involved in these experiments would have to have conducted one unpublished, nonsignificant study per month, every month for 28 years. To some of the critics of psi this is more plausible then the existence of psi!

The Relationship Between Psi and Religion

Earlier research on the relationship between psi beliefs and religious beliefs demonstrates very mixed results. One hypothesis states that the relationship between religious beliefs and belief in psi is positive. This has developed from the reasoning that paranormal experiences are found in many religious texts; therefore it will not be hard for religious people to make the jump from believing in say heaven and hell to believing in ESP. Many scientists tend to view religion and the paranormal as one and the same, i.e., they both "violate known laws of science" (Orenstein, 2002, p. 302).

On the other side of the debate is a second hypothesis in which researchers reason that the relationship will be negative primarily because religious leaders tend to discourage belief in psi that is not specific to their religion, for example, the belief in reincarnation may be viewed as conflicting with traditional church teachings of heaven and hell. Writers such as Greeley (1975) and Wuthnow (1978) have "suggested that church authorities have a self-interest in disparaging paranormal claims because they fear that these claims will provide an alternative source of revelation and legitimacy that is not under the control of the church" (cited by Orenstein, 2002, p. 302).

Research on the relationship between religion and paranormal beliefs is ambiguous. Tom Rice (2003, p. 95) found "that the correlations between belief in religious phenomena and other paranormal phenomena are largely insignificant." He also concluded that standard social background factors are not good predictors for identifying psi believers. Thus, religion, socioeconomic status, education, age and gender were not predictors of belief in cognitive anomalies.

Orenstein (2002) and McKinnon (2002) found that religious and paranormal beliefs are positively correlated but this was not the case for participants that claimed to attend church regularly. This was a factor that Rice (2003) did not control for; it appears that both the hypotheses mentioned earlier are correct. People that are religious or spiritual are more likely to believe in psi, but the relationship turns to a negative one when we account for church attendance. This could be due to the fact that church leaders discourage their members from believing in psi abilities.

The Relationship Between Psi and Jungian Personality Types

The empirical relationship between psi and personality is less complex than the relationship between religion and belief in psi, and between religion and personality. The research tends to be consistent with its findings that people who believe in psi are more like to exhibit psi ability, this is often referred to as the sheep/goat effect (Schmeidler and McConnell, 1958) in which sheep are the believers in psi and goats are sceptics. "Goats" tend to demonstrate no anomalous cognitive ability or they demonstrate a phenomenon called psi-missing. Psi-missing occurs when people demonstrate *below* chance missing scores; i.e., say a participant has a 50% chance of *guessing* an answer correctly and that person (most likely a goat) only gets 45% of the answers correct this is significantly below chance. The theory then is that "goats" use their psi ability to get a low score, whereas "sheep" tend to obtain positive deviations or scores above the expected average score.

Extroverts have also been empirically proven to exhibit psi abilities when compared to introverts (Rao, 2001). There is some speculation on why these personality traits differ on paranormal abilities, but the general consensus is that extroverts tend to be more in-tune with other people, therefore more open to their psi abilities. Introverts tend to live more in an inter world and are not as good at "reading" other people or their environment in general. The iNtuitiveness measure of the Myers-Briggs Type Inventory (MBTI) is also likely to correlate positively with psi belief and ability; partially because of the overlap in the operational definitions of psi and iNtuitiveness (N). N's are characterized as relying on their "gut feelings" (Myers,

1991), being open to such feelings is, in and of itself, a sixth sense. The N's counterpart the Sensors (S) are characterized as the types that have to "see it to believe it", therefore it is reasonable to assume that participants that are N will more likely believe in psi (which leads to psi ability as well) and S types will be less likely to believe in anomalies that are outside of the five senses.

The Relationship Between Religion and Personality

In general, the literature review finds that personality types are not a good predictor of religiosity, but rather different types of personalities use religion in different ways. For example, Ross (1996) found that iNtuitive religious types tend to emphasize the undefinability of religious beliefs and are more open to religious change, as opposed to Sensing types who find religious doubt more upsetting, and emphasize structure and ritual.

The Present Study

This research study is unique in that it combines religiosity, the paranormal and personality in ways that has not been done before. While religiosity and personality and belief in psi and personality have been studied before, the interrelation between the three have not been explored. This study is conducted in a Southeastern American University, with primarily church going participants. This study is a replication of a study done in India, to explore cross-cultural perspective on this issue (see previous chapter 18).

Hypotheses

1) We expect to find a significant positive correlation between religiosity and paranormal beliefs in non-church attendees, and a negative relationship between religious church attendees and belief in psi. This leaves the third group which is people who are not religious or spiritual and who do not attend church, no significant correlation is expected between this group and belief is the paranormal.

2) Based on the sheep/goat studies we expect to find that the higher one scores on the religiosity scale (and does not attend church) he/she is more likely to believe in psi and therefore exhibit psi abilities. The "goats", i.e., the church goers who do not believe in psi are less likely to exhibit paranormal abilities or report paranormal experiences.

3) Extroversion should be a predictor of psi and psi ability and Introversion

4) iNtroversion should not be a predictor.

5) Intuitiveness should be a predictor of psi belief and ability.

6) Sensing types should be a negative predictor of psi.

Methods

Participants

A total of 282 participants filled out the survey (153 females, 92 males, and 37 in which the gender was not specified). The age ranged from 18 to 56 with a median age of 19. The participants were college students attending a midsized South-eastern American university. As Hood and Morris (1985) have noted when researchers draw from a sample in this area it results in a highly fundamentalist population that is not necessarily representative of the U.S. as a whole. The participants received extra course credits for participating in this study.

Materials

The *Religiosity Survey* questionnaire is developed from the *Multidimensional Measure of Religiousness/Spirituality for use in Health Research* (MMR/S), published by the Fetzer Institute (1999) in collaboration with The National Institute on Aging (NIA) in California. This is a 29 item 4 point Likert scale that utilizes revise scores with option number five being "not sure". The scale ends with one open ended question asking participants what is the most import thing they do to cope with depression.

The *Survey of Paranormal Experiences* (SPE) questionnaire is based on an ESP Survey developed by John Palmer, at the University of Virginia. This scale consists of 24 dichotomous questions, with answer options of "yes", "no", and "not sure". Like the former scale this one ends with an open ended question asking participants to share their paranormal experiences.

The *How Intuitive Are You* measure was developed by K.R. Rao (Rao, in press). This is the measure of psi ability (please note that the term *intuitive* here refers to paranormal ability and it should not be confused with the MBTI personality type of iNtuitiveness). This scale is made up of 12 items in which the force choice method asks participants to "guess" the target. The targets were generated at a later date after all the surveys had been collected, which is a measure of precognition. This scale has a free response measure at the end of which the participants are asked to relax and visualize whatever comes to mind and write about it.

Myers-Briggs Type Indicator (MBTI) was created by Katherine Cook Briggs and her daughter Isabel Briggs Myers. The theoretical base for the scale is Carl Jung's theory of personality. The MBTI (Form G) is meant for older populations (20 years or more), it consists of 126 items which measure four dichotomies:

1. Extroversion (E) and Introversion (I)
2. Sensing (S) and iNtuition (N)
3. Thinking (T) and Feeling (F), and
4. Judging (J) and Perceiving (P).

Design and Procedure

The data were collected by three graduate students at a midsized Southeastern American university aided by five undergraduate assistants. The participants were told simply that this was a research project dealing with religiosity and the paranormal. These surveys were completed in a classroom setting consisting of 20 to 100 participants at a time. The participants were given explicit instructions on the proper order in which to fill out the surveys. First the consent forms, packets and answer sheets were handed out which contained the *Religiosity Scale*, *Paranormal Experiences Scale*, and *How Intuitive are You Scale* (in that order) participants were allowed to get started on that packet and then handed the MBTI. This helped insure that the MBTI was filled out last. Participants were also asked not to write on the packets, and to use the answer sheets provided. When the participants returned the completed surveys the consent forms were separated from the answer sheets to guarantee anonymity.

It was predetermined that the surveys needed to be completed in this order because of the lengthiness of the measures used in this study. It took an average of one hour to properly complete the surveys. The MBTI, being the longest of the four, needed to come last because we did not want the participants to be fatigued while filling out the first three scales. There was no debriefing and no one refused to participate.

Data Scoring and Analyses

Due to the nonexperimental research design of this study, a Pearson correlation analysis of the variables under study was conducted. After eliminating the data from four participants due to problems with response validity (e.g., answering every question the same on a reverse scored scale), answers from an additional 7 participants were deleted only on the MBTI. This scale was the last to be completed and the lengthiest of the measures, causing 7 participants to run short of time and/or give up on completing the scale. The final sample consists of 278 participants on all measures but the MBTI, for which there were 271 participants.

All questionnaires were scored according to the scoring procedures specified by the test developers. Data analysis involved an examination of the average response per item for all psychometric scales.

Results

Hypothesis 1: Among the non-church attending subjects, the scores obtained on religiosity and paranormal questionnaire correlate positively.

The overall correlation between the religiosity scale and paranormal experiences was $r = -.11$, $p = .16$, (two-tailed) which is negative but statistically insignificant. However, a partial correlation controlling for church attendance, gives $r = .19$, $p < .01$, (one-tailed) and provides support to our hypothesis. (See table 1, below for a correlation matrix displaying the results). It would seem that church attendance is an important variable that vitiates the positive relationship between beliefs in the paranormal and religiosity of the person.

Hypothesis 2: Among the non-church attending subjects the religiosity scores correlate significantly with ESP scores.

This hypothesis is not supported by the data as the correlation between religiosity and ESP scores among the non-church attendees is $r = -.03$. For the entire population the correlation is $r = -.07$, which is also completely insignificant. There appears to be no difference between church attendees and those who do not attend church regularly, as far as the anomalous ability as tested in the present study is concerned.

Hypothesis 3: Extroversion scores correlate positively with paranormal experience scores, and introversion scores correlate negatively with paranormal experiences.

Paranormal experience and extraversion yielded a correlation of $r = .09$, $p = .15$, one-tailed. Paranormal experience and introversion yielded $r = -.07$, $p = .24$, one-tailed. No significant relationship was found between extroversion and paranormal experience or introversion and paranormal experience, even though both the correlations are in the expected direction.

Hypothesis 4: ESP scores correlate significantly positive with extroversion and significantly negative with introversion scores.

Extroversion did not correlate significantly with ESP scores, $r = .06$, ($p = .35$, one-tailed). Also the correlation between introversion and ESP scores, though negative as expected, is not significant ($r = -.08$, $p=.22$, one-tailed).

Hypothesis 5: Intuitiveness correlates significantly with paranormal experiences scores, whereas sensing correlates negatively with paranormal experiences.

The Sensing and iNtuition scales on the MBTI correlated, as predicted, with paranormal experiences. Sensing was negatively correlated with experiences of the paranormal ($r = -.37$, $p < .01$, two tailed) and iNtuition was positively correlated with paranormal experience ($r = .34$, $p < .01$, two tailed). Sensing types tended to report less anomalous experiences, and iNtuitive personality types tended to report having more anomalous experiences.

Hypothesis 6: ESP scores correlate positively with intuition and negatively with sensing scores.

No significant relationship was found between Sensing and ESP scores ($r = -.02$, $p = .77$, one-tailed) or between INtuition and paranormal ability ($r = .02$, $p = .76$, one-tailed).

To summarize, two out of the six hypotheses were supported, while there is no evidence from our data to support the other hypotheses. The strongest relationship was between the Sensing and iNtuition measures of the MBTI and the reporting of paranormal experiences. As predicted, Sensing types tended to report less anomalous events when compared to iNtuitive participants. There was a tendency for religious church attendees to report less paranormal experiences when compared to religious non-church attendees. Extroversion and Introversion appear to have no relationship with reported paranormal events. The paranormal abilities measure yielded no significant results with this sample on any of the variables studied.

TABLE 1 : RESULTS

N=278	Religi-osity	Contro-lling for Church attendance	Extrove-rsion	Introve-rsion	Sensing	Intuition
Paranormal Experience	-0.11	0.19**	0.09	-0.07	-0.37**	0.34**
Paranormal Abilities	-0.07	-0.03	0.06	-0.08	-0.02	0.02

* correlation is significant at the .05 level (1-tailed);** correlation is significant at the .01 level (1-tailed)

Based on previous literature the amount of reported paranormal experience should correlate positively with the measure of paranormal ability. A post-hoc analysis was conducted to see if this was indeed the case with this sample. A Pearson correlation between the reported paranormal experience scores and the ESP scores obtained in the "How Intuitive Are You" yielded a correlation of $r = .11$ $p = .07$, (one-tailed). This relationship appears to be in line with our expectation, even though this study did not have a powerful enough sample to adequately detect the effect in question. The problem most likely lies in the anomalous abilities measure itself and the way it was administered. The weakest results appear to come from this ESP test measure, as indicated by the insignificant hypothesized results above as well as by the overall ESP results which are not different from chance expectation.

Discussion

First, it was predicted that the higher people rate on the Religiosity Scale, but do not report attending church regularly, the more likely they report paranormal experiences. We did indeed find this trend. The relationship between religiosity and the reported paranormal experiences was marginally negative; however, when church attendance was controlled for, the relationship became significantly positive. Thus, considering the drastic change in the relationship, when controlling for one question (How often do you attend religious service such as church?), provides support for the hypothesis that people who attend church regularly are less likely to report cognitive anomalies when compared to religious non-church attendees.

Second, previous research has found that people who believe in psi are more likely to exhibit psi ability (Rao, 2001); therefore, if non-attending religious participants are more likely to believe in psi, then it follows that they should also be more likely to demonstrate psi abilities. The results indicate that this may not be the case, for this sample; non-church attendees did not demonstrate significantly more paranormal ability than did the church goers.

Extroversion and introversion were not strong indictors of reported anomalous experiences or abilities. Essentially, we found no relationship between these variables. It was predicted that extroverts would report more anomalous events and that they would demonstrate anomalous abilities; whereas, introverts would report less paranormal events and not do as well on the abilities measure. The results indicate that there is no relationship between these variables.

INtuitiveness, as predicted, had a positive relationship with paranormal experiences. INtuitive participants tended to report more anomalous events. Sensing, on the other hand, correlated negatively with reported psi experiences. Participants who scored high on the Sensing scale tended to report fewer anomalous events. INtuitive participants tend to listen to their "gut feeling" and may learn to rely on such feelings, even when making major decisions in their lives. It makes sense then that these people who are open to this "sixth sense" would take note of such experiences; therefore, being more likely to report such anomalies, as was found in this study. On the other hand, Sensing types have to "see it to believe it". If something is not clearly tangible to them they may not take notice of it; hence, they would be less likely to report such abstract events as the paranormal. INtuitive and Sensing participants appeared to have no relationship with the anomalous abilities measure.

Limitations of the Study

The fact that most religious people consider themselves to be spiritual as well as religious makes it hard for researchers to make a clear distinction between religiousness and spirituality (Zinnbauer and Pargament, 2005). This may be one of the reasons why we did not see as large a distinction as predicted with religious church attendees in relation to psi abilities. In other words, the distinction between religious/church attendees and spiritual/non-attendees is a fine line. The scales and sample used in this study may not have been sensitive enough to detect a difference between the paranormal abilities of church attendees and those who do not attend regularly.

The fact that the sample is a fairly conservative evangelical population most likely confounded the results. If the majority of the participants attend church regularly, then they may tend not to believe in the paranormal (i.e., we may have ended up with a population of goats or unbelievers). This could, in turn weaken the results of the psi ability measure, because goats tend not to do as well on psi tests as sheep or believers in psi.

Nevertheless, these results do demonstrate some of the trends that past research has found. Further research needs to be conducted with larger and older populations. One of the major limitations of this study was the use of college freshmen as the primary participants. Other areas outside of the Southeastern part of the U.S. should be sampled in order to be able to generalize these results outside of this particular area.

Another problem with this study is that the participants took this survey just before finals week. Many of the open ended responses indicated that the subjects were stressed and/or tired. Previous research indicates that stress is not an ideal condition for psi. Many studies have shown that participants perform better when relaxing or meditating (Braud and Braud, 2001). This may be another explanation for why we did not find the results we were looking for with the psi abilities measure.

Being that the surveys were not counterbalanced we may have had an order effect. The reliabilities for the MBTI were sufficient indicating that even though the participants were fatigued they managed to answer in a consistent manner even though this survey was filled out last. Never-the-less, we might have gotten different results had the surveys been in a different order.

Future Research

Additional research is needed to more fully prove or disprove the results of this study. This study should be replicated with a larger, older, more diverse population, and under better conditions that are more conducive to psi (i.e., not just before final exams). Beyond the replication of this study it would be useful to further investigate gender differences. For example, do men and women differ on the types of paranormal experiences reported? It would also be interesting to investigate whether or not any differences exist between the different denominations of Christianity.

Regarding the bigger picture, psi research should continue to conduct experiments which are designed to investigate the circumstances that are optimal for cognitive anomalies to exist. Now the question is how does psi work? With the technologies of today we can study brain activity, which allows us to look at the biological basis of psi. Many studies have been conducted to prove the existence of anomalous abilities (some of which were mentioned in the literature review section of this paper). The next step is to move beyond this; theories need to be (and are now being) formulated that speculate why and how such phenomenon exists (Rao, in press). Then, as is the case with all good research, these theories must be tested.

Conclusion

In accord with the previous research we can conclude that religious people who do not attend church regularly tend to report more paranormal experiences. Some evidence was found to support the hypothesis that religious church attendees tend to report less paranormal experiences. It appears that the psi abilities measure was too weak to be able to draw any reliable conclusions. Similarly, extraversion and introversion, for this sample, were not good indicators of reported paranormal experiences. However, the Sensing and iNtuition personality types were good indicators of reported paranormal experiences; with Sensing types tending to report less paranormal occurrences when compared to iNtuitive types.

REFERENCES

Braud, L.W. & Braud, W.G. (2001). Further studies of relaxation as a psi-conducive state. In K.R. Rao (Ed.). *Basic Research in Parapsychology* (2nd edn.). Jefferson, NC: McFarland & Company Inc. Publishers.

Fox, J.W. (1992). The structure, stability, and social antecedents of reported paranormal experiences. *Social Analysis,* 53, 417-431.

Gallup, G.Jr. & Lindsay, M.D. (1999). *Surveying the Religious Landscape: Trends in U.S. Beliefs.* Harrisburg, PA: Morehouse Publishing.

Greeley, A.M. (1975). *The Sociology of the Paranormal: A Reconnaissance.* Beverly Hills, CA: Sage Publications.

Hansel, C.E.M. (1989). *The Search for Psychic Power: ESP and Parapsychology Revisited.* Buffalo, NY. Prometheus books.

Hood, R.W. Jr. & Morris, R.J. (1985). Boundary maintenance, social-political views, and presidential preference among high and low fundamentalist. *Review of Religious Research*, December, 27(2), 1-12.

Hyman, R. (1996). Evaluation of a program on anomalous mental phenomena. *Journal of Scientific Exploration,* 10, 31-58.

Koenig, H.G., McCullough, M.E. & Larson, D.B. (2001). *Handbook of Religion and Health.* New York, Oxford University Press.

McKinnon, A.M. (2002). The religious, the paranormal, and church attendance: A response to Orenstein. (A. Orenstein, Journal of the Scientific Study of Religion, 2002) [Electronic version]. *Journal for the Scientific Study of Religion*, 42, 299-304.

Myers, I.B. (1991). *Introduction to Type: A Description of the Theory and Applications of the Myers-Briggs Type Indicator.* Palo Alto, CA.: Consulting Psychologists Press

Orenstein, A. (2002). Religion and paranormal belief. *Journal for the Scientific Study of Religion*, 41, 301-311.

Paloma, M.M. & Gallup G. (1991). *Varieties of Prayer: A Survey Report*. Philadelphia, Trinity Press International.

Radin, D. (1997). *The Conscious Universe: The Scientific Truth of Psychic Phenomena*. New York: Harper Edge.

Radin, D.I. & Ferrari, D.C. (1991). Effects of consciousness on the fall of dice: A meta-analysis. *Journal of Scientific Exploration*, 5(3), 61-84.

Rao, K.R. (2001). *Basic Research in Parapsychology,* (2nd edn.). Jefferson, NC: Mcfarland & Company Inc. Publishers.

— (in press). *Cognitive Anomalies-phase I.* Visakhapatnam, Institute for Human Science & Service.

Rice, T. (2003). Believe it or not: Religious and other paranormal beliefs in the United States. *Journal for the Scientific Study of Religion*, 42, 95-107.

Ross, C.F.J., Weiss, D. & Jackson, L. (1996). The relation of Jungian psychological type to religious attitudes and practices. *International Journal for the Psychology of Religion*, 6, 263-279.

Schmeidler, G.S., & McConnell, R.A. (1958). *ESP and Personality Patterns*. New Haven: Yale University Press.

Spilka, B., Hood, R.W. Jr., Hunsberger, B. & Gorsuch, R. (2003). *The Psychology of Religion: An Empirical Approach*. New York Guilford Press.

Utts, J. (2001). An assessment of the evidence for psychic functioning. In K.R. Rao (Ed.). *Basic Research in Parapsychology* (2nd edn.). Jefferson, NC: Mcfarland & Company Inc. Publishers.

Wuthnow, R. (1978). Peak experiences: Some empirical tests. *Journal of Humanistic Psychology,* 18 (3), 59-75.

Glossary

Sanskrit and Parapsychology Terms

***abhiniveśa*:** Clinging to life, will-to-live; an urge for survival or for self-preservation.

agent: The one who transmits a telepathic message.

***ahaṃkāra*:** The ego or self-referencing function/feelings and thoughts about self at empirical level. Egoism or self-conceit; the false "I"; "I" am-ness. It is the self-arrogating principle "I" that is projected by the mind. Awareness of oneself, or of individuality; ego self.

aiśvarya (variant spellings: ***aishwarya***, ***aishwaryam***): A form of distant mental influence in which will-power is exerted and then left to work itself out; an instance of so exercising the will. In Sri Aurobindo's *Record of Yoga*.

alpha: A distinctive brain-rhythm or brain-wave which occurs mainly in the occipital region of the cortex, and is associated with feelings of drowsiness, relaxation and disengaged attention with a relatively high amplitude. It has a frequency range of between 8 and 13 Hz (cycles) per second.

altered state(s) of consciousness (ASC): Expression popularized by Charles T. Tart which can refer to virtually any mental state differing from that of the normal waking state such as those found during dreaming, hypnosis, trance and meditation.

anicca: Many-sidedness of reality; transience.

aṇimā: A *siddhi* in which something of the nature of the subtle body is introduced into the physical body. (Term is defined in the senses in which they are used in Sri Aurobindo's *Record of Yoga*.)

anomalistic psychology: Term first used by Leonard Zusne and Warren Jones (1982) to indicate that part of psychology that investigates paranormal and occult phenomena

anomalous cognition (AC): Another term for remote viewing (RV) and ESP when some individuals are able to gain access to information from events outside the range of their senses.

anomalous mental phenomena (AMP): Another term for parapsychological phenomena or psi.

anomalous perturbation (AP): Another term for psychokinesis (PK), direct influence of mind over matter.

anomaly: A phenomenon that is unexpected according to conventional scientific knowledge, sometimes preferred to "paranormal".

antaḥkaraṇa: "Inner instrument"; subtle inner organ; mind. In Advaita Vedānta, it is conceived to include the mind and the intellect and refers to the functional mind as opposed to *jīva ātman*, the passive witness.

asamprajñāta samādhi: A trans-cognitive state of consciousness in which one is conscious without being conscious of anything; state of pure consciousness; highest superconscious state where the mind and the ego-sense are completely annihilated.

āsana: Yogic physical posture, especially as recommended in Haṭha Yoga as one of the aids to concentration.

asmitā: Ego consciousness; I-ness; the sense of "I am"; "I exist".

aṣṭasiddhi: Eight supernormal powers; a traditional list of *siddhi*s, modified by Sri Aurobindo and grouped into two "siddhis of knowledge" (*prākāmya* and *vyāpti*), three "siddhis of power" (*aiśvarya*, *īśitā* and *vaśitā*) and three "siddhis of being" or physical *siddhis* (*aṇimā*, *laghimā* and *mahimā*). (Term is defined in the sense used in Sri Aurobindo's *Record of Yoga.*)

ātman: The individual spirit or self; principle of life and sensation; subjective moment of consciousness. With capital Ā(tman), the universal Spirit or the supreme soul of the universe.

autoganzfeld: Laboratory *ganzfeld* technique in which many of the key procedural details, such as selection and presentation of the *target* and the recording of the evaluation of the target-response similarity given by the *percipient*, are fully automated and computerized, so as to reduce as far as possible errors such as motivational errors that could bias the manual operations.

***avidyā*:** Generally, ignorance, or nescience; ignorance of one's true nature.

bhāva: Emotion; subjective state of being (existence); heart-mind.

bio-PK*:* Term used to refer to *psychokinetic* effects on living systems such as those involved in psychic healing and PK effects on germination of seeds and growth of bacteria. It is also labeled as DMILS, or direct mental influence on living systems.

Brahman (***Brahma***): The transcendent reality that manifests in the universe. (Term is defined in the sense used in Sri Aurobindo's *Record of Yoga.*)

buddhi: Intellect; power of comprehension. Derived from the root verb *budh*: to enlighten, to know; one of the four aspects of the internal organ; the determinative faculty controlling the sense organs; the "psychic" component of the mind.

catuṣṭaya: A group of four, especially any of the seven divisions of the *sapta catuṣṭaya*, each consisting of four terms. (Term is defined in the sense used in Sri Aurobindo's *Record of Yoga.*)

chance: A state characterized by complete unpredictability.

citta: The mind (as conceived of in Yoga); the mental mode turned towards objects; has the capacity to understand and serve as a storehouse of impressions left behind by past experiences.

citta-vṛtti: Fluctuations or modifications of the mind; activities of the mind (*citta*), such as thinking, imagining, recollecting and so on.

clairvoyance: ESP of objects and events as distinguished from ESP of thoughts and mental states of persons.

clairvoyant: A person endowed with a special ability for *clairvoyance*.

cold reading: A set of statements claiming to be paranormally received, which are in fact no more than information gleaned from facial gestures, clues in conversation, etc. of the person seeking the reading.

control: Is an experimental procedure, condition, introduced to prevent the influence of unwanted factors that could contaminate the hypothesis under investigation.

decline effect: A frequently observed decline of scoring in ESP experiments when subjects are tested over a period of time or scoring decline during the course of an experimental session.

déjà vu: The feeling or illusion of having previously experienced an event or place which in reality was not encountered before.

dhāraṇā: Contemplation or continued concentration of mind on an object; a Yogic term meaning anchoring the stream of thoughts to a particular object of thought. This is described by Patañjali as a step in the course of restraining the processes of consciousness; one of the eight stages of Rāja Yoga.

dharma: Duty; the righteous way of living, as enjoined by the sacred scriptures and the spiritually illumined; characteristics; duties appropriate for one's station in life; doing one's duties is considered one of the four major goals of life, along with *artha*, *kama*, and *mokṣa*.

dhyāna (jñāna): Meditation, contemplation, specifically defined in Yogic terminology as a steady and homogenous flow of thoughts; the seventh rung in the eightfold ladder of yoga.

differential response: A parapsychological response pattern first labelled as such by K.R. Rao; an often-observed tendency to score positively on one condition and negatively in the other in the same ESP experiment consisting of two different conditions such as two kinds of targets.

direct mental interaction with living systems (DMILS): A term used to describe instances where one person tries to influence a biological system paranormally.

displacement: ESP responses to targets other than those for which the calls were intended.

dveṣa: Aversion/avoidance for something, implying a dislike, repulsion, antipathy or hatred.

effect size: (ES) is a name given to a family of indices that measure the magnitude of a given effect. Unlike significance tests, these indices are independent of sample size.

ekāgra\ekāgratā: One-pointed focus and concentration.

electrodermal activity: Refers to changes in the skin's ability to conduct electricity.

electroencephalography: A technique for amplifying and recording the fluctuations in electrical voltage in a living brain using electrodes attached to key positions on the person's head.

electromyography: The measurement of the electrical waves associated with the activity of skeletal muscles.

ESP cards: A special deck of cards, developed for testing ESP. A pack of 25 cards, each containing one of five symbols — circles, cross, square, star or wavy lines.

ESP: See extrasensory perception.

experimenter effect: An experimental outcome which results not from manipulation of the variable of interest per se, but rather from some aspect of the particular experimenter's behavior, such as unconscious communication to the subjects, or possibly even a psi-mediated effect working in accord with the experimenter's desire to confirm some hypothesis.

extrasensory perception (ESP): The acquisition of information about, or response to, an external event, object or influence (mental or physical; past, present or future) otherwise than through any of the known sensory channels; used by J.B. Rhine to refer to such phenomena as *telepathy, clairvoyance* and *precognition*.

ganzfeld: Refers to a technique for homogenous, unpatterned sensory stimulation. Audiovisual ganzfeld may be accomplished by placing halved ping-pong balls over each eye of the subject, with diffused light focused on the eyes and unstructured sounds (such as "white" or "pink" noise) fed into the ears. Placing the subject in such an environment creates an altered state of consciousness in the subject. Sometimes subjects report a total blank out consequent on the deprivation of patterned sensory input.

general extrasensory perception (GESP): A non-committal technical term used to refer to instances of *extrasensory perception* in which the information paranormally acquired may have been derived either from another person's mind (that is, as in *telepathy*), or from a physical event or state of affairs (that is, as in *clairvoyance*), or even from both sources.

glossalalia: Speaking in "tongues," that is, in a language which is either unknown to linguistic science, or completely fabricated; it usually occurs in a religious context or is attributed to religious inspiration, as from the Holy Spirit; not to be confused with *xenoglossy*.

goat: Term originally used by Gertrude Schmeidler to describe a subject who rejects the possibility that *extrasensory perception* could occur under the conditions of the given experimental situation; this somewhat narrow meaning has been extended to refer also, or alternatively, to persons who do not believe in the existence of ESP in general (that is, under any conditions!).

guṇa: Attribute; property, quality, or characteristic arising from nature (*prakṛti*) itself; as a rule, when "*guṇa*" is used, it is in reference to the three fundamental qualities, "strands" or interacting components of *prakṛti*, the primordial materiality of the universe: *sattva* – purity, light, harmony, *rajas* – activity, passion and *tamas* – dullness, inertia, and ignorance.

hypnagogic state: Term referring to the transitional state of consciousness experienced while falling asleep, sometimes characterized by vivid *hallucinations* or imagery of varying degrees of bizarreness; sometimes used to refer also to the similar state of awareness experienced during the process of waking up.

hypnosis: A condition or state, commonly resembling sleep, which is accompanied by narrowing of the range of attention, is characterized by marked susceptibility to suggestion, and can be artificially induced.

intuition: Somewhat ill-defined term referring to the faculty of coming to an idea directly, by means other than those of reasoning and intellect, and indeed often outside of all conscious processes; the source of these messages is often said to be in the normal, mundane, unconscious, but it is often also said to be the result of *mystical* or *paranormal* processes. The word sometimes refers to the process, sometimes to the product of intuition.

***īśitā* (*ishita*)**: A form of distant mental influence which brings about the fulfilment of needs or wishes not formulated in a deliberate act of volition. (Term is defined in the sense used in Sri Aurobindo's *Record of Yoga*.)

jīvātman: The individual self/spirit.

jñānam brahma: *Brahman* realized as universal consciousness. (Term is defined in the sense used in Sri Aurobindo's *Record of Yoga*.)

judging: The process whereby a rating or a rank-score (that is, "1st," "2nd," "3rd," and so on) is awarded to one or more responses produced (or *targets* used) in a free-response test of *extrasensory perception,* in accordance with the degree of correspondence obtaining between them or one or more targets (or responses); also, the attempt to match, under blind conditions, a set of targets with a set of responses.

kaivalya: Literally, isolation. In the Sāṃkhya and Yoga systems, the term implies the state of release from the unending chain of actions and its consequences through the isolation or detachment of the self (*puruṣa*) from *prakṛti*; perfection, state of pure consciousness, transcendental state of unconditioned freedom; free and unencumbered by the manifestations of *prakṛti*, which normally cloud consciousness as it is reflected on the *buddhi*.

kleśa: Defilements; Afflictions one encounters, pain or suffering arising from disease; various obstacles or hindrances that disturb the equilibrium of the mind.

kośa: Sheath; bag; scabbard; a sheath enclosing the soul; body. The Advaita Vedānta conceives of the *jīva* or person as a multilayered entity composed of five nested sheaths, with the body on the outside (*annamaya*), followed by bodily functions (*prāṇamaya*), sensory capacities (*manomaya*), cognitive functions (*vijñānamaya*), and finally blissfulness at the core (*ānandamaya*).

kṣipta: Wandering, active.

laghimā: The *siddhi* of "lightness" in the mind and body, related to the phenomenon of levitation. (Term is defined in the sense used in Sri Aurobindo's *Record of Yoga*.)

lucid dream: A dream in which the dreamer is conscious of the fact that they are dreaming.

mahat: The great principle; the essential principle of being; the first evolute from *prakṛti*; intellect. The principle of cosmic intelligence or *buddhi*; the intellectual principle as source of *ahaṃkāra*.

mahimā: The *siddhi* of "greatness" of physical and mental force, which imparts an abnormal non-muscular strength to the body. (Term is defined in the sense used in Sri Aurobindo's *Record of Yoga*.)

nāma-rūpa: Psycho-physical personality; name and form; the nature of the world.

near-death experience (NDE): Term applied to experiences undergone by persons who either seem to be at the point of death (or who are even formally declared dead) but then recover, or who narrowly escape death (as in a motor car accident) without being seriously injured; it has been suggested that there is, upon coming close to death, a "core" NDE made up of certain common elements, such as a feeling of indescribable peace, a sense of being out of one' s body, a movement into a dark void or down a tunnel, seeing a brilliant light, and entering that light; there may also be reported the experience of so-called "panoramic memory" (the "life review"), the encountering of an "unseen presence," or being greeted by deceased relatives or religious figures.

nididhyāsana: Uninterrupted and persistent contemplation; profound and continuous meditation. It is the last of the three stages of Vedāntic realization. The state of being so completely absorbed in contemplation of *Brahman* that no other thought enters the mind a frausenolental state of noncognitive knowing or realization.

nirguṇa: Without attributes or qualities (*guṇas*). According to Advaita Vedānta, *Brahman*, the ultimate reality, is said to have a qualityless substrate behind or beyond the perceptible and intelligible world.

nirodha-samāpatti: Cessation of all overt mental activities.

niruddha: Complete control and transcendence of sense processes that enables one to achieve *kaivalya* or perfection; restraint; suppression; non-reaction; non-response; dissolving, control.

nirvāṇa (nibbāṇa): Liberation; final emancipation; the term is particularly applied to the liberation from the bondage of karma and the wheel of birth and death that comes from knowing *Brahman*; absolute experience; the final state into which beings enter when, becoming Enlightened, they are no longer bound by the consciousness of an illusory ego; release/freedom of the personal soul from the physical world (*saṃsāra*). The term usually refers to the state of perfect calm, repose or bliss resulting from the absolute extinction of all desires. It is often used synonymously with other terms such as *kaivalya*, *mokṣa*, and *mukti*. It is the supreme state of being in Buddhism.

out-of-[the]-body experience (OBE, or OOBE): An experience, either spontaneous or induced, in which one's center of consciousness seems to be in a spatial location outside of one's physical body; Celia Green distinguishes two types of such "ecsomatic experiences: the "parasomatic" in which the person appears to possess a duplicate body, sometimes connected to the physical body by a "silver cord;" and the "asomatic" in which the person feels to be entirely bodiless; in either case, many experients claim to perceive their physical bodies lying inert, to see and hear people while remaining unperceived themselves, and to perceive objects and events normally beyond the range of their physical senses; of special interest to parapsychologists on account of its alleged connection with clairvoyance, and to students of survival as providing an example of what disembodied existence could be like. The term "OBE" is preferred by parapsychologists for the phenomena also known as "astral projection," "traveling clairvoyance".

paramātman: The Supreme Self; Universal Brahman; God.

paranormal: A concept applied to any phenomenon which in one or more respects exceeds the limits of what is deemed physically possible on current scientific assumptions; often used as a synonym for "psychic," "parapsychological," "attibutable to psi," or even "miraculous" (although shorn of religious overtones).

paraphysics: Subject investigating paranormal physical effects as in the case of pryehokinecis (PK).

parapsychological: Involving or pertaining to parapsychology or paranormal processes.

parapsychology: Term coined in German by Max Dessoir (1889) and adopted by J.B. Rhine in English to refer to the scientific study of paranormal or ostensibly paranormal phenomena, that is, psi; except in Britain, the term has largely superseded the older expression "psychical research;" used by some to refer to the experimental approach to the field.

past-life regression: A process in which a hypnotized person is mentally "taken back" (or "regressed") by the hypnotist to one or more apparent previous life-times, thus suggesting reincarnation.

paṭiccasamuppāda: (Skt. pratītyasamutpāda) Principle of dependent arising in Buddhism.

percipient: Broadly speaking, someone who perceives or who has a perception-like experience, in particular, the person who experiences or "receives" an extrasensory influence or impression; also one who is tested for ESP ability.

post-mortem communication: A communication or message said to be from a deceased to a living person, usually delivered through a medium.

prākāmya: A heightened power of mind and senses by which the consciousness can exceed the limits normally imposed by the body and project itself into other persons and objects to know what is in them; an instance of the exercise of this faculty. (Term is defined in the sense used in Sri Aurobindo's *Record of Yoga*.)

prakṛti: A term used in the dualistic ontology of the Sāṃkhya system to designate the "material" as opposed to the sentient principle called *puruṣa*. Sometimes translated as "primordial materiality". Nature (Sāṃkhya); causal matter; the fundamental power (*śakti*) of God from which the entire cosmos is formed; the root base of all elements or the primal substance out of which all things evolve.

pramāṇa: Instruments or means of acquiring valid knowledge; an epistemic criterion for validating a cognition; valid cognition.

prāṇāyāma: Control of the subtle life forces (breath/*prāṇa*), often by means of special modes of breathing. Therefore breath control or breathing exercises are usually taken to mean *prāṇāyāma.*

pratyāhāra: Fifth rung in the *Rāja yoga* ladder; abstraction, control or withdrawal of the senses from their objects.

precognition: A form of extrasensory perception in which the target is some future event that cannot be deduced from normally known data in the present.

precognitive telepathy: The paranormal acquisition of information concerning the future mental state of another conscious being.

premonition: A feeling or impression that something is about to happen, especially something ominous or dire, yet about which no normal information is available.

psi (Ø): A general blanket term coined by R.H. Thouless and B.P. Wiesner used either as a noun or adjective to identify paranormal processes and paranormal causation; the two main categories of psi are *psi-gamma* (paranormal cognition; extrasensory perception) and *psi-kappa* (paranormal action; psychokinesis), although the purpose of the term "psi" is to suggest that they might simply be different aspects of a single process, rather than distinct and essentially different processes.

psi phenomenon: Any event which results from, or is an instance of, the operation of psi; examples are the forms of extrasensory perception and psychokinesis.

psi-conducive: Favorable to, or facilitative of, the occurrence of psi, whether it be manifested as *psi-hitting* or *psi-missing.*

psi-hitting: The use of psi in such a way that the target at which the subject is aiming is correctly identified in a test of extrasensory perception; or influenced, in a test of psychokinesis), more frequently than would be expected if only chance were operating. Hence, "psi-hitter" is a subject who exhibits a tendency to psi-hit.

psi-missing: The use of psi in such a way that the target at which the subject is aiming is "missed" (that is, responded to incorrectly, in a test of extrasensory perception; or influenced in a direction contrary to aim, in a test of psychokinesis) more frequently than would be expected if only chance were operating; the term is also sometimes used, misleadingly, to refer simply to non-significant negative scoring. Hence, "psi-misser" is a subject who displays a tendency to psi-miss.

psychic(al): Refers to an individual who possesses psi ability of some kind and to a relatively high degree; it is nowadays applied to paranormal events, abilities, research, and so on, and thus means "concerning or involving psi," or "parapsychological".

psychical research: The original term for "parapsychology," still widely used, especially in Britain.

psychokinesis (PK): Paranormal action; term coined by Henry Holt and adopted by J.B. Rhine to refer to the direct influence of mind on a physical system that cannot be entirely accounted for by the mediation of any known physical energy.

puruṣa: Literally, man, or a human being. In the dualistic ontology of the Sāṃkhya system, implies the self, consciousness or the sentient principle of reality as distinguished from *prakṛti*, the material principle. This principle manifests itself in the form of innumerable "souls" that reside in all kinds of living creatures. It is pure consciousness, consciousness-as-such.

qualitative experiment: Any test for extrasensory perception which uses target material and forms of response which do not allow a definite probability-value to be attached to the response items made; examples are most free-response tests, tests of psychometry, mediumistic utterances, and so on; statistical evaluation of such data must therefore proceed in an indirect fashion, by assigning a probability-value to the matching-performance of a judge.

quantitative experiment: Any test for psi which uses targets each of which has a specific prescribed value for the probability of its occurrence; such a test therefore allows for direct statistical evaluation of the results obtained.

quantum mechanics: Quantum mechanics is the study of mechanical systems whose dimensions are close to or below the atomic scale, such as molecules, atoms, electrons, protons and other subatomic particles. Quantum mechanics is a fundamental branch of physics with wide applications.

rāga: Attraction, attachment/affinity for something, implying a desire for it. This can be emotional (instinctual) or intellectual. It may range from simple liking or preference to intense desire and attraction.

rajas: One of the three components or "strands" or *guṇas* of *prakṛti* as conceived in Sāṃkhya philosophy. *Rajas* is the active principle, roughly equivalent to energy; one of the three primal qualities—described as red, the principle of activity; restlessness; passion, desire for an object or goal.

random number generator (RNG): An apparatus (typically electronic) incorporating an element (based on such processes as radioactive decay or random "noise") and capable of generating a random sequence of outputs; used in tests of psi for generating target sequences, and in tests of psychokinesis may itself be the target system which the subject is required to influence, that is, by "biasing" the particular number or event output; a binary RNG has two equally-probable outputs; the term "RNG" is increasingly being used to refer to any system which produces naturally random outputs, such as bouncing dice, radioactive decay, or even, perhaps, the brain.

recurrent spontaneous psychokinesis (RSPK): Expression coined by William G. Roll to refer to paranormal physical effects which occur repeatedly over a period of time, especially used as a neutral description of poltergeist disturbances.

reductionism: Reductionism can either mean (a) an approach to understanding the nature of complex things by reducing them to the interactions of their parts, or to simpler or more fundamental things or (b) a philosophical position that a complex system is nothing but the sum of its parts, and that an account of it can be reduced to accounts of individual constituents.

reincarnation: A form of survival in which the human soul, or some aspects of self, is, after the death of the body, reborn into a new body, this process being repeated throughout many lives.

remote viewing: A neutral term for general extrasensory perception introduced by Russell Targ and Harold Puthoff, especially in the context of an experimental design in which a percipient attempts to describe the surroundings of a geographically distant agent.

retroactive PK: Psychokinesis occurring in such a way as to be an instance of retroactive causation; to say that event A was caused by retroactive PK is to say that A would not have happened in the way that it did had it not been for a later PK effort exerted so as to influence it. Sometimes abbreviated to "retro-PK;" also referred to as "backward PK" or "time-displaced PK".

retrocognition: Term coined by Frederic Myers to refer to a form of extrasensory perception in which the target is some past event which could not have been learned or inferred by normal means.

RSPK: See *recurrent spontaneous psychokinesis.*

samādhi: The eighth step in Patañjali's Rāja yoga. A set of altered states of consciousness, where the aspirant is one with his object of meditation; profound absorption; a state of being where every activity of the mind ceases completely as advanced state of meditation; absorption in the self; oneness; the mind becoming identified with the object of meditation; the state of superconsciousness; the meditator and the meditated, thinker and thought become one in perfect absorption of the mind.

saṃskāra: The impressions left behind by experiences and actions that are said to shape future experiences and behavior; rites of passage, cognitive schemas; innate tendencies; impressions in the mind from previous births.

saṃyama: Constraint; self-control; an all-complete condition of balance and repose; onepointedness of mind; the triple practice of *dhāraṇā, dhyāna* and *samādhi* in Patañjali's Rāja yoga.

sapta catuṣṭaya: The seven quaternaries, an outline of the elements and stages of the spiritual discipline whose practice is documented in the *Record of Yoga*. (Term is defined in the sense used in Sri Aurobindo's *Record of Yoga.*)

sarvam brahma: *Brahman* realized as all existence. (Term is defined in the sense used in Sri Aurobindo's *Record of Yoga.*)

sattva: One of the three components, "strands" of *guṇas* of *prakṛti* as conceived in Sāṁkhya philosophy. *Sattva* is said to be characterized by illumination, subtlety and lightness as opposed to darkness and heaviness. Purest property of mind.

sensitive: A person who frequently experiences extrasensory perception and who can sometimes induce it at will.

sheep: Term originally used by Gertrude Schmeidler to describe a subject who does not reject the possibility that extrasensory perception could occur under the conditions of the given experimental situation; this somewhat narrow mean-ing has been extended to refer also, tentatively, to persons who believe that ESP exists as a genuine phenomenon.

sheep-goat effect (SGE): Term first used by Gertrude Schmeidler to describe the relationship between acceptance of the possibility of extrasensory perception occurring under the given experimental conditions, and the level of scoring actually achieved on that ESP test: subjects who do not reject the possibility ("sheep") tend to score above chance, those rejecting the possibility ("goats") at or below chance; the terms "sheep" and "goat" are nowadays often used in a more extended sense, and "sheep-goat effect" may thus refer to any significant scoring difference between these two groups as defined by the experimenter.

siddhi: Attainment; spiritual perfection; psychic power; supernatural power.

smṛti: Memory; recollection; "that which is remembered." In this latter sense, *smṛti* is used to designate all scriptures except the *Vedas* and *Upaniṣads* (which are considered of greater authority).

spontaneous case: A discrete incident of ostensible spontaneous *psi*.

suṣupti: Deep, dreamless sleep is one of the four major states of consciousness recognized by Vedānta. The other three states are *jāgṛti* (wakeful), *svapna* (dream), and *turīya* or the "Fourth" state.

svapna: Dream state; dream is one of the four states of consciousness recognized by Vedānta. The other three states are *jāgṛti* (wakeful), *suṣupti* (sleep), and *turīya* or the "Fourth" state.

tamas: One of the three components or "strands" of *prakṛti* as conceived in Sāṃkhya philosophy, *tamas* is said to be characterized by heaviness, inertia, and darkness; ignorance.

target: An item that is the focus of an ESP or PK response.

tattva: "Thatness." Principle; element; the essence of things; truth; reality.

telekinesis: Older term for "psychokinesis," coined by Alexander Aksakof (1895/1890), and still preferred in the former USSR; Soviet Union and Eastern Europe.

telepathy: Term coined by Frederic Myers to refer to the *paranormal* acquisition of information concerning the thoughts, feelings or activity of another conscious being; the word has superseded earlier expressions such as "thought-transference."

trial: The smallest unit of data to be analyzed.

***trikāladṛṣṭi* (*trikaldrishti*)**: Vision of the past, present and future ("the three times"), especially precognition, with or without the aid of telepathic data supplied by *prākāmya* or *vyāpti*; "trikaldrishti of time" refers to foreknowledge of the precise time when an event will take place. (Term is defined in the sense used in Sri Aurobindo's *Record of Yoga*.)

turīya: The state of pure consciousness. In the *Upaniṣads* and the system of **Vedānta**, *turīya* implies the "Fourth state" of consciousness, ever present and unchanging witness- consciousness, which is said to be devoid of intentionality or subject-object split and provides direct experience of *Ātman-Brahman*.

utthāpanā: The freedom of the body from fatigue, strain and heaviness that results from mastery of the physical *siddhi*s of *aṇimā*, *laghimā* and *mahimā*. (Term is defined in the sense used in Sri Aurobindo's *Record of Yoga*.)

vairāgya: Dispassion; detachment, absence of desire; a sense of non-attachment or nonego involvement or indifference towards and distaste for all worldly things and enjoyments.

vāsanā: Desires, especially originating from drives or other inborn tendencies.

vaśitā (***vashita***): A form of distant mental influence in which the will is concentrated in order to control the movements of a person or object. (Term is defined in the sense used in Sri Aurobindo's *Record of Yoga*.)

vijñāna: Gnosis, supermind; a faculty of knowledge superior to the rational intellect, uniting a "concentrated consciousness of the infinite Essence" with a "knowledge of the myriad play of the Infinite". (Term is defined in the sense used in Sri Aurobindo's *Record of Yoga*.)

vijñāna (***vinñāna***): Consciousness.

vikalpa: Cognitive differentiation, abstraction, and imagination; also doubt and indecision; mental construct; conceptualization.

vikṣipta: Occasionally steady; distracted.

viparyāya: Processes of consciousness involved in incorrect cognition or in the experience of illusions, such as the experience of seeing two moons.

viveka khyāti: Discriminative knowledge of pure consciousness and its content.

vṛtti: Mental actions; the modification of the inner sense (mind) which happens to take place when the faculty of internal organ reaches the object through the external sense organ; thought-wave; mental whirlpool; a ripple in the citta (mind substance); mental concept. A process of consciousness or a mental event of any of the following categories: cognitive processes such as perceiving and thinking which involve valid cognition, cognitive processes (such as having illusory perceptions) which involve erroneous or distorted cognitions, imagining and constructing, sleeping, and recollecting.

vyāpti: The telepathic faculty by which thoughts, feelings, etc. are received from others (receptive *vyāpti*) or transmitted to others (communicative or effective *vyāpti*); an instance of the exercise of this faculty. (Term is defined in the sense used in Sri Aurobindo's *Record of Yoga*.)

xenoglossy: Term coined by Charles Richet to denote the act of speaking in a language ostensibly unknown to the speaker.

We sincerely acknowledge the Parapsychological Association for granting permission to use parts of the parapsychology glossary from their website www.parapsych.org/glossary_a_d.html1

Contributors

Dr. Sarath Nath Arseculeratne, Colombo, Sri Lanka. MBBS (Ceylon, 1955); Dip. Bacteriol. (Manchester, UK 1962); D.Phil. (Oxford, UK, 1965); D.Sc. (Hon. U. Ruhuna) Professor of Microbiology, Universities of Peradeniya & Kuala Lumpur; Visiting Professor Harvard University, Boston, USA & Kelantan, Malaysia. His other interests are in parapsychology, science education, science history, scientific literacy.

Prof. William Braud is a researcher, writer, and educator in the areas of inclusive, integrated psychology; transpersonal and spiritual studies, and consciousness studies. Dr. Braud is professor and dissertation director within the Global Doctoral Program of the Institute of Transpersonal Psychology in Palo Alto, California.

Prof. James Carpenter received his Ph.D. in clinical psychology from Ohio State University. He has published widely in the area of parapsychology, and has served on the board of directors of the Rhine Research Centre for seven years, and was president for three years.

Lynne Hill-Clarke graduated from Fort Lewis College in 2000 with a B.A. in Psychology. In 2006, she received a M.S. in Research

Psychology from the University of Tennessee at Chattanooga. Lynne is currently a member of The Society for the Scientific Study of Religion and the Psychology of Religion Division 36. She is pursuing a career in the mental health/non-profit field.

DR. MATTHIJS CORNELISSEN came to India as a qualified physician in 1976 to study the confluence of Yoga and psychotherapy. He is a member of the editorial team overseeing the publication of The Complete Works of Sri Aurobindo, and teaches Integral Psychology at the Sri Aurobindo International Centre of Education in Puducherry.

PROF. ARJUNA DE ZOYSA professor in the Dept. of Mathematics and Philosophy of Engineering at the Open University of Sri Lanka. As a founder member of an NGO group called Vidyartha, Prof. De Zoysa has been involved with facilitation and participation in a number of projects, dealing with the philosophy and practice of Traditional Knowledge (TK). His interest in traditional knowledge systems has led him to explore areas in spiritual healing, metaphysics and Buddhism.

PROF. SUITBERT ERTEL Professor Emeritus at the Georg-Elias-Müller Institute of Psychology and a member of the Society of Scientific Exploration, of the Parapsychological Association of the Gesellschaft für Anomalistik and of the Gesellschaft für Psychologie. He specialized in the fields of psycho-astrology, of solar correlations, of morphic resonance and of psychometrics of anomalous abilities.

JACKSAN J. FERNANDES completed his Masters of Arts in counselling psychology from Mangalore University. Presently, he is a Ph.D. research scholar at the Institute for Human Science & Service, Visakhapatnam. He holds a diploma in the theory and practice of yoga, from the Institute for Yoga and Consciousness, Andhra University. His interests are in the area of psychology of religion and yoga.

RICHARD HARTZ studied philosophy and South Asian Languages and Literature at Yale and the University of Washington. He has lived in India since 1979. He is a member of the Sri Aurobindo Ashram Archives and is currently on the editorial board of the Complete Works of Sri Aurobindo.

MR. JAMES E. KENNEDY began his career at the Institute of Parapsycho-logy. After a master's degree in public health, he has continued his interest in parapsychology. In recent years he has focused on two topics: why are psi effects apparently capricious, and how do psi experiences affect people. These two topics have converged on the subject of spirituality and psi.

DR. SONALI BHATT MARWAHA earned her M.A. and M.Phil. in clinical psychology, with a focus in neuropsychology. Interest in aspects of normal behaviour, led her to undertake a theoretical analysis of Belief Systems, Self, and Emotions, for her Ph.D. thesis. Her current areas of interests include the interface between philosophy, religion, and psychology, with a focus on the materialist perspective. Her recent publications include *Towards a Spiritual Psychology* edited with Prof. K. Ramakrishna Rao (Samvad, India, 2005), and *Colors of Truth: Religion, Self, and Emotions, Perspectives of Hindu, Buddhist, Jaina, Zoroastrian, Islam and Sikhism* (Concept, India, 2006).

DR. EDWIN C. MAY earned his Ph.D. in low-energy, experimental, nuclear physics in 1968. From 1975 to date, however he has been active in psi research most of which was within STAR GATE—the 20-year, $20M US Government's program of which he was the director for its final 10 years. Dr. May has provided both theoretical insight and a substantial number of significantly positive experimental results, which span topics from remote viewing to physiological evidence for precognition.

DR. SANGEETHA MENON is a philosopher with a doctorate awarded for the thesis entitled "the Concept of Consciousness in the Bhagavad Gita". She is working as Fellow at the National Institute of Advanced Studies since 1996. Dr Menon has been working in the area of consciousness studies for over twelve years. Her core research interests are Indian ways of thinking in classical philosophical schools, Indian psychology and Indian dramaturgy and current discussions on 'consciousness'.

DR. H.R. NAGENDRA was a Mechanical Engineer from IISC Bangalore, in the early part of his career. He did his post-doctoral work at the University of British Columbia, Canada and the Marshall Space Flight Centre, NASA, USA. An enduring interest in yoga led him to shift careers in 1975. Presently he is the President, Vivekananda Yoga Anusandhana Sansthana (VYASA) & Vice-Chancellor, Swami Vivekananda Yoga Anusandhana Sansthana, (deemed University), SVYASA, Bangalore.

DR. ROGER NELSON has a Ph.D. in Experimental Psychology. His focus is on the interaction of consciousness with the physical world. He was Coordinator of Research at the Princeton Engineering Anomalies Research (PEAR) laboratory at Princeton University from 1980 to 2002. He is the founder of the Global Consciousness Project (GCP), and has directed the project since its inception in 1997.

PROF. K. RAMAKRISHNA RAO is a philosopher, psychologist and educationist with vast experience in national and international arena as a teacher, researcher and administrator. An acknowledged international authority on Indian psychology, consciousness studies and psychical research, Professor Rao has published nearly two hundred research papers and twelve books, the most recent ones include *Consciousness Studies: Cross-Cultural Perspectives* (McFarland, 2002), *Towards a Spiritual Psychology* edited with S. B. Marwaha (Samvad, India, 2005) and *Handbook of Indian Psychology* edited with Anand Paranjpe and Ajit K. Dalal (Foundation Books, 2008). He was the Founder, Head and Professor, Department of Psychology and Parapsychology and Honorary Director in the Institute for Yoga and Consciousness at Andhra University. Dr Rao worked with Dr J.B. Rhine at the Duke University and later headed his Foundation for Research on the Nature of Man as its Executive Director. In addition to teaching and research Professor Rao served in several top level administrative, executive and advisory positions, including the Vice-Chancellor of Andhra University, Chairman of the A.P. State Commissionerate of Higher Education. Professor Rao is the founder President of the Institute for Human Science and Service. Currently the Chairman of the Indian Council of Philosophical Research, Professor Rao received numerous national and international honors and recognition for his work, which include Doctor of Letters (Honoris Causa) degrees from Andhra and Kakatiya Universities and Doctor of Science (Honoris Causa) degree from Acharya Nagarjuna University.

DR. SERENA RONEY-DOUGAL did a Ph.D. thesis in Parapsychology at Surrey University. She has had over 30 years of study and experience in scientific, magical and spiritual explorations of the psyche, has lectured and taught courses, seminars and workshops in America, Britain and Europe; has written numerous articles both technical and popular, and two books; Where Science and Magic Meet and The Faery Faith. She is a founder of Friends of Bride's Mound and The White Spring Trust.

DR. KARAN SINGH, currently a Rajya Sabha Member, was the youngest member to be inducted into the Union Cabinet, at the age of 36, in 1967. Since then he has a long career in political life. Dr Karan Singh was for many years Chancellor of Jammu and Kashmir University as well the Benaras Hindu University. Dr Karan Singh is an author of distinction, having written a number of books on political science, religion, philosophical essays, travelogues and poems in English. His fascinating autobiography, his book on Sri Aurobindo entitled Prophet of Indian Nationalism, important collections of his writings entitled One Man's World and India and the World and his Essays on Hinduism have been widely acclaimed. With his deep insight into the Indian cultural tradition, as well as his wide exposure to Western literature and civilization, Dr Karan Singh is recognized as an outstanding thinker and leader in India and abroad.

DR. JERRY SOLFVIN was trained in mathematics, psychology, and social science. His interest in parapsychology and yoga go back to the 1970's, when he conducted meditation and psi research at the Psychical Research Foundation at Duke University. He is currently affiliated with the Centre for Indic Studies at University of Massachusetts Dartmouth where he explores his special interest in Eastern and Western perspectives on the science and spirituality dialogue.

DR. K.M. TRIPATHI a postgraduate from Banaras Hindu University (BHU) with specialization in Clinical Psychology and Mental Testing, earned the doctoral degree with his work on Personality and Behaviour Pattern in Psychosomatic and Neurotic Disorders and Role of Yoga and Ayurveda in their Management. Since 1989, Dr Tripathi has served as the Assistant Director of Yoga in Centre for Yoga, Malaviya Bhawan, and Benaras Hindu University and since 1997 he is the Senior Assistant Director.

Name Index

Subject Index

Q

R

Sheep-goat effect (SGE), 77, 87